Brothers Across the Ocean

Brothers Across the Ocean

British Foreign Policy and the
Origins of the Anglo-American
'Special Relationship' 1900-1905

Iestyn Adams

I.B. TAURIS
LONDON · NEW YORK

Revised paperback edition published in 2012 by I.B.Tauris & Co Ltd
6 Salem Road, London W2 4BU
175 Fifth Avenue, New York NY 10010
www.ibtauris.com

Distributed in the United States and Canada
Exclusively by Palgrave Macmillan
175 Fifth Avenue, New York NY 10010

ISBN: 978 1 84885 963 0

A full CIP record for this book is available from the British Library
A full CIP record for this book is available from the Library of Congress

Library of Congress catalog card: available

Printed and bound by CPI Group (UK) Ltd, Croydon, CR0 4YY
From camera-ready copy edited and supplied by the author

Contents

The Limits of Rapprochement

Side by Side on the World Stage

Acknowledgements

During the researching and writing of this volume, I have incurred a number of debts, which it is my pleasure to acknowledge. First and lasting thanks must go to Dr Keith Wilson at the University of Leeds, whose encyclopedic knowledge, keen interest and constant enthusiasm did far more than help me to avoid a number of pitfalls, clarify my thought processes and highlight archival sources that I might otherwise have missed. It was he who first suggested tackling Lansdowne – and I'm very grateful he did.

I am deeply indebted to Robert Smith, curator of the Lansdowne Papers at the British Library, for guiding me through a fascinating assortment of Lansdowne's letters, memos and private journals. Extracts taken from this previously little used collection run throughout the book.

My final words of thanks must go to all those who helped to sustain me throughout the writing of this book. I am deeply indebted to Gill and John Adams, for enduring encouragement and support, to Andrea Myers and Ritchie Lane, to Mark and Coco Shears, and to Groucho, Chico, Harpo and Zeppo Marx for light relief. Thanks also go to Andrew Cothliff for providing the final graphic design and being generous with his time and talent.

My wife, Colette, has been my constant companion and fondest critic. For patiently reading every word and for staying the course without complaint, she deserves front-rank recognition for sacrifices above and beyond ... I hope she knows how grateful I am.

FOR COLETTE AND CAI

Introduction

THE OPENING FIVE YEARS of the twentieth century, when Lord Lansdowne presided at the Foreign Office, was a critical period in the reconsideration and adjustment of British foreign relations. After the enthusiastic imperialism that marked the previous century, a growing anxiety began to prevail that Britain's resources were over-stretched and, more significantly, that her sprawling Empire could no longer adequately be protected. The recognition that British global hegemony was under increasing attack had been a gradual process. By 1894, however, the major European Powers, eager for imperial adventure and busy with naval expansion, had formed into two opposing blocks while Britain remained perilously isolated.[1] Traditionally evading entangling alliances, the abortive attempts of the late 1890s to join the Triple Alliance (primarily advocated by Joseph Chamberlain at the Colonial Office) represented one aspect of a new policy of accommodation, a policy that gained added impetus once Lansdowne was appointed Foreign Secretary on November 12 1900. Under Lansdowne, foreign affairs would primarily be governed by a rueful acknowledgement of Britain's relative decline (particularly the vulnerability of her scattered and ever-expanding Empire during a period of exceptional turbulence) and the consequent need for international allies.[2]

Lansdowne's arrival at the Foreign Office coincided with a particularly anxious period in British external relations. In South Africa, a difficult, bitter and internationally unpopular war against the Boers still raged, while, in China, British interests came under increasing threat in the wake of the Boxer uprising. By 1905, however, much had changed. Britain had concluded two important international agreements – with Japan in 1902 and France two years later – which served to lessen the immediate danger. At the same time, the Foreign Office made strenuous attempts to remove long-standing causes of friction with otherwise friendly Powers, most significantly the United States.

For the first time, the attempt to effect a closer understanding between the two 'Anglo-Saxon' races was regarded in high Government circles as a serious policy objective. The Americans, suddenly emerging from the Spanish-American war of 1898 as a major world Power, might be induced to become Britain's unofficial global partner, thereby safeguarding British interests in the Western Hemisphere whilst ensuring freedom of commerce in the East. More than any other nation, then, the United States was becoming seen as Britain's natural, and potentially most rewarding future ally.

This book will reconsider the motives and attitudes with which Lansdowne, the Foreign Office and the last pre-war Unionist Government approached Anglo-American diplomacy. Not only is the majority of previous research now well over thirty years old, but Lansdowne's influence on the Anglo-American *rapprochement* has hitherto excited insufficient interest.[3]

Considering the key role played by the Foreign Secretary in the formulation of foreign policy, it is a little surprising that no historian has systematically examined Lansdowne's approach to American affairs. He was, after all, a pivotal figure during an extremely important period of Anglo-American relations, a man who fully understood the requirements of the age and, most significantly, exerted a strong voice in the final determination of Britain's external relations. Naturally, diplomacy is never solely the business of the Foreign Office (Lansdowne was always ready to consider outside views) and, for this reason, an attempt has been made to incorporate the influence of two Prime Ministers (Lord Salisbury and Arthur Balfour), the Colonial Office, Admiralty and Committee of Imperial Defence. A close analysis of the way Lansdowne and his colleagues managed American diplomacy, it is hoped, will provide an alternative account of the 'special relationship' during a critical period of transition.

Until the very last years of the nineteenth century, Anglo-American relations were marred by mutual antipathy, suspicion and distrust. While the two nations fought only once during the century, in 1812, diplomatic atmospheric conditions tended invariably to be rather bitter, cold and frosty. As the American people swept across the North American continent – slowly but inexorably consolidating their future as the greatest of all the world Powers – Great Britain remained the one great and tangible enemy. Not only was Britain in possession of a dominant navy, vastly outnumbering all her competitors in size, technology and strength, but her extensive Western Hemispheric possessions provided a perfect platform from which an attack on the United States might easily be launched.

A series of angry incidents perpetuated the uneasy relationship. After the bitter Oregon boundary dispute of the 1840s, Britain betrayed a partisan sympathy for the South during the American Civil War, culminating in the construction of three Confederate cruisers in British ports.[4] During the 1880s, Canadian-American hostility rose sharply and placed Anglo-American relations under an almost constant strain. A series of acrimonious fisheries and sealing disputes raged throughout the decade, emphasising a growing rivalry between the two great North American Powers and leaving Britain in a rather delicate position. In early 1886, Senator William B. Allison told Sir Lionel Sackville-West, Britain's Minister in Washington, that,

'if the Commercial relations with Canada were placed upon the footing of the inter-state commerce of the Union great benefit would accrue to the North Western States; – But the opinion was general that this would sooner or later be obtained by the incorporation of Canada with the United States.'⁵

Sackville-West himself became the object of American antagonism two years later, for his unwise expression of support for Grover Cleveland's Democrats during the 1888 electoral campaign, and was summarily ejected from the country. During the period of quiet that followed, however, Anglo-American relations underwent a notable, if tentative improvement. Together, the two nations concluded a fisheries *modus vivendi* in 1888 and, in 1893, entered into arbitration on sealing questions in the Behring Sea (see chapters eight and nine). At the same time, the British public began to take a real interest in American affairs and James Bryce's epic treatise, *The American Commonwealth*, first published in 1888, was perhaps its most visible manifestation. Bryce contended that,

> 'America has still a long vista of years stretching before her in which she will enjoy conditions far more auspicious than any European coun-try can count upon. And that America marks the highest level, not only of material well-being, but of intelligence and happiness ... will be the judgement of those who look not at the favoured few for whose bene-fit the world seems hitherto to have framed its institutions, but at the whole body of the people.'⁶

By 1893, the British Legation at Washington had been upgraded into an Embassy. The veteran diplomat Sir Julian Pauncefote succeeded Sackville-West in 1889, and now became Britain's first Ambassador to the United States. It 'marks an epoch in the growth and perpetuation of the good will which exists between the two coun-tries', he happily remarked.⁷ The Ambassador's confidence, as it turned out, was rather premature and, when an acrimonious dispute erupted in 1895 over the law-ful boundary line between British Guiana and Venezuela, a relapse to the old state of hostility suddenly seemed inevitable.

The Venezuelan crisis of 1895-1896 initially confirmed every suspicion and prejudice that marked Anglo-American relations. Cleveland's attitude from the start was both bellicose and aggressive – as a stern champion of the Monroe Doctrine, he automatically assumed British wrong-doing, and determined that the small, defenceless Latin American state should be protected. Secretary of State Richard Olney, however, undoubtedly went too far when he released his famous note of July 20 1895, which pressed for arbitration. Olney's belief that 'the United States is practically sovereign on this continent', and that the 'distance and three thousand miles of intervening ocean make any permanent political union between an European and an American state unnatural and inexpedient', was guaranteed to anger a British Government that still ruled over many loyal western colonies.⁸ Accordingly, Salisbury scornfully dismissed the approach, and withheld his official rejoinder until early December. Angered by Britain's apparent indifference to a quick settlement, meanwhile, Cleveland handed an inflammatory message to

Congress on December 17, indirectly threatening war should Britain refuse to accept American demands. This proved to be the turning point. Naturally shaken, Salisbury ruefully accepted arbitration and the crisis quickly receded.[9] An arbitral tribunal convened in Paris in the summer of 1899 and, on October 3, delivered its verdict: the disputed territory, in the main, belonged to British Guiana.

'I have very little doubt that there are plenty of malign influences at work in the U.S. to promote war.' So wrote Sir William Harcourt, leader of the Liberal Party, on January 26 1896.[10] While American ire took some time to fade – strong anti-British sentiment was a prevalent and disquieting factor in the United States' election campaign of 1896 – there were encouraging signs that a more friendly relationship was emerging. In 1897, Pauncefote and Olney successfully negotiated a general arbitration treaty, although it failed to pass the Senate. Then, in the spring of 1898, the United States went to war with Spain.

The Spanish-American war proved critical to the transformation of the Anglo-American bond. Choosing to regard McKinley's intervention in Cuba as a humanitarian mission to protect the oppressed Cubans, Britain assumed an attitude of benevolent neutrality toward American endeavours, while other European nations, and particularly the Catholic states, laid their sympathies with Spain.[11] The United States' post-war enthusiasm for Britain, however, was based on serious misconceptions. Britain, in fact, neither opposed European intervention to prevent the war, nor blocked hostile German designs at Manila.[12] She had, on the other hand, allowed the United States access to her ports, intelligence gathering at Gibraltar and use of the Hong Kong cable.[13] America's rising imperialism was encouraged in Britain, which supported the annexation of Hawaii, the Philippines and the Samoan island of Tutuila. 'The friendship shown the United States by Great Britain during the late war', one American writer happily remarked, 'and the corresponding good will aroused toward the mother country is by all odds the greatest gain derived from the success of American arms'.[14]

Now, a new set of idealistic race notions began to take over as the new mode of popular Anglo-American expression, and 'Anglo-Saxonism' (the notion of a common and superior racial heritage) suddenly became a tangible phenomenon. In *Anglo-Saxons and Others*, published in 1900, American Aline Gorren maintained that Anglo-Saxons had 'a covenant with the Deity, and all the privileges and all the obligations that go with the position.'[15] That Britain and America broadly had the same attitude to world affairs simply served to confirm this philosophy.

Of great significance to the future of Anglo-American friendship was the strong influence of Anglo-Saxonism on two rising British politicians. Arthur J. Balfour, Salisbury's nephew and Leader of the House of Commons in the 1890s staunchly supported Anglo-American solidarity. Speaking at Manchester at the height of the 1896 Venezuelan crisis, he stressed that,

> '[t]he idea of war with the United States carries with it some of the unnatural horror of a civil war. ... We may be taxed with being idealists and dreamers in this matter. I look forward with confidence to the time when our ideals will have become real. ... The time will come, the time

must come, when someone, some statesman of authority, more fortunate even than President Monroe, will lay down the doctrine that between the English-speaking peoples war is impossible.'[16]

Balfour sounded a similar note to Henry White, American Chargé d'Affairs in London, in December 1900. 'I am, as you know, a most earnest advocate of a harmonious cooperation between the two great Anglo-Saxon States', he explained. 'Such at all events is my creed ... and I am firmly convinced that the more fully it be accepted, the better for the interests of humanity.'[17]

Colonial Secretary Joseph Chamberlain was equally swayed. During a public speech in May 1898, he spoke of Britain's duty:

'to establish and to maintain bonds of a permanent amity with our kinsmen across the Atlantic. They are a powerful and generous nation. They speak our language, they are bred of our race. ... I do not know what arrangements may be possible with us, but this I know and feel, – that the closer, the more cordial, the fuller, and the more definite those arrangements are, with the consent of both peoples, the better it will be for both us and for the world. And I even go so far as to say that, terrible as war may be, even war itself would be cheaply purchased if in a great and noble cause the Stars and Stripes and the Union Jack should wave together over an Anglo-Saxon Alliance.'[18]

One of the first results of the new Anglo-American cordiality was the establishment of a Joint High Commission in August 1898, intended to resolve all outstanding Canadian-American disputes. While that body broke up in acrimony seven months later over the emotive Alaska boundary issue,[19] the Alaskan *modus vivendi* of October 1899 served, temporarily at least, to remove a major source of friction. When the Boer War erupted that month, the United States remembered the Spanish-American conflict and remained steadfastly neutral. Popular American sentiment, it is true, took the Boers' side, but a blend of practical politics and race sentiment prevailed.[20] Accordingly, while a storm of protest burst forth from Europe, McKinley allowed the Boer envoys a polite reception in Washington, but refused to press for mediation. The American Government could have given no greater proof of its friendly feelings for Britain and for her imperial designs – the new age of Anglo-American relations had begun.

In the opening years of the next century, however, the bond's true strength would be seriously tested. Two major sources of potential friction remained unresolved and negotiations on the right of the United States to construct a ship canal across the Central American Isthmus, and the final delineation of the Alaskan-Canadian boundary, continued to threaten a return to international hostility. Although British and American statesmen increasingly perceived a mutuality in their strategic concerns, the diplomatic relationship was far from secure. Indeed, the *rapprochement* was suddenly strained in the winter of 1902, when Britain and Germany imposed a naval blockade off the Venezuelan coast, and in the latter stages of the Russo-Japanese war. The manner in which diplomats, on both sides of the Atlantic, met these difficulties would determine the future of the emerging Anglo-American 'special relationship'.

Faced by the malevolence of continental Europe, meanwhile, Britain's external relations came under increasing strain. As the Dual Alliance (France and Russia) and Triple Alliance (Germany, Austria-Hungary and Italy) established an uneasy balance of power, Britain remained awkwardly isolated. In Africa and the Far East, fervent expansionist aspirations created diplomatic friction and colonial rivalry; with the scramble for Africa reaching its climax, French and German imperialism threatened Britain's territorial ambitions. The ill-judged Jameson Raid on Johannesburg further highlighted British unpopularity,[21] while, during Lord Kitchener's reconquest of the Sudan three years later, Major Jean B. Marchand, a French Officer, hoisted the Tricolour over Fashoda and challenged Britain's claim to the Upper Nile. A limited Anglo-German treaty temporarily brought Britain closer to the Triple Alliance in 1898, but there was little chance of a lasting settlement.[22] In this light, Europe's hostility to the Boer War, which erupted in October 1899, was both predictable and disappointing.[23] Despite her vast colonial possessions and dominant navy, Britain had never felt so alone.

Far Eastern affairs were similarly disquieting. In China, the Germans seized the port of Kiao-Chow on November 14 1897 and began an undignified race for international concessions; by spring 1898, the Chinese had been compelled to hand over Port Arthur to the Russians and Wei-hai-Wei to Britain. Russian expansion equally endangered British interests in both Near and Far East. Against a determined invasion by vast Russian armies, India was vastly unprepared,[24] while less critical regions (Persia, Afghanistan and North China) had already proved susceptible to Russian domination. The Boxer uprising of 1900 worsened matters yet further. While European military contingents, sent to quash the rebellion, delayed their departure from Peking, Russia occupied Manchuria and stubbornly refused to budge. In this maelstrom, Lord Salisbury could do no more than try to maintain China's integrity, whilst stoutly defending British interests. This would prove an onerous task and one too great for Britain to manage alone.

Meanwhile, the 1900 "Khaki Election" returned the Unionists with a large majority. Salisbury stayed on as Prime Minister, but yielded control of the Foreign Office to Lansdowne. Chamberlain remained at the Colonial Office (and Sir Michael Hicks Beach at the Treasury), Lord Selborne came in as First Lord of the Admiralty and St. John Broderick took Lansdowne's old War Office job. These were to prove dramatic changes – the new-style Cabinet was filled by men who appreciated Britain's international woes and the problems generated by her scattered possessions. From the Admiralty, Selborne told Hicks Beach that,

'Leaving out of account altogether the rapidly increasing Navies of Germany, Japan, and the U.S., we must keep at least equal to France and Russia combined ... The aggregate of the French and Russian Navies governs the number of our ships. ... The fact that France and

Russia are constantly improving the armament of their ships and increasing their reserves makes it imperatively necessary that we should not allow the same process in our navy to be checked.'[25]

With great haste, major policy reconsiderations began to take place. The Boer War had revealed Britain's lack of preparedness for a major foreign conflict, so military and naval matters were now intensively rethought. Balfour, succeeding Salisbury in 1902, replaced the inadequate Defence Committee with the Committee of Imperial Defence, a body of shifting personnel that considered the Empire's entire military and naval requirements. Similar changes took place at the Admiralty, where Selborne and Sir John Fisher undertook a radical adjustment of naval resources; Fisher, Lord Esher and Sir George Clarke busily discussed War Office reform.[26] Lansdowne's sensitive approach to Foreign affairs was just as significant. The Anglo-Japanese alliance and Anglo-French agreements did much to ease the pressure on Britain's stretched navy and secure her Far East and Northern African interests. Suddenly, Anglo-American friendship was a serious policy objective and, in retrospect, one of Lansdowne's most enduring achievements.

Henry Charles Keith Petty-Fitzmaurice, Fifth Marquis of Lansdowne, was born into genteel aristocracy on January 14 1845. Descended from a long line of prominent Whigs, he was destined from birth to assume a public career alongside the greatest politicians of the day. At first glance, Lansdowne's personality seemed perfectly to fit the traditional mould of the eminent Victorian peer. By temperament rather staid and formal, he believed in the importance of tradition, protocol and prestige. In the event, however, he was to prove rather a prisoner of his upbringing, harbouring few political ambitions, considering politics an onerous, if serious duty, and vastly preferring to spend his days fishing the waters of his great English and Irish estates, Bowood and Dereen.

In the Unionist Cabinet, filled with powerful personalities, Lansdowne was a quiet and thoughtful figure, committed and dependable rather than brilliant. Lacking Salisbury's presence and international standing, Chamberlain's compelling charisma or Balfour's wit and political flair, he nevertheless brought an intense understanding and a talent for compromise to the field of foreign affairs. To his biographer, Balfour gave this retrospective impression of his old Foreign Secretary:

'I shouldn't call him very clever. He was – I don't quite know how to put it – better than competent. ... Lansdowne had the mentality of the great Whigs – remember he was descended from a great line of them. But one must qualify even that a little, he wasn't quite an Englishman. His mother was French – she was a Flahault. I always felt a sort of Continental quality of mind in Lansdowne. I was always very fond of him.'[27]

When Lansdowne was appointed Foreign Secretary, he was fifty-five and had thirty-two years of public service behind him. As a Liberal peer, he began his

Parliamentary life in 1868, accepting William Gladstone's offer of a junior Treasury position. Four years later, he was appointed to the War Office as Under Secretary of State and transferred to the India Office following Gladstone's electoral victory of 1880. Two months after accepting his post, however, Lansdowne opposed the Liberals' Irish policy and abruptly tendered his resignation. Increasingly inclining towards the Conservatives by 1883, he reluctantly consented to Gladstone's wish that he become Governor-General of Canada. '[M]y heart fails at times when I think of it', he wrote to his mother on May 18, 'but the years will pass by, and when they are gone, I believe we shall all of us admit that it would have been wrong to refuse.'[28]

Once in Ottawa, Canadian-American relations naturally occupied much of the Governor-General's time. The fisheries dispute was then at its height as, in 1886, American revenue cutters began seizing Canadian sealing vessels, while British warships also entered the fray in the North Atlantic fishing grounds.[29] Significantly, Lansdowne's tenure as Governor-General imprinted on his mind a firm appreciation of Canadian loyalty to the Mother Country. In his private journal, he listed the main reasons for this loyalty, which were: 'pride in common history, sense of protection, continuity of nat[ional] life, personal respect for the sovereign, admiration for [the] British constitution, [and the] abhorrence of needless revolution.'[30] Then, on December 31 1887, whilst still in Ottawa, Salisbury offered Lansdowne the Viceroyalty of India.[31] 'I am offered a magnificent post', he told his mother on February 8 the following year, 'the most responsible and honourable in the service outside England.'[32] After a long colonial career, he finally returned home in January 1895, whereupon Salisbury quickly offered him the post of Secretary for War in his new Unionist Administration.

Although Lansdowne had acquired an extensive experience of foreign affairs, his appointment to the Foreign Office in November 1900 was regarded as something of a disappointment. After the seeming failure of British arms in South Africa, the War Office (and Lansdowne in particular) came under intense criticism. Lord Esher noted that,

> 'The new appointments have been well-received on the whole. Lansdowne only has come in for a large share of abuse. Why, no one can explain, who knows him and his sound diplomatic instincts and his experience. I saw him yesterday. He was unmoved by criticism. He has been accustomed, as an Irish land-lord, to be pelted by the Press.'[33]

Before the outbreak of hostilities, Lansdowne's War Office career had made little impression. One observer, the diarist Henry W. Lucy, labelled him a 'hide-bound redtape-fettered War Minister.'[34] For the clear inadequacy of her military preparation before the South African conflict, however, Britain's budgetary requirements (and an out-dated military outlook) must primarily shoulder the blame.[35] Still, when Lansdowne wrote to the Queen in October 1900, having been offered the Foreign Office, he acknowledged that, 'as Secretary of State for War he must often have seemed to Your Majesty to fall short of expectations.'[36] Herself unsure about the wisdom of the appointment, Victoria responded by directing Salisbury to maintain his close supervision over foreign affairs. Every Foreign Office dispatch and telegram, she understood, should first be submitted to the Prime Minister for his consideration. Salisbury, however, failed to fulfil his side of the bargain and the new international priorities assumed at the Foreign Office owed far more to Lansdowne than to the Prime Minister.[37] It was Lansdowne's desire for foreign allies, and for friendly, courteous exchanges, that altered the course of British diplomacy. Indeed, Salisbury's rather overbearing diplomatic style became for Lansdowne a source of complaint; in August 1900, for example, he wrote to Secretary for India Lord George Hamilton that 'Salisbury is very provoking: he deals with the Ministers and Sovereign of [the Japanese] Meyi [sic.] powers as if they were Hatfield solicitors.'[38]

Lansdowne's relationship with Balfour was, by contrast, mutually sympathetic. Both men were internationalists, fascinated by foreign, imperial and defence questions. Key diplomatic issues were invariably shown to the Prime Minister for his consideration. Selborne and Chamberlain completed the 'inner circle' of ministerial policy-makers.[39] A broad consensus marked diplomatic decisions (Lansdowne seriously disagreed with his colleagues only once post 1902, when his desire to assist Japan in the event of a Russo-Japanese conflict received overwhelming disapproval). Under Balfour, diplomacy was pragmatic and flexible; its formulation was conducted in an atmosphere of mutual respect.

Perhaps because of his heritage, Lansdowne was personally unmoved by the popular appeal to Anglo-Saxonism; the complete absence of expressions on race sentiment in his private correspondence suggests a balanced view of cultural philosophy.[40] He was, however, prone to use Anglo-Saxon terminology in public, specifically, when Anglo-American cordiality came under threat. As the canal negotiations concluded in 1901, he spoke of Britain's friendship with her 'brothers across the ocean'; during the Venezuelan blockade a year later, he was 'constantly reminded of the friendly feelings by which the two great Powers – Great Britain and her kinsmen across the sea – were united.'[41] Unlike Balfour and Chamberlain, Lansdowne's brand of Anglo-Saxonism was a valuable (and rather cynical) device. Whereas Balfour dreamed of an Anglo-American alliance to 'open a new era in the history of the world'[42] – Lansdowne saw only its practical worth.

Throughout the tariff reform crisis of 1903, which almost destroyed the Balfour Administration, Lansdowne was similarly unwilling to think in idealistic terms. Siding neither with tariff reformers nor free traders, he instead lent his wholehearted support to Balfour's middle course.[43] As a realist amongst idealists, Lansdowne was driven by clear diplomatic goals, grounded in national self-interest and by the need to secure Britain's strategic objectives with concrete alliances. Having just arrived at the Foreign Office, he immediately outlined his desire for international cordiality. To Sir Frank Lascelles, Britain's Ambassador in Berlin, he explained that,

'I shall undertake the duties of my new office without, I hope, too many preconceived ideas, but I plead guilty to one – the idea that we should make every effort to maintain, and, if we can, to strengthen the good relations which at present exist between the Queen's Gov[ernmen]t and that of the [German] Emperor.'[44]

In a similar vein, he penned this dispatch to Sir Edmund Monson in Paris: 'I am sure few will not suspect me of using a mere phrase when I express the hope that our cooperation may be successful in maintaining the best relations between this country and that to which you are accredited.'[45] Significantly, Lansdowne's opening letter to Sir Julian Pauncefote, long-serving Ambassador to Washington, betrayed equally fervent hopes for American friendship.

> 'On the eve of my assumption of office,' he explained, 'I cannot resist telling you how sincerely I congratulate myself on my good fortune in finding you still at your post. Nothing could be more reassuring to me than this reflection ... Of my earnest desire to cooperate with you in maintaining good relations with the Government of the United States, you will, I am sure, not be in any doubt.'[46]

The future of the Anglo-American relationship, during a critical transitory phase, was thus left largely in Lansdowne's hands. His responses to the increasingly strident tone of American diplomacy were broadly based on global considerations of the changing balance of power, the inevitability of the United States' emergence as a great nation and Britain and the United States' apparently similar diplomatic outlook. Accordingly, he tended to approach American affairs in a conciliatory manner – provided that Britain was neither obliged nor expected to sacrifice her vital interests.

Lansdowne's arrival at the Foreign Office in late 1900, however, coincided with a particularly uneasy period in Anglo-American relations, as the United States – impatient for an American-built canal across the isthmus of Central America – pushed strongly for Britain to revise the canal treaty of 1850. During the Isthmian Canal dispute, Anglo-American friendship would be sorely tested but, ultimately, would emerge unscathed.

Canal Rights and Debt Collection in Latin America

1

No Apology, No Explanation

Prestige Diplomacy and the Isthmian Canal, 1900-1901

O N DECEMBER 12 1900, Arthur Balfour wrote to Henry White, the American Chargé d'Affairs in London, of his earnest hope to see the burgeoning Anglo-American friendship furthered. Every indication, he explained pointed towards 'a fundamental harmony, – a permanent sympathy', between the two countries, 'compared to which all merely political alliances with other States should prove to be the evanescent result of temporary diplomatic convenience.'[1] While many politicians, on both sides of the Atlantic, had been converted to the cause of Anglo-American harmony, however, they understood that its presence was only precariously established and could as easily fade as flourish. In fact, even as Balfour wrote his missive, an acrimonious dispute was brewing concerning the terms under which the United States would be permitted to construct a canal across the isthmus of Central America.

Historians generally acknowledge that these discussions were critical to the future of the 'special relationship', but their explanations of Foreign Office diplomacy have shown less unanimity.[2] Yet Lansdowne's actions throughout the affair were generally consistent. The fundamental decision to concede to the United States the right to construct a canal had been made by the Cabinet prior to Lansdowne's arrival at the Foreign Office. Britain had no burning interest in the issue, neither were the Senate's amendments to the Hay-Pauncefote treaty considered to have any practical significance. While Lansdowne never wavered from this position, he refused to concede legitimate treaty rights in a manner that would damage British prestige.

The treaty created by John M. Clayton and Sir Henry Bulwer in April 1850 stated that the United States and Great Britain must undertake the future construction of a ship canal across Central America in co-operation. Both nations agreed not to erect fortifications in the Canal Zone, nor to 'assume, or exercise any domination over Nicaragua, Costa Rica, the Mosquito coast, or any part of Central America'.[3] Furthermore, the treaty stated that, should Britain and the United States ever be at war, the free passage of their vessels should still be guaranteed through the canal. In 1850, the treaty had little impact. Indeed, over the next fifty years, Britain exhibited little interest in the prospect of an isthmian canal.

Her vast commercial fleets had prospered under the dominance of the British flag and the Suez route, opened in 1869, had made even Far Eastern markets easily accessible to British merchant shipping. On the other side of the Atlantic, however, the move to build the canal suddenly intensified at the turn of the century. In 1850, the United States had been preoccupied with westward expansion, but, by 1900, the isthmian issue had risen to national significance. During the Spanish-American war, the problems of linking America's naval squadrons on the West coast with those in the Caribbean were clearly demonstrated as the U.S.S. "Oregon" took two months to sail from San Francisco, around the Straits of Magellan, into Caribbean waters. Needing the Clayton-Bulwer Treaty to be abrogated, so that a canal could quickly be constructed and the same problems would never recur, John Hay approached Ambassador Sir Julian Pauncefote in late 1898; the result was the Hay-Pauncefote Treaty of February 1900.

It gave to the United States the right to construct, regulate and manage the isthmian canal, although the provisions respecting neutrality remained firmly in place: the 'canal shall be free and open, in time of war as in time of peace, to the vessels of commerce and war of all nations, on terms of entire equality.'[4] Both men were confident that their agreement was fair to both nations. Neither expected the widespread protest that was quickly to emerge.

'[T]he Panama canal under a European guarantee must smash the Monroe Doctrine in the head; must secure South America to Europe and shut us up in the north.' The prominent American writer Henry Adams confided these fears to John Hay in December 1900 and anxiously predicted that the United States would be forced to 'submit or fight, and either horn gores us to death.'[5]

While Adams' fears of an aggressive and united Europe threatening the Western Hemisphere were somewhat beside the mark, his belief that the canal must be wholly American had growing support. The Hay-Pauncefote Treaty, published in March, had been received by the American people, increasingly confident and aware of their strength, as a needless concession of vital interests. Particular hostility was focused on the neutrality provision and the implicit admission that foreign Powers had a legitimate interest in the Canal Zone, even in time of war. That 1900 was an election year did little to ease the situation. Keen to make ground on McKinley, the platform of the Democratic party demanded,

> 'the immediate construction, ownership and control of the Nicaragua
> Canal by the United States and condemns the Hay-Pauncefote Treaty
> as a surrender of American rights and interests not to be tolerated by
> the American people.'

The text ended with an attack on Britain and the supposed pro-British sentiments of the McKinley administration. As Pauncefote noted, 'It condemns the "ill concealed Republican Alliance with England which must mean discrimination against other friendly nations and which has already stifled the nation's voice whose liberty is being strangled in Africa."'[6]

Such sentiment found great support and nowhere was the nationalistic spirit more evident than in the Senate. In the months following publication, a series of amendments sought to bring the canal under exclusive American control. Of these, Senator Cushman K. Davis introduced the most well known, although hardly the most extreme. In times of conflict, Davis argued, the United States must have the right to send troops into the Canal Zone to maintain order.

Other senators, particularly William Hepburn and John T. Morgan, called for nothing less than the total abrogation of the Clayton-Bulwer Treaty, with or without Britain's consent. McKinley, meanwhile, continued to press for a quick resolution. During December, while the Inter-Oceanic Canal Commission determined which route would be most satisfactory, Hay engaged in earnest negotiation with representatives from Nicaragua, Colombia and Costa Rica, to secure for the United States the right to construct and control a canal in those countries. While McKinley denied that treaties had actually been signed – he feared the accusation that such arrangements would constitute and infringement of the Clayton-Bulwer Treaty – he admitted that 'overtures' had indeed been made.[7]

In his Message to Congress on December 3, the President noted Britain's friendly attitude towards his country and pressed the Senate to ratify the treaty without delay.[8] Pauncefote now happily noted the amicable relations between State Department and British Embassy and even played down the Senate's actions:

'The attitude of the administration towards us is all that could be desired', he noted, 'but they have to contend with the bad influences of certain unscrupulous politicians who stir up opposition to any and every treaty with Great Britain. The President however is stronger now than he was last session and I hope I may be able soon to report some satisfying results.'[9]

McKinley's support lacked conviction, a fact bemoaned in Pauncefote's increasingly sour dispatches to the Foreign Office. '[T]he President thinks it his duty to obey the *vox populi*,' the Ambassador warned Lansdowne on December 21, predicting that McKinley would 'give way to popular clamour for the abrogation of the Clayton-Bulwer Treaty.'[10] Pauncefote's anxieties were soon confirmed. In no mood for a direct confrontation with the Senate, McKinley announced that he would accept the treaty with or without the Senate amendments.

The result of the Senate's vote was never in doubt. On December 16, the great majority of the House agreed to adopt the Hay-Pauncefote treaty, but asked for serious modifications. Article III, which invited other Powers beside Great Britain and the United States to adhere to the treaty, was stricken out altogether. While the abrogation of the Clayton-Bulwer Treaty was finally made explicit, the most significant alteration was the addition of a single paragraph respecting the future neutrality of the isthmian canal, in which it was stated that:

'It is agreed, however, that none of the immediately foregoing conditions [concerning neutrality] ... shall apply to measures which the United

States may find it necessary to take for securing by its own forces the defence of the United States and the maintenance of public order.'[11]

Hay fully expected the result. In April 1900, he told his friend John J. McCook that, when the canal treaty had been published, 'I felt sure no one out of a mad house could fail to see that the advantages were all on our side. But I underrated the power of ignorance and spite, acting upon cowardice.'[12] Now, hearing of the Senate's actions, he fell into a barely concealed state of despair. Writing to Balfour of his sincere feelings of regret, Hay commented that the amendments 'deform and disfigure the Treaty; they take much from the grace and value of the concession which Great Britain has made us.' Disillusioned and disappointed, Hay was quick to blame 'those who want to hurt the President; those who want me out of the Cabinet ... [those] who think it is always good politics to attack England; and a certain number of honest narrow minded patriots who know no better.'[13] Still, Hay understood that he was hardly in a position to reverse the Senate's decision and that nothing further could be done until Britain's response was received in Washington.

In sharp contrast to American enthusiasm, Britain's position regarding the canal issue was rather equivocal. While the Board of Trade generally favoured its construction – arguing that British trade could only benefit from the new shipping route – Admiralty experts feared the effect of a strengthened American navy upon Britain's naval predominance and hoped the canal would never be built. The increased dominance that Washington would exercise over Central America and the Caribbean was less than encouraging: British possessions in the region had already become largely dependent on the United States and were in danger of being swallowed up altogether. On July 18 1899, British Guiana concluded a reciprocal tariff arrangement with the United States; by late 1900, 39 per cent of its total trade was with that country.[14]

A similar trend was apparent in Jamaica. Acting-Governor Sydney Olivier reported that the 'value of exports from Jamaica which go to the United States continue to increase in total value and in proportion to the whole amount of the trade', adding pointedly that the 'exports to the United Kingdom diminish steadily.' By 1900, 64 per cent of Jamaican exports went to the United States, while 43 per cent of imports came from that country[15] For those advocating imperial unity, such figures caused great anxiety.

The decision to negotiate with the United States for a new canal treaty, however, was made on diplomatic rather than commercial or imperial grounds and, however unappealing the prospect, the British Government quickly recognised the need for compromise for the sake of Anglo-American friendship. Thus, Canadian demands – that canal negotiations should only take place alongside similar discussions on the Alaskan boundary issue – were quickly disregarded. '[I]t is recognised by public opinion here that [the] claim of [the] United States for the revision of the Clayton-Bulwer Treaty is legitimate,' Joseph Chamberlain told Lord Minto, Canada's Governor-General, in January 1900.[16]

That Britain was now resigned to the imminent construction of the canal became clear when the Hay-Pauncefote treaty was signed the following month. Salisbury, in fact, was rather pleased with the arrangement. Writing to Queen Victoria, he contended that, while the treaty 'relaxes in some degree the Clayton-Bulwer treaty,' it did so 'without injuring in any way the essential interests of Great Britain.'[17] The Americans, he admitted, had a legitimate grievance, since the Clayton-Bulwer Treaty was unsuited to present conditions, yet his primary concern was the mood of the American people. Had Britain refused to modify her position, he noted, the United States may have been 'disposed to insist that the Clayton-Bulwer Treaty should be thrown over altogether.'[18]

Now that the canal treaty was finally signed, Salisbury's attention turned to other important foreign questions. Pauncefote kept his superiors apprised, but there is little evidence that the canal occupied much official Foreign Office business until mid December, a month after Lansdowne succeeded Salisbury. In late 1900, British statesmen were generally indifferent to the canal discussions. The ongoing struggle against the Boers, coupled with international negotiations in Peking, preoccupied both Government and people. As a result, British newspapers dealt with the Senate and the canal in a short, simple and factual manner. Such apathy was, for *The New York Times*, perfectly understandable: because of the war, it remarked, 'it is scarcely surprising that the public refused to be cajoled into taking a burning interest in the Nicaragua Canal.'[19]

When journalists did venture their opinions, however, they wholeheartedly advocated rejecting the Senate's amended treaty. On December 15, a *Manchester Guardian* reporter blamed the 'vacillating attitude of the Administration, and of its weakness in not insisting upon the [Hay-Pauncefote] treaty as it stood.' *The Times'* position was similarly direct. Its reporter in Washington commented that 'the humiliation of England will be complete if she submits to the terms the Senate has striven to impose on her.'[20]

On December 9 1900, Pauncefote sent a telegram to the Foreign Office with the news that the Hay-Pauncefote Treaty, together with amendments, was about to come before the Senate for ratification. The Ambassador urged acceptance, even if it should be amended beyond recognition, 'owing both to the improbability of any practical effect resulting from the [Davis] amendment and to the popular cry for a canal wholly American and without any restrictions whatever.'[21] The Cabinet had not discussed the subject since February, and was now forced quickly to assess its position. On December 14, Lansdowne handed a hastily written and largely pessimistic memorandum to his colleagues. If 'we refuse to accept the amendment of the Convention,' he explained, 'it seems probable that Congress will pass a bill on the lines of the Hepburn Bill virtually abrogating the Clayton-Bulwer Treaty.'[22]

Nevertheless, Lansdowne, supported by Salisbury, was prepared to risk just such a diplomatic confrontation, and, Pauncefote's advice disregarded, the Cabinet quickly agreed that they would reject the treaty should the amendments be passed. It 'was resolved that if we were asked whether we could consent to the proposed amendment, to answer in the negative', Salisbury informed the Queen, 'but otherwise to take no further action: preferring to rely upon the Clayton Bulwer treaty until it should actually be infringed.'[23] Directions in this sense were soon relayed to the British Embassy in Washington, together with an explanation. Admitting that he was unsure whether the amendments 'would have any practical effects injurious to our interests', Lansdowne told Pauncefote that,

> 'we have, it seems to me, to consider the moral as well as the material results which would follow from the virtual abrogation of the Clayton Bulwer Treaty with our consent, and the Cabinet held strongly that we ought not to acquiesce in this.'

Significantly, the Foreign Secretary refused to discount the possibility of further discussions with the United States. He went on:

> 'We are however only at the beginning of this affair and it is clear that for the present we shall do well to maintain reserve as to the conduct which we shall follow. The situation may alter at any moment. Much, it seems to me will depend upon the manner in which we are approached by the U.S. Govt., whenever it considers that the time has come for eliciting our views.'[24]

On December 24, Lansdowne sought a further indication of Admiralty opinion concerning the naval and strategic implications of the isthmian canal. The response was prompt, pointed and unwelcome: 'it is not really in the interests of Great Britain that it [the canal] should be constructed.'[25] Lansdowne now prepared a dispatch for the State Department listing Britain's objections to the amended treaty, but the delivery of the note was delayed on Pauncefote's advice until late February, when Congress adjourned.[26]

Significantly, Lansdowne's rejection was based, in the main, on the methods adopted by the Senate, rather than the substance of its amendments. Several British government officials, it is true, fully realised the need to placate the United States (and, soon, to pursue a policy of strategic withdrawal from the Western Hemisphere), but the practicality and desirability of surrendering Britain's rights to brash American demands could not be admitted; the Senate's high-handed actions were alone enough to warrant a rebuke. In a private note written in September 1912, during the Panama Tolls dispute, Lansdowne explained that his rejection had been primarily 'a question of principle.' The Clayton-Bulwer treaty was an internationally binding contract, he wrote. 'We objected to the attempt to abrogate [it] without a previous attempt to ascertain our views.'[27] On February 19 1901, Lansdowne explained the situation in a secret letter to the Washington Embassy, in which he stated that,

> 'from the U.S. Govt. we have had no hint of a desire to negotiate – no official intimation that the Senate amendments were offered, as Mr.

Choate told me privately, for our consideration. They have been thrown down upon the floor with an intimation that we are expected to pick them up and swallow them.'

Lansdowne went further and informed Pauncefote that Britain would have been more inclined to accept the amendments,

'if the U.S. Govt. had approached us differently, had endeavoured, e.g., to show us that the Davis amendment was not intended to interfere with the neutrality of the Canal and that they were ready to reconsider its language, and, if necessary, to add safeguards ... we have surely a right to ask that our temperate criticisms shall be examined and discussed with equal temperance'.[28]

By rejecting the amendments, then, Lansdowne intended to give the United States a lesson in diplomatic courtesy. The Foreign Office, without doubt, remained keen to maintain the fragile Anglo-American friendship, but felt that the Senate had asked for and expected too much. During an interview with a *New York Times* reporter, one undisclosed 'high authority' at the Foreign Office explained that Britain 'would not have abrogated the Clayton-Bulwer treaty for any other nation in the world. Unless all the traditions of British foreign policy are reversed, I fail to see how we can afford to give away any more advantages, even to America.'[29] In a similar vein, Lansdowne relayed to Pauncefote his conviction that Britain had gone as far as she could 'without loss of self-respect.'[30]

Although Lansdowne was primarily concerned by the diplomatic slight, he could hardly fail to criticise the amendments themselves. On January 14, he held an interview with Joseph Choate, the United States' Ambassador in London, where he labelled the Davis amendment 'dangerously vague', since 'it was open to the United States at any moment, not only if war existed, but even if it were anticipated, to take measures which, in their own judgement, might be suitable for the purpose of protecting themselves.'[31] Intervention might not only take the form of defence against European aggression; the protection of American rights and property in a notoriously unstable region could result in the constant presence of United States' forces: the isthmian canal zone would be United States' property in all but name. A more serious cause for concern was the removal of Article III, which had invited the adherence of foreign Powers. As a result, Lansdowne argued that other nations would receive preferential treatment, not having to respect the canal's neutrality. Lansdowne told Choate that,

'while the United States would have a Treaty right to interfere with the canal in time of war, or apprehended war, and while similar rights would be enjoyed by other Powers, this country alone, in spite of her enormous possessions on the American Continent, in spite of her Australasian Colonies, and her interests in the East, would be absolutely precluded from resorting to any such action.'[32]

In conclusion, Lansdowne refused to accept the possibility of agreement until the implicit discrimination of Britain was removed from the text. Choate countered quickly, commenting that the matter was of little practical importance and even accusing Lansdowne of 'regarding the subject in too critical a spirit.'[33]

Indeed, as far as practical politics were concerned, the issue really was relatively unimportant and both men probably understood this. After rejecting the Hay-Pauncefote Treaty because it gave other Powers a legitimate position in the Canal Zone, the United States was hardly likely to allow foreign nations freedom of action in the region, whether they adhered to the new treaty or not. Still, since the United States could not openly admit this, Lansdowne determined to stand firm, demanding that a suitable alternative must be found.

Despite his deep reservations, however, it is likely that Lansdowne's actions would have been very different had the Administration in Washington backed the Senate. In the event, Britain was quick to notice the friendly position taken by the State Department, which, on December 8, sent a notice to the nation's press that roundly criticised the Senate. After an agreement had been effected through the proper diplomatic channels, the statement went, it would be intolerable 'to throw over the terms which it [the State Department] had accepted and which are considered to be a perfectly fair disposition of a matter that has been a standing cause of irritation for years.'[34]

The startling division of opinion was not lost on Pauncefote, who informed Lansdowne that the 'bitter contest' between Administration and Senate was 'a surprise to the outside world and I believe to the President and his Cabinet.'[35] McKinley continued to take a passive role and the State Department, unwilling to rubber stamp the amended treaty; delivered it to British authorities and allowed the amendments to speak for themselves.[36]

Official policy aside, this was too important an issue to let rest and Henry White, Joseph Choate, even John Hay himself, all engaged in private communication with British officials to sort out the mess. Hay openly confessed his belief that the Senate had mangled his canal treaty, but urged Britain to accept the treaty for the sake of Anglo-American friendship.[37] White adopted a reassuring tone. To Balfour, he explained that 'no hostility to this country [Britain] appears to have been intended by the Senate in inserting the amendments in question.' Moreover, the amendments would only become significant during an Anglo-American conflict, a possibility that the American Chargé d'Affairs positively refused to entertain.[38] Choate joined the fray in a specially convened interview at the Foreign Office, a meeting that emphasised his rather awkward position. Realising that he could not deliver an official statement – and had no hopes of being able to do so in the foreseeable future – Choate nevertheless attempted to press Lansdowne informally to accept the amendments. The latter, in turn, was as bemused as he was irritated. 'The United States Govt. is behaving in a singular fashion over the amendments question', he told Pauncefote on January 17:

> 'After having requested ... a special interview for the purpose of explaining them to me, Mr. Choate told me that he was "absolutely

uninstructed" by his Govt., that all he had to say was for himself alone, and that he expected me not to repeat it except to Lord Salisbury! Of course I told Mr. Choate that although I should not – after what he had said – attribute his views to the U.S. Govt., I felt bound to lay them before the Cabinet for what they were worth. He appears to me mortally afraid of "giving himself away". I suppose Hay has the same feeling, and that while they wish probably to assure us and explain the amendments away, they intend, publicly, to show the amendments on the table of the F.O. … without a word of apology or explanation. I am very sorry that Hay has shown so little courage.'[39]

Still, Lansdowne continued to believe in Hay's friendly feelings towards Britain. A secret letter to Pauncefote, written on February 19, was particularly revealing. 'I do not attach too much importance to the extravagance of individual Senators,' Lansdowne remarked, 'above all I should be sincerely grieved if Mr. Hay's resignation were to be the result of what has taken place.'[40] Such fears were understandable. While Hay remained at his post, Britain could rely upon temperate and friendly diplomacy by the State Department; Hay's presence was vital for the canal issue to reach a peaceful settlement.

On January 15, Lansdowne predicted to the Cabinet that, if Pauncefote continued to use 'firm but conciliatory language', the US Government would quickly make fresh proposals.[41] Given the Cabinet's pessimism one month earlier, Lansdowne's new confidence must have caused great surprise. It seems likely that a conciliatory message from Hay, received just days before, played a significant role in increasing Lansdowne's optimism. Hay stressed that Britain had 'completely misunderstood' the Senate's actions of December 1900. That body had 'merely sought to suggest certain modifications which it deemed necessary in the text of the Treaty, and to submit them for our consideration.'[42] This was an interesting departure. Now, Lansdowne concluded that Britain's rejection would inspire further discussions, rather than create an acrimonious stalemate.

Choate became a frequent visitor at the Foreign Office during the early weeks of 1901. Unaware that the Cabinet had already decided to reject the treaty, he attempted to extract from the Foreign Secretary a clarification of British intent, stressing that 'the President and Secretary of State regarded the situation with considerable anxiety'.[43] Lansdowne, in turn, hinted that Britain favoured rejection and listed his grievances in a private interview on January 14. His concluding remarks were unequivocal, and deserve to be quoted at length:

'It was, I would not conceal from him, a very great disappointment to us to find that further changes were now insisted upon, all of them to the advantage of one side. He must not suppose that this feeling of disappointment was only entertained by prejudiced or ill-informed people; it was, moreover, aggravated by our experience of previous negotiations with the United States, which has on more than one occasion come to nothing, not, I thought, from any fault of ours.'[44]

Lansdowne's direct manner barely concealed his intention. Nevertheless, while Choate could have hardly been in any doubt about Britain's intent, he continued to press Lansdowne for a direct answer and the Foreign Secretary's refusal to be pinned down became a serious cause for complaint. Choate now accused Lansdowne of breaking off the informal discussions that had taken place between the two men. More than ever sure of his position, Lansdowne reacted with polite disdain. The Ambassador 'had expressly warned me against treating the observations which he then made as having any official authority', he commented wryly. 'I was not, therefore, breaking off negotiations with him, because no negotiations between us had begun.'[45]

On March 4, one year after it had been signed, the Hay-Pauncefote treaty quietly expired. The Senate accepted the news with resignation, expecting that further discussions would take place. Senator John T. Morgan alone continued to plead for the total abrogation of the Clayton-Bulwer treaty. The Alabaman Senator claimed that, although Britain was apparently willing to negotiate, she had no actual intention of permitting the canal to be built, thereby relinquishing her control over maritime trade. 'Great Britain, through Liverpool, which is the commercial centre of the world, is being enriched, and the United States, because of the lack of the Nicaragua Canal, is contributing to the enrichment of Great Britain.' Should Congress act on his advice, Morgan argued, it would prove 'that it was not chained to Britain.'[46]

Whilst the Senate remained as anxious as ever to facilitate the construction of the isthmian canal, it favoured a more temperate route than Morgan's firebranding. No further action could be approved until Britain's intentions were clarified. There would not be long to wait; in early March, rumours began to appear in American newspapers of an imminent response from the Foreign Office. *The New York Times* now predicted that an amicable compromise might be found: 'it is likely that it [Britain's reply] will be taken in good part, and that negotiations will be resumed for the conclusion of a new treaty'.[47]

Pauncefote called at the State Department at midday on March 7, and gave Hay a copy of Lansdowne's February 22 dispatch, which listed British grievances, but remained firmly courteous – Lansdowne's desire not to offend American sentiment was manifestly apparent. Most importantly, Lansdowne hinted that Britain would welcome further discussion and 'would sincerely regret a failure to come to an amicable understanding in regard to this important subject'.[48]

Pauncefote soon informed the Foreign Office that, although Hay was 'very depressed on the subject', he had 'naturally anticipated that His Majesty's Government had rejected the amendments made by the Senate'[49] – Lansdowne's carefully worded note had succeeded in appeasing American hostility. The Washington reporter for *The Times* commented that 'reasonable Americans do think the British attitude reasonable.' This was also the opinion of *The New York Times*, which commented that the 'tone of the reply is distinctly friendly throughout' and admitted that Britain's position was perfectly understandable.[50]

Naturally, less temperate opinions were expressed by those bitterly disappointed at the apparent failure of America's great undertaking. 'I think

Lansdowne's position is mischievous and ridiculous', Theodore Roosevelt told Henry Cabot Lodge, the outspoken Senator for Massachusetts. Henry Adams went even further and labelled the Foreign Secretary 'a vexation'. His appointment to the Foreign Office had been 'a blunder almost as serious as the Boer War.'[51]

The fear that Lansdowne's rejection might have angered the United States prompted a further declaration of Britain's friendly attitude on the canal issue. Balfour, speaking in the House of Commons on March 14, remarked that, although the Foreign Office had not initiated fresh negotiation, Britain 'would be ready to consider in a friendly way any proposals made for that object by the Government of the United States.'[52] Hay responded, as Lansdowne had predicted, by approaching Pauncefote on March 26, seeking 'an early opportunity to converse ... in regard to a possible basis of agreement.'[53]

Happily, the basis for a new treaty emerged with surprising speed. Hay had a set agenda: in Pauncefote's words, this was to 'carry out the same object in a manner which would conform better with Diplomatic usage and conciliate the views of all parties.' While British authorities welcomed Hay's activities, Pauncefote noted that the new treaty had little chance, 'unless the Suez Canal rules [respecting neutrality] were restored in their integrity and proper provision were made to obtain the agreement of the other powers to the Neutralization of the Canal'.[54] On May 4, Britain received the new proposals. Three days later, Lansdowne wrote to Pauncefote that there were 'as you point out ... several provisions which seem to require modification.'[55] However, the Foreign Secretary saw that negotiations could not proceed indefinitely and that the time had arrived for Britain to discard many of her previous objections.

Lansdowne's memo of July 6 says it all. A copy of this note was telegraphed to Pauncefote, who quickly assented to its content,[56] before it was shown to the Cabinet on July 8. Lansdowne's message was simple. Now that 'we are approached in a very different spirit by Mr Hay,' it was possible 'to deal somewhat less strictly with him so far as matters of form are concerned.'[57]

The right of the United States to abrogate the Clayton-Bulwer Convention could now be admitted, Lansdowne explained, providing the general neutrality of the canal was maintained. Furthermore, he now referred to the Senate's 'antagonistic' neutrality amendment as only a 'slight change from the original Treaty' and remarked that 'I do not know ... that this change of form is one to which we need seriously object.' Britain's objection to the construction of American forts along the Canal Zone was similarly played down:

> 'The Rule against fortification was, I believe, of no practical value to us: the United States would not be likely to spend money on expensive works at the mouth of the canal or throughout its course, nor, if they did, would the control of the canal in time of war depend upon the presence or absence of such works.'

If these arguments surprised the Cabinet, they hardly represented a fundamental departure for the Foreign Secretary, who had long considered the amendments to have only theoretical significance. However, while he was fully prepared to yield, Lansdowne worried about the diplomatic effect of such wholesale concessions and commented that 'however much we may desire an amicable settlement, it will be impossible for us to abandon the strong position which we took up in our dispatch of the 22nd February'.[58]

Throughout the ensuing negotiations, therefore, Lansdowne resolved gradually to abandon the high ground. The Powers should still be invited to adhere to the new treaty and Lansdowne, determined that Britain should not suffer sole discrimination, refused to give way entirely on this point. Luckily, discussions on this subject quickly resulted in an amicable compromise. Lodge, living in London that summer, met the Foreign Secretary on July 19 and observed that the United States 'were now prepared to take upon themselves the sole responsibility not only for constructing the canal, but for maintaining its neutrality.' As Lodge himself noted, this 'changed the situation considerably'.[59] No longer suffering the onerous responsibility of guaranteeing the neutrality of the isthmian canal, Lansdowne declared himself generally satisfied.

The informal negotiations now began to show great promise and, with the chances of an amicable settlement increasing, feelings of relief and optimism spread in British diplomatic circles. Pauncefote, who had returned to Britain for the summer to join Lansdowne, Choate and White in serious discussion, was especially pleased with the progress of negotiations. He told a reporter for *The Times* in July that,

> 'when I return to the United States at the end of October I hope to take with me a Nicaragua Treaty to meet the views of both the President and the British Government ... I believe that the differences of opinion between the two nations are capable of settlement in an agreement fair to both.'[60]

Hay was equally enthusiastic. 'Lord P[auncefote] sailed for this side yesterday,' he told Clarence King on October 27, 'bringing with him the British assent to my new Canal Treaty. I have got everything I asked for, after a whole summer of good-natured negotiation.'[61] In the meantime, with the success of the canal treaty apparently secured, Henry Cabot Lodge took the opportunity to send Lansdowne a copy of his article "The Treaty-Making Powers of the Senate" which argued that Britain had misunderstood the Senate's intentions when amending the canal treaty. The amendments, Lodge explained, were not intended as absolute demands, rather they had been intended for Britain's perusal and modification. The article went further by criticising Lansdowne personally. The United States had a right to expect that such 'a statesman of long experience ... should understand thoroughly the constitutional provisions and modes of governmental procedure in the United States.'[62]

Of course, Lodge's explanation was hardly new. It will be remembered that, as early as January 8, John Hay had informed Lansdowne that the Senate had only sought to suggest modifications to the canal treaty. At this time, the Foreign

Secretary requested Pauncefote's opinion. While such an interpretation was indeed possible, Pauncefote replied, 'the President has not adopted a course of action consistent with that view.'[63] The amendments, after all, had been handed to Britain without an explanation from either McKinley or the State Department. It appeared, therefore, that the Administration had bowed to the Senate's demands and accepted the treaty as amended. Lansdowne now had to consider how he would reply to Lodge. Fully understanding that, at this crucial stage, it was important not to create further friction by entering into an unprofitable and potentially bitter argument, the Foreign Secretary instead restricted himself to expressions of goodwill, and commented that 'I am glad to have before me an exposition of it [the constitutional point] by one so well qualified as you are to inform the public on such a subject.'[64]

Lansdowne continued to pursue a policy of gradual concession and proposed further slight modifications to bring the treaty in line with the Suez Canal Convention of 1888. In reply, Hay admitted the strength of Britain's case, but reminded Pauncefote that it was useless to discuss changes to which the Senate would not agree. While 'this is a consideration which we have no right to bring forward in discussing a matter of principle with a friendly Power', Hay admitted, 'we ourselves must always bear in mind the conditions under which we labor.'[65] In fact, both Lansdowne and Salisbury shared Hay's desperation for the canal issue to be quickly settled and, with little ceremony, the changes proposed by the Foreign Office were summarily abandoned. Sufficient minor modifications had been made to the treaty to satisfy the Foreign Secretary and Cabinet and, on October 7, Salisbury informed Lansdowne that he was 'quite content' with the new treaty.[66] In a final memorandum for the Cabinet, dated October 16, Lansdowne expressed his personal desire to accept the new treaty:

> 'I shall be glad to know as soon as possible whether these proposals have the approval of the Cabinet. It is, as I have pointed out, important that the United States' Government should be made aware of our decision without loss of time, and, unless I learn from any of my colleagues ... that they desire further alterations in the draft, I propose ... to inform the United States' Chargé d'Affairs that His Majesty's Government are prepared to accept the draft as amended.'[67]

Lansdowne received only one reply. Chancellor Sir Michael Hicks Beach had no intention of prolonging negotiations by suggesting further alterations, but worried about the manner with which the British public would receive the new canal treaty. The Americans, he wrote,

> 'not merely from their natural love of crowing, but also in order to get the Senate to ratify, are certain to say that we have yielded everything. You must, I think, be able to show that this is not the fact: and therefore I should hope that you will have a dispatch ready for publication at the proper time, proving it.'[68]

On both sides of the Atlantic, influential supporters made the case for ratification. Lodge prepared to return to the United States in October to defend it whole-heartedly in the Senate.[69] This was hardly required, since Hay had remained in constant communication with several Senators during the preceding months whilst negotiating the new treaty. Ratification was already effectively ensured. After the shooting of President McKinley on September 6, moreover, the mood of Anglo-American relations suddenly became more conciliatory. To the American people, still suspicious of her motives, Britain's expressions of condolence came as a pleas-ant surprise. It is worth noting that the Foreign Office's dismayed reaction was absolutely sincere. Hearing of McKinley's relapse, Lansdowne wrote that the President's 'death would be a calamity for the whole world and a very great mis-fortune to this country. I trust we may escape it.'[70] It was to be a futile hope, as McKinley's death on September 14 was followed by the inauguration of Theodore Roosevelt, that unpredictable 'cowboy', to the White House.

Meanwhile, on November 18, Hay and Pauncefote signed the new Canal Treaty, which, with little delay, was ratified by the Senate. The final agreement entirely satisfied the American demands, yet managed to appease both nations. To the United States was given the right to maintain 'such military police along the canal as may be necessary to protect it against lawlessness and disorder.'[71] Moreover, the phrase that had allowed foreign vessels free passage through the canal in wartime was omitted in the new treaty; temporary deneutralisation by the United States was thereby permitted.[72]

Britain gained little, although she was no longer expected to guarantee the canal's neutrality alone. Most importantly, if the terms of the treaty uniformly favoured the United States, the Foreign Office had not surrendered any vital inter-ests that it had not already decided to abandon in February 1900. Personally, Lansdowne declared himself pleased with the final result. By rejecting the amend-ments, he had forced the United States to pursue temperate and traditional diplo-macy. Because of this, Britain could surrender insignificant treaty rights without loss of self-respect. Lansdowne's firm, but courteous approach to American affairs, it appeared, had been fully vindicated.

On November 27, an eminently contented Foreign Secretary spoke publicly on the subject during a speech at the Drill-hall in Darlington. Lansdowne began by emphasising his respect for the new President. 'Like our brothers across the ocean,' he explained, 'we regarded with the most friendly predispositions the dis-tinguished man who had succeeded to the Presidency of the U.S.' He continued:

> 'Throughout the [canal] negotiations, the question had been discussed by both sides in no narrow or one-sided spirit, but with a genuine desire on our part that this great enterprise should be conducted to a suc-cessful issue; that the principles of neutrality of the canal for which we had contended should be maintained: that it should be opened and free to the commerce of the whole world; and that these objects should be achieved under conditions honourable and convenient to both sides alike. (Cheers.)'[73]

Lansdowne – who rarely gave public speeches – evidently intended this timely address not merely for the British audience, but to be heard as strongly on the other side of the Atlantic. Now that the issue had reached an amicable conclusion, it was vital that the two nations resume their amicable relations and the enthusiastic response in Washington that greeted the new canal treaty was a natural cause for celebration. On December 19, Pauncefote wrote of his conversation with the Secretary of State:

> 'He [Hay] begged me to thank you and to express again to you the deep sense entertained by him and his Govt. of the broadminded and generous statesmanship displayed by H. M. Govt. throughout the negotiations of the Canal Treaty and which has led to so happy a result.'[74]

Parliamentary support for the new treaty was equally effusive. Throughout the affair, MPs had shown little interest in proceedings, and only a handful of questions were asked on the subject throughout the whole of 1901. Now, in the Lords on January 16 1902, Earl Lytton expressed his hope 'that all future discussions on points of difference between the two countries may be discussed in the same friendly spirit, and may be crowned with an equally satisfactory result.' Earl Spencer noted that 'we must rejoice that His Majesty's Government have had the courage to carry through this treaty, and I congratulate them upon it.'[75]

Those who had created the new treaty were similarly pleased. The popular belief, that, by abandoning insignificant treaty rights, Britain had furthered Anglo-American harmony, created a celebratory mood in official circles. In November, Pauncefote happily wrote to the Foreign Secretary of the cordiality towards Britain harboured by the American people. 'There is a general feeling,' he noted, 'that our attitude has been generous and friendly and that the Treaty will do much to keep up our good relations.' In a rather expansive mood, he remarked that, 'for ourselves we have surrendered no right worth keeping and have saved for the world at large the great principle of the Clayton-Bulwer Treaty, which Congress would undoubtedly have scattered to the winds, had we not come to terms.'[76] On January 30 1902, Pauncefote told his friend, Sir Charles Dilke, that,

> 'no one better than yourself can appreciate the far reaching importance of the result obtained and of the benefit which we gain therefrom ... the improvement of our relations with the U.S. instead of a return to the old state of international rancour. We have given up nothing worth keeping at the present day and indeed the new Treaty is just as good as the Clayton-Bulwer Convention and better suited to existing conditions.'[77]

For his part, the Foreign Secretary felt similarly inclined towards self-congratulation. With one of the great Anglo-American issues resolved, Lansdowne began to anticipate further amicable discussions on other outstanding diplomatic questions, primarily the vexing Alaskan boundary dispute. 'The conditions are favourable and indeed they may never be more so', he told Pauncefote on December 31. 'How delightful it would be if you should be able, before you leave Washington, to give us that clean slate which we all so much desire.'[78]

At the same time, the dismay with which Pauncefote's diplomatic colleagues in Washington reacted to the success of the canal treaty became a secondary cause for satisfaction. The Ambassador penned a rather smug dispatch on December 19 explaining that 'it was hoped no doubt that the Treaty would ... be mangled in the Senate and the Entente Cordiale would perish with it. If we now settle the Alaska Trouble they will be in despair'.[79] Whether the new Canal Treaty gave to Britain or to the United States the advantage was, for many European Powers, wholly insignificant. Of greater concern to the great Powers was the prospect of closer Anglo-American friendship and possible co-operation between the two nations in other areas of the globe. 'What you tell me with regard to your foreign colleagues is very suggestive,' Lansdowne replied on December 31. 'I have received two or three disinterested ... warnings from similar sources as to the danger with which the proposed [Isthmian Canal] Convention was believed to bustle.'[80]

The feeling that the canal negotiations had set an unwelcome precedent did not, however, escape everybody. Goldwin Smith, who had long advocated a stronger Anglo-American understanding, believed that Britain was simply no longer able to resist American demands in the Western Hemisphere. Writing to Sir Charles Dilke in November, Smith foresaw an impotence in British diplomacy on the American continent: whatever 'the Americans concede short of their extreme demands must be conceded to international rights and their own reputation, of which, to do them justice, they are not regardless.'[81]

Negotiations on the Alaskan question would determine whether the United States was to exhibit friendship or force in its future diplomacy with the Foreign Office and whether Britain was indeed defenceless against American pressure in the Western Hemisphere. Before negotiations on the Alaskan boundary question could reach a conclusion, however, an unexpected crisis in Anglo-American relations developed, in late 1902, when Britain's naval intervention against the Castro Administration in Venezuela threatened suddenly to destroy the growing, but ever fragile *rapprochement*.

2

That Disreputable Little Republic

Great Britain and Venezuela, 1901-December 1902

WHEN THE NEWS that Britain and Germany had undertaken a joint
naval action against Venezuela reached the House of Commons in mid
December 1902, there was a dismayed and incredulous response. That
Britain should use the might of her navy to extract a relatively insignificant sum
from the Castro Administration seemed positively unbelievable. It was, said Mr.
Schwann, Member of Parliament for Manchester, 'like using a Nasmyth hammer
in order to crack a nut.' More critically, anxiety was expressed concerning the
potentially damaging consequences that such action might have on the Anglo-
American relationship. Lord Charles Beresford[1] argued that 'whatever we do, we
ought to be most careful to cement friendly feeling with the Government of the
United States. We should do nothing of any kind, sort, or description that would
be in the least way provocative of irritation or animosity on the part of the United
States.' It was a matter of general agreement that, although America was not likely
to interfere in the dispute, public opinion, always a powerful determinant in the
national policy of the United States, could at any moment become enraged 'which
may make the position more serious for this country.' In short, the proposed action
was considered to be both ill-conceived and dangerous.[2]

This interpretation has been generally accepted in historical circles ever
since. It is now almost unanimously accepted that the Unionists were slow to
appreciate the dangers of involvement in disputes with Central and South
American countries and that Britain should have listened to the bellicose tone of
America's foreign policy, particularly her much publicised determination to protect and advance the Monroe Doctrine.[3] Furthermore, little thought, it is argued,
was given to the ever fragile Anglo-Saxon unity: 'now Balfour and Lord
Lansdowne were upsetting the delicate balance of this mighty combination,'
writes Élie Halévy, 'a combination not so much political as sentimental.'[4]

Yet an alternative explanation of the dispute seems worthy of consideration.
The evidence suggests that, while Lansdowne and Balfour did worry about inflam-
ing American opinion, the danger was simply not apparent in the final months of
1902. The precedent shown in European quarrels with both Guatemala and the
Dominican Republic suggested that the United States would raise no serious
objections, provided that whatever measures of coercion were adopted, they

would be both moderate and short-lived. In December 1902, one Congressman told Sir Michael Herbert, Britain's Ambassador in Washington after the death of Sir Julian Pauncefote, 'you can spank Venezuela if you like. She deserves it; but don't take too long about it.'[5]

The 1902-3 Venezuela blockade, then, was not so much ill-conceived as badly managed and it was primarily the indiscretions committed by both navies, at La Guaira and Puerto Cabello, that caused the surge of anger throughout the United States. British and German statesmen, however, failed to appreciate the wiles of President Castro and the extent of his defiance. It was easy to think of Castro as a 'tin-pot' dictator, whose decrepit navy was unable to withstand two mighty European nations, but Castro never held any hope of naval victory. Instead, he skillfully began influencing popular opinion in the United States and his late appeal for arbitration – carefully sent through the United States' Government – was an effective means of ensuring American interference.

The boundary dispute between British Guiana and Venezuela ended as the twentieth century began. On October 3 1900, the boundary was finally laid out, almost a year after the judicial tribunal published their findings. It was a quiet end to a quarrel that had threatened to mar Anglo-American relations. American writer and lecturer John Bassett Moore now admitted that 'I believe I was the first person in this country to consider the boundary dispute on [its] merits, and it is not improbable that I may yet be the last'.[6] It was perhaps natural, now that Britain could forget the troublesome dispute, that complacency should begin to manifest itself in official circles. Sir Walter J. Sendall, Governor of British Guiana, wrote that the 'award has been received here with a universal feeling of satisfaction, and I cordially agree with you in thinking that the thanks of the Colony are due to those whose labours have been attended with so favourable a result.' Chamberlain, in response, expressed pleasure that the matter was finally settled.[7]

Yet Castro began playing up as soon as the boundary line was settled. His country in turmoil and his position under constant threat, he refused to pay international debts and initiated discriminatory measures against foreign nationals and shipping.[8] In February 1901, soldiers from the Venezuelan gunboat "Augusto" landed on Patos, an island claimed to be part of the colony of Trinidad and, as such, under dubious British authority. Reports complained of the 'seizure of persons and property of certain individuals, some of whom are British subjects.'[9]

A protest was sent, but received no reply. Instead, the outrages continued. In April, Sir Alfred Moloney, the Governor of Trinidad, complained of the 'illegal activity' of Venezuelan 'guardacostas', again trespassing on Patos, and burning the British sloop "Marie Teresa" in Guiria.[10] The cool response from Venezuela was to become typical. After a meeting in April between Venezuela's Foreign Minister, General Diego B. Ferrer and Sir William Haggard, Britain's Minister in Caracas, the latter explained that,

'I concluded the interview by urging his Excellency to lose no time in bringing to justice the authors of the various outrages on British subjects. He replied that the inquiry was actually being held into these cases, but he in no way pledged himself as to its result.'[11]

As Haggard correctly predicted, the inquiry came to nothing. These were not to be isolated incidents. During the ensuing months, Venezuelan forces repeatedly detained or destroyed British ships and harassed British subjects, while Haggard's successive representations to the Castro administration – he made seventeen in all – were steadfastly ignored. To Lansdowne, Haggard complained that, in the light of the Venezuelans' refusal to 'entertain any question with Her Majesty's Legation save one in which they conceive their own interests to be concerned, I do not expect to [receive a reply] until the present situation changes.'[12]

Initially, the Foreign Office showed remarkable restraint. The German Minister at Caracas, von Pilgrim-Baltazzi hinted in September 1901 that Haggard had raised the subject of possible Anglo-German co-operation against Castro, but there is no evidence that this proposal was taken seriously. Certainly, Haggard did not repeat his idea to the Foreign Office.[13] By December, after another excursion by Venezuelan soldiers on Patos and the detention of the "Pastor", Haggard confined himself to the suggestion that 'the repeated violation of territory may make it desirable to record a further strong remonstrance against any infraction of the sovereign rights of Great Britain.'[14] After witnessing the results of previous representations, this clearly was a hopeless gesture.

Neither did Lansdowne show any desire to sanction strong punitive measures against Castro. Dismissing Venezuelan arguments that sought to establish their legitimate ownership of Patos as not 'of sufficient importance to call for a reply', he refused to bar Venezuelan ships from Britain's territorial waters, feeling that there were insufficient grounds for such a move.[15] Meanwhile, Haggard's frustration continued to mount. In one confidential dispatch, he remarked that 'I cannot hold out to your Lordship the prospect of any change so long as General Castro remains in power', and added that 'until that moment His Majesty's Legation will be deprived of its *raison d'être* as a means of official communication with the Venezuelan Government and remains in the somewhat absurd and useless position in which it has been for the last five months.'[16]

That Castro was not the kind of man with whom Britain could conduct proper diplomacy was quickly becoming evident. His arrogant and high-handed behaviour had not only offended the Foreign Office, but even General Ferrer admitted that his President 'was a very difficult man to deal with, very wrong-headed when he got an idea into his head.'[17] Others were less kind; contemporary observers described Castro as 'the greatest international nuisance of the twentieth century', a man with 'no concept of justice.'[18] Given the fact that diplomacy had produced such meagre rewards, it was now vital that Britain take a more determined stand.

The nature of the stand, however, still needed consideration. In January 1902, the Foreign Office began discussing with its German counterpart the possibility of undertaking the coercion of Venezuela in co-operation, but at this time their proposals were both tentative and vague.[19] The truth was that, for different reasons, neither country wanted to use force. Until May 1902, Britain's military involvement in South Africa ensured that disputes with South American republics took second place. While it was true that British resources were stretched and that a sizeable fleet could not be spared, however, the implicit decision not to punish Castro during the war was not merely logistic. Involvement in another dispute would have been unpopular with the British public, tired of foreign conflicts. At the same time, Lansdowne could not ignore the danger that an aggressive policy might reawaken the hostility of Europe, which had accentuated British isolation and established in official circles a sense of international weakness. After Vereeniging,[20] however, Britain was in a stronger position, both strategically and diplomatically, and could afford to play the aggressor.

That Britain might be obliged to intervene in South American affairs to protect her interests led the Foreign Office, in early 1902, initially to resist an Admiralty request to reduce the Pacific Squadron. It was not, after all, solely Venezuelan affairs that worried Lansdowne, but the general unhealthy state of Latin American politics and the Foreign Office was perfectly willing to undertake limited coercive measures to protect the lives and property of British subjects overseas. Sir Evan MacGregor, the Admiralty's Permanent Secretary, wrote of the 'great development which is taking place in certain foreign Navies' and advocated the need for the greater concentration of Britain's fleets.[21] With little delay, MacGregor received the following reply from Sir Francis Villiers, Assistant Under Secretary at the Foreign Office:

> 'in the disturbances which so frequently occur at, or near, South American ports, the presence of one of H[is] M[ajesty's] Ships is invaluable for the protection of British property and sometimes life, and even, on some occasions for the restoration of order.'

He went on:

> 'Lord Lansdowne would therefore be glad to be informed to what extent it is proposed to reduce the Pacific Squadron and whether the reduction would restrict to any considerable degree the assistance hitherto afforded by H[is] M[ajesty's] Ships in those regions.'[22]

MacGregor's note of reassurance stressed that only one sloop would be removed, leaving three cruisers and a single sloop. This would not 'restrict to any material extent, the assistance hitherto afforded by His Majesty's Ships'. Relieved, the Foreign Office consented on March 12. Provided the Pacific Squadron would still be able to deliver an effective response, Lansdowne declared himself satisfied.[23]

In the meantime, it was obvious that an armed response was the only effective means of resolving the Venezuelan dispute, but Lansdowne still inclined towards leniency. In June the "General Crespo", a Venezuelan gunboat, sank the British sloop "In Time". Moloney responded angrily and suggested that the "General Crespo" should itself be seized, but Lansdowne demurred, replying on

July 1 that 'stronger evidence would undoubtedly be necessary in order to justify so drastic a measure as the seizure of the Venezuelan gun-boat.' Instead, he proposed to instruct Castro that 'His Majesty's Government may be obliged to cease extending the hospitality of British ports to Venezuelan cruisers.'[24] A mild threat at most, it nonetheless represented a departure from Britain's position over the last year. However, later in July, Lansdowne finally accepted the need for more energetic measures, following the seizure of the "Queen", detained under the charge of gunrunning. '"We clearly cannot let this pass"' the Foreign Secretary declared on July 19. The need to use force against Castro had at last been admitted.[25]

The rapid evolution in British thinking during June and July explains Lansdowne's reaction to the German proposal of July 23 that Germany and Britain together carry out the coercion of Venezuela. Although cautious, the Foreign Secretary was conspicuously relieved at this unexpected assistance. 'Unless His Majesty's Government received explicit assurances that incidents of this nature shall not recur,' he wrote on July 29, 'and unless the Venezuelan Government promptly pay to the injured parties full compensation ... His Majesty's Government will take such steps as they are entitled to demand from the Venezuelan Government.' That the initiative had steeled Lansdowne's resolve was confirmed as he sounded out Admiralty opinions in early August.[26]

Lansdowne might have accepted the notion of Anglo-German co-operation, but neither he nor his newly-appointed superior, Arthur Balfour, was initially prepared to sanction any coercion beyond the seizure of Venezuela's gunboats.[27] The viability (and wisdom) of a naval blockade of Venezuelan ports became a matter of serious discussion amongst British statesmen and strategists. Despite Admiralty endorsement, Lansdowne worried about possible international complications that might follow such a move, particularly with the Americans. '[A] belligerent blockade might involve us in troublesome questions with other Powers', he told Sir Frank Lascelles in late October.[28] Balfour wholeheartedly shared Lansdowne's anxiety. To King Edward, he explained that:

> 'This disreputable little Republic has been committing a series of outcries on us and on the Germans: and some ... action is absolutely necessary in order to exact reparation. ... A blockade has been suggested: but a blockade injures not only the countries blockaded, but the neutrals who trade with it:– and on the whole it seems better, if it be practicable, to seize the Venezuelan gunboats in concert with the Germans.'[29]

This was not to say that a blockade was entirely ruled out. In a Cabinet memorandum, printed on November 24, Lansdowne stressed that the seizure of gunboats would be the primary method of coercion, but if 'this should fail to produce the necessary effect, further measures will be taken the exact nature of which is still under consideration.' In the same note, Lansdowne formally announced the Anglo-German partnership. 'Joint action, if undertaken,' he explained, 'will be maintained, unless terminated by mutual consent until the demands of both

Governments have been satisfied.'[30] In effect, then, Britain was tied to Germany until the dispute ended. At the time, the dangers of such a firm contract were hardly appreciated by members of the British Government, believing that decisive action against Venezuela would bring about a quick and satisfactory settlement. If Lansdowne and Balfour really believed that the seizure of Venezuelan gunboats would be enough to bring Castro to reason, however, they woefully misread the extent of Castro's defiance. As it turned out, Lansdowne was forced to sacrifice diplomatic caution in mid December and a last-minute decision was made to sanction a blockade of Venezuelan ports.[31]

The restraint shown by Britain during 1901 and 1902 had many causes. In part, it was a result of British preoccupation with South Africa and a consequence of Lansdowne's cautious approach to international affairs. Another contributing factor, which played a significant role in delaying the use of force against Castro, was consideration of American sentiment. Britain had begun to view Anglo-American friendship as a major foreign policy priority and, for this reason, Germany's personal attack upon the well-liked and trusted Sir Julian Pauncefote came as a severe blow. In response to George Smalley's statement in *The Times*, stating that Britain had been America's greatest friend during the Spanish-American war, Germany accused Pauncefote of taking a line – rather in advance of his diplomatic colleagues – in order to prevent the war entirely. The venerable Ambassador protested, and was able to report on February 28 that,

> 'I have been fairly treated by the more respectable Press, and nobody believes that I ever said or did anything with an unfriendly intent towards the United States. Accordingly I have received the most warm and gratifying expressions of sympathy and support from the President, the Secretary of State, members of the Cabinet, prominent Senators ... and from society in general who believe that there was a plot against me.'[32]

The Pauncefote case caused a tangible wave of panic throughout British circles. To Lansdowne, Chamberlain voiced his hope that the Foreign Office would rebuff the accusations. 'The situation in the United States is rather critical', he explained. More significantly, it was now more important to conciliate the United States than Germany.[33] While Pauncefote's behaviour in 1898 has since been called into question,[34] however, the incident caused no lasting damage, and was treated as little less than slander in Washington. In the event, Pauncefote himself was the only casualty. '[T]he shock of the sudden attack', Sir Thomas Sanderson, Permanent Under Secretary at the Foreign Office, wrote to Lascelles on June 2, the 'fuss and worry and controversy had the most painful effect on him and one from which his health never recovered.'[35]

Britain's restraint in the Venezuelan affair had very specific roots. Of the Americans' sensitivity regarding South America, Lansdowne was of course aware. Speeches by such influential Americans as Theodore Roosevelt and Henry Cabot

Lodge expressed an increasing desire to protect the Monroe Doctrine, if necessary with force. At the recent Pan-American Exhibition at Buffalo, both Roosevelt and Lodge stressed that 'renewed and formal notice should be served upon Europe that the United States were more than ever determined to "jealously maintain the doctrine of Monroe."' As President, Roosevelt continued to urge upon his countrymen the need for a powerful navy to repel European aggressors on South American soil. Speaking in Vermont in 1902, Roosevelt again explained his position: 'Shame on us if we assert the Monroe Doctrine, and then, if our assertions shall be called into question, show only that we made an idle boast and that we are unprepared to back our words by deeds.'[36]

It is often argued that remarks of this sort provided a tangible argument against armed action off the Venezuelan coast. In fact, when it came to Latin American debt, Roosevelt tended to side with Europe. As Vice-President, he declared: 'If any South American country misbehaves towards any European country, let the European country spank it.'[37] His position is easily explained: it was due to the chronic state of revolt prevalent in Central America, and the tendency towards non-payment of debts by unreliable dictators that provoked in Europe and in the United States a similar degree of resentment. In December 1902, the editor of *The New York Times* wrote that 'We do not, Monroe Doctrine or no Monroe Doctrine, "stand for" fraudulent debtors, any more than we stand for nests of pirates or highwaymen.'[38] Moreover, once the canal treaty was signed in November 1901, the United States, more than any other nation, wanted to see calm restored in the area. Consequently, Roosevelt was consistently to speak out against Latin American debtors. The President's 1901 Message to Congress stated that 'We do not guarantee any State against punishment ... provided that punishment does not take the form of the acquisition of territory by any non-American power.'[39] Hay was yet more explicit to Pauncefote. On December 2, the latter relayed Hay's remarks to Arthur Larcom, Chief Clerk to the Foreign Office's American Department:

> 'the U.S. suffered quite as much as other nations from the misconduct of the Republics in question and their disregard of national obligations, They had the folly to imagine that European Powers are debarred from enforcing their rights against them by the Monroe Doctrine and he hoped they would soon have a rude awakening from that dream, as the President disclaimed any such fallacy.'

A much-heartened Pauncefote concluded that the 'only remedy I can see is to try to induce the U. S. Govt. when a strong case arises to intimate as much to the offending Republic, and if it be still obdurate to resort to force'.[40]

With such approval, the fear of stepping upon the somewhat blurred edges of the Monroe Doctrine soon evaporated in Europe and a succession of punitive measures followed. The Guatemalan dispute began early in 1901, when President Manuel Estrada Cabrera's regime defaulted on payment of the Republic's external debt to foreign bondholders. In Britain, the decision to exert pressure on Cabrera was not taken lightly. At the Admiralty, Lord Selborne predicted grave consequences; writing to Lansdowne he argued that 'you will see that a real danger exists there especially [since] the American Government is beginning to take such a close interest in Central America.' However, Selborne's fears, that the United States 'could give the Lion's tail a very disagreeable twisting' proved to be unfounded.[41] Cabrera's resistance crumbled in mid 1902 in the face of pressure from Britain, Germany, France and Belgium, so there was no need to resort to force. The proposed measures against Guatemala, significantly, provoked nothing but indifference in American political circles. Hay saw no cause for alarm 'inasmuch as it is within the right of the creditor nations to require payment of debts due to their nationals.'[42] The total failure of this episode to excite the wrath of the United States – and particularly the agreeable, friendly response of the State Department – was not forgotten.

Moreover, during the formulation of her response to the Guatemalan situation, Britain showed far more consideration towards the United States than has previously been suggested. One historian has argued that there is no evidence that the Foreign Office consulted the State Department regarding Guatemala.[43] On the contrary, as early as April 1901, Pauncefote brought the matter to Hay's attention and called for 'a kind of solidarity as it were among foreign Powers by means of mutual assistance to recover just debts.' The British Ambassador even went so far as to say that 'this is certainly a case where the powerful assistance of your Government would be justly bestowed.'[44]

Neither was Britain reticent about consulting Washington about the dispute with the Dominican Republic that flared up in 1902. Pauncefote enquired whether the Americans would 'feel disposed to take joint action with His Majesty's Government in support of the British and United States bondholders, whose interests appear to be alike injured by the attempts of the Dominican Government to evade their obligations.' Hay's evasive reply, which did not question the right to exert punitive measures but rather dodged the question of Anglo-American cooperation, was attributed to 'the traditional policy of the United States to avoid any action in conjunction with a European Power.'[45] It did not matter that both the dispute with Guatemala and that with the Dominican Republic were settled peaceably: what was of fundamental importance to the Foreign Office was the trend shown by Roosevelt's administration and all signs unmistakably pointed towards the resigned acceptance by the State Department of the right of European nations to coerce defaulting republics in Latin America.

Furthermore, Castro was considered in the United States to be even more troublesome than most Latin American despots. An article in the *Washington Post* in October 1902 argued that Venezuela was 'particularly hostile to the United States', a surprising fact 'in view of the fact that this country almost went to war with Great Britain over the question of British encroachment on Venezuelan soil.'[46] Something needed to be done to protect US interests in the region and the resulting formation of the West Indian Squadron in October was a strong statement of intent. Arthur Raikes, Britain's Chargé d'Affairs at the Washington Embassy, temporarily in control following the death of Sir Julian Pauncefote, wrote that the State Department was contemplating further strong measures in the isthmus. Raikes reported that it was only Castro's last-minute decision not the carry out his threat to cut cable communication that now prevented the United States landing a strong force of marines.[47] This was probably an empty threat. If Roosevelt really intended to land troops in Central America, it was a sharp departure from the non-interventionist policy that the United States had maintained since the Venezuelan boundary dispute of 1896.

Castro's unruly behaviour gained speed as the year ended. With his few dilapidated gunboats he attempted to establish a blockade of the Orinoco. On July 29, Lansdowne directed Arthur Raikes to ascertain the State Department's response. Accordingly, the Chargé d'Affairs sent a note to Hay stressing that,

'as it is quite impossible for the Venezuelan Government to render effective the blockade which they have notified, with the resources at their disposed His Majesty's Government are of [the] opinion that they will be justified in declining to accept such notification as creating a state of blockade, and [ask] whether the United States Government would join in making a communication to this effect to the Venezuelan Government.'[48]

With the State Department still deciding whether or not to recognise the blockade, the British cruiser "Phaeton" sailed down the river, broke through the weak cordon of Venezuelan ships and entered Ciudad Bolivar. The British colony there was 'found to be almost destitute'.[49] The "Phaeton" had singlehandedly exposed the weakness of Castro's navy, yet the State Department continued to vacillate, neither recognising the blockade nor attempting to break through. In December, it was reported in *The New York Times* that 1,375 ships of all nationalities had entered and left the Orinoco without incurring any damage while American vessels languished in Port of Spain with their cargoes spoiling.[50] It was an embarrassing situation that highlighted Roosevelt's refusal to intervene in Latin American affairs, even when American interests were directly threatened.

If the United States was unprepared to punish Castro, it was not blind to his motives, so it is not surprising that Roosevelt dismissed Castro's declaration of peaceful intent in mid November 1902. Aware that measures were now underway in Europe against him, Castro stressed that 'Venezuela entertained a cordial, sympathetic friendship for the United States, and desired that the closest relations should exist between the two countries.' A late appeal to the Monroe Doctrine would have no effect, replied the State Department, remarking that '[t]he United States does not propose to see Venezuela oppressed or spoilated. That is certain. But neither does it propose to uphold Venezuela, or any other State, in wrongdoing.'[51] The Germans, informing Washington of their intent to coerce Castro, were told that 'no difficulties need be anticipated' from the United States Government and, in November, Sir Michael Herbert, newly-appointed Ambassador in Washington, reported that both the President and Hay had spoken 'encouragingly' regarding the imminent action against Castro.[52]

As soon as it became clear that the measures of coercion would go ahead, however, Roosevelt and Hay suddenly became decidedly cool. Hay repeated his opinion that the United States 'could not object to [European nations] taking steps to obtain redress', but stated that his government 'regretted that European Powers should use force against Central and South America.'[53] It is doubtful whether this remark was intended to push Britain into a change of policy; rather, it can be taken as a further indication that the United States would not countenance the protracted presence of European warships off the Venezuelan coast. Whatever Hay's intention, American anxiety in late 1902 was neither visible nor strong enough to warrant a change of British plans. Herbert mentioned the Venezuelan affair infrequently. He was clearly more concerned about the Alaska boundary question, which, during 1902, constituted the greatest threat to Anglo-American friendship. Furthermore, even in the dispatches he did send about Venezuela, his remarks were usually reassuring. On December 4, he wrote that the Venezuelan Government was 'quite aware that they cannot count on the support of the present [American] Administration.'[54] It has been suggested that Herbert misread the mood of the United States and that, had Pauncefote still been alive, better information would have come from Washington.[55] This does Herbert an injustice. Undoubtedly some Americans were against the coercion of Castro, but this was not a popular opinion in the United States before the blockade began. Roosevelt's statements on Venezuela had been highly encouraging and every recent European quarrel with Latin America had completely failed to arouse strong American indignation.

To minimise the danger, Lansdowne emphasised Britain's very limited objectives. He quickly prohibited the occupation of Venezuelan soil, explaining that 'if the occupation were prolonged, troublesome international questions might arise between the Powers concerned and the United States Government.'[56] In the Commons, Balfour and Under Secretary of State for Foreign Affairs Cranborne pledged their support for the Monroe Doctrine, Cranborne commenting that the blockade 'is in no way an infraction of the Monroe Doctrine, and they [the United States] recognise that no nation in the world had been more anxious than England to assist them in maintaining that doctrine.'[57] With this guarantee made, Britain delivered a final ultimatum to Venezuela on December 7. Lansdowne saw little cause for concern, light-heartedly explaining to the United Club that he,

'did not think we had an inveterate antipathy even against Venezuela. (Laughter.) If the republic would desist from committing outrages against British subjects and British property, if she would pay her just debts to her creditors, if she would reply to diplomatic representations made to her in perfectly courteous language, we need have no quarrel whatever with her; he would even say, if she would be content to put herself on a moderate allowance in the matter of revolutions. (Laughter.) Venezuela in the last 70 years had, he believed, indulged in the luxury of no fewer than 104 revolutions. Three revolutions in two years seemed to him to be altogether unreasonable. (Laughter.)'[58]

These were not the kind of remarks one might have expected from a statesman who had just sanctioned the use of armed force. This, certainly, was the opinion of Earl Spencer, who responded in the House of Lords. 'I doubt whether the noble Marquess was right to be playfully sarcastic and jocular ... with reference to this small country,' Spencer remarked. In response, Lansdowne merely replied that he supposed he 'might perhaps have said that in more tragical [sic.] accents.'[59]

Lansdowne clearly had no fear of Venezuela and Roosevelt's apparently benevolent attitude removed his final doubts. It was symptomatic of Lansdowne's caution, however, that he should devote part of his speech to the theme of Anglo-American unity. He was 'constantly reminded of the friendly feelings by which the two great Powers – Great Britain and her kinsmen across the sea – were united.'[60] Such a blatant appeal to Anglo-Saxonism, coming when it did, was hardly coincidence and, like his earlier speech at Darlington during the latter stages of the canal negotiation, was primarily intended for American ears.

When British and German warships sailed for Venezuela, then, it was understood that the United States, whilst not actually supporting the European Powers, would stand aside. Roosevelt amicably agreed to the suggestion that the American representative at Caracas, Herbert Bowen, should take control over British and German interests after the departure of Haggard and von Pilgrim-Baltazzi. In fact, Bowen's influence was quickly required when an infuriated Castro rounded up the British and German subjects unfortunate enough still to be in Caracas and threw them into prison. Through Bowen's interference, Castro was soon brought to reason (the Venezuelan President's position was fragile enough and the approbation of the United States would have left him defenceless). In the House of Lords, Lansdowne noted that 'I think your Lordships will agree that we are much indebted for the good offices of the United States Minister at Caracas in these difficult circumstances.'[61]

Yet it was at this crucial point that many British officials began to doubt the wisdom of the Anglo-German partnership. In November, Herbert wrote to the Foreign Secretary that 'I wish we were going to punish Venezuela without the aid of Germany for I am not sure that joint action will be palatable here.'[62] Herbert had good reason to lament Britain's choice of ally. Many in the United States tended to associate Germany with a grasping and opportunistic race, although the President, keen not to offend German-American voters, carefully avoided a public expression of this view. Of particular concern was the expansion of German naval building, especially since the Kaiser's foreign ambitions seemed to include the acquisition of colonies in South America.[63]

Lansdowne certainly understood the extent of America's suspicion: a similar suspicion prevailed in Britain, largely the result of the breakdown in Anglo-German negotiations over the preceding months. Furthermore, as in the United States, Britain tended to look upon Germany's naval expansion building program with extreme disquiet. In September, Hugh Arnold-Forster, Parliamentary Secretary for the Admiralty and later to become Secretary for War, argued that against 'England alone is such a weapon as the modern German navy necessary; against England, unless all available evidence and all probability combine to mislead, that weapon is being prepared.'[64] Despite this, Lansdowne tended to defend the Germans. His admission to Herbert on December 4 that it 'is perhaps unlucky that we should be harnessed to them [the Germans] but it was quite inevitable,' was primarily due to the anti-Germanism prevalent in Britain, rather than the result of his own personal misgivings. All correspondence between London and Berlin regarding Venezuela was reassuring; diplomatic dispatches from the German Foreign Office insisted that the Kaiser had no intention of landing troops on Venezuelan soil and was as anxious as Lansdowne not to offend Roosevelt. Because of this, the Foreign Secretary concluded the dispatch by happily recognising that the 'Germans are working fairly well with us in regard to the Venezuelan difficulty.'[65]

On December 9 1902, the action finally began. (At this late stage, Italy joined the coercing Powers. However, since the Italians' role in the dispute was relatively insignificant, it can be ignored in this account.) Meanwhile, to the great disappointment of the Foreign Office, naval matters began to present unforeseen difficulties. The instructions given to the British and German squadron commanders urged caution and co-operation. As the first gunboats were seized, however, signs of bad management became immediately apparent. While the British squadron acted in accordance with its Government's wishes – seizing three gunboats and sending the crews ashore – their German counterparts managed to sink two ships off La Guaira. Explaining the incident to Balfour, German Ambassador Paul Metternich maintained that 'for naval reasons no other course was open, as the two wretched little boats could not be kept afloat.'[66]

Whatever the truth – and it was true that Castro's navy was in a lamentable condition – it was clearly a mistake not to make a public defence as American opinion reacted angrily and laid the blame squarely on Germany. 'It would be futile to attempt to deny that a bad impression has been created in this country', the Washington reporter for *The Times* remarked. He concluded that while 'it is not the presence of British and German warships that is objected to', what 'is objected to is the sinking of Venezuelan warships, which gives the expedition a punitive character.'[67] The editor of *The New York Times* was yet more explicit. Admitting the justice of British and German claims, and supporting their right to seize gunboats, customs houses and duties, he concluded that 'It can hardly be denied that they [Britain and Germany] went beyond these proper limits when they actually … destroyed armed vessels belonging to the Government of Venezuela.'[68] In London, too, there was a reaction. Arnold-Forster wrote to Cranborne to suggest that a full explanation was in the public interest. 'I should not make any allusion to the Germans,' he argued, 'but merely state what our own Officers have done.'[69] ·

The bombardment of the Venezuelan fort at Puerto Cabello on December 13 by the British warship "Charybdis" and the German "Vineta" caused a further, and more serious reaction. Increasingly suspicious, many Americans assumed that London and Berlin had secretly determined to punish Castro. Indeed, Commodore Montgomerie's actions hardly reflected the caution of his Government and certainly would not have received its approval. The incident began when a mob of angry Venezuelans stormed the British merchant vessel "Topaze", hauled down its flag and kidnapped its captain. Montgomerie, aboard the "Charybdis", sent a message to Venezuelan authorities at Puerto Cabello demanding immediate satisfaction. Only one hour after sending this message, however, both warships began firing on the fort and, forty-five minutes later, troops were sent ashore to quell Venezuelan resistance. Again, *The New York Times* was incensed. 'The shelling of the port of Puerto Cabello was perfectly characteristic of this ill-managed affair', he wrote; negotiations 'are now needed without delay.'[70] In official circles, too, mounting anger was evident. While the mood of the House of Representatives was becoming 'restless and irritated', Hay feared 'bellicose resolutions' from the House that would bring the dispute into the American political arena.[71] Still, the reaction concentrated almost solely on German misdemeanours and overlooked Montgomerie's indiscretions. The American Government was apprehensive about German designs, 'although not suspicious of us', wrote Herbert.[72] Similarly, *The New York Times* noted that 'there may be European powers who would not be unwilling to make a test of the efficiency of the Monroe Doctrine. Great Britain is surely not one of these Powers'.[73]

Nevertheless, that the mismanaged naval incidents had caused a surge of anger in the United States could not be denied. Britain's response was twofold. Firstly, the Government reasserted its support for the Monroe Doctrine. On December 15, Balfour explained the situation to Edward VII, commenting that:

'The two difficulties are German co-operation and American jealousy! Neither can, Mr. Balfour fears, be avoided. But the dangers incident to both can be mitigated by careful steering. American jealousy may best be dealt with by saying in public what the Government has, as your Majesty knows, long determined on in private, namely that, for military reasons, if for no others, we should abstain from landing ... on Venezuelan soil.'[74]

Lansdowne made this assertion in the House of Lords on the 16th, strenuously repeating his belief in the Monroe Doctrine. 'It is thought this is done for America', *The New York Times* noted on the 17th. As a secondary precaution, Britain attempted to distance herself from the German naval operations. Britain's attitude towards her ally had become surprisingly equivocal and Sir Michael Herbert confessed that he regarded 'with malevolent satisfaction' the 'explosion of feeling against Germany.'[75] Now Balfour stressed to the House of Commons that the two fleets 'will be acting with the same object, they will not be acting as one force',[76] a clear indication that Britain would not be dragged into a diplomatic crisis with the United States because of the German navy.

3

Difficult Money Matters

The Diplomacy of the Venezuela Blockade, 1902-1903

ON DECEMBER 13 1902, the United States' Government forwarded a last-minute appeal for arbitration from President Castro and called for a prompt reply. Returning from Bowood on December 15, Lansdowne attended the House of Lords, where he explained that Castro's request was under consideration.[1] During a meeting with Paul Metternich at the German Embassy that day, the Foreign Secretary learnt that, in Berlin, there were 'considerable objections to encouraging the idea of arbitration.' Metternich was comforted by the fact that 'the proposal was merely passed to us, and not in any way supported by the United States' Government.' Lansdowne hardly needed convincing and voiced his own reasons for refusal. Firstly, he saw dangers in accepting a vague proposal without a guarantee that Castro would act with good faith during and after arbitration. Secondly, the proposal came too late and 'the Venezuelan Government should not have waited until we had given them three distinct warnings, and finally been driven to coercive measures.'[2] Still, the matter was serious enough to warrant an interview with Henry White. Asked whether it was true that the proposal was merely forwarded and not actually recommended by Roosevelt, the American Chargé d'Affaires replied that 'this was no doubt the case', but spent the following week pleading with British officials that they accept Castro's offer for the sake of Anglo-American friendship.[3]

However pertinent the objections to arbitration, the progress of the naval action, and particularly the bombardment of Puerto Cabello, had been difficult to defend to an angry and bewildered House of Commons on the 15th. More importantly, the United States now seemed on the verge of active interference. The Germans, as Lansdowne remarked to Sir Frank Lascelles, now urged action in the matter 'without waiting until Washington "exchanged the rôle of post-office for one of a more active character."'[4] When White met Lansdowne on December 17 – handing him a timely dispatch from Roosevelt urging upon the European Powers the desirability of resorting to arbitration – it naturally made a deep impression. White immediately relayed Lansdowne's response to the State Department: 'the cabinet gladly accept the principle of arbitration for the purpose of settling the dispute with Venezuela.'[5] At the Cabinet meeting held the following day, arbitration, in principle, was formally accepted.

As it was, Roosevelt's intervention, if timely, was received with considerable distaste. '[T]he message from the U.S. suggesting arbitration was rather impertinent', Balfour told the Cabinet on December 18.[6] The Prime Minister, keen that British diplomacy should not be seen to yield to Washington, tended to play down the effect of the President's message. The decision to accept arbitration had provisionally been made between Lansdowne and Metternich, he explained to the King, before White delivered Roosevelt's note to the Foreign Office. It was, Balfour argued, primarily a result of the angry reaction to the Anglo-German partnership.[7] Nevertheless, Balfour was far too shrewd a statesman to voice his annoyance in public and realised that the irritation of an unpredictable nation and an equally unpredictable President had to be assuaged. So prominent officials in London rather self-consciously repeated their wholehearted support for the Monroe Doctrine, while Balfour privately approached his American friends to reassure them of his own personal goodwill. In a letter to the wealthy industrialist Andrew Carnegie, Balfour repeated his Government's promise not to land troops in Venezuela, and added that 'the Monroe Doctrine, to which we have not the smallest objection (rather the reverse!) could not therefore in any way be violated either in letter or spirit.'[8]

The Cabinet had accepted arbitration in principle, but it would be something of an exaggeration to suggest that Britain had retreated in the face of American pressure. The December 18 declaration – coming so soon after Roosevelt's intervention – suggested that British policy was inspired by the United States. Roosevelt, however, had neither dictated the terms nor extracted valuable concessions from the Foreign Office.[9] While Lansdowne expected the decision to be 'received with satisfaction by the U.S.',[10] the scope of arbitration suggested in Castro's appeal was summarily and firmly rejected. Crucially, first-rank claims, dealing with the offences committed by the Venezuelan navy against British merchant shipping and sailors, were excluded from adjudication. Still more, Castro was expected to admit general liability before arbitration could proceed. In other words, Venezuela must settle what Balfour labelled 'the real cause of the present troubles' before the second-rank (or pecuniary) claims were settled by arbitration.[11] On December 23, Lansdowne gave White a note listing the grievances to be excluded and argued that his Government 'could not admit that there was any doubt as to the liability of the Venezuelan Government with respect to them.'[12] With regard to the remaining claims, Britain would accept arbitration without reserve.

This was by no means a departure in British thinking. In fact, there exists a striking resemblance between the demands set out in Lansdowne's memorandum of December 23 and those he outlined before the naval operations had even commenced. As early as November 17, Lansdowne made the distinction between first and second rank claims, the latter being those that might be settled by a Mixed Commission.[13] In a note for the Cabinet on November 24, Lansdowne further stressed that, whereas payment would have to be made by Venezuela 'of the amount due for seizures of ships and for maltreatment of British subjects', the 'heavier claims for damage to property ... will be referred to a Commission.' He also made it quite clear that, from Venezuela, 'a general admission of liability will be required.'[14] If Castro chose to accept Britain's demands, therefore, Lansdowne would score a diplomatic success.

In the interests of a quick settlement, which would bring the unpopular part-nership to an end before the blockade caused more trouble, Lansdowne indicated his willingness to accept a degree of compromise, telling White on December 18 that Venezuela's payment of first-rank claims 'need not necessarily be large, recog-nition of the principle rather than the amount of payment being the question.'[15] Encouraged by what he saw as a significant departure in Britain's diplomacy, White was nonetheless disappointed to learn that Lansdowne had no intention of raising the naval action until Castro accepted these demands.[16] While the presence of European warships had aroused the resentment of the American people, the naval action had been instrumental in bringing President Castro to reason. Far from retreating in the face of American disapproval, Britain and Germany now prepared to increase the pressure on Venezuela and, on December 20, they announced the establishment of a formal blockade. Their warships, joined by a single Italian vessel, moved into position around Venezuelan ports and the mouth of the Orinoco on Christmas Day.

Yet the climate of Anglo-American diplomacy had changed. Britain's acceptance of arbitration was hardly a major concession, but was received with great enthusiasm both at home and in the United States. 'I regard this as a great triumph,' Roosevelt told Albert Shaw on December 26, adding that:

'of course nothing that they [the blockading Powers] have done or threatened to do so far has in any way or shape conflicted with our contention as to what the Monroe Doctrine means. But the chances of complication from a long and irritating little war between the European powers and Venezuela were sufficiently great to make me feel most earnestly that the situation should be brought to a peaceful end if possible.'[17]

Britain's public support for the Monroe Doctrine, voiced particularly by Lansdowne and Lord Cranborne, the Under Secretary of State at the Foreign Office, had clearly encouraged the American people. As early as December 17, the Washington reporter for *The Times* wrote that Americans 'recognised the friendly correctness' of Britain's attitude, and added pointedly that 'if there were a Lansdowne in Berlin also, it is felt that things would look considerably better.'[18] The shrewd suggestion that Roosevelt be asked to arbitrate proved equally popular.[19] *The Times*, arguing that the proposal had come, in the first instance, from Britain, commented that it was 'one link in the ever-strengthening chain of friendship between England and the United States.'[20] If the suggestion was intended to flatter the President and placate American popular opinion, it was undoubtedly successful, yet it also had a more selfish aim. Only the United States had sufficient authority over Castro to ensure Venezuela's good behaviour during negotiations. After Roosevelt publicised his refusal to arbitrate, Lansdowne wrote ruefully to Sir

Michael Herbert that 'if he had undertaken the job we might probably have got through with a minimum of pedantry and red tape', later adding that 'an Award by him would have carried with it a strong moral sanction.'[21] Despite refusing the role of arbitrator, Roosevelt suggested that negotiations might begin at Washington in the New Year. The Foreign Office quickly consented to what it considered an unusual proposal, having little to lose by such an arrangement: if the talks in Washington proved to be abortive, the Powers could always refer the dispute to the judicial tribunal at The Hague.

Meanwhile, in a move that clearly surprised the Foreign Office, Castro attempted once more to appeal to the Americans by conferring full powers of negotiation on the United States' Minister at Caracas, Herbert W. Bowen. Immediately, Haggard wired a strongly worded warning to the Foreign Office, explaining that 'Mr Bowen is a mischievous man, and ... it would be suicidal to allow him to have a voice in any settlement.'[22] Despite Lansdowne's clear confidence in Haggard's consular abilities, however, he chose to ignore the warning and quickly dismissed the telegram as the result of a personal quarrel between the two men in Caracas. To Herbert, he explained that 'even assuming him [Bowen] to be a bit of a rogue and an accomplice of Castro, I do not see that that is an insuperable objection. A Venezuelan commissioner pure and simple would probably be worse still.'[23]

Once assurances were received from the State Department that Bowen was not acting under their authorisation, and was in no way supposed to represent the United States, Lansdowne saw no reason to complain.[24] Foreign Office dispatches to Herbert prohibited any discussions until Castro unreservedly accepted Britain's conditions and it was assumed that Bowen, or any representative for Venezuela for that matter, would have little room in which to manoeuvre.

Now that an understanding had been arrived at, fears that Venezuela would turn into a diplomatic disaster soon evaporated. Guardedly optimistic, Lansdowne wrote to the Duke of Devonshire that 'Venezuelan matters are moving rather slowly but I think satisfactorily', but 'I see no prospect of Christmas holidays.'[25] From Washington, Herbert also expressed satisfaction, reporting that, if arbitration were to go ahead, it would be 'almost safe to affirm that the friendly relations between Great Britain and the United States, instead of being impaired, have, if anything, been strengthened by the Venezuelan incident.'[26] Over the following weeks, the primary concern of Anglo-American became the establishment of a tribunal to resolve the Alaskan boundary issue, and correspondence on Venezuela accordingly lapsed. 'The F.O. is not very communicative about the Venezuelan affair', Devonshire complained on December 30, 'there has not been a word in the F.O. telegrams or other papers to show what has been going on between us and the German or U.S. governments'. In reply, Lansdowne simply pointed out that 'there have been, as you will see ... very few papers to send.'[27]

With the new year, the Alaskan boundary continued to command Lansdowne's attention, leaving Venezuela unresolved. Still, Roosevelt's impatience was becoming increasingly apparent and the danger of unwanted American interference could not easily be dismissed. 'I should be rather afraid of the U.S. Government being too officious in its attempts to bring us together', Lansdowne explained on January 1.[28] In a subsequent dispatch to Herbert, Lansdowne stressed his overall sense of optimism, but added that,

> 'it would be a misfortune if the U.S. Govt. were to exhibit too much interest in the proceedings, and anything like officiousness on their part, and, still more, the appearance of dictation, would do endless harm here and perhaps spoil the game altogether. You may possibly see your way to giving Mr. Hay a hint in this sense. He seems to me to be always friendly, but his colleagues may be less so.'[29]

Lansdowne's position was clear: Britain's demands were perfectly explicit and would suffer no further modification. Consequently, American intervention was both unwelcome and futile. Lansdowne told Balfour that he 'feared it was open to the interpretation that they [the United States] were forcing arbitration upon us.'[30] As far as Britain was concerned, Castro must make the next move. Until the blockading Powers received a water-tight promise from Venezuela that the Anglo-German demands had been accepted without reserve, negotiations could not begin and the blockade would remain in force. As Lansdowne put it, Britain 'could not ... considering the past conduct of the Venezuelan Government, afford to remove the pressure, which had apparently brought them to a tardy recognition of their obligations'.[31] In the meantime, seeking a quick resolution of their own, the Foreign Office briefly considered the possibility of selling Venezuela's captured gunboats to pay first-rank claims, but discarded the scheme when, on January 9 1903, Bowen informed the blockading Powers that Castro had seen reason and accepted their terms.[32]

Now, with a real prospect of successful negotiations in Washington and an amicable conclusion to the Venezuelan dispute, the Foreign Secretary happily foresaw an early settlement, which was in everyone's interest:

> 'the blockade is beginning to punish them [Venezuela], and I have told Harry White that we cannot raise it until a settlement has been arrived at. Bowen will probably be keen to come to terms with you. The U.S. Government will, I should think, be of the same way of thinking, and we shall be delighted to be rid of the question.'[33]

Of course the dispute was never so straightforward. Although the blockade was successful in restricting Venezuelan trade, and thereby damaging her economy, it also carried great risks: interference with neutral vessels, for example, risked inciting diplomatic friction. On January 22, Henry White informed Lansdowne that two American vessels had indeed complained of discrimination, and called for an investigation to be made by British authorities.[34]

While such incidents were unavoidable and could at least be defended, it was absolutely essential that there should be no further military confrontations between European warships and Venezuela's garrisons. Such an incident, arousing the anger of the United States, would destroy the chances of a quick settlement and strengthen Castro's position. Discouraging reports of minor clashes involving German ships, however, were already arriving at the Foreign Office:[35] if Lansdowne really believed that the troublesome period of the Venezuela dispute had passed, he had greatly underestimated the situation.

As it turned out, Lansdowne's optimism was to be shattered by a particularly tactless naval blunder committed by German warships. Negotiations had not even begun when, on January 21, the Venezuelan fort of San Carlos at Maracaibo was subjected to a severe bombardment and eventually destroyed. Venezuelan soldiers sparked the incident by opening fire on the German warship "Panther", but the destruction of San Carlos was universally condemned as an act of needless brutality. From the United States came a predictable violent outburst of anger; *The New York Times* declared that 'worse international manners than Germany has exhibited have rarely come under observation of civilized man.'[36] The January 26 edition *Manchester Guardian* sounded a similar note:

> 'None of the explanations given at Berlin tends to diminish the disagreeable impression caused by the bombardment ... High Government officials in the United States do not conceal the surprise and displeasure caused by the action of Germany ... The feeling here is that an agreement is likely to be hastened by the general odium into which Germany may perceive she is falling if she persists in gun practise at mud forts for the mere sake of prestige.'[37]

In Washington, Sir Michael Herbert was aghast. Worried that American anger would not solely be directed at Germany, he predicted 'a strained situation' that might 'place the President in a position of serious embarrassment.'[38] Luckily, despite an initial straining of diplomatic relations, the genuine horror with which Britain reacted to the San Carlos incident soon soothed American irritation. Balfour told White that the attack had 'much annoyed and perturbed' him and impressed upon the American Chargé d'Affaires his desire for a settlement.[39] While Admiralty officials stressed that 'His Majesty's ships should not be implicated in any indiscreet or violent action, and that matters should be kept as quiet as possible pending negotiations',[40] Lansdowne approached Metternich on January 26 and demanded an explanation:

> 'I told his Excellency that I was far from desiring to hurry over what were, I hoped, the final stages of this troublesome negotiation. He must, however, I thought, be aware that a great deal of irritation has been created both in this country and in the United States by the German bombardment of San Carlos. ... I told his Excellency that I should be grateful for any information as to what had occurred, but that there was undoubtedly an impression that the reprisals had been excessive.'[41]

An alarmed Metternich offered to make enquiries and his superiors, from Count Bernstorff to the Kaiser himself, guilelessly expressed their determination to co-operate fully in the future – solicitous behaviour that had little effect on the Cabinet, now thoroughly disgusted and disillusioned with their wayward ally.

Although the Foreign Office had been unwilling to enter discussions before Castro accepted its terms, it was quite prepared to pursue a moderate policy once negotiations began. Lansdowne told Lascelles on January 15 that 'it did not seem to me desirable that we should attempt at this stage to press President Castro ... Castro had, by accepting our conditions, admitted that it was essential that arrangements should be made for the settlement of the first-rank claims.'[42] The German Foreign Office's refusal, on the other hand, to enter negotiations until payment for first-rank claims had actually been effected was a real cause for concern. When negotiations eventually began, it seemed that the German Government were determined to effect the complete humiliation of Venezuela by submitting a series of new and entirely unexpected claims. Herbert watched anxiously, writing to Lansdowne that 'it appears to me to be scarcely fair that Germany should, at this late hour, make fresh conditions',[43] and suggesting that, if her ally continued to act in such an uncompromising manner, Britain might raise the blockade without consulting Berlin.[44]

Naturally, Lansdowne had no desire to endanger the Anglo-German part-nership, thereby offending a powerful European Power, so he spent much time at the German Embassy advocating the need for moderation. On January 27, the German Ambassador handed the Foreign Secretary a proposal that Venezuela's custom-houses might be seized to obtain a greater hold over Castro. Such an extreme measure risked inciting Roosevelt's displeasure and was soon dismissed by the Foreign Office. Lansdowne, explaining that the proposal was 'most objection-able', repeated his desire that negotiations should, at all costs, proceed smoothly.[45] Painfully aware that Washington was watching their every move, Cabinet members were at a loss to explain the Kaiser's objectionable tactics: the Duke of Devonshire asked Lansdowne whether Britain, in the light of the new demands, was 'absolutely bound to the Germans and unable to accept anything to which they do not agree'. Furthermore, since the Admiralty had deprecated the bombardment of San Carlos, Devonshire concluded by enquiring 'does this give us no ground for dis-solving the partnership?'[46]

On January 30, Lascelles wrote to Lansdowne that 'the tone of the English Press, and the attacks made on the Government, merely because they had taken part in a common action with Germany were abominable.' The angry press reac-tions in Britain, and particularly in the United States, 'has surprised and fright-ened people here to such an extent that they have become as anxious as we can be to put an end to the business as soon as possible.' This was just what Lansdowne wanted to hear. He replied that the two nations had worked well together and, playing down the Cabinet's concerns, concluded that:

'We have ... always guarded ourselves by desiring Herbert to consult his German colleague freely. Metternich, no doubt under instructions, has

shown himself considerate and anxious to meet our views. I do not
wonder that the German Ministers are taken aback at the violence of
the anti-German feeling which is exhibited here.'[47]

In one respect, Lansdowne was correct to dismiss the significance of Germany's
behaviour during the negotiations at Washington: Germany had jeopardised the
success of the discussions, but Herbert Bowen's obstructive actions were even
more serious. Far from working to secure an amicable settlement, Bowen sought
to break the Anglo-German partnership and to appeal to the United States to save
Venezuela from European aggression. Herbert was disgusted. Describing Bowen
as 'blustering, insolent, untrustworthy', he nonetheless recognised that his actions
were having an effect on the American mind:

> 'the picture of the American defending poor Venezuela from the greed
> and avarice of the three Powers appeals strongly to the average
> American. He [Bowen] has done me personally a good deal of harm
> in the eyes of the American public by the lies he has started about me
> ... This I do not care about, but what I do mind is the manner in which
> he has influenced public opinion in America, which is always fickle and
> quick to move against England.'[48]

Bowen soon refused to deal separately with the blockading Powers, favouring
equal negotiations with every country having a genuine cause for complaint.[49]
Naturally, Britain and Germany vehemently refused, arguing that since
Venezuela's sudden acceptance of her international obligations was the direct
result of Anglo-German naval operations, it was only fair that British and German
claims should be settled before the others. Lansdowne telegraphed Herbert that,
although Britain's first-rank claims were 'trifling in amount, [they] are of the first
importance in principle'. Herbert should, therefore, demand immediate payment.[50]
With no prospect of agreement in sight, Lansdowne appealed once more to the
American President. If he would not arbitrate the entire dispute, might he at least
arbitrate the question of preferential treatment for Britain and Germany?
Roosevelt's refusal, on the grounds that arbitration by the United States would
compromise her own claims against Castro, was expected, but nonetheless disappointing,[51] especially in the light of reports that Congress viewed the continuing
delays with mounting distaste.[52]

Increasingly dismayed at the deadlock, Lansdowne confided to Lascelles: 'I
am convinced that with a little good will on both sides, an immediate settlement
upon [an] equitable basis might easily have been obtained.'[53] He should have heeded
Haggard's warnings, Lansdowne confessed, and Bowen 'might have settled the
whole business in 48 hours if he had wished to do so'.[54] In the meantime, he saw
no clear way forward and wrote to the Balfour on January 29 that,

> 'The telegrams from Washington are so unsatisfactory that I have given
> up leaving London. ... I am disturbed by Herbert's reports of Bowen,

who is, I am afraid, not behaving well. Unless you can suggest some
ingenious mode of turning the difficulties which have arisen, I should
be disposed to instruct Herbert that we have come to the conclusion
that we had better give up the attempt to settle at Washington and that
he is now to arrange with Bowen the preliminaries at the Hague.'[55]

Meanwhile, British frustration with Bowen and with the progress of negotiations
was not lost on the Americans. 'Herbert can't deal with him [Bowen], and goes to
bed with rage,' Henry Adams remarked. 'Absolutely, Lansdowne is now at a loss
whether to break with Bowen, or beat him blue.'[56] Adams was not so very far from
the mark. Although desperate to leave the capital and his troubles at the Foreign
Office, affairs in Washington forced Lansdowne to remain at his post. Suffering
from illness and overwork, he collapsed on January 29, later confessing to Balfour
that the Venezuela negotiations had left his brain reeling.[57]

Lansdowne's dejection was mirrored in the official reports of the
Washington Embassy. In early February, Naval Attaché Dudley de Chair detailed
the possible repercussions of the Venezuelan blockade, argued that it would guarantee the passage of the Naval Appropriation Bill and concluded that the
inevitable US response would be to construct a more powerful fleet. 'There is little
doubt but that our difficulties in Venezuela are influencing public opinion in this
country,' he remarked ruefully.[58] Herbert sounded a similar note:

> 'I feel myself bound to warn your Lordship that a great change has
> taken place in the feeling of this country towards us ... and that our
> good relations with this country will be seriously impaired if this
> Alliance with Germany continues much longer. The time has come, in
> American opinion, for us to make the choice between the friendship of
> the United States and that of Germany.'[59]

Faced by Bowen's obstruction and mounting American anger, Lansdowne decided
in early February that the Hague was the only remaining option and that that
option should immediately be taken up. On February 2, he raised the possibility
that, if the only obstacle to a settlement was the payment of first-rank claims, he
was fully prepared to 'accept payment in some other form which would insure
prompt settlement.'[60] This effort, however, proved abortive and, with the opening
of Parliament imminent – promising severe attacks on the Government's
Venezuelan policy – an arrangement was urgently required.

Lansdowne was in a difficult position. He could not cut his losses by lifting
the blockade with Castro still defiant: whatever happened, the appearance of victory over Venezuela was vital to Britain's international prestige. On the other
hand, continuing the blockade indefinitely was a far more alarming prospect. 'I
fully realise [the] importance of not allowing [the] present situation to be indefinitely prolonged', Lansdowne assured Herbert on February 3. Four days later, in
a secret telegram, the Foreign Secretary was yet more explicit: 'for Parliamentary
and other reasons, it is absolutely necessary that there should be no further delay

in effecting a settlement ... As soon as the preliminaries of reference have been sat-isfactorily arranged we should, of course, be ready to raise the blockade.'[61]

Eager to prevent a breach in Anglo-American relations, British officials con-tinued to express unabated goodwill towards the United States. On January 30, Cranborne played down the nature of Britain's unlucky co-operation with Germany. There 'was no German alliance', he explained, only 'certain arrange-ments to govern our common action [and] we could not leave in the lurch those who took common action with us.'[62] Speaking in Birmingham, Austen Chamberlain labelled Anglo-American tension, 'a calamity not merely for the two nations but for the whole of the civilised world ... [there] was no nation in the world with whom we were so closely knit as with our cousins across the Atlantic.'[63] Charles Beresford, then in New York, reaffirmed Britain's desire for Anglo-American friendship:

> 'He stated that the Monroe Doctrine originated with Great Britain and had always had the support of the British Government. ... He saw no necessity for any formal [Anglo-American] alliance each country being perfectly able to take care of itself but spoke of a "natural alliance" to be brought about by closer relations.'[64]

Although Britain would not back down on preferential treatment (unless Venezuela pay compensation to Britain and Germany for their expenses incurred during the naval operations), Lansdowne was prepared to see the question of sep-arate treatment settled by the Hague Tribunal. Such a concession was only worth-while if it would end the distasteful Washington negotiations and facilitate the sig-nature of a protocol to refer the dispute to the Hague. Lansdowne forestalled German objections by summoning Paul Metternich to the Foreign Office on February 9. During the interview, Metternich was told 'with the utmost frankness the gravity of the situation and importance of immediate settlement.' Lansdowne politely remarked that, while Britain 'had no intention of deserting Germany', he did not think that the 'position of Germany would be enviable if negotiations fell through'.[65] These comments, coupled with Roosevelt's plain speaking to the German Ambassador in Washington, did the trick and Germany reluctantly signed the protocol.

Whilst the payment of first-rank claims was still to be effected and the ques-tion of preferential treatment for the blockading Powers was still in doubt, the scope of Anglo-German claims had not significantly changed. By signing the pro-tocol on February 13 1903, however, the unpopular naval action could finally be concluded and the blockade was officially lifted the following day. 'As regards our friendly relations with the U.S.', Herbert remarked to Lansdowne, 'the settlement with Venezuela has not been arrived at a day too soon!'[66]

Now that the Venezuelan dispute was over, recriminations in Britain began in earnest. When the Parliamentary session of 1903 began, it became clear that the Government's popularity had diminished. Sir Henry Campbell-Bannerman, leader of the opposition, remarked on February 17 that the Venezuelan 'cloud has happily passed, but it was a very black cloud, and most of us think it was a cloud that might have been avoided.'[67] Lord Tweedmouth's criticism in the House of Lords was typical: 'from which ever point of view you look upon it, the policy of the Government has been unusual, ill-considered, rash, and likely to lead to misunderstanding and difficulty, if not danger.'[68] Other attacks were more personal and Lord Lansdowne, considered to be the architect of Britain's misguided Venezuelan policy, came under particular abuse. In the Lords on March 3, Lansdowne remarked that the State Department had been both friendly and considerate throughout, a statement that left the Washington reporter for *The Times* scathingly unimpressed:

> 'by what sedulous and skilful [*sic.*] appeals to American public opinion this Government was able to maintain throughout the friendly attitude to England, Lansdowne seems totally unaware. He was content to know that all was smooth on the surface, heedless of the continuing risk of explosion from the volcanic forces which his own policy had stirred. The official view possesses his mind.'[69]

According to George Smalley, it was 'nothing to the British Foreign Secretary that by his entanglement with Germany he for some weeks put a great strain on American goodwill to England.'[70] The main difficulties had arisen, Sir William Harcourt argued, from 'the character of our claims and the character of the German claims, and the grounds and nature of the arrangement between the two countries with regard to enforcing those claims.'[71] One observer commented that 'it was generally thought that they [the British Government] had been forced out of an undesirable position by public opinion, without which they were quite prepared to carry out the wishes of the Kaiser.'[72] Lansdowne's biographer even argued that the bombardment of San Carlos was 'impelled by an uncontrollable spirit of Frightfulness'!'[73] Campbell-Bannerman, a more astute critic, suggested that Britain had been 'bound hand and foot to Germany, of whose claims both in nature and extent we were ignorant, and whose aims and ideas in American policy are far from being identical with ours.'[74]

It was Cranborne who made the closest thing to a public apology for Britain's actions. After denying that Britain had coerced Castro merely to collect debts, Cranborne conceded that the dispute,

> 'was a mess.– (Hear, Hear.) Warlike operations were always a mess, and he could assure them that no one disliked warlike operations more than the Secretary for Foreign Affairs and those who served under him. Undoubtedly it was a mess, but we must not be afraid of that. It was necessary in order to defend our interests.'[75]

In private, however, British officials tended to blame Germany for the crisis. From Washington, Sir Michael Herbert wrote to Edward Hamilton that 'I had a difficult task for I do not like the Germans or their policy, and I disapproved [of] every-thing they did during the negotiations.'[76] Similarly, Sir Francis Bertie wrote to Lansdowne of a conversation he had just had with Admiral Morris, during which the latter 'said that he thought it a very strong order that the Germans should have been so exacting in regard to the payment of their claim. My answer was that in our dealings with the German Government we had always found them difficult in money matters.'[77]

Lansdowne alone defended Germany. They had, he argued, generally behaved well: 'although they have been fussy and fond of raising unnecessary points … they have almost invariably given way to us.'[78] In the face of serious crit-icism in the Lords, Lansdowne patiently defended the Anglo-German collabora-tion. Firstly, a blockade would have been much harder for Britain to effect single-handed. More importantly, he explained, 'I should have regretted any action on the part of His Majesty's Government which might have had the effect of increasing the estrangement produced between the two countries by the events [of the South African war].'[79] That Lansdowne still hoped to see closer relations between London and Berlin is clear, but, in defending Germany, he had a more particular aim. Tension between the two countries threatened their joint backing of the Baghdad railway scheme, so strenuously supported by the Foreign Secretary. The wave of anti-German feeling following the Venezuelan blockade, however, ensured that Britain would pull out of the scheme. Viscount Esher rightly predicted in April that 'the Government will flinch. They are very timid just now. The Germans will go on just the same and the railway will ultimately be made, only we shall be out of it. We never learn by experience.'[80]

Britain coped rather well during the Venezuelan dispute. While admitting the necessity of concession, the Foreign Office steadfastly refused to abandon its most significant demands in the face of American pressure. The co-operation with Germany made a temporary tension in Anglo-American relations unavoidable; the Washington correspondent for *The Manchester Guardian* reported that '[i]ncreasing wonder is expressed here that England should so long abide by so awkward an alliance, leading to nothing but friction.'[81]

Britain's response was calculated to appeal to the American mind. Firstly, the temporary nature of Anglo-German co-operation was frequently emphasised and the existence of a greater understanding between the two countries vehemently denied. Secondly, the Foreign Office emphatically refused to become implicated in Germany's naval indiscretions. As Herbert told Edward Hamilton, Britain had 'come out of it all right because we acted fairly and consistently from the begin-ning and the Germans did not.'[82]

Constant communication between the Foreign Office and the American Embassy had been of crucial importance in retaining the 'special relationship' throughout these difficult weeks. 'I have always found every readiness and even desire on the part of Lord Lansdowne and his subordinates to give me the fullest information as to the instructions sent to Sir Michael Herbert', wrote White.[83] Most importantly, Britain had wholeheartedly maintained her support for the

Monroe Doctrine. On the same day that the blockade was lifted, Balfour spoke at Liverpool. During his speech, the Prime Minister commented that 'the Monroe Doctrine has no enemies in this country that I know of.'[84] For his part, the Foreign Secretary remarked that it 'ought to be evident, even to the most prejudiced mind, that so far as the U.S. was concerned our conduct has been strictly correct from start to finish.'[85] It was because Americans understood Britain's friendly feelings towards their country that the troublesome dispute with Venezuela did no lasting damage and was quickly forgotten.

4

A Marvellously Elastic Doctrine

The Search for Anglo-American Concord in Latin America, 1903-1904

BRITAIN IS TO-DAY our only real friend, even with the masses', Andrew Carnegie wrote in July 1903. 'In [the] Venezuelan invasion, Britain was all right, poor Germany the real enemy.'[1] While most British officials supported the view that the crisis had been sparked by German misbehaviour (not by Britain's thoughtless infringement of the Monroe Doctrine), Latin American affairs remained disturbingly chaotic, always threatening to spark another crisis into which Britain might be obliged to intervene. The Venezuelan experience and the scare of serious diplomatic confrontation had left Britain in a rather delicate position with regard to her future Latin American policy, yet her interests in the region could not simply be abandoned. So entered a rather unsatisfactory period, during which Balfour postponed a policy decision until the Americans clarified matters, or until another crisis forced the issue.

British thinking, post-Venezuela, was increasingly solicitous towards the Americans' legitimate interest in Latin American affairs. 'It ought to be an object of British policy, in the operations we are forced to undertake on the other side,' Sir Edward Grey told the House of Commons in July 1903, 'as far as possible to make an understanding with the United States our first object, and, if possible, an understanding with the United States alone.'[2] Captain Greville, a spokesman for the Government, stressed that Britain welcomed American interference:

> 'the United States could see their way to the adoption of some effec-
> tive course by which these almost periodical difficulties arising between
> the great Powers and some of the States of South America could be
> prevented, I think I may say it would meet with a cordial concurrence
> in this country.'[3]

Balfour went further, effectively calling for the United States to police Latin America. Stressing his wholehearted support for the Monroe Doctrine and welcoming Roosevelt's involvement in South America, he explained that:

> 'I believe it would be a great gain to civilization if the United States of
> America were more actively to interest themselves in making arrange-

ments by which these constantly recurring difficulties between European Powers and certain States in South America could be avoided ... the United States of America can perform no greater task in the cause of civilization than by doing their best to see that international law is observed, and by upholding all that the European Powers and the United States have recognized as the admitted principles of international comity.'[4]

Roosevelt, however, was initially reluctant to assume any such responsibility and the State Department refused to prohibit European Powers from future coercive action. The President's strained silence (largely due to internal political considerations) theoretically left the door open to European intervention and the anti-foreign attitude exhibited by several South American Republics – and by Venezuela in particular – suggested that intervention would again become necessary. In the event, Roosevelt provided no real alternative to naval coercion and, while the Foreign Office was naturally anxious not to overstep the line, Lansdowne was prepared to take his chances until the President made a definite statement of intent and sanction further armed measures off the Latin American coast.

On December 29 1902, Martin Garcia Mérou, the Argentine Minister in Washington, relayed a message to the State Department from Louis Drago, Minister of Foreign Relations, concerning the alarming Anglo-German blockade of Venezuela. Clearly worried that European Powers might undertake a similar action against the Republic should it fail to pay its debts, the message pleaded for the United States to take preventative measures to protect South America from foreign aggression. The Argentine people 'felt alarmed at the knowledge that the failure of Venezuela to meet the payments of its public debt is given as one of the determining causes of the capture of its fleet, the bombardment of one of its ports, and the establishment of a rigorous blockade along its shores.' Should such proceedings succeed, they would 'establish a precedent dangerous to the security and the peace of the nations of this part of America'. In conclusion, Drago explained that the real danger of military intervention for the purpose of debt collecting was prolonged territorial occupation, something guaranteed to offend the United States:

'Such a situation seems obviously at variance with the principles many times proclaimed by the nations of America, and particularly with the Monroe Doctrine, sustained and defended with so much zeal on all occasions by the United States, a doctrine to which the Argentine Republic has heretofore solemnly adhered.'[5]

The State Department's first reaction was one of caution and John Hay ensured that his reply was delayed until the Venezuelan blockade had been lifted. The memorandum sent to Mérou on February 17 merely repeated Roosevelt's words of December 2 1902, that no 'independent nation in America need have the slightest fear of aggression from the United States'. However, it 'behooves each one to maintain order within its own borders and to discharge its just obligations to foreigners.'[6] The inference was clear: Venezuela had been punished for her own sins and South American states could not expect the United States to shield them from just retribution.

Despite the setback, the Argentine Republic continued to push the State Department to make a definite statement on the future of debt collection in South America. On March 12, Herbert sent the Foreign Office notice that Mérou had asked 'for the conclusion of an alliance between the Argentine Republic and the United States in order to support the Monroe Doctrine, and to prevent the collection of debts in the Western Hemisphere by force.' As Herbert reported, Acting Secretary of State Francis B. Loomis was dismissive. Resenting this blatant attempt to direct American diplomacy, Loomis informed German Ambassador von Sternburg 'that the United States Government were not in favour of the Argentine proposal.' On Herbert's dispatch, one Foreign Office official noted that the United States 'on their part appear to have been more embarrassed than grateful and to have confined their reply to a pious wish for increased resource "to an impartial Arbitral Tribunal."'[7]

Although the State Department's refusal to defend South America from European debt collecting was naturally welcomed by the Foreign Office, it was vital that Britain obtain a satisfactory declaration of Roosevelt's intentions. Herbert soon approached Hay to clarify matters. During their meeting of March 21, Herbert found Hay in a confiding mood, the latter listing to the British Ambassador his reasons for rejecting the Argentine proposal. 'Had he consented to support the view that the collection of debts must not be made by force, it would have prevented the United States from ever taking action of that kind in the future.' However, he quickly emphasised that 'if he had openly declared that the United States could not oppose the recovery of debts by force, European Powers would probably have been encouraged to resort to the same methods which had recently been employed against Venezuela.'

Hay made no attempt to hide the embarrassing position in which the State Department found itself and could not advance a definite policy. Herbert pressed on. Britain would gladly enter into arbitration with the South American Republics, he explained, but 'if the latter Governments showed unwillingness to agree, how were they to be coerced?' Hay politely avoided a direct response, and the British Ambassador left the interview unsatisfied.[8] Later that day, he attended a White House dinner, and found the President more forthcoming. '[H]e thought the people of the United States were opposed to the collection of debts by force,' Herbert explained, 'and that the United States Government would probably sooner or later have to adopt that view.' Although Roosevelt was inclined at that time not to undertake the policing of the entire Continent, Herbert shrewdly concluded that,

'Although neither the President nor Mr. Hay can consistently oppose the collection of debts by force, public opinion in this country, as reflected in the newspapers and magazines, shows a decided trend towards a further extension of the marvellously elastic doctrine originated by President Monroe.'[9]

Roosevelt betrayed his intentions to Hay, explaining that 'the American people will never consent to allowing one of the American Republics to come under the control of a European power by any such subterfuge as exercising this control under color of a pretense to the guaranteeing or collecting a debt.'[10] This hardly resolved the immediate situation however. In the meantime, the Argentine proposal was criticised, not only by the United States, but by other South Americans. On March 30, the *Correio da Manha*, a Brazilian newspaper published in Rio, argued that the Argentine Republic had wholly misjudged the situation 'which in many parts of the continent the mistakes and wrongdoings of the governments are creating.' More importantly, the article continued that:

> 'the case of Venezuela, the most recent and of the most positive eloquence as a notice to the nations of South America, caused a kind of chorus of clamoring or of protests to explode that had been lying dormant in certain Americans who, with respect to the great power at the North, live forever midway between fear of the expansionist policy of Washington and the plaintive desire and request for Yankee tutelage.'[11]

Even the Argentineans were despondent. In his annual message to Congress, the Argentine President defended the proposal, but dismissed its significance: 'It is understood that the Republic has not gone in search of protectors or alliances, but has merely stated its views respecting European intervention in a section of this continent'.[12] All that anyone could do was wait for the US to arrive at a decision.

During this period, the Foreign Office busily engaged in obtaining satisfactory terms for Britain in the long-running Venezuelan arbitration. Once the Anglo-Venezuelan protocol was signed on February 13, Lansdowne hoped for a quick resolution that would both satisfy British prestige and please the United States. Discussions continued in Washington for a Mixed Commission Agreement to settle the details of arbitration, but Bowen's presence continually threatened disruption; his refusal to accept a proposal giving preferential treatment to the blockading Powers was followed by a shrewd comment to the American press that such treatment would simply prolong Anglo-German co-operation. American opinion was incensed. '[T]he opinion has been freely expressed during the last two weeks that the people of this country are weary of Britain's protestations of friendship,' Herbert ruefully explained, 'and that the time has come for Great Britain to choose between Germany and the United States.'[13] In the face of such hostility, Lansdowne quickly advanced the following modification.

> 'If preferential or separate treatment is not given to Great Britain, Germany and Italy, the Tribunal may consider whether any and what

compensation should be made by Venezuela to these Powers for the expenses which they have incurred in connection with the blockade.'[14]

Standing firm against Bowen, Lansdowne told Herbert to insist upon the immediate payment of thirty per cent of the custom revenue from La Guayra and Puerto Cabello.[15] Foreign Office resolve, however, was tempered by the determination to effect a quick settlement. While the confiscated gunboats were restored to Venezuelan authorities in late March, Lansdowne proposed that Roosevelt appoint the umpire to adjudicate the question, should the Commission be deadlocked: the President named Frank Partridge – who had served as United States' Minister in Caracas – on May 16.[16] Of greater significance was Lansdowne's new suggestion on the subject of preferential treatment. 'If preferential or separate treatment is not given to the Blockading Powers,' he told Herbert on April 1, 'the Tribunal shall decide how the said revenues shall be distributed among all the creditor Powers, and its decision shall be final.'[17] An outcry from the Germans was fully expected, insisting that the blockading Powers must secure preferential terms as a reward for their naval endeavours. Lansdowne countered the difficulty by meeting Metternich on April 2 and emphasising the desperate need for compromise. To Sir Frank Lascelles, Lansdowne described the interview:

'I did not think the views of the German Government could be maintained ... it seemed desirable to obtain from the Tribunal a complete finding upon all points. It would clearly be inconvenient to have a decision which would oblige us to commence a fresh discussion upon the question of distribution, and which, especially if a separate settlement was not given, might involve an interminable and undignified wrangle among all the creditor Powers.'[18]

Considerations of American sentiment had become, for the Foreign Office, the governing factor in the Venezuelan negotiation. On April 6, Lansdowne sent a telegram to the Washington Embassy with the news that Britain considered the repayment of expenses caused by the blockade 'not a matter to which much importance is attached.' Asking Herbert to determine the American reaction, Lansdowne concluded that 'His Majesty's Government are prepared to defer to the opinion of the majority among the creditors.'[19]

Meanwhile, on April 9, Herbert recounted Hay's strong opposition to the question of preferential treatment. '[H]e was bound, if he was forced to do so, to say that they did not meet with his approval', Hay remarked, 'although he has had no instructions from his Government, [he] tells me privately that he thinks that we have no right to press the amendments.'[20] To satisfy both the United States and Germany, Lansdowne now proposed another compromise. While a general agreement should be signed by all creditor Powers and Venezuela, the blockading Powers might conclude separate arrangements with Bowen. Since the Anglo-German action had primarily been responsible for bringing Castro to reason, the blockading Powers deserved some reward: separate arrangements would secure for

Britain and Germany an opportunity for just compensation. On the other hand, the proposal for concurrent negotiations would satisfy critics that Britain and Germany did not make their acceptance of arbitration dependent on receiving preference. Realising that Britain's desire for compromise had ended hopes of a better settlement, Metternich relayed Germany's consent on May 6 and the separate Hague Agreements were signed on the following day.[21]

For the undue delay in the Washington discussions, Lansdowne squarely blamed Bowen and his ally, Wayne McVeagh. In a private message to Herbert, the Foreign Secretary labelled the two men 'pestilent fellows'. Remarking that the latter, who had dealt with the American claims against Venezuela, was 'inclined to be ugly', Lansdowne explained that McVeagh's belief 'seemed to be that Germany was trying to elude the arbitration and that we were conniving. Whether he seriously believed this, not knowing my man, I cannot say'.[22] In fact, Lansdowne's complaint was both strategic and disingenuous. He sought to dismiss the strain between Britain and Germany and, in particular, Britain's annoyance at Germany's persistent refusal to accept compromise. Nevertheless, now that the details of the terms for arbitration had been agreed, and with the Tribunal due to convene at the Hague in early November, the Foreign Secretary finally could afford to relax.

If Britain expected that affairs in South America would quieten, she was to be disappointed. In June, a truculent President Castro issued a decree, informing the Powers that Venezuela was closing her ports and customs houses to foreign trade. Immediately, Lansdowne directed Herbert to assess the State Department's response. '[T]he recent decree of the President of Venezuela is equivalent to a declaration of blockade of the ports named,' Hay explained, concluding that the American Government 'do not intend to recognise this, as it cannot be effective.'[23] This was pleasant reading, and Lansdowne soon telegraphed Sir Outram Bax-Ironside, Britain's newly-appointed Minister in Caracas, that Britain joined the United States in refusing to recognise the blockade.[24] The confiscation of more British ships was a matter of far greater concern. On September 18, Bax-Ironside relayed a serious incident, in which the British sloop "Virginia" had been seized by the Venezuelan gunboat, "23 de Mayo".[25] A later dispatch gave details of a further seizure. Not only had the "23 de Mayo" seized the "Alemania", an American vessel manned largely by British sailors, but the "Virginia" had now been sold by Venezuelan authorities at Carúpano. These actions, Bax-Ironside maintained, 'reminded one, perforce, of the acts of the Venezuelan Government towards British shipping prior to the blockade.' It was difficult to propose a satisfactory solution, but Bax-Ironside hinted at the need for decisive and immediate action:

> 'It is difficult to bring home to President Castro the gravity of such seizures', he explained, 'and such acts committed by officials of the Venezuelan Government, but if they are allowed to continue we shall, I fear, soon have to chronicle grave acts, similar to the seizure of the "Queen," the "In Time," and the "Indiana."'[26]

Lansdowne was faced by a clear dilemma. Castro's unruly behaviour must have left him both disappointed and depressed, yet he was understandably keen not to initiate a further conflict. Firm action would still be taken in the event of proven wrongdoing by Venezuela, but further punitive measures so soon after the Anglo-German blockade would only reawaken international outrage. For this reason, the official Foreign Office reply, sent in early November, authorised a full investigation before submitting an official protest. In particular, the Foreign Secretary asked the Legal Adviser at the British Legation to determine:

> 'the legality or otherwise of the actions of the Venezuelan authorities. This will involve a consideration ... of the exact position, whether within or without Venezuelan territorial waters, of the vessel when seized; of the papers (if any) which she had on board ... and of the provisions of the Venezuelan law which are said to be applicable to the case.'[27]

Fresh incidents continued to arise. The Colonial Office notified Lansdowne that Venezuela had seized the British vessel "Urabanti" and asked that another representation be made to Castro. 'In these circumstances,' Lansdowne told Bax-Ironside, 'although the facts as at present known are insufficient to justify an actual protest, you should ... request the Venezuelan Government to investigate the matter, and let you know the result.'[28] In the meantime, no action should be taken.

As a final twist to the long-running Venezuelan dispute, meanwhile, the Hague Tribunal determined in February 1904 that the blockading Powers should get preferential treatment after all. Castro must compensate all claimants, but Britain, Germany and Italy should receive priority – the final Award therefore fully justified the blockade. Arthur Larcom, who attended the Tribunal, explained that Britain should be satisfied 'both in respect of the fact that the Award was unanimous, and that it was arrived at on grounds of abstract justice and was obviously wholly unbiased by any considerations of a political nature.' Lansdowne spoke of his 'great pleasure' and, from Berlin, Lascelles emphasised Germany's 'pleasure that [the] recourse to the Hague Tribunal had produced so satisfactory a settlement of German claims.'[29] Such a resounding victory, however, could be depended upon to surprise and offend the other interested nations. Penfield, the American representative at the Hague, had concluded his arguments on November 13 1903 by stating that, while 'the point of honour must in certain events demand the arbitrament of war, he was not convinced that the resort to it by Great Britain in the present instance had been justified.'[30] Americans now worried that the preferential treatment ruling would set a dangerous precedent.[31]

While British officials continued to investigate Venezuela's naval seizures, President Castro took heart from the evident policy of non-intervention and his anti-foreign diplomacy even gained impetus. A confidential dispatch from the British Legation in Caracas complained that,

> 'no effort is left untried to annoy and bleed enterprises established here with foreign capital ... All European interests are suffering considerably

from the retrograde and narrow-minded policy of the President and
his entourage ... Foreigners of all nationalities who are in a position to
do so are leaving the country, and many natives express open discontent
at the present state of affairs.'[32]

From Bax-Ironside's account, it was clear that the Anglo-German blockade had
failed to curb Castro's lawlessness. In February 1904, he informed Lansdowne that
Castro had demanded the recall of Baron Aliotti, the Italian Chargé d'Affairs in
Caracas: 'your Lordship will perceive that the attitude of President Castro and his
Government continues to remain a strongly anti-foreign one', he concluded.[33] Still,
evidence of Castro's bad faith continued to drop in Lansdowne's in-tray.
Regarding the confiscation of the "Urabanti", Venezuela now stubbornly denied
Britain's right to intervene, 'in view of Article II of the law defining the rights and
duties of foreigners in Venezuela of the 11th April 1903'. Lansdowne replied that
Britain had already protested against the law and stressed that 'His Majesty's
Government have declined to recognise ... any law framed with the purpose of
limiting their rights to protect British subjects in Venezuela.'[34]

Now, intervention was not an option. Britain's response to crises in the
Western Hemisphere was more than ever directed by American opinion, and the
United States' Presidential election, taking place in November, acted as a further
deterrent against intervention. In the summer of 1904, Roosevelt came under
attack from the Democrats, who accused him of rampant imperialism – a British
vice – and a tendency to '"mark time to England's step"'. Sir Mortimer Durand,
who had replaced Herbert at the Washington Embassy, explained that '[w]e know
how untrue this is, but it is what the Democrats are saying, and we may be sure
that Roosevelt and Hay will be anxious to clear themselves from the reproach.'
Anxious as he was to meet the President, Durand worried that even his presence
in Washington might harm Roosevelt. 'The Government is always sensitive about
us,' he noted ruefully, 'and while a Presidential campaign is going on it is abnor-
mally so.'[35]

To quieten his critics, Roosevelt stressed his presidential achievements,
dwelling on the strength of the American Navy and the resultant protection given
to the Monroe Doctrine. In a letter to the Chairman of the Republican
Notification Committee, given to the British Embassy in September, Roosevelt
pointed out that the navy 'has been and is now the most potent guarantee of
peace, and it is chiefly because it is formidable and ready for use.' Roosevelt
emphasised his total support for the Monroe Doctrine. '[H]e says that it has been
strengthened and upheld by the present Administration,' Durand explained, 'and that
never before has it been acquiesced in abroad as it is now.'[36] Britain took the point
– the 'special relationship' might not survive another naval mission against Castro.

A more serious dispute arose in Venezuela in mid 1904 as Castro moved
against the New York and Bermudez Asphalt Company. Although primarily an
American concern, the dispute threatened British investment in the company,
which also employed several British subjects. Since 1887, the company had

exploited the asphalt concession in the Guanoco region of Venezuela. Ten years later, what was to become a long running litigation entered the Venezuelan courts, when the lucrative concession was contested. The affair took a more serious note when President Castro received evidence that the company had lent its support to the revolutionary movement headed by Manuel Antonio Matos. Quick as always to react, Castro confiscated company property in April 1903 and began legal proceedings.[37] While this behaviour was strongly deprecated by both the United States and Great Britain, the affair only became critical when Venezuela placed an embargo on the asphalt lake on July 21 and appointed a custodian to take over the company's affairs.[38] On July 23, Bax-Ironside sent an urgent dispatch to the Foreign Office. Enclosing a plaintive letter from Captain Robert K. Wright, Managing Director of the New York and Bermudez Asphalt Company, Bax-Ironside maintained that 'the Venezuelan Government have illegally and unjustifiably placed an embargo on the property of the Company, and have appointed a custodian or receiver ... without having served any writ, summons, or notice on the Company or its representative of any such intended action.'[39]

For the first time, Castro's anti-foreign behaviour was directed primarily against the United States. Through his reckless defiance, Castro even succeeded in alienating Bowen. Now the American Minister telegraphed the State Department in July, suggesting that the United States should act immediately to defend the company's interests. 'In his official correspondence,' Bax-Ironside noted on August 22, Bowen 'states that intervention is, in his opinion, absolutely necessary.'[40]

British officials were naturally curious to see how the State Department would react; they were equally keen that the United States should sanction firm action against Venezuela. A protest by the State Department was summarily ignored. The Venezuelan Government simply replied that 'legal action must be allowed to take its course.'[41] In the face of such obstruction, Bax-Ironside now sent a lengthy dispatch to the Foreign Office proposing a severe reaction:

> 'The only logical conclusion to the present situation appears to be the adoption of coercive measures by the United States' Government against the Venezuelan Government: should such measures by undertaken, it is to be hoped that they will prove of a more effective nature than the late blockade. In my opinion, such intervention should, in order to be effective, take the form of President Castro's deposition.'

As British officials hoped, Castro might finally have gone too far. Bax-Ironside predicted the abolition of stringent taxes under a new President, freedom of commerce and a general policy of non-intervention against foreign Companies. Considering the widespread chaos prevailing in the region, such predictions were rather optimistic. Accordingly, the Chargé d'Affairs suggested that his proposal be forwarded to the State Department, noting that 'they may be grateful for moral support under the present electoral circumstances.'[42] Had Roosevelt sanctioned American interference in Venezuela so soon before the election, however, he would have underlined his image as an imperial adventurer, rather than the protector of Latin America. Nonetheless, from his private correspondence, it is clear that Roosevelt did not intend indefinitely to remain passive. 'It looks to me as if Castro is riding for a fall, and my present impression is that if he has to have a fall, we had better give it to him,' he told Hay on August 30. To retain his popularity during the campaign, Roosevelt concluded that 'I should want action deferred until after [the] election.'[43]

Without securing American approval or co-operation, the Foreign Office delayed its decision. 'The Bermudez Company must be regarded as an American concern,' Lansdowne told Bax-Ironside, 'but you should lend such support as you properly can, as British capital is also involved.'[44] Then, grave information received by the Foreign Office in early August completely altered the situation. The Company's British employees had been forced to continue working at the asphalt lake and urgently needed protection. On August 3, the *Port of Spain Gazette* announced that the men were 'made to work by force of arms.' It went on:

> 'In one case, when a man named Bryant, a carpenter, refused [to work], he was tied by his thumbs and fourteen Mauser rifles placed on his body, and when released he was in a state of physical exhaustion. ... several acts of injustice are reported as having been done to British and American subjects by the Venezuelan troops'.[45]

Lansdowne acted swiftly. On August 6, he directed Bax-Ironside to 'request an immediate inquiry and stringent orders to that official [the company's Venezuelan Receiver] to abstain from any improper treatment of British workmen.' Should this appeal fail, he was prepared to authorise coercion. On August 9, Sir Francis Villiers directed the Admiralty to make a British warship available from the North America and West Indies Squadron to sail for Guanoco. Two days later, Sir Evan MacGregor replied that the "Tribune" had been sent to Trinidad and was awaiting further instructions.[46]

Once more, Britain had taken the lead against Castro. More significantly, she had done so without securing American approval. Although an outcry from the United States was not expected, the Foreign Office found itself once more on the brink of authorising armed action against Venezuela, thereby risking another long-running and acrimonious dispute in South America. While it is impossible to determine whether the Foreign Secretary actually intended to proceed with force, he was playing a dangerous game if he expected the presence of the "Tribune", so close to the Venezuelan coast, to bring Castro to his senses. Fortunately for Britain, Castro surrendered. On August 21, Bax-Ironside telegraphed the Foreign Office that he had received an important note from Venezuelan Authorities. '[N]o cruelty took place during the recent incident at Guanoco,' the note read. Venezuela, Bax-Ironside concluded, had recently freed the British labourers and sent them to Trinidad: the 'question need no longer, therefore, be considered of an urgent nature.'[47] In reply, Lansdowne simply stated that the Foreign Office considered the presence of the "Tribune" at Trinidad no longer necessary.[48] For the Foreign Office, the sudden crisis had vanished.

American authorities, meanwhile, were still struggling to find a satisfactory response to the situation. On August 17, Bax-Ironside reported that the American Legation at Caracas had been directed to deliver a third official protest. The ensuing, predictable defiance led to talk of US coercion, but there is no evidence that this was seriously considered. During an interview between Villiers and White, the New York and Bermudez Asphalt Company issue came under serious discussion. As Lansdowne informed Durand, Villiers 'called attention to the importance of the interests of Great Britain in that country and to the anxiety naturally aroused by the state of affairs there.' Ridgely Carter, an American Embassy official, called at the Foreign Office on August 31 to explain that, although a protest had been sent, 'no decision had been reached as to the course which would ultimately be taken, and no forcible action was at present contemplated'.[49] Until the Presidential elections, then, Castro was safe.

A continuation of Anglo-Venezuelan hostility was fully expected. Indeed, in late September, an unsavoury incident occurred on the boundary between British Guiana and Venezuela, during which a group of British gold prospectors was captured and imprisoned by Venezuelan police. An angry dispatch from Sir James Swettenham, Governor of British Guiana, reported 'a serious aggression on British territory by an armed force of Venezuelans'. Accordingly, the Colonial Office requested that Lansdowne 'take such steps as may to him appear best for obtaining from the Venezuelan Government an apology and reparation for this outrage'.[50] Lansdowne requested that Venezuela explain the incident and release the prisoners.[51] In fact, the release had already taken place. Sir Frederick Hodgson, Britain's Governor at Barbados, noted that, during an interview with Dr. Tirado, Chief Venezuelan Boundary Commissioner, the latter had stressed that 'the men were at work on the Venezuelan side of the frontier, and that there had been no violation of British territory by the Venezuelan police.' Hodgson even concluded that the affair was 'being dealt with in a very friendly spirit.'[52] This was something of a surprise. Used to dealing with Venezuelan truculence, Venezuela, it seemed, had genuine cause for complaint. Lansdowne sought further information and Hodgson asked for copies of the Mining Laws and Regulations of Venezuela,

'as I desire to make salient points of them known to gold prospectors, and to acquaint them that they have to be observed in connection with work in Venezuela equally as this Colony's laws and Regulations have to be observed here [British Guiana], and that if they contravene them they cannot expect any protection from this Government.'[53]

Still, Lansdowne inclined to support the prospectors, directing Bax-Ironside to 'urge [the] Venezuelan Government to appoint and instruct [a] Commissioner at once, as further delay is undesirable.'[54] Yet it proved impossible to determine exactly where the arrests had taken place, while a secondary clash between gold diggers and Venezuelan authorities in December suggested that the British prospectors had been, and remained at fault.[55] Accordingly, the British Government was content to let the matter drop.

While the Foreign Office deliberated its future approach to diplomacy in South America, naval and defence experts reacted to the rising threat from foreign navies and stressed the urgency of withdrawing British forces from the Western Hemisphere. Defence experts, tending to regard the Caribbean as a relatively unthreatened region, decided to withdraw all but one cruiser squadron.[56] This would be sufficient to safeguard British interests from anything but an attack by the United States. Meanwhile, the question of maintaining the West Indian garrisons came before the Committee of Imperial Defence. On November 25 1903, the Committee considered the position in Bermuda, and decided that:

'(1.) The island must not be left undefended, if only because it is necessary to protect it from attack by a European Power.
(2.) The present defences are sufficient to protect the island against any Power other than the United States.
(3.) It would scarcely be possible for a hostile force to land until the guns had been silenced from the sea – in any case, except in the event of war with the United States, only a small raiding force could be landed, against which the present fortifications and garrison would probably be sufficient.'[57]

Discussions on the future of the Bermuda garrison continued on July 8 1904. Clearly influenced by the ongoing Anglo-American *rapprochement*, the Committee revised its Caribbean strategy and decided that an 'attack from the United States need not be taken into consideration. Only the possibility of a raid by cruisers of a European Power need be considered.' Not only was an infantry battalion withdrawn from Bermuda, but the CID authorised the removal of all white soldiers from Jamaica and a reduction of troops in Trinidad. Withdrawal was taken a step further on November 22 when St. Lucia's defences were abandoned. '[T]he maintenance of a garrison there would now merely invite attack', the Committee concluded.[58] If Britain retained sufficient forces to deal with lesser disputes, the abandonment of the West Indian garrisons announced Britain's willingness to concede regional hegemony to the United States.

The decision of the Venezuelan court regarding the New York and Bermudez Asphalt Company was delivered on October 4 1904. 'In the course of the proceedings', it stated, 'the defendants have not produced any evidence in their favour, therefore the reasons on which the court ordered the sequestration remain in force.'[59] In late October, the United States sent Castro a fourth official protest, demanding that the property of the New York and Bermudez Asphalt Company be restored to its rightful owners. [I]t seems scarcely possible,' Bax-Ironside remarked, 'that, from the point of view of their own dignity, the United States Government will again address this [Venezuelan] Government on the subject, unless such a communication takes the form of an ultimatum.'[60] More forceful measures against Venezuela became clear in early December, when Bax-Ironside telegraphed news that parts of the American-European, the American South Atlantic and the Caribbean Squadrons were due to meet off Culebra Island, east of Puerto Rico, to carry out manoeuvres and target practice. 'A feeling is prevalent here,' he explained, 'that the assembly of so large a fleet in the neighbourhood of the Venezuelan sea-board will tend considerably to strengthen the hands of the United States' Government in any action which they may see fit to take to support the interests of the Asphalt Company.'[61] The free hand the United States had allowed Castro was coming to an end. Once Roosevelt secured re-election, he used his 1904 Annual Message to announce serious extensions to the Monroe Doctrine:

'It is not true that the United States feels any land hunger or entertains any projects as regards the other nations of the western hemisphere save such as are for their welfare. All that this country desires is to see the neighbouring countries stable, orderly, and prosperous. ... If a nation shows that it knows how to act with reasonable efficiency and decency in social and political matters, if it keeps order and pays its obligations, it need fear no interference from the United States.'

Despite his protestations of friendship, Roosevelt was quick to issue a stern warning to the Latin American Governments:

'Chronic wrong-doing, or an impotence which results in a general loosening of the ties of civilized society, may in America, as elsewhere, ultimately require intervention by some civilized nation, and in the western hemisphere the adherence of the United States to the Monroe Doctrine may force the United States, however reluctantly, in flagrant cases of such wrong-doing or impotence, to the exercise of international police power.'[62]

Finally, the United States assumed responsibility for maintaining order in South America. Britain's immediate reaction was one of natural enthusiasm and tangible relief. One British journalist, J. Fred Rippy, stated that Roosevelt had 'enforced a new and much less one-sided view of the Monroe Doctrine, a view equally acceptable to the non-aggressive Powers of Europe and to all such South American States as pay their debts, keep their word, and act with decency.'[63] What results were to follow from Roosevelt's Corollary, however, were not immediately apparent. Negotiations with Venezuela about the New York and Bermudez Asphalt Company continued well into 1905 – rather than sending in warships, the State Department tended acted with greater consideration for Castro's republic, refusing to offend South America by overpowering Venezuela.[64] On April 2, Roosevelt explained to Hay that the United States must keep its temper. 'Castro is an unspeakably villainous little monkey,' he wrote, 'and on ethical grounds, as well as to give exercise to the United States Army, I should like to send an expedition against him'. However, 'this at present would be inadvisable in such a mundane world as ours, alike from the standpoint of internal and international politics.'[65] In mid November, Elihu Root – who succeeded John Hay as Secretary of State – told the American Chargé d'Affairs in Caracas that the State Department would 'render every proper assistance within our power toward bringing any negotiation between the company and the Government of Venezuela to a conclusion which will be in accordance with substantial justice.'[66] As a means of settling the long-running dispute (already well over a year and a half old), this clearly fell a long way short. The European Powers would have to wait further to determine whether the Roosevelt Corollary carried any weight.

The Anglo-German blockade and its aftermath had a distinct effect on Lansdowne's diplomacy in Central and South America. The blockade taught the Foreign Office that it must conduct such drastic measures without the assistance of other European nations. Still more, Britain's strong wish not to offend the United States led to an increased sensitivity for American opinion, and a desire for the two Powers to act in harmony. Nevertheless, it is equally clear that the Foreign Office considered itself free to pursue a strong policy in the region, at least until Roosevelt gave a definite statement of intent. When the question of hemispheric responsibility had been in doubt, Britain would, in the last resort, undertake naval operations in South America to protect her interests. The Roosevelt Corollary, however, largely brought this to an end. Although its worth was yet to be proved, Britain welcomed Roosevelt's strengthened Monroe Doctrine. Once the United States had made clear their determination to police the entirety of South and Central America, affairs in the region calmed down and the possibility of another serious dispute, though never wholly disregarded, no longer was considered imminent.

Under Lansdowne, British interest, and intervention, in South American affairs underwent a rapid change. From the signature of the Hay-Pauncefote Convention to the acceptance of Roosevelt's Corollary, the Foreign Office displayed a willingness to give to the United States total control of the continent. In part, this was a forced decision (the strain on Britain's military and naval resources will be covered in the next chapter), yet the widespread belief that Britain had no significant interests in South America that she risked losing was equally important – if Roosevelt was prepared to defend British subjects and interests against Latin American despots, that was one less area of the globe for Britain to police.

For these reasons, Lansdowne's diplomacy in South America was generally successful. The Venezuelan blockade had been unfortunate; Campbell-Bannerman called it 'a paltry quarrel, apparently involving a comparatively insignificant sum', and had betrayed 'every element of foolishness and recklessness in the situation'.[67] Lansdowne nonetheless pursued a strong policy for which he, and his German allies, were suitably rewarded. Through careful steering and protestations of friendship for the United States, Lansdowne achieved a satisfactory relationship between the two Powers in Latin America. If the Foreign Office could pursue a similar course with regard to Anglo-American questions in North America, the ever-strengthening 'special relationship' between Britain and her 'brothers across the ocean' might finally be cemented.

America and Canada

5

Responsibility, Strategy & Paranoia

Imperial Considerations in Canada, 1895-1905

URING LANSDOWNE'S TIME at the Foreign Office, the nature of Britain's relationship with Canada was influenced by the requirements of Anglo-American diplomacy. The radical reconsideration of British global strategy – primarily to meet the powerful Franco-Russian combination – ensured that British forces would withdrawn from the Western Hemisphere.[1] Once this decision had been made, Britain was obliged to rely upon the United States to ensure the continuing safety of Canada and other North American colonics. In consequence, both from hope and from necessity, British officials tended to disregard the United States as a potential enemy. As we have seen, Balfour's convictions lay strongly towards Anglo-American harmony. On December 20 1899, he wrote to Alfred Thayer Mahan, the well known American expert on sea power, that:

> 'It becomes more and more obvious – to me at least, as it is I think to you – that our interests, both in the narrow and in the wide use of that term, are identical. We have not only the same ideas of progress, freedom, civilisation, religion, morality, but we have the same interests in peace'.[2]

Even without Balfour's idealism, British military and naval experts fully understood the necessity of placating the United States. Lord Selborne, First Lord of the Admiralty, told Lansdowne in late 1901 that the maintenance of a two power standard for the British navy would be impossible 'if the United States were to use all their resources to develop their naval strength.'[3] Roosevelt's campaign for a stronger American navy to enforce the Monroe Doctrine made Anglo-American harmony all the more desirable. Still, Britain simply could not afford to abandon Canada, her only truly important possession in the Western Hemisphere. Canadian assistance in South Africa, and the potential future of a burgeoning trade between the two countries, inspired in Britain a campaign for closer imperial ties. In turn, the Unionists made a brave, though ultimately futile attempt to balance imperial responsibility with the new global strategy. Although Lansdowne's role was not always significant, these events largely determined his approach to Anglo-American diplomacy and his views on Britain's North American colonies.

'The nineteenth century belonged to the United States, the twentieth century belongs to Canada.'[4] So claimed Sir Wilfrid Laurier, the Canadian Prime Minister, at Toronto on May 20 1902. In the event, Laurier's prediction that Canada might overtake her southern neighbour proved to be somewhat optimistic, but her rapid economic growth indicated a bright and successful future.

Signs of a changing Anglo-Canadian bond were already apparent in the opening years of the twentieth century. Beginning to appreciate the Dominion's vast potential as a trading nation, many Canadians now looked towards economic expansion and the conclusion of trade agreements with Powers besides the Mother Country. In particular, Canada made tentative steps towards achieving a reciprocal trade agreement with the United States. In 1896, Sir Richard Cartwright, Canada's Minister of Trade and Commerce, met Joseph Chamberlain in Massachusetts to advance the proposal for such an arrangement. The Colonial Secretary was concerned that Canadian-American unity would sever the Dominion from her imperial connection and noted that Cartwright's plan was a 'practical refutation of the expressions of loyalty and imperial patriotism ... so gladly accepted by the British public'.[5]

The worry that economic considerations had compromised Canada's loyalty to the Empire were prevalent in Britain and the signs of such a shift were readily apparent. Canadian imports of American goods had doubled during the 1890s until, by 1900, their value had risen to $102,224,917.[6] 'It is always difficult to get any correct analysis of the real feeling between Canada and the United States', the newly-appointed Canadian Governor-General, Lord Minto, told Lansdowne in 1898, 'no doubt the people we know are intensely loyal, but I used to feel pretty certain that trade interests had decidedly affected patriotism in some districts.'[7] Lansdowne hardly needed persuading. As Governor-General in the 1880s, he had been quick to highlight what he then considered to be Canada's inevitable shift towards the US. If the Dominion 'is to have closer trade relations', Lansdowne noted in his Canadian journal, 'it will be to her advantage to establish them with [the] U.S. rather than with [Britain]. It is easier for her to deal with a country sep-arated from herself by ... a 3000 [mile] frontier than with one divided by 3000 [miles] of ocean.' In another entry, Lansdowne explained that the natural alliance of Canada 'is with [the] U.S. in spite of free trade with [the] U.K.'[8]

By the time he arrived at the Foreign Office however, Lansdowne's pes-simism had largely evaporated, a direct result of Canada's reaffirmed loyalty to the Empire. In 1897 the Dominion Government gave a 25 per cent preference to British goods. Although Sir Wilfrid Laurier hardly expected that the arrangement would be reciprocated, he made no secret of his desire to bring about a closer commercial bond between the colonies and the Mother Country. Accordingly, the Canadian Premier pressed for the termination of an agreement, concluded between Britain and Germany on May 30 1865, which entitled German goods to the same treatment in the colonies as those from Britain. The British Government, anxious to encourage imperial commerce and equally keen to deter trade between the colonies and foreign competitors, denounced the treaty in July 1897. A Colonial Conference had convened in London that summer, during which Laurier repeated his opposition to the Anglo-German treaty. When the Conference ended, Salisbury informed the German Foreign Office that Britain wished to see the treaty terminated.[9] Significant amendments were made the following year to the Canadian Tariff Act, insisting that the Dominion should only adopt preferential trade agreements with Britain and her Colonies. Of yet greater interest to Laurier was Sir Michael Hicks Beach's imposition of a Corn Registration Duty in 1902. Britain, it seemed, had finally accepted the need for protective tariffs. Attending the Colonial Conference in July, Laurier again pressed for imperial preference.[10] While Canada had not totally abandoned the idea of a reciprocal trade arrangement with the United States, Laurier's desire to strengthen the imperial bond could hardly be misinterpreted.

The surge of Canadian loyalty that followed the outbreak of war in South Africa underlined the true strength of her patriotism. By the end of the conflict, more than eight thousand Canadian volunteers had joined their British counterparts in the fight against the Boers, at a cost of over two million dollars. That the enlistment had been voluntary was yet more encouraging and gave great weight to Sir Charles Dilke's remark that the Canadians were 'perhaps the most loyal of all the peoples under the British Crown.' In *The British Empire*, published in 1899, Dilke concluded that, should the United States seek to annex the Dominion, she would find Canada 'a hard morsel to digest.'[11] Canada's contribution to South African success was a timely reminder of the intense patriotism that prevailed throughout the country. 'A much larger force could have been recruited,' Sir Frederick Borden, Canada's Minister of Militia, informed the War Office on November 10 1899, 'and my chief difficulty was to restrain those who seemed determined to force their services upon me and would scarcely take no for an answer.' Clearly relieved, Lansdowne sent an enthusiastic reply: 'The war has been popular with the great mass of our people, and nothing has added to its popularity more than the support which the great Colonies have already given us.'[12] The resurgence of loyalty to the Empire in Canada inspired the desire for closer ties. In October 1901, Minto remarked that, 'I believe that feelings have been stirred by the S. African war which if properly directed here [in Canada] would certainly do much to unite in one common cause all the outposts of the Empire.'[13] Joseph Chamberlain, returning from his South African trip in 1903, now began advocating an interdependent imperial economy. Before discussing this radical reform programme, however, it is necessary to turn to the question of Canadian defence.

The War Office had long entertained hopes that Canada, along with the other colonies, might be persuaded to assume her imperial responsibilities and help Britain meet the needs of the Empire. Responding to the many strains on Britain's naval and military resources, the Unionists determined that they should attempt to strengthen the imperial connection by inviting direct colonial contribution to the imperial purse. If the colonies contributed to their own defence, Britain could make vital reductions in imperial spending. For the Treasury, its finances already stretched, such measures were crucial. However, in 1896, Canada was in no mood to consider defence questions. Her own militia was badly organised, poorly trained and totally unprepared for war.[14] In February, a report arrived at the War Office complaining of the chaotic nature of Canadian military affairs. 'I fear there is not much to be done,' Lansdowne – then Secretary for War – told Joseph Chamberlain, 'the tendency for job promoting, contracts &c. is ingrained.'[15] Borden's arrival at the Department of Militia in 1896 did much to highlight defence considerations in Canada and Lansdowne determined to push for greater organisation. In 1898, he appointed Colonel Edward Hutton as Borden's military adviser. During an interview between the two men, Lansdowne, 'considered from his own experiences in Canada that much might be done', Hutton recalled, 'and that the Canadian Government just now were anxious to improve their forces and to make it sound and efficient.' Lansdowne then tentatively steered the conversation towards the contribution that Canada might make to the Empire, hinting at 'the idea of raising a regiment in Canada for Imperial purposes upon imperial rates of pay.' Given the state of Canada's militia, Hutton simply replied that he 'considered the idea utopian.'[16] Despite this, many in Britain continued to advocate the need for a greater imperial contribution,[17] but, despite Borden's influence and the South African war, the pace of change was frustratingly slow.

Hugh Arnold-Forster (Secretary for the Admiralty and later Secretary for War in Balfour's Cabinet reshuffle of 1903) stepped up the campaign in 1902, pushing for a colonial contribution towards the upkeep of the British navy: 'It is of the highest importance that in view of the immense strain upon the United Kingdom, the Colonies, which derive so much benefit from the protection offered by the Navy, should be induced to contribute towards the Navy, both in men and money.' Arnold-Forster even named a satisfactory sum: Canada and Australia should deliver an annual payment of £300,000 while New Zealand and South Africa might pay £100,000 each.[18]

The Canadian Government, however, was reluctant to assume any such responsibility. With reason, Canada argued that there simply was no tangible threat to her borders. The majority were convinced that Canada's only potential enemy, the United States, was unlikely to initiate a war, but a minority took the American threat seriously – and it was undeniable that the relationship between Canada and the US had worsened over preceding years.

In May 1898, a protocol signed by Pauncefote and Hay established a Joint High Commission to resolve all outstanding sources of Canadian-American dispute. Sessions began at Quebec in August 1898 and reconvened in Washington in November. Six jurists sat on each side, with Canada's case headed by Britain's Lord High Chancellor, Lord Herschell, whom Hay labelled 'more cantankerous than any of the Canadians'.[19] After lengthy discussions, negotiations stalled – on February 20 1899, official talks ended.[20] This turn of events worried those who already feared Canada's annexation, a minority that included such prominent men as the academic and strenuous anti-imperialist Goldwin Smith, who, in late 1901, wrote to Sir Charles Dilke of his pessimism concerning Canada's future:

'Canada, in the event of war with the United States, is indefensible', he explained. 'She has an open frontier, allowing for indentations, of something like 4000 miles. For 800 miles in the North West the frontier is only a political line. A hostile gunboat on Lake Superior would command the Canadian Pacific Railway and cut it in two.'

For Goldwin Smith, Canadian integrity was not threatened solely by war. Instead, he predicted the peaceful incorporation of Canada into the United States; the Dominion's 'extension to the Pacific,' he remarked, 'destroying all geographical and commercial unity, while each province is attracted by nature to the country South of it, has made ultimate annexation, it seems to me, a certainty.'[21]

To counter Canada's tendency to ignore its own defence, meanwhile, Minto suggested that two Canadian garrisons be handed over to the Dominion – the military stations at Halifax (Nova Scotia) and Esquimalt (Vancouver Island) were the last outposts in Canada still manned by British troops. In mid 1901, Minto explained to Lord Roberts, Commander-in-Chief of the British army, 'that the solution of the unsatisfactory military position here is to hand over Halifax & Esquimalt to the Dom[inio]n. Govt. retaining certain Imperial control over them.' This, he concluded, would 'place the defence and military position of Canada on a footing of such importance that the people of Canada would be bound to recognize it.'Speaking to Sir Richard Cartwright in November, Minto again raised his proposal. Cartwright 'did not jump at it', Minto noted, '[he] thought the expense would be very great, probably $1,000,000'.[22] In the near future, however, Canada would have to compromise or risk a serious rupture in Anglo-Canadian relations.

At the same time, the size, allocation and efficiency of the British navy were suddenly called into question. The old two-power standard was no longer adequate and, although a Franco-Russian combination was seen as the greatest immediate threat, the Admiralty also worried about German and American naval ambitions.[23] In the "Balance of Naval Power in the Far East", Selborne noted that,

'I have already given to the Cabinet my reasons for thinking that this standard would be beyond the strength of this country if the United States were to use all their resources to develop their naval strength, and that it is inadequate if applied to a possible war against France in alliance with Russia. ... I am strongly in favour of concentrating our strength, as far as possible, at the spot at which the final issue will be fought out; but some risks would be too great to run even for this object.'[24]

The Anglo-Japanese agreement of January 1902 lessened the strain in the Far East and Selborne now began urging a significant shift in naval policy. Writing to Balfour in April 1902, he remarked that it 'is impossible that the Cabinet should be without a naval policy or leave the Admiralty without instructions.' The time had now arrived, for Britain to initiate a radical reappraisal of her naval strategy:

'I candidly admit that I had not ... realised the intensity of the hatred of the German nation to this Country. I have consulted Lord

Lansdowne and I find that he shares my sense of the importance of the question and my anxiety to arrive at a fixed policy. He desires, however, and I fully agree with him, that before I bring this subject before the Cabinet you and Mr. Chamberlain and he and I should meet and discuss the matter thoroughly.'[25]

Selborne and Lansdowne now discussed the realities behind the apparent German threat. Selborne's 'conundrums', sent through Lansdowne to Sir Frank Lascelles on April 22, asked for a clarification of Germany's true motives. 'Will it be safe for England to be content with a Navy just equal or a little superior in numbers to France & Russia combined,' he enquired, 'and have nothing in hand as against the German Navy?' He went on:

'In the case of England being engaged in a war with France and Russia what would be the attitude of (a) the German Government (b) the German people, towards England? And what use if any would be made of the naval strength of Germany?'

It was, replied Lansdowne, likely that Germany would 'stick to her role of the honest broker, taking advantage, if you like, of our difficulties ... but without pooling her ironclads with those of France & Russia'. Lascelles agreed. The Germans 'are alive to their interests', he remarked on April 25, 'and they understand that, if England were to cease to exist as a Great Power, they would be at the mercy of Russia and France, if those two Powers united against them.'[26] The Kaiser's unpredictability continued to jangle the nerves of the British Government so, to ease the immense naval strain, Selborne strove for all possible efficiency. In May, he sent a letter of complaint to Lansdowne in which he maintained that:

'Whenever you tell me that the Navy can in any way assist your diplomatic action in a matter of real importance you will never find me name difficulties; on the contrary I will always help you to the utmost of my power. On the other hand you can I think help me greatly by reducing the number of calls on the Admiralty which are really not absolutely necessary. I do not think the F.O. at all realise the way in which the efficiency of the navy is impaired by these unnecessary calls upon it.'

Selborne found in Lansdowne a strong ally. Both men recognised the inadequacies of Britain's global strategy and accordingly aimed to redirect her resources. A no less significant event in the reshaping of British strategy was Salisbury's retirement on July 10. Balfour, who succeeded Salisbury, had a deep interest in foreign and defence questions and, urged by Selborne and St. John Broderick, Secretary for War, to reorganise the Defence Committee, established the Committee of Imperial Defence in December 1902.[28] It was a clear sign that, under Balfour, imperial strategy would receive intensive thought.

Imperial problems resurfaced at the 1902 Colonial Conference, when protection and defence contributions came to the fore. A resolution accepted 'that the
principle of preferential trade between the United Kingdom and His Majesty's
Dominions beyond the seas would stimulate and facilitate mutual commercial
intercourse'. This 'would, by promoting the development of the resources and
industries of the several parts, strengthen the Empire'. Although he had long fostered the idea, Joseph Chamberlain chose the moment to lend his wholehearted
support to protection. Not only would protection strengthen Britain's scattered
Empire, but, by doing so, it would secure the Empire's future, basing the imperial
relationship on something more concrete than loyalty. However, his hopes were at
least temporarily dashed as the next resolution admitted that it was not then practical
to expect a general system of free trade between Britain and her colonies.[29]

Still, Britain was quite prepared for Canada to grant her further economic
concessions. To the existing thirty three per cent preference on British goods,
Laurier added an additional preference on selected articles, whilst raising duties on
foreign imports. Perhaps for this reason, Canada made no contribution to imperial
defence. Although other colonies were obliged to make payments – Sir Robert
Bond of Newfoundland agreed that his Government would pay £3,000 annually
for the Newfoundland Royal Naval Reserve – Canada remained the last significant
colony not to forward any defence funds.[30] To a greater contribution, the colonies
would not agree. It was one thing for Britain to equate colonial contributions with
imperial unity, but many colonies resented paying for a navy for which they had
neither use nor need.[31] The Conference thus ended as a limited success, without
resolving the many issues raised during its sitting.

In determining both the future of the imperial tie and the continuing relationship between Britain and her Western Hemispheric possessions, 1903 was a
pivotal year. The Alaska boundary question (see the following chapter) threatened
to disrupt the amicable state of Anglo-Canadian relations; at the same time, fundamental changes were proposed to the imperial bond. In May, Chamberlain
began his famous campaign for tariff reform. At Birmingham, Chamberlain
stressed that upon Britain's immediate policy decisions,

'depends the tremendous issue whether this great Empire of ours is to
stand together, one free nation, if necessary, against the world, or
whether it is to fall apart into separate States, each selfishly seeking its
own interests alone – losing sight of the common weal, and losing also
all the advantages which union alone can give.'

Chamberlain's message was clear; the future of the Empire depended on Britain
recognising the need for reciprocal tariffs with the Colonies. Concluding his
speech, the Colonial Secretary remarked that:

'I say it is the business of British statesman to do everything they can,
even at some present sacrifice, to keep the trade of the colonies with

Great Britain; to increase that trade, to promote it, even if in doing so
we lessen somewhat the trade with our foreign competitors.'[32]

This was pure ideology. To Lord Chancellor Halsbury, Chamberlain explained
that 'I advocate for the union of the Empire. I know it involves a big fight but I
would rather fall in such a course than [see] any member of our party victorious.'[33]
It is not necessary to discuss Chamberlain's campaign for Colonial preference in
any great detail here.[34] It is important to note, however, that through his determination to ensure the imperial tie, he almost destroyed Balfour's Administration. In
the Cabinet, Charles T. Ritchie, Chancellor of the Exchequer, Lord George
Hamilton at the India Office and the Duke of Devonshire all opposed preference,
while the Prime Minister – with Lansdowne in support – stoutly defended a middle
course. The very credibility of the Government was at stake, as free-traders and
tariff-reformers engaged in a free for all that ended with the resignations of
Chamberlain and Devonshire in September. J. A. Spender, writing for the
Westminster Gazette, lampooned Government policy with the character "Greville
Minor" Highlighting the comical chaos of the Cabinet, Minor noted that,

> 'It is strange enough to wake up in the morning and read in one's
> Times a vehement letter from the Colonial Secretary advocating a fun-
> damentally new line of policy for which the Government disclaim all
> responsibility, and which a majority of his colleagues actively disavow
> ... Ministers speak with the utmost freedom of each other, and none of
> them apparently are under the slightest obligation to support or
> approve, or even pretend to support or approve, what others of them
> are doing.'[35]

For his part, Balfour appreciated the dangers of the tariff issue. While he made no
secret of his support for retaliatory tariffs, however, he was disappointed that the
question could not be delayed. Writing in June, Balfour explained that 'my efforts
have been devoted to lessening, so far as I can, evils which I fear cannot be wholly
avoided.' Significantly, the Prime Minister laid the blame for the sudden crisis
squarely on Canada. 'The question might ... have continued to slumber,' he
explained sadly, 'until some economic catastrophe aroused public opinion, had it
not been for the Colonial Conferences of 1897 and 1902; for the overt action of
Canada in giving a preference to this country, and for the diplomatic controversy
which thereupon ensued with Germany.'[36]

The German-Canadian fiscal dispute suddenly re-emerged in 1903. Angry
at Laurier's rejection of the preferential tariff, Germany retaliated by withdrawing
her most-favoured nation clause with Canada and, in April, threatened to remove
the clause from Britain should other colonies follow the Canadian example. In
response, Ottawa actually raised the Canadian tariff on German goods.[37] An esca-
lating commercial dispute seemed likely, those in favour of tariff reform welcoming
the Canadian action and those advocating free trade refusing to countenance economic retaliation. Clearly, it was necessary to calm a dangerous situation and

Lansdowne's response was firm. 'We did not regard it as loose talk [but] did not propose to rush into a war of tariffs', he noted. In all, the affair had been both 'clumsy and absurd'. Significantly, in this undated note, Lansdowne declared himself wholeheartedly against preference. 'Canada is in fact worse off for having given us preference', he remarked. 'Other colonies will be worse off.'[38] Meanwhile, Devonshire, a staunch free trader, renewed his protests. According to John Sandars, Balfour's Private Secretary, Devonshire considered that Britain 'had no legitimate case of complaint against Germany!'[39] In response, Lansdowne argued that the affair was a one off and would not bring about widescale retaliation. 'I infer that it does not commit us finally to retaliation,' Devonshire acknowledged, 'and therefore do not dissent.'[40] For this reason, German objections were disregarded by the Foreign Office and the Canadian preference was maintained.

Despite Canada's determination to strengthen imperial trade relations, the Dominion made her desire perfectly clear to effect reciprocity with the United States in food stuffs and raw materials. 'In respect to the possibility of such reciprocity eventually alienating Canada from the Mother-Land,' Laurier told Minto in June 1903, 'he said that he was not in the least apprehensive, but the only thing which he thought might cause friction in that direction would be obstruction on the part of the Mother-country to any desire for reciprocity in the part of Canada with the U.S.'[41] It was only the American tariffs that had kept Canada from seeking closer co-operation with Washington: 'the result of the U.S. tariffs has been to drive Canada into British markets', the Governor-General told Arthur Elliott on July 5. If McKinley had not imposed such tariffs, the result would have been different and Minto stressed that 'if there had not been complete commercial union between the U.S. and Canada by this time there would have been something very near it, with annexation not very far off.'[42] Fortunately, Roosevelt had no intention of abandoning protection, while the minority who supported free trade tended to couch their arguments in naive and sentimental terms. In *Free Trade and Protection*, published in 1903, American economist Henry George maintained that,

> 'With the abolition of our custom houses and the opening of our ports to the free entry of all good things, the trade between the British Islands and the United States would become so immense, the intercourse so intimate, that we should become one people, and would inevitably so conform currency, and postal system and general laws that Englishman and American would feel themselves as much citizens of a common country as do New Yorker and Californian.'[43]

In Ottawa, Minto worried about the effect that even a limited reciprocity on raw materials and food stuffs would have on Anglo-Canadian relations. 'Do you think a reciprocity Treaty with the U.S. might ultimately lead to [a] risk for [the] British connection', he asked Sir John Willison, editor of the Toronto *Globe*, on July 4, 'might it not indicate the thin end of the wedge for commercial union?'[44] In fact, such anxiety was unfounded and even Canadian officials considered reciprocity unlikely to succeed. Willison's reply stressed that that there 'is no general feeling for reciprocity with the United States, any early revival of such feeling is not likely, & at last Canadians feel a *real* confidence in their own country.' At the same time, W. S. Fielding, Canada's Minister of Finance, shrewdly observed that the State Department 'would demand to be placed on the same terms as British goods in respect to any preference, which would ... be an impossible proposition.'[45] Because the Canadian people recognised that Canadian-American reciprocity was unrealistic, and because they still cherished the hope of imperial preference, the move for trade discussions with Washington was soon abandoned. There were other reasons for pulling away from the United States. Not only had Roosevelt offended the Dominion during the long-running Alaska boundary negotiations, but worrying signs re-emerged during 1903 that the United States had not quite abandoned the idea of Canadian annexation. Minto's letter to Chamberlain of December 14, three months after the latter had resigned from the Colonial Office, showed the Governor-General in a more optimistic mood; the 'feeling against the U.S. is so strong at the present moment,' he explained, 'that Canadians generally refuse to consider the possibility of closer connection with them'. However, should Britain consistently refuse preference, that there might be a severe reaction:

> 'she [Canada] will simply accept the rebuff & look elsewhere,' he remarked, 'her tendency will at any rate be away from closer Imperial connections, it will in the first place, if she feels strong enough, be towards independence – otherwise temptations in the direction of commercial union with the U.S. will play a great part.'[46]

On February 27 1903, Sir Michael Herbert sent the Foreign Office worrying news that a section of American opinion still hoped to see Canada annexed by the United States. A resolution, introduced in the House of Representatives by David A. De Armond of Missouri, requested 'the President to ascertain upon what terms Great Britain would be prepared to cede to the United States all or any part of Canada.' De Armond's proposal, to integrate the Dominion 'into one or more States and [to be] admitted into the Union upon an equality with the other States, the inhabitants thereof in the mean time to enjoy all the privileges and immunities guaranteed by the federal constitution', was, as Lansdowne noted, 'a remarkable Resolution.'[47] There was little cause for alarm – De Armond's scheme failed to gain significant political support – yet it sparked a definite response in Britain, worried that Roosevelt's own desire for Canadian annexation might re-emerge.[48]

In June, a secret report was prepared by Colonel Hubert Foster, Military Attaché to the Embassy, detailing the 'measures which would probably be taken by the United States in the event of their attempting the invasion of Canada.' Foster's arguments were largely hypothetical and not a response to a particular or immediate threat. Nevertheless, the Foreign Secretary gave the matter his full attention. Noting that the report was both 'extraordinarily interesting and carefully prepared', Lansdowne concluded that its perusal would serve to 'open the eyes of some of the critics of the British W.O. to read this description of the feeling which prevails in the U.S.'[49] Although he considered the possibility of an Anglo-

American conflict over Canada remote – Villiers noted the sections of the report 'which show how entirely unprepared the U.S. are for immediate military operations'[50] – Lansdowne was not yet ready entirely to dismiss it.

In early winter, the withdrawal of Britain's military and naval forces from the Western Hemisphere came under serious consideration in the Committee of Imperial Defence. On November 25, the Committee decided that the garrisons at Bermuda, St. Lucia and Jamaica should not be left entirely undefended (such a move would invite an attack from European warships) but not to increase their strength to repel an American invasion.[51] The inference was clear. Britain's strategy for defending the Western Hemispheric possessions relied on the improbability of an Anglo-American war and admitted that, should such a conflict arise, the garrisons would be completely indefensible. Canadian defence, however, was more complicated. Minto, who in 1901 had advocated the transfer of the garrisons at Halifax and Esquimalt to Canada, was no longer convinced. In April 1903, he sent Broderick a proposal that the two commands should be amalgamated under one imperial officer. Broderick agreed. 'I fear I am quite opposed to withdrawing English troops or General from Halifax', he commented. 'Some day it may be a material link – & I think between ourselves, Chamberlain who hankered a little after this, hardly realises the change it would make.'[52]

For a number of reasons, this opposition was short-lived. Intervention in the South African war had given Canada's militia a sense of purpose and Borden's efforts were equally successful in raising the profile of Canadian defence. Moreover, after the decision of the Alaskan tribunal had been delivered on October 20, the Dominion realised that Britain could not be relied upon to support her interests against the United States.

A concurrent move for change was taking place in Britain, where Arnold-Forster (Broderick's successor at the War Office) sought to reduce imperial commitments. With the same aim, Admiral Sir John Fisher had already begun withdrawing British squadrons from the Western Hemisphere.[53] The inevitability of a Russo-Japanese conflict suggested an urgent need to re-allocate British forces. Worried that the alliance with Japan might bring Britain into the fight, the Committee became preoccupied in late 1903 and throughout the following year by the Russian threat. Accordingly, when Borden visited London in December, asking that the garrisons' defences be handed over to Canada, he found an amenable audience. Meeting Arnold-Forster, he 'dwelt much upon the desirability of Canada's taking over Esquimalt and Halifax' and explained 'the Canadians would appreciate and live up to the responsibility imposed on them.' Arnold-Forster declined his official support, but remarked in his diary that 'I really think the thing might be done without disadvantage.'[54] Then Borden turned to the CID, which favourably considered the idea, provided that the 'armament at Halifax and Esquimalt [was] maintained adequately, and in conformity with modern requirements.'[55] In a Cabinet memo, Balfour happily noted that now 'the Colonies are beginning to awake to their Imperial obligations' and concluded that only War Office incompetence could prevent effective colonial assistance towards matters of imperial defence.[56]

While the threat of war with the United States was considered unlikely, it was nonetheless treated as a matter for serious discussion. On July 8 1904, the Committee of Imperial Defence agreed to strip the Canadian garrisons of much of their strength, not because an American attack was impossible, but because the garrisons, unless vastly strengthened, could not defend vital coaling stations in the region. Lord Roberts and Major-General James Grierson anxiously protested. Together, the Commander-in-Chief and the War Office's Director of Military Operations inserted a Secret Addendum to the Committee Minutes. It stated that,

> 'we consider that it is important, in the event of war with the U.S. alone, to hold Halifax, and that, as the present scheme provides for a defence which is likely to be successful against any land attack which would be made by the U.S. in the preliminary stage of a war, that [the] standard of defence should be approximately maintained.'[57]

Military opinion carried great weight in the Committee, but the policy of withdrawal was upheld and, on November 22, it was agreed to act upon the decisions made on July 8.[58] Meanwhile, at the Admiralty, Fisher proposed a radical solution to the problem of Canadian Defence: the Dominion should be abandoned in the event of war. In December, Fisher sent Lansdowne a letter expressing his feelings in his characteristically blunt fashion. The latter immediately handed the note to Selborne and asked for his opinions. 'I learnt for the first time, that Fisher is most violently hostile to Canada and everything Canadian,' Selborne remarked. 'He said that under no conceivable circumstance could he escape an overwhelming and humiliating defeat by the U.S. and therefore he would leave Canada to her fate and no matter what cause of quarrel or merits of the case he would not spend one man or one pound in the defence of Canada.' Selborne generally agreed with Fisher on strategic matters, but this was political suicide. Accordingly, he told Fisher that he must state the personal nature of his proposal should he raise it during a Committee meeting. In the meantime, on January 1, the Prime Minister sent a suggestive reply to Selborne. 'Everything really turns upon the cause of the quarrel which is to lead to this hypothetical war,' he explained, 'and the strength of the Canadians' wish to remain either independent, or part of the British Empire, but in no case a province of the U.S.A.' Balfour appreciated the need for discussion, but stressed his opinion that Canadian defence questions were primarily theoretical. In conclusion, he directed Selborne to make a further study of Canada's defensive capabilities, 'whatever view we make take of the probability, or (as I should prefer to put it,) the improbability of war.'[59]

Once the CID gave its support to the transfer of the Halifax and Esquimalt garrisons to Canada, there was no reason for delay. Minto returned to London in December 1904 and explained to the Committee that Laurier had officially requested that Canada take over the defences.[60] The following month, Arnold-Forster suggested that a dispatch be sent to Ottawa, stating that 'we welcome the offer of the Canadian Government to undertake the responsibility (& cost) of the garrisons of those places', and recommended that the transfer take place on April

1.[61] However, the Committee was preoccupied by events in the Far East and delayed its formal decision until June 28; the transfer took place in July. While the garrison at Esquimalt was abandoned as a military station, the

> 'standard of defence of Halifax should be sufficient to deter a fleet, including battleships, which could not afford to incur serious losses, from attacking the sea defences, and to enable the attack of an organised expeditionary army, landed in the vicinity, to be resisted for a considerable period.'[62]

Britain's presence in the Western Hemisphere had all but disappeared, yet Canadian defence continued to receive attention in the CID. In part, this was due to an unwillingness entirely to dismiss the American threat. More importantly, Balfour and Alfred Lyttleton, Chamberlain's successor at the Colonial Office, were reassuring Canada that, not only would she continue be protected, but the Anglo-Canadian bond was vital to the British Empire. Balfour stated that,

> 'any discussion of this question must be prefaced by affirming the principle that, in the event of danger, Canada has a right to the support of the whole resources of the Empire. The question is, how best to distribute our Imperial forces in peace time with a view to carrying out our heavy obligations both to Canada and to the Empire as a whole.'

Turning to matters of detail, the Committee agreed that, since British ships would inevitably be barred from sailing up the St. Lawrence river in wartime, due to the 'far superior local resources of the U.S.', a fleet of submarines might be stationed at Halifax. There was no tangible threat – this was intended to placate the Canadians, anxious about the withdrawal of Britain's North Atlantic squadron from Halifax. Lyttleton remarked that 'he had already been obliged to give explanations as regards the withdrawal of the Pacific squadron [from Esquimalt]' and that he 'wished to be able to inform the Canadian Government that existing pledges ... would be fully maintained, and that the general principles of Imperial defence ... remained unchanged.' There was little chance that such measures would be approved. Again, Fisher strenuously voiced his opposition, shrewdly arguing that 'if submarines were stationed at Halifax in numbers obviously in excess of the requirements of local defence, it would be clear that they were maintained against the U.S. alone, and they would be regarded by that Power in a serious light.'[63] Fisher won the day: no changes to Canadian defence were approved.

By 1905, Britain had all but abandoned her military presence in the Western Hemisphere and conceded regional hegemony to the United States. While the possibility of an Anglo-American war had not been entirely disregarded, the Balfour Administration saw little cause for concern. This explains Lansdowne's frequent absence from CID meetings on the subject of Canadian defence. Of the fourteen meetings held between 1903 and 1905 that dealt with Western

Hemispheric strategy, the Foreign Secretary attended only twice. If the process of withdrawal was met with general satisfaction, however, the Anglo-Canadian bond became rather fragile. Not only had Britain lessened her imperial presence, but her Alaskan diplomacy and unwillingness to commit to retaliation offended the Canadian people who expected more from the imperial connection. Since preferential tariffs had achieved nothing by way of reciprocity, the chances were that Canada would look elsewhere to secure her commercial future. While Laurier would not initiate reciprocity discussions with Washington, Minto commented, 'what will he do if the U.S. do make reciprocity proposals I cannot say. He [Laurier] is in a position to say "we have made advances to the Mother Country, & have met with no response – here are the U.S. making proposals and we must look out for ourselves."'[64] Once the need to placate the United States was admitted, and once preference was abandoned, there was little that Britain could do to ensure Canadian loyalty yet, on April 19 1905, Borden issued a stern warning. The American people still wanted to see reciprocity with Canada, he reminded Chamberlain; there was a popular belief in the Dominion, that

> 'the true policy of Canada is to enter reciprocal trade arrangements with the United States ... be assured that there is much which tends to bring Canada into closer trade relations with the United States. The vast immigration from the western states to our North Western Territories, in the increasing investment of United States capital in the development of Canadian industries, the remarkably conciliatory and appreciative tone of the United States statesmen, newspapers and business men towards everything Canadian – all these have a certain influence which may become very strong if our kinsmen in the British Islands continue to slumber.'[65]

Throughout Lansdowne's time at the Foreign Office, the readjustment of Britain's global strategy made relations with Canada tentative and dilatory. As we shall see, these considerations played a significant part in diplomacy during the Alaskan boundary dispute. 'Lord Lansdowne has once more shown what value he sets on American goodwill', the New York reporter for *The Times* noted in early 1903 with the Alaskan dispute in its latter stages.[66] Indeed, Lansdowne's pro-American attitude was destined to offend and disappoint Canada, her Governor-General and even, in part, the Colonial Office. '[W]hilst fully recognising the necessity of the present position', Minto told Lansdowne in March 1903, 'I am always afraid that the day may come when we shall be bound in honour to show our teeth.'[67] However, until the retention of Anglo-American harmony became less vital for Britain (or until Britain became strong enough to resist the United States) there was little chance that such action would be contemplated to protect Canada, or any of Britain's North American possessions.

6

Last of the Great Disputes

The Alaska Boundary, 1901-February 1903

IN JUNE 1900, the Fourth Congress of Chambers of Commerce of the Empire sent a resolution to Lord Salisbury for his urgent attention. '[I]t is of vital importance to British and Canadian Trade on the Pacific Coast to press forward a settlement of the Alaska Boundary question', the note read, 'and this Congress while recognising the endeavours of Her Majesty's Government to effect an adjustment would urge the desirability of renewed efforts in order to accomplish that object.'[1] Salisbury hardly needed convincing: the Foreign Office fully appreciated the importance the Alaskan issue, for economic and diplomatic reasons. In December, Pauncefote wrote to Lansdowne, recently-appointed Foreign Secretary, of his keen hope that he would be 'of utility in disposing of the two important and difficult questions (the only two happily) which threaten to disturb the Entente Cordiale [between Britain and the US], namely Alaska and Nicaragua.'[2] Negotiations on the canal issue were well underway; its successful conclusion would make an Alaskan settlement crucial to Anglo-American harmony.

The background is briefly this: the boundary between Alaska and Canada became a significant issue in 1897 following the discovery of gold in the disputed Yukon territory on the Alaskan panhandle. Canadian officials had long considered the matter insignificant and were now eager to obtain access to the Pacific coast to facilitate the country's trade. As a result, the ambiguous boundary line (and, specifically, the Anglo-Russian treaty of 1825 that marked the frontier) was called into question. The treaty, as it turned out, was based upon a number of geographical inaccuracies. It directed the frontier to follow a line of mountains 'situated parallel to the coast', and that,

> 'whenever the summit of the mountains which extend in the direction parallel to the coast from the 56th degree of latitude to the point of intersection of the 141st degree of west longitude shall prove to be at a distance of more than 10 marine leagues from the ocean the limit between the British possessions and the line of the coast which is to belong to Russia ... shall be formed by a line parallel to the windings of the coast, and shall never exceed the distance of ten marine leagues therefrom.'[3]

After further exploration, however, it became evident that there was no line of mountains from which the boundary could be drawn. Still more, it was unclear whether the boundary was intended to run around the coastal inlets or across their mouths. If the latter case were the true interpretation then Canada could justly claim access to the Pacific, and, specifically, the legitimate ownership of such crucial Pacific ports as Dyea, Skagway and Pyramid Harbour.

The Alaskan question was raised during a meeting of the Joint High Commission in 1898, but initially made little headway. In a wave of acrimony, it was primarily Alaskan considerations that broke the Commission, which was dissolved in February 1899. The situation in the Yukon, meanwhile, continued to worsen. Searching for the richest deposits of gold, the ever-growing swarm of miners on the Alaskan panhandle paid little regard to the vague frontier; increased competition resulted in a series of bitter clashes between miners and local authorities. While the United States' Government remained adamant in its refusal to countenance any form of arbitration that would bring into discussion regions long populated by American settlers – including Dyea and Skagway – the constant threat of a flare up in the Yukon made a temporary compromise vital. As a result, it was resolved on October 20 1899, to adopt a *modus vivendi* that would keep the situation quiet until a more permanent settlement could be reached.

Discussions for that object continued into the new year. On January 22 1900, Joseph Choate sent Salisbury a note stressing that the mode of arbitration that had been used during the Venezuelan boundary dispute could not be used for Alaska. 'Surely the Tribunal which is to pass upon such a question,' he remarked, 'should not be enabled to compromise it, but should be required simply to decide it.'[4] Salisbury countered by inviting a completely independent tribunal to determine whether the boundary should run around the coastal inlets or cut across them: 'His Excellency states that once this question has been determined neither party would probably desire to go to the expense and trouble of an Arbitration as to the exact location of the boundary line.'[5] Such a scheme had little chance of acceptance. The American Government was not likely to give foreign umpires the power to settle such important territorial questions. Still more, Salisbury's proposal reaffirmed the State Department's opinion that Canada had no legitimate grievance, but had brought up the boundary question merely to obtain access to the coast. With neither side inviting compromise, the establishment of a permanent boundary line appeared to be a long way distant. On Choate's dispatch, one Foreign Office official noted that an 'indefinite prolongation of the modus vivendi seems the probable result.'[6]

Enter Lansdowne. Determined to pursue a new, more conciliatory policy towards the United States, Lansdowne saw the Alaskan issue as an unnecessary source of friction that blocked the chances for a permanent Anglo-American understanding. Yet Lansdowne's desire to maintain and further the 'special relationship' only partly explains his Alaskan diplomacy. Throughout the negotiations, the Foreign Secretary acted with notable carelessness towards the Canadians, for whom the Alaskan issue was of the most critical importance. There is little evidence that he sought anything more than a rudimentary knowledge of Canada's case and, far from displaying sympathy towards the Canadian Government, Lansdowne dealt with Sir Wilfrid Laurier with both impatience and irritation. For a statesman who had spent five years in Ottawa as Governor-General, this lack of sympathy was perhaps surprising.[7] Regard the Alaska boundary as a diplomatic, rather than an imperial or judicial matter, he determined to clear the obstacles to settlement. Throughout the controversy, his conviction was unshaken: in this case, Britain could only concede significant Canadian interests for American friendship.

On May 10 1901, Hay gave to Pauncefote a new draft proposal recommending that an arbitral tribunal should be created to settle the troublesome Alaska boundary question. Six impartial jurists would sit on the tribunal, which would discuss the legitimate ownership of the disputed region that the Anglo-Russian Treaty had failed to clarify. Primarily, the commission would determine firstly whether there should be an unbroken coastal strip, and, secondly, who should own the Portland Channel.

Pauncefote quickly relayed the news to the Foreign Office and expressed his hope that Britain might react favourably to this, as yet, tentative initiative: there was now 'a more hopeful prospect of successful negotiation than has yet presented itself', the British Ambassador explained.[8] While Foreign Office officials were genuinely pleased at the Americans' determination to move the Alaskan issue forward, they sought clarification. In particular, they asked for further information to clarify the scope and finality that would be given to the judges' decision. On June 13, a memorandum – prepared by Senior Clerk Arthur Larcom – enquired whether the tribunal was,

> 'merely to report as to the proper boundary basing themselves upon the Treaties, or should the Treaties not supply materials for making a sufficient recommendation, are they free to recommend what seems to them a proper boundary, and make any recommendation which may seem proper to them?'[9]

The answer to Larcom's enquiry came quickly enough. After an enlightening conversation with Hay in July, Pauncefote reported that the judges would be allowed little power beyond that of interpreting the treaty of 1825. 'If power be given to them to depart from the strict interpretation of the Treaty,' Pauncefote wrote, 'the Arbitrators will take refuge in a compromise which the Pacific Coast people violently oppose.' That partisan interests should exert such control over American diplomacy was naturally disappointing. Pauncefote realised, however, that a sudden eruption of violence in the disputed boundary region might endanger the amicable state of Anglo-American diplomacy and asked that Britain not withhold her acquiescence. After all, if negotiations were to end in a deadlock – a likely enough outcome – the judges might still advance proposals for future consideration. These 'would, of course, have only a moral force, but it would facilitate further negotiations for a friendly settlement.'[10]

Naturally, Lansdowne would have preferred a tribunal that would take every aspect of the dispute into account, but rejecting Hay's scheme and thereby inviting American hostility appears not to have been seriously considered. Lansdowne sent Pauncefote's dispatch to Lord Chancellor Halsbury in July. Asking for the latter's views, Lansdowne remarked that 'I am disposed to agree with Lord Pauncefote.'[11] Halsbury concurred that Britain should indeed accept the proposal. However, one serious obstacle remained and Lansdowne rightly predicted a strong protest from Ottawa. Because of this, the Foreign Secretary began the task of persuading Sir Wilfrid Laurier and the Canadian Administration that they swallow their objections and accept the American initiative.

The initial response from Canada was encouraging. 'I am delighted at the prospect of arrangements with the U.S. – contained in your recent secret cable,' Governor-General Minto told Chamberlain on August 3. 'I certainly hardly hoped for the opening that appears.'[12] However, this was only a personal view. Minto was obliged to wait for Sir Wilfrid Laurier's reaction since the latter was then travelling along the lower St. Lawrence and, therefore, was temporarily out of contact. Once communications had been re-established, Minto's tone underwent a rapid change. On August 7, he ruefully cabled the Colonial Office that Laurier 'has replied that he considers [the] United States' proposal most insidious.'[13] In a secret telegram to Chamberlain, written on August 24, Minto expanded by relaying the substance of Canada's objection. Laurier, wrote Minto, noted the two areas of dispute upon which the tribunal was to adjudicate. His grounds for refusal were based on the State Department's,

> 'false interpretation of the Treaty of 1825, by which [a] quantity of territory undoubtedly belonging to Canada, and extending some fifteen miles beyond [the] provisional frontier would be brought into arbitration, while [the towns of] Dyea and Skagway would be exempt from the perils of arbitration.'[14]

Meanwhile, to prevent the possibility of deadlock, Laurier privately forwarded an alternative proposal, that there should be five, rather than six jurists. Britain and the United States should appoint two members each, while the fifth would be nominated by both countries. Moreover, the Canadian Premier sought to expand the scope of the proposed tribunal beyond that of the mere interpretation of the 1825 treaty, to include the consideration of 'all issues arising from subsequent events.'[15] In the meantime, the Canadian Government stoutly refused to deliver an official response.

Laurier's refusal to accept the terms of Hay's tribunal was, naturally, a great obstacle to settlement, and Britain, although keen to settle the matter and to work amicably with the State Department, could hardly ignore the strength of Canadian feeling so soon after accepting her assistance in the South African war. However, if Laurier believed that his counter proposals would meet with success, or even that the British Government would give their wholehearted support, he was sadly mistaken. Inevitably, those in Washington would react to the counter proposals with stony silence. While she would dutifully pass to the State Department whatever objections Laurier might raise, Britain felt obliged to insist that Canada recognise the need for compromise. Chamberlain, anxious that discussions should begin without delay, asked Minto to make every effort to quash Canadian resistance. At the very least, Laurier should be pushed into delivering an official response. The satisfactory progress of negotiations for the isthmian canal, and the friendly mood of Anglo-American relations, should not be wasted, Chamberlain reminded Minto in early October: 'if we are to have any indirect advantage therefrom we ought to be in full possession of their [the Canadians'] views on [the] draft Treaties at [the] earliest possible date.'[16] The advantage must only be indirect, since the British Government had long determined not to delay the canal agreement to get better terms for Canada in Alaska. 'Her Majesty's Government are deeply conscious of the valuable support received from Canada in the present crisis [in South Africa],' Chamberlain had told Minto in January 1900, adding that 'it is recognised by public opinion here that [the] claim of the United States for the revision of the Clayton-Bulwer Treaty is legitimate.'[17] Now, with the Hay-Pauncefote Canal Treaty in its later stages, Lansdowne became more than ever determined not to endanger its success. Sir Francis Villiers, Assistant Under Secretary at the Foreign Office, wrote to his Colonial Office colleagues, on September 19 1901, of Lansdowne's determination,

> 'that the communications to the Dominion Government should not in any way imply that His Majesty's Government associate the settlement of the Alaskan Boundary and other primarily Canadian questions with that of the Interoceanic Canal question, or that the negotiations for the ... Treaties are interdependent.'[18]

Canada now finally began to appreciate the weakness of her position. The State Department adamantly refused to widen the scope of arbitration and the British Government would not allow the issue to be indefinitely prolonged. One-sided concessions must therefore be the only result, with Canada's claims slowly evaporating in the face of American pressure. What was worse, Laurier realised that any further obstructive tactics he conceived could only damage imperial ties. For this reason, he indicated in October that Canada would reluctantly accept adjudication by six jurists in order to facilitate further discussion.[19]

Meanwhile, Laurier began searching for an alternative solution to satisfy both Canada and the US. A Colonial Office dispatch soon fell on Lansdowne's desk, repeating Laurier's objections but giving reason for cautious optimism. Chamberlain wrote that he 'had reason to believe that the Dominion Government would be prepared ... to accept pecuniary compensation' rather than territorial compromise.[20] Canada had abandoned her claim to Dyea and Skagway, looking for compensation 'in another direction'. Larcom explained that,

> 'Sir W. Laurier is, I understand, loath to use the word "financial" in this connection on account of the probable political outcry, and Lord

Minto's tel. gives expression to this unwillingness to put the dots on the
i.s – but the fact may facilitate matters.'[21]

Laurier's sudden desire to effect a compromise was undoubtedly unexpected. It
seems likely that his reasons were twofold. Firstly, Canada realised that without
some concessions on her part, there would be no settlement. The timing of the initiative, however, was largely a reaction to a serious scare on the boundary line. In
mid November, rumours began to circulate that American miners in the Yukon
were contemplating a revolt against the local government. 'I inform you at once,'
Minto secretly cabled on November 20, 'in order that possible complications with
the United States may be avoided.'[22] The news was, in fact, greatly exaggerated,
but it served to underline the unpredictable climate in the Yukon and the very real
possibility of a sudden crisis in Anglo-American relations. It was difficult to ignore
such a warning.

The canal treaty, signed on November 18 1901, removed a significant source
of Anglo-American friction and, most importantly, opened the door for the settlement of the Alaskan issue. 'It would be wise not to delay much longer' regarding
Alaska, Pauncefote told Lansdowne in December. 'It is the last of the ...great disputes which have been for so many years a source of constant menace to our good
relations.' Everything should be done, he concluded, to bring about a settlement.[23]
Lansdowne needed very little persuasion. Witnessing the enthusiasm on both sides
of the Atlantic to the Hay-Pauncefote treaty, he looked forward to a quick resolution on the Alaska boundary. 'How delightful it would be,' he replied on December
31, 'if you should be able ... to give us that clean slate which we all so much
desire.'[24]

While the Canadians busily evaluated their position, Pauncefote met Hay to
relay the substance of Laurier's objections to the proposed tribunal. Hay was in a
state of despair and 'despondent as to the prospect of any agreement for an arbitration.'[25] Indeed, the optimism that the Secretary of State had shown in May
1901 evaporated soon after McKinley's assassination in September. McKinley had
left the boundary negotiations in Hay's hands, but McKinley's volatile successor
was to prove far more determined to pursue a strong foreign policy to uphold
United States' interests.

Roosevelt soon made his opposition to arbitrating the boundary line – and
to Hay's draft treaty – perfectly clear. 'The President considers the claim of the
United States is so manifestly clear and unanswerable,' Pauncefote explained in
March, 'that he is not disposed to run the risk of sacrificing American territory
under a compromise that is the almost certain result of an arbitration.' Roosevelt
'would not be indisposed to submit the points involved to a Tribunal of which the
members should merely record their reasoned opinions. This, he thought, would
be a step in advance and facilitate a settlement.'[26] Naturally, neither Colonial nor
Foreign Office saw matters in the same light and shared Hay's disappointment.
They had been willing to accept Hay's proposal because it offered a final and amicable solution to the boundary question; the tribunal as suggested by Roosevelt

would simply prolong an unsatisfactory situation and invite the possibility of a diplomatic crisis should the tense situation in the Yukon deteriorate. Because of this, Chamberlain reacted to the news with regret.[27] Meanwhile, the President continued freely to publicise his firm opposition to any form of arbitration. In May, he sought out Arthur Raikes, Britain's Chargé d'Affairs in Washington, in order to explain his views. Raikes, who temporarily headed the British Embassy after Pauncefote's death, wrote to Lansdowne that, after a desultory conversation, Roosevelt,

> 'suddenly changed the subject to the Alaska boundary and said "your people were good to us in 1898 and I have not forgotten it, so I do not want to raise the Alaskan question until your troubles in South Africa are over for then I am going to be ugly". This he said with his customary vehemence and he had I know used similar language on a previous occasion.'

Raikes went further, anxious that the Foreign Office should understand the strength of Roosevelt's opinion. During a meeting with Colonel Gerald Kitson, Military Attaché to the Washington Embassy, Kitson had told Raikes that,

> 'in a conversation which he had with Senator Lodge, the latter told him that the President had recently declared in the presence of two Senators that if any trouble arose in the territory in dispute he would occupy it with United States troops. To which one of the Senators rejoined "If you would make that declaration, sir, from the steps of the White House, your nomination for the next Presidency would be assured."'[28]

Roosevelt's plain speaking had its desired effect. Lansdowne showed Raikes' note to Chamberlain, Salisbury, Balfour and the King. 'This is not pleasant reading', the latter remarked with something of an understatement.[29] Although Lansdowne naturally wanted to retain the friendship of the Dominion Government, Canada's claims were insignificant when compared to the maintenance of Britain's good relations with Washington. Still more, the Foreign Secretary was clearly able to recognise the importance of a timely gesture of friendship. Consequently, Lansdowne made an indirect intimation to Roosevelt that he was willing openly to consider the American proposals.

In June, Lansdowne took an opportunity to write to Sir Cecil Spring Rice. As a good friend of the President, Spring Rice would be certain to relay the news. 'I am deeply impressed with the gravity of the Alaska problem', the Foreign Secretary explained, 'and I will take an opportunity of speaking to Mr. Choate about it. I would give a great deal to get it amicably disposed of.'[30] No time was wasted and, meeting the American Ambassador later that month, Lansdowne suggested that, since Minto and Laurier were both in London to attend the King's coronation, informal talks might begin immediately. Somewhat surprisingly,

Choate's initial response was evasive. Referring to the elections due to take place in the United States that November, he doubted whether the timing of discussions would be advantageous. However, Lansdowne, more than ever determined to see the boundary question quickly concluded, was disinclined to wait until the new year for something to happen. Although he had 'no desire to provoke a discussion prematurely,' he worried that 'so long as the question remained open, there was a risk of serious trouble arising should there be discoveries of gold at any point within the disputed area.'[31]

At Hay's direction, Choate soon relented and agreed to enter discussions, to take place at the Foreign Office over the following weeks. Indirectly, the talks had an effect. While the parties failed to arrive at a definite solution, the American Ambassador was quick to note the willingness of the Foreign Office – and even Laurier himself – to accept a compromise. In July, Lansdowne informed Raikes that Laurier had finally abandoned his country's claim to Dyea and Skagway. Moreover, the Foreign Secretary wrote of Laurier's fears:

> '[T]he Canadian Government were so apprehensive of the dangers which might arise from the discovery of gold within the debatable region, that they would gladly accept a "compromise line," drawn either provisionally or as a permanent arrangement ... I told Mr. Choate that I could well understand Sir Wilfrid Laurier's feelings, and it seemed to me that we ought to take advantage of the dead season in order, at all events, to prepare the way for a settlement.'[32]

Laurier's proposal was encouraging, but the Canadian Premier remained doggedly determined to reject the tribunal if it should have the limited scope previously laid out by the State Department. Lansdowne was hardly disposed to stand in the way of a new treaty, but considered himself duty bound to give the Canadians some degree of support. His insistence upon a more complete arbitration was relayed in a lengthy note to Raikes, intended for Hay's consideration. '[A]ll questions which depend for their solution upon the interpretation of the Treaty [of 1825] should be simultaneously referred to arbitration,' Lansdowne explained, 'to determine the true meaning of that instrument, and this, not merely with regard to the Lynn Canal or any other particular point, but in respect of the whole line, throughout its entire length.' Writing with the twofold purpose of mollifying Canadian opinion and warning the State Department that Britain would not abandon her rights simply to placate the American people, the Foreign Secretary added that this 'appears to be the only way in which it [the boundary] can be satisfactorily and permanently settled.'

The Foreign Office, Lansdowne continued, was quite prepared to accept a degree of compromise concerning the field of arbitration: 'His Majesty's Government are not wedded to a particular formula, and are prepared to consider any reasonable modifications to the rules suggested ... which the United States may consider the special circumstances of the case ... call for.' Most significantly, when Lansdowne referred to what he labelled the 'main question', he made it quite clear that the United States must accept a degree of compromise. This question, Lansdowne wrote,

> 'involves the ownership of the heads of inlets in general, and of the Lynn Canal in particular. That Canal derives its present importance from the fact of its forming the natural approach to the gold-bearing regions of the Canadian interior, which are accessible by sea in those latitudes through the ports of Dyea, Skagway and Pyramid Harbour. ... Their ownership must therefore constitute in the view of the United States' Government, the chief object of the arbitration. ... The suggested reservation therefore seems equivalent to a declaration on the part of the United States' Government that they will accept arbitration only on condition that the principle objects of the reference shall be theirs in any event, and that Great Britain will be so covenant before the parties go into court.'[33]

Sir Michael Herbert arrived in Washington in September 1902 to assume his post at the Embassy. Meeting Roosevelt for the first time as Ambassador, Herbert described his reception as one of the best yet shown to a diplomat. Indeed, Lansdowne's choice of Herbert had been largely the result of the latter's friendship with the President.[34] Whatever personal feelings might exist, however, it had little effect on practical politics or on Roosevelt's desire to press ahead with the Alaskan issue. During their first interview, the President stressed that the only arbitration he might consider acceptable was an Anglo-American Jurist Tribunal that would 'merely record their reasoned opinions' and carry no formal weight. 'If we had only Hay to deal with,' Herbert noted ruefully, 'the dispute could be settled in five minutes, but with the Senate and the President opposed to him he is powerless.'[35] Lansdowne, if disappointed, was willing to consider Roosevelt's initiative. As a temporary measure, it was considerably better than prolonged stalemate. Still more, Lansdowne could take comfort knowing that the scheme would probably be accepted in Ottawa. As a result, he replied on November 3 that,

> 'I am not sure at all that if we cannot obtain arbitration in some more satisfactory form, it might not be worth while to try the "Anglo-American Eminent Jurist Tribunal." ... I do not think it could do any harm, and in the meanwhile it would hold the field and perhaps keep things quiet for us.'[36]

Hearing the news, the Canadian Government gave its conditional consent. '[M]y Ministers, while declining to give their final assent to the proposal,' Minto telegraphed Chamberlain on November 18, 'would be disposed to consider it favourably, provided that the reference to a Tribunal should include all aspects of the question.'[37] With these views in mind, Lansdowne directed Herbert on December 6 to inform Hay of Britain's assent, providing the scope of the tribunal was wide enough to satisfy the Canadians.[38]

With a general agreement secured, discussions could now turn to more specific issues, particularly regarding the composition of the tribunal. For his part,
Hay made it quite clear that he considered the dispute primarily Anglo-American
and favoured the inclusion of only one Canadian on the commission. Herbert,
relaying Hay's remarks to the Foreign Office on December 9, was inclined to go
even further. 'Is it necessary that any Canadian should be named?' he enquired:

> 'A tribunal composed of three members of the U.S. Supreme Court
> and three eminent English judges would carry more weight with the
> Senate. I have strongly urged that all three American judges should be
> members of the Supreme Court, but owing to pressure of business
> before the Tribunal this may be difficult.'[39]

Imperial considerations weighed heavily on Lansdowne's mind. Hoping to conciliate
the Canadian Administration, he quickly proposed the following modification. 'In
my view it is absolutely necessary to have a Canadian on the Committee. But I
should say one was enough.'[40] A solitary Canadian would hopefully placate the
Dominion Government, but leave the ultimate decision-making to the big boys –
Britain and the United States.

Although such a solution was eminently acceptable to the Foreign Office,
however, it was heavily criticised by the Colonial Office. '[T]here would be a better
prospect of arrangement if all three members were Canadians', Joseph
Chamberlain maintained, 'because any conclusion arrived at ... would stand more
chance of acceptance.'[41] Lansdowne was quite prepared to modify his position, but
the possibility of appointing only Canadians to the tribunal was never seriously
considered by the Foreign Office. Without at least one British representative, there
could be no other result than an acrimonious stalemate and a further delay to the
settlement of the troublesome boundary question. 'I should not like to have three
Canadians', Lansdowne told Herbert in December, 'but we shall never be allowed
to exclude them altogether, and the C.O. is very colonial about this.'[42]

From Washington, the tone of Herbert's reports continued to show great
optimism. Convinced that the United States would appoint their best men, the
British Ambassador became rather carried away with the prospect of an amicable
and lasting settlement that would clear the path for an even greater understanding
between the two nations. Herbert awaited the Canadian response with great anxiety
and hoped that they could be persuaded to be reasonable. 'The settlement of the
Alaska question is of such paramount importance in connection with the improvement of the relations between the two countries', Herbert wrote on December 12,
'that I earnestly hope that Canada will not hold out in regard to the composition
of the commission.' Of great importance was the precedent which a successful settlement would set; Herbert now envisaged a 'kind of Anglo-American Supreme
Court' that might settle all future disputes, although he admitted that the idea was
a little unrealistic.[43]

If Herbert's enthusiasm was understandable, considering his relatively
recent appointment to Washington, British official circles tended towards greater

circumspection. Sir Montagu Ommanney, Permanent Under Secretary at the Colonial Office, wrote to Lansdowne on January 6 1903 that 'I cannot help thinking Sir M. Herbert is a little influenced by the idea of [an] Anglo-American Supreme Court, though he does speak of it as utopian.' The true state of the Alaskan negotiation was less than encouraging: 'I foresee so much difficulty in regard to the composition of that Tribunal', Ommanney explained, 'that I should greatly have preferred leaving the question severely alone.'[44]

The anxieties of the Colonial Office jarred with Herbert's naive enthusiasm: the former was by far the more realistic position. Roosevelt's stern opposition to the proper arbitration of the Alaska boundary issue remained the critical determining factor and, to those who fully understood the situation, left little hope for a Canadian victory. When Ommanney telegraphed Herbert's views to Lord Minto on January 12, however, he was guardedly optimistic, and stressed that the success of the Alaskan Treaty would 'depend largely on [the] composition of the Tribunal.' Herbert's idea, he concluded, advocated:

> 'three judges of [the] United States Supreme Court, with [the] Lord Chief Justice [of] England [the] Chief Justice of Canada and [a] Judge of [the] High Court [of] Great Britain on our side, as constituting a Tribunal commanding in [the] highest degree [the] confidence of all concerned.'[45]

In the meantime, Theodore Roosevelt's determination to protect American interests in Alaska became, if anything, stronger with each passing month. In January, Roosevelt received a report from G. T. Emmons, a retired Lieutenant in the American Navy that gave a detailed account of the boundary question, including maps, affidavits and photographs. The report evidently made a deep impression on the President, and Roosevelt wrote to Hay on January 14 that:

> 'It seems to me that there is good reason for believing that the boundary we should have by rights would take in more land even than the boundary as claimed on the Russian and American maps ... I have not considered the question as one open to reasonable doubt, and for that reason have refused to permit any arbitration upon it.'[46]

Now that Hay and Herbert were busily engaged in the drafting of a new treaty, it was vital to obtain the official consent of the Canadian Administration. In response to an enquiry from the Washington Embassy, Lansdowne made a further effort to elicit Laurier's views: 'the Canadians are very dilatory' he told Herbert on January 13.[47]

Two days later, Lansdowne received an unexpected telegram from the British Ambassador, relaying the news that Laurier intended once more to publicise his objections to the Alaska treaty and to submit further counter proposals to the State Department. Calling for the tribunal to be composed partly of foreign jurists, or, should this meet with disapproval, asking for the entire question to be referred to the Hague, Laurier's initiative was both badly timed and doomed to failure. Herbert was horrified. Asking for instructions, he explained that 'time presses' and told Lansdowne that it 'is a tactical mistake at this hour to repeat objections as to the composition of the tribunal.' While the Foreign Secretary would not actually prohibit Laurier from making his ill-conceived approach, he was quick to express his firm sense of disapproval. 'It is very difficult to overrule the Canadian Gov. who evidently wish their proposal to be urged,' Lansdowne scrawled on Herbert's dispatch, 'but it seems to me a pity to urge it.'

Since these very proposals had already been forwarded to Hay by the British Embassy on more than one occasion, Lansdowne recommended that the Canadians should ask themselves 'whether they really think it worth while to ride for a fall as well as irritate the U.S.'[48] On the same day, the Foreign Secretary relayed his official approval to the Canadian approach, simply because, as he informed Herbert, Laurier attached great importance to 'having it on record that such a proposal has been put forward even if it be not accepted.' On these terms, the Foreign Office was prepared to forward Laurier's proposal 'and allow it to take its chance.'[49]

Dutifully, Herbert notified the State Department and soon reported Hay's extreme disappointment. 'He [Hay] says that he could only repeat what he had frequently intimated to me,' Herbert wrote on January 18, 'that the President was unable to accept any form of arbitration other than that proposed in the Treaty.'[50] This was no real surprise. Indeed, it seems likely that Laurier had initiated the protest as a last gesture of defiance and to satisfy his Cabinet. During a meeting between the Canadian Premier and Minto on January 19, Laurier emphasised that, while opposition to the treaty was prevalent in the Cabinet, he recognised the need for acquiescence. 'He [Laurier] is, as he has said in former conversations, dissatisfied especially with the number of the proposed tribunal', Minto noted in his journal, 'and thinks it may result in an even expression of opinion on either side, but at the same time is fully impressed with the absolute necessity of accepting the terms proposed.'[51]

That Canada's resistance had finally evaporated now became clear; her official acceptance of the Alaskan treaty was given on January 21.[52] Two days later, Edward VII gave his assent to the terms of the proposed treaty. Sir Francis Knollys, the King's Private Secretary, wrote to Lansdowne that Edward 'thinks the proposed Alaska arrangement is an excellent one and he quite approves of your authorising Sir Michael Herbert accordingly.'[53] At last, the path was cleared for a lasting settlement.

The Hay-Herbert Convention was concluded on January 24 1903. By the terms of the treaty, six impartial jurists were to be appointed, each to sign an oath 'that he will impartially consider the arguments and evidence presented to the tribunal and will decide thereupon according to his true judgement.' After the exchange of ratifications, two months would be allowed for the parties to prepare their arguments and formal discussions would take place in London four months later, six months after ratification. Article IV of the Convention listed the exact questions on which the jurists were to adjudicate, directing their efforts toward an evaluation of the precise location of the Portland Channel and asking them to answer the question whether,

> 'it [was] the intention and meaning of [the] convention of 1825 that there should remain in the exclusive possession of Russia a continuous fringe or strip of coast on the mainland, not exceeding ten marine leagues in width, separating the British Possessions from the bays, ports, inlets, havens, and waters of the ocean'.

Significantly, in Article VI, it was stated that the decisions arrived at were to be final and binding.[54] Unless there was deadlock, therefore, the tribunal would bring the long-running boundary question to an end. Although the progress of negotiations was encouraging, strong opposition from representatives of the North-Western states temporarily threatened to endanger the future of the Hay-Herbert Convention. 'These opponents of the Treaty maintain that there is nothing in the boundary question on which to arbitrate', *The Times* remarked on February 6, adding that both Roosevelt and Hay were in a state of despair, having given up all hope that the treaty would pass the Senate.[55]

In London, Lord Cranborne suggested that Britain should delay publication, since there was little point presenting the treaty to Parliament if it should then fail to be ratified. Lansdowne agreed, noting ruefully that 'it seems doubtful whether after all the treaty will be ratified.'[56] With an agreement in sight, the treaty's supporters made one final effort to win over the intransigent Senators, reminding the House that the United States' Government, no matter what the verdict, would permit no loss of territory to Canada. This was a persuasive argument and, to the relief of both State Department and Foreign Office, the convention passed in the Senate on February 11.

Great enthusiasm greeted the Hay-Herbert treaty on both sides of the Atlantic. British Parliamentary opinion was effusive. Relieved that Britain had entered the final stages of negotiation, the nature and strength of the Canadian claims received scant attention. Instead, the treaty was seen as a total diplomatic triumph. '[A]ny steps towards the settlement of a question which might have involved us in serious difficulty with the United States must be welcomed by both countries', the Duke of Roxburghe noted on February 17, a view wholeheartedly supported by Earl Spencer and Sir Henry Campbell-Bannerman. In the House of Commons, Captain Grenville of Bradford spoke in a similar vein, emphasising that:

> 'it will probably be agreed that any English Government would do all within its power to come to an amicable settlement of this long standing controversy, consistent with the material interests of Canada, and the Government deserves our congratulations at having arrived at such an agreement with the Government of the United States.'[57]

Journalists shared the sense of relief and vigorously supported the Alaskan treaty. 'It is probably on the whole a greater diplomatic triumph for all concerned than was the Hay-Pauncefote treaty or any other of recent times', *The Times* commented on January 26. 'It is, moreover, frankly accepted here as one more proof of England's friendship.' For its part, *The New York Times* was similarly glowing: 'This treaty is but another witness and new pledge of the friendship of the two great English-speaking nations,' it remarked happily.[58]

In both countries, the widespread approval was a result of the conviction that the Hay-Herbert Convention had ended a potential source of friction between Britain and the United States. Indeed, the Senate's ratification led most observers to believe that the Alaskan issue was now all but concluded. On February 12, Herbert telegraphed the Foreign Office to explain that the Senate's actions regarding the Alaska treaty had 'removed a great weight off my mind.' Lansdowne, equally satisfied, replied that the ratification 'has had a good effect here and we are all very pleased.'[59] However, until that time when the Alaskan Commission delivered its final judgement, the possibility of a return to diplomatic friction remained a significant threat and subsequent events were to prove that the official and popular reaction to the Hay-Herbert Convention had been a little over optimistic.

7

Alaskan Settlement

The 'Special Relationship' in Crisis,
February-October 1903

O N FEBRUARY 18 1903, Theodore Roosevelt made public the names of the three American nominations to the Alaskan tribunal. The appointments of Secretary of War Elihu Root and Senators Henry Cabot Lodge of Massachusetts and George Turner of Washington were guaranteed to cause an outrage. Lodge, who had spoken publicly against Canada's contention; Turner, who represented the interests of the Pacific North-West; and Root, politically tied to Roosevelt, were hardly the jurists of repute for which the Hay-Herbert Convention had called. For Canada, well used to the high-handed diplomacy of her southern neighbour, it seemed obvious that Roosevelt had chosen his judges solely to ensure that the United States lost no territory through the negotiations. For this reason, the American argument – that three unbiased judges simply could not be found – carried little weight.[1] '[T]he selection of Mr. Lodge and Mr. Turner gives great offence to the Canadian people,' the Ottawa correspondent for *The Times* noted in mid February. 'One of the Ministers said to-day that it was evident the United States wanted to convert the proceedings into a farce.'[2] Herbert was aghast, having genuinely believed that the jurists would either be eminent judges or members of the Supreme Court. '[I]f the President honestly thought that the three men named were "eminent jurists"', he told John Hay on February 19, 'I of course had nothing more to say.' Five days later, Herbert declared himself 'disgusted and disheartened', adding that 'all my illusions are gone in regard to men in whom I believed.'[3] From Ottawa, Minto expressed a similar sense of outrage. Describing Roosevelt's choices as 'most unfortunate', he explained that 'in my opinion it would be quite impossible for any good to agree to this composition of the tribunal.'[4]

Lansdowne, warned in advance about the appointments, was dismayed, but inclined toward temperance. A coded dispatch from Herbert, relaying the news, had been sent to the Foreign Office four days before the names became public. 'This is much to be regretted', Lansdowne remarked with characteristic understatement, 'and will render the selection of the British members of the Commission somewhat difficult.'[5] Nevertheless, on February 19, the Foreign Secretary wrote a note on Herbert's telegram asking the Colonial Office not to act impulsively. 'Disappointing as these American appointments are we must take them seriously', he maintained. 'Lodge and Root are both influential men and any attempt to cast ridicule or contempt upon their selection would have a very bad effect.'[6] Lansdowne's first suggestion, relayed to Herbert in a note dated February 20, called for the appointment of 'an ex-judge, a politician of the Asquith or Haldane type and a Canadian.'[7]

Due to its consideration of American opinion, however, the Foreign Office soon dismissed the idea as impractical. The United States would react with indignation should Britain appoint inferior men and the Foreign Office was more than ever determined not to risk a rupture in Anglo-American relations in the immediate wake of the Venezuelan crisis. As we have seen, Britain's untimely participation in the Anglo-German blockade of Venezuela had caused a clear diplomatic strain in Washington, while the blockade had been raised on February 14, only four days before Roosevelt announced his Alaskan appointments. Now, then, was not the time for further friction. Consequently, in his dispatches to Ottawa, the Foreign Secretary was carefully reassuring tone: at all costs, the tribunal must proceed. On February 21, he told Minto that the news had 'come upon us as a terrible blow', but pointed out that,

> 'I am however strongly of [the] opinion that the case is not one in which we ought to show temper, and that it would be a mistake to reply by selecting three mediocrities as our representatives ... I am discussing the question with the Lord Chancellor and Balfour, and I hope we may be able to get together a good team.'[8]

It only remained for Lansdowne to convince Chamberlain and the Colonial Office. Angry at the appointments and determined to protect Canada from the Roosevelt's brash diplomacy, the Colonial Office was contemplating a serious protest. On February 20, a secret communication from Sir Montagu Ommanney was passed to the Foreign Office. It noted that, should Britain appoint three already committed representatives, as Roosevelt had done, there would be certain deadlock. Yet 'it would be obviously unfair to invite impartial Judges to form half of a tribunal for the judicial consideration of questions upon which their colleagues are already committed to a particular view.' With no satisfactory alternative in sight, Ommanney concluded that 'it should be seriously considered whether, in these circumstances, His Majesty's Government should proceed with the ratification of the treaty.'[9]

If it really was necessary for Britain to exchange ratifications, the Colonial Office emphasised that three Canadian members must be selected to sit on the Alaskan tribunal. Ommanney informed the Foreign Office that he intended to send a message to the Canadian Government that 'it seemed impossible that the Lord Chief Justice or any of the highest English Judges should be Members of the Tribunal.' At once, Lansdowne grasped the possible consequences of such behaviour and refused to allow the Colonial Office a free hand. 'It seemed very undesirable that the C.O. should commit themselves in any way,' Sir Francis Villiers replied on February 19.[10] No official dispatch, jeopardising Britain's relations with

Washington or strengthening Canada's resistance, could be sanctioned by the Foreign Office and Lansdowne was determined that the two offices must present a united front. For this reason, he directed Villiers to ask 'Sir M. Ommanney not to send any further instructions to Canada without his concurrence.'[11]

In Washington, Herbert shared Lansdowne's sense of urgency and busily sent a number of dispatches, to Ottawa and to the Foreign Office, detailing the strength of American feeling on the Alaska issue and the utmost necessity of its quick and amicable conclusion. While he felt dismayed and betrayed by Roosevelt's appointment, Herbert understood the futility and short-sightedness of protest. '[T]he more I appreciate the temper of the politicians in regard to the Alaska boundary,' he explained, 'the more I realise the paramount importance of having the question settled.'[12] Herbert soon took an opportunity to warn Sir Wilfrid Laurier that the rejection of the American jurists would have grave results. 'The President's appointments are all approved here,' he told the Canadian Premier on February 23, 'and such action on the part of Canada would create a political outcry against her ... and make the President more popular than ever.'[13]

Ultimately, the Foreign Office was prepared to use whatever means were necessary to persuade Laurier to accept the appointments. On February 24, a dispatch drafted by Lansdowne and intended for Lord Minto's attention, made every effort to minimise the significance of Roosevelt's actions. Senator Lodge had, Lansdowne noted, played an important role in ensuring the ratification of the Hay-Herbert Convention. Still more, the Foreign Secretary remarked, somewhat disingenuously, that it was,

> 'no doubt true that ... Messrs. Lodge and Turner have taken a strong line in reference to the Boundary question. It may upon the other hand be contended that the language which they have held does not do more than pledge them to resist any attempts to surrender American territory and that it would not necessarily preclude them from dealing impartially with such questions as those enumerated in Article IV of the Convention.'[14]

This was hardly plain speaking. In fact, Lansdowne's words were so blatantly transparent that he felt obliged to withdraw the paragraph from the draft sent to the Colonial Office. Nevertheless, if the Foreign Secretary recognised the need for greater subtlety, he had become determined that the Canadians needed to understand the disastrous consequences that rejecting the nominations would have on Anglo-American harmony. It would 'sow the seeds of lasting ill will between the two countries', which naturally would be a 'gave misfortune in the interests of both countries and the Dominion of Canada.'[15] Accordingly, a copy of the proposed dispatch, reworded by Villiers, was given to the Colonial Office on February 25.[16] Lord Onslow, Under Secretary at the Colonial Office, quickly evaluated the note and offered a number of amendments. 'I do not think it necessary for us to comment on the position in the U.S. of the three gentlemen they have selected, whose position and views are doubtless fully known to the Canadian Ministers', he replied on February 26. 'Nor do I think it useful to say much to them about the relations between the U.K. and U.S.A. or we shall lay ourselves open to the charge that we are ready [to] sacrifice Canadian interests to promote good feeling between England and America.'[17]

The official dispatch, sent by Onslow to Minto on February 26, was, in effect, a compromise between Foreign and Colonial offices. If Lansdowne's insistence had prevailed, that Canada must accept the American appointments, the Colonial Office were equally adamant that Britain should not gloss over what was, naturally, an embarrassing and uncomfortable situation. Consequently, the Colonial Office transmitted to the Governor-General an honest, if persuasive, account. Onslow conceded that the nominations were disappointing, but contended that 'arguments against the personal fitness of the three American representatives, however convincing, would fail to lead to any practical result.' The difficult situation could only be solved with the assistance of the Dominion Government and, for this reason, the Colonial Office now officially requested Canada's concurrence. The dispatch, however, concluded with a note of optimism, for which Villiers had been primarily responsible. The British Government preferred that the tribunal should proceed,

> 'in the confident hope that it would not prejudice Canadian or British interests, since, even in the event of failure, much important information on the controverted points would be collected and placed before the public, thus facilitating a reasonable settlement of the question at some future date.'[18]

Minto soon intimated that Laurier and his colleagues would relent. In order to preserve the dignity and weight of their case, Laurier asked that the British Government nominate, as their representatives, the Chief Justice of England and two judges from the Canadian High Court.[19] The Foreign Secretary was perfectly agreeable. The appointment of two Canadians would be a suitably conciliatory gesture to deflect Canada's irritation away from Britain. During the Cabinet meeting on March 3, Lansdowne successfully pressed the nominations. 'There was at first a disposition to show temper and to reply by appointing three Commissioners of quite a different stamp', Lansdowne told Minto on March 5.[20]

Later that month, Chamberlain published the names of the British representatives in the House of Commons. Making it absolutely clear that the appointments had been suggested by the Canadian Government and had not been imposed upon them, the Colonial Secretary named Lord Chief Justice Alverstone, Sir Louis A. Jetté of Quebec and Judge J. Douglas Armour from the Canadian Supreme Court. Due to Armour's death, Allen B. Aylesworth became the final British appointment.[21]

Meanwhile, to Laurier's dismay, Britain exchanged ratifications with the United States on March 3, before Canada had delivered her official consent. The Foreign Office had undoubtedly been somewhat forward in authorising the exchange. Inspired by a desire to see the tribunal begin at the earliest possible date, and recalling previous frustrating delays, Lansdowne had simply been unwilling to wait for an official Canadian response. Moreover, it was necessary to show Roosevelt that Britain, rather than Canada, was in control of negotiations. The Foreign Secretary now had to face Canadian hostility: Laurier had just made up his mind to accept the appointments, Minto told Lansdowne on March 8: 'then comes the news in the papers ... saying that the exchange of ratifications had taken place ... this puts the fat in the fire here, on the grounds that the treaty was still under the consideration of my Ministers.' What was worse, Minto worried that Laurier and his colleagues were beginning to display a distinct lack of trust in the British Government. The Foreign Office had shown itself willing to 'sacrifice Canada for the friendship of the U.S.'[22] Canadian interests, simply put, had been treated with contempt.

Britain was fully prepared to apologise. To their colleagues, the Foreign Office blamed the King for the misunderstanding and Villiers was quick to inform the Colonial Office in this sense. 'You will of course remember how the King insisted upon ratifying,' Villiers told Lansdowne on March 8. 'Once his ratification [was] signed we could not delay the exchange.' Lansdowne agreed, but worried about the increasing friction between Britain and Canada. The incident, he remarked, 'was a rather unlucky proceeding and gives the Canadians an opportunity of which they will avail themselves.'[23] To protect the Foreign Office from the accusation that Britain had carelessly abandoned Canada for Anglo-American harmony, the Foreign Secretary drafted a further dispatch for Minto's attention. '[T]here was no intention of treating Canadian interests with discourtesy,' he explained on March 10. However,

> 'It seemed to them [the British Government] of the utmost importance that the Convention should be concluded and the Canadian Government shared this view ... Much as His Majesty's Government deplore the American selections, they had held from the first, as Lord Minto is aware, that it was impossible to break off upon this ground, and they find with great satisfaction that this view is shared by the Government of the Dominion.'[24]

Such arguments did nothing to mollify the Canadians. Nevertheless, Laurier was in no position to withhold Canada's assent at this late stage. On March 9, Minto relayed the news to the Colonial Office that Laurier had reluctantly given his official assent to the Hay-Herbert Convention. Not surprisingly, Laurier firmly emphasised his Government's angry and bitter reaction to what it considered crude diplomatic behaviour on the part of the British Government. Minto noted with regret that the Canadians:

> 'have felt called upon not only to express their dissatisfaction at the recent exchange of ratifications at Washington before their official consent had been given, but practically to indicate that their assent had been rendered unavoidable by His Majesty's Government.'[25]

The high-handed manner with which Canada had been treated remained a great cause for complaint. On March 30, Chamberlain passed to Lansdowne a letter from William Fielding, Canada's Minister of Finance. 'There is much indignation in the public mind now,' Fielding remarked angrily, 'there will be more when all the facts become known.'[26] While the Foreign Office might have regretted the incident, it made no further effort to defend itself. Only in a private minute to Villiers, dated April 9, did Lansdowne make an effort to explain the incident. The Canadians had indeed been presented with a choice, he noted, but 'the 'choice' which in our view was open to them was the choice of [the British Commissioners'] names.' Lansdowne concluded by stressing that 'We had no reason to suppose that there was any question [about] ratification at this late stage.'[27] Unwilling to enter into an unprofitable and unwarranted dispute with the Canadian Government, Lansdowne hoped that Laurier would see reason. The terms for the Alaska boundary tribunal were now firmly settled and, with only two months in which to prepare the details of the Canadian contention, it was time to focus on the details of the case.

The preparation of Canada's case, which was entrusted to Clifford Sifton,[28] Canada's Minister of the Interior, took longer than expected. Under the terms of the Hay-Herbert Convention, the exchange of arguments was to take place on May 3, two months after ratification. Due to difficulties in collecting the requisite documents (and also due to the inherent weakness of the Canadian case), the Foreign Office enquired whether the State Department would agree to an extension. On March 13, Herbert sent a formal enquiry to the Assistant Secretary of State, Francis B. Loomis, asking for the exchange to be delayed until May 31 or even June 30.

Ten days later, once Sifton had reassured the Foreign Office, Herbert withdrew the request and the exchange of arguments took place on the due date.[29] However, with the American arguments in his hands, Lansdowne felt obliged to ask once more for a delay. '[I]t will no doubt be recognised by the United States' Government that it is desirable that all the facts and documents connected with the question should be fully examined', he told Choate in early May, 'so that both sides may be presented to the Tribunal in as complete a form as possible.' Choate replied that such a move 'was strongly deprecated by the United States' Government', while Hay described the proposal as 'extremely inconvenient.'[30]

Eager to see the matter settled, the State Department was irritated by what it considered stalling tactics. Moreover, it emphasised that the American Commissioners could not remain in Britain later than the end of October and, consequently, that discussions must begin, as directed in the Hay-Herbert Convention, on September 3. Consequently, Hay refused to assent to Lansdowne's proposal, that Britain might take photographs of the original American documents. While the Secretary of State would allow Sifton access to these papers, he stressed that there must be 'no delay in the delivery of the Counter-Case or printed Argument, or in the hearing of the oral argument.'[31] Such a position was not only unreasonable; it set a dangerous precedent for future arbitration. Lansdowne quickly relayed his conviction to Herbert that no 'precedent exists, so far as His Majesty's Government are aware, for making the production of original documents dependent on a condition of this nature.' Britain's interest in ending the boundary issue would only go so far and, reacting to a point of prestige, Lansdowne concluded with the hope 'that the United States' Government will, on further consideration, agree unconditionally to the desired production of the original documents, and that it may thus be possible to avoid the necessity of calling a special meeting of the Tribunal in order to consider the point.'[32]

It appeared at first that Britain might indefinitely maintain her objections and force a delay. However, while desiring to uphold the historical precedent, the force of American pressure was hard to ignore. While Lansdowne recognised the necessity of assisting the Canadians throughout the negotiations, he had long determined not only that the tribunal must meet, but that it should also deliver a satisfactory and lasting outcome. Similarly convinced that the tribunal should take place on time, Roosevelt informed Hay that:

'I don't want the thing pending during a presidential campaign, and moreover if the English decline to come to an agreement this fall, under any pretense [sic.], I shall feel that it is simply due to bad faith, – that they have no sincere desire to settle the matter equitably. I think they ought to be made to understand that there must be no delay; that we have come to a definite agreement with them and that the agreement must be kept on their side as well as on ours, and that we shall expect them to live up to it without fail.'[33]

In accordance with Roosevelt's directive, Hay was obliged to insist upon the terms of the Hay-Herbert Convention. On August 5, Joseph Choate reminded the Foreign Secretary that Lodge and Root must return to the United States before November 9, to attend the special Session of Congress: 'I am again specially instructed to repeat the notice already given to His Majesty's Government that the Government of the United States desires and expects the Tribunal to assemble on the 3rd September.'[34]

In the face of such determination, Lansdowne's resistance crumbled. Writing to Senator Lodge, the Foreign Secretary explained that there was 'no desire on our side to waste a moment of time' and hinted that it had been the Canadians, rather than the Foreign Office, who had pressed for the delay. 'So far at any rate as H.M.'s Govt. are concerned you may rely on our doing our best to expedite matters', Lansdowne remarked eagerly. 'But we are not masters of the situation.'[35] On August 13, the Foreign Secretary's submission became official. A dispatch was sent to Arthur Raikes, indicating that Britain agreed to the commencement of discussions on September 3.[36]

Throughout the United States there was a great optimism that America's territorial contention would be upheld. That Canada had no case and that Laurier's motives were, at the least, questionable, was almost universally asserted. 'How would you like Scotland to be flaunting the Stars and Stripes along the border, boasting its allegiance to the Republic,' Andrew Carnegie wrote to Balfour on July 23, 'raising what you considered trumped-up claims to territory ... which she only does because she knows Britain is in reserve behind her?'[37] Meanwhile, State Department officials, who had long held similar views, were greatly encouraged by the details of the Canadian case. On May 22, John Hay told Henry White, American Chargé d'Affairs in London, that the department was 'in very good spirits', adding that the verdict 'depends on whether Lord A[lverstone] goes on the Bench with an imperial mandate or not. If he goes there with an open mind, we consider our case won.'[38]

Roosevelt now determined that British officials should appreciate his insistence on the kind of complete Alaskan settlement that would satisfy the United States. In June, the President wrote to Oliver Wendell Holmes, the Supreme Court Justice, and stated that Holmes might show the letter to Joseph Chamberlain. Should the tribunal deliver an unsatisfactory result, Roosevelt declared his intention to 'take a position which will prevent any possibility of arbitration hereafter.' This was to be stated in the President's Message to Congress, and would 'render it necessary for Congress to give me the authority to run the line as we claim it, by our own people, without any further regard to the attitude of England and Canada.'[39]

During a meeting between Holmes and Chamberlain in early August, the former dutifully presented Roosevelt's letter. Chamberlain's reaction was swift: sufficiently impressed with the gravity of the situation, he immediately relayed the news in a confidential note to the Prime Minister. 'I told Mr. Justice Holmes that I had heard the letter with the greatest regret,' Chamberlain noted, 'as the spirit it showed seemed to me unworthy of the head of a great country.' It was evident to Chamberlain that Roosevelt's position hardly accorded with normal diplomatic practice; he declared:

> 'while I made no complaint that President Roosevelt should take a strong view on the matter in dispute, exactly as we did in the dispute with regard to the boundary in Venezuela, it seemed to me impossible to preserve friendship if one side accompanied his assent to arbitration by saying that if arbitration went against him he would take the matter into his own hands.'

In reality, Chamberlain was as worried as he was irritated. For the sake of an Alaskan victory, it appeared, Roosevelt would risk destroying the 'special relationship' and the President's defiant note, placing the responsibility for averting a diplomatic confrontation squarely with Britain, created a palpable wave of anxiety. For years, the fragile *rapprochement* had never been so threatened.

Chamberlain fully understood the gravity of the situation and proposed that Alverstone be immediately informed.[40] This proved a turning point, as Britain determined quickly to settle the dangerous Alaskan issue, whatever the cost to Canada and the imperial connection. Roosevelt's intention, to scare Britain into a satisfactory settlement, was therefore undoubtedly successful. In the meantime, the President continued to exert a strong personal presence. If the Alaska

Commission, beginning its deliberations on September 3, was never quite the impartial instrument for which the Hay-Herbert Convention had called, the American representatives were further kept in line through constant communication with the President and American Embassy. Eager that his contention be upheld, Roosevelt wrote several pointed letters to Lodge and Root: a good example, sent to the latter on October 3, expressed the President's sincere wish that Britain 'could understand that this is the last chance, and that though it will be unpleasant for us, if they force me to do what I must do in case they fail to take advantage of this chance, it will be a thousandfold more unpleasant for them.'[41]

On September 10, one week after the Alaskan tribunal began its deliberations, Herbert relayed an encouraging rumour from Washington. John Foster, who had prepared the American argument, appeared to be in favour of a compromise 'according to which the Canadians should be given their claim in the South the Americans getting their own way in the North.'[42] Lansdowne must have known that neither Roosevelt nor the American commissioners would consider the scheme, let alone accept it. Nevertheless, he responded with alacrity. Foster's suggestion, Lansdowne told Herbert on September 14, 'would be – as a matter of practical politics – the best solution for all concerned'. However, with the judicial discussions now underway, he demurred from making an official statement on the subject. 'The point is one which will require the most delicate handling,' he explained, 'and if there is to be any discussion as to the possibility of bringing about such an arrangement, the F.O. had better not be officially concerned in it.'

Instead, Lansdowne looked in another direction for a settlement and intimated to the British Ambassador that he has not been completely inactive over the preceding weeks. In a particularly suggestive passage, the Foreign Secretary referred to 'other means of arriving at the desired result', adding that 'I have already taken steps to ensure that these shall not be neglected.'[43] Even to the British Ambassador, Lansdowne evidently was unwilling to explain his true intentions. Dismissing the idea of a further approach to the United States, neither could Lansdowne hope to influence the Canadian jurists. It may be inferred, therefore, that the Foreign Secretary, as early as September, had made some kind of approach to the sole British representative, in order to ensure a satisfactory settlement for Britain.[44]

When Alverstone entered the fray, he was already inspired by the desire to find a reasonable agreement consistent with the interests of both parties. Indeed, the Chief Justice appeared to be the only member of the Commission who sought to deal with the points in question in an impartial manner. Elected as President, Alverstone sought a compromise that would satisfy both his American and Canadian colleagues. While he soon conceded the strength of the American case regarding the coastal inlets, it proved all but impossible to bring either Jetté or Aylesworth into line. Such intransigence was difficult to overcome and, for this, Alverstone received much sympathy from British official circles. 'What an awful time you must be having!' Austen Chamberlain remarked on October 7.[45] If the

Canadian Commissioners were behaving unreasonably, the same could easily be said for the Americans. On October 14, John S. Sandars, Balfour's Private Secretary, had a lengthy interview with Alverstone, during which the latter expressed his frustration. To the Prime Minister, Sandars reported that Alverstone,

> 'tells me that he is now in a very tight place. The Americans have behaved very badly. They got him to express an opinion favourable to their contention in respect to the Lynn Canal region; they on their part yielding the Portland Canal. ... He has formed the most adverse opinion of Lodge and Root.'

Although the American representatives would not accept anything other than the complete acceptance of their main contentions, Alverstone stated that the matter was 'not quite hopeless'. Still more, it seems clear that, during the interview, Sandars himself stressed the utmost necessity that the parties arrive at a definite settlement. 'He quite appreciates the grave consequences to Canada if no decision is reached,' Sandars explained, 'but as he says, he cannot give everything away, especially when the evidence would not sustain him in doing so.'[46] Balfour was clearly discouraged by the Americans' unreasonable posture and by Alverstone's failure to produce a settlement. He told Sandars on October 15 that 'I am vexed about Alaska and grieved at the unfavourable impression produced by our American friends upon Webster [Alverstone]'. The Prime Minister concluded by remarking that 'I do not know Root. Lodge I know, and like. Of course he is a strong politician, and has deeply committed himself on this very question.'[47]

Once Alverstone had agreed to accept the American contention that the boundary line should follow the coastal inlets, the only important questions to be resolved concerned the exact location of the Portland Channel and the size of the coastal strip that would belong to the United States. On these issues, even Roosevelt had admitted that the Canadian contention might have some merit. '[T]here might be an arguable question as to the possession of the islands in the Portland Channel,' he wrote to Holmes in July, 'and also as to the boundary line where there were on the main land no high mountains within the ten mile limit.'[48] The Canadian Government, Commissioners and even the Governor-General, remained adamant that theirs was the stronger case, and Minto told Arthur Elliot on October 18 that:

> 'On the Portland Canal I do not think the U.S. have a leg to stand upon – though they have erected store houses there, placing in them stone slabs with "this is the property of the U.S." engraved upon them! on what I believe will be proved to be distinctly Canadian soil. In fact what Sir Wilfrid & I hope for is – to lose in the North & gain in the South'.[49]

To pacify Jetté and Aylesworth, Alverstone insisted that all four islands in the Portland Channel should be given to Canada and that the coastal strip, to belong to the United States, should be as narrow as possible. However, while the

Americans were prepared, in the last resort, to abandon the islands, they whole-heartedly refused to accept Alverstone's contention on the second point. When a deadlock appeared to be the only result, Alverstone suddenly changed his mind and, siding with the American Commissioners, cleared the path for a final settle-ment. Such an abrupt about-turn by Alverstone needs explaining. It is likely that further pressure from Roosevelt led Lansdowne, amongst others, to make every effort to persuade Alverstone into concession. On October 14, Choate met Lansdowne at the Foreign Office, to repeat the President's determination to bring about a lasting settlement. The American Ambassador remarked that,

> 'there was a supreme necessity for this boundary question to be settled by this Commission, and there never would be another opportunity, that the President, in signing this Treaty had gone as far as he could possibly go; that he would never in the event of this Commission failing, consent to an arbitration for the settlement of this boundary'.[50]

The timing of Alverstone's submission indicates that the meeting had a profound effect on his final decisions. On October 14, the Chief Justice remained insistent that the mountain range, from which the boundary would be drawn, ran close to the sea. The following day, he told Root that he would make every effort to effect an award.[51] According to Lodge, Alverstone was 'looking very anxious' on the morning of October 15. 'We went into conference at eleven,' Lodge recalled, 'argued fruitlessly for some time, and then came to a pause. Then Lord Alverstone said openly what he had already said to Root and myself privately, that we must prepare a [boundary] line.' Accordingly, on October 16, the American delegates handed Alverstone their frontier contention, which was quickly accepted.[52]

Choate had stressed the importance of British concessions, but he could hardly have expected the speed with which Alverstone intended to comply. After Alverstone's public change of heart during the conference meeting of October 15, the American Ambassador quickly sought Lansdowne's views. Choate, Lansdowne explained, 'appeared surprised when I told him that Alverstone was not "riding to orders" and would certainly resent a suggestion that he should decide the question referred to him otherwise than according to the evidence.' Naturally, Lansdowne could not admit to the American Ambassador that he had been responsible for Alverstone's change of heart. Instead, he expressed himself 'in favour of a reasonable give and take settlement as between the two Governments, but stuck to my opinion that it was impossible for me to press the [Commissioners].'[53]

While there is no conclusive evidence to indicate that Lansdowne and Alverstone had met on the 14th, we have already seen that an interview took place between Sandars and the British Commissioner on that date, during which the for-mer made no pretence about the need for a settlement. Still more, it was Choate belief that Lansdowne had been playing a greater part in the final stages of the Alaskan negotiation than he was prepared to admit. In a dispatch to Hay, Choate described the interview of October 15, during which Lansdowne 'professed not to know what was going on in the Commission'. After the two men examined the issues in detail, Choate reported that the Foreign Secretary,

> 'went on in a way that indicated to my mind that he knew the exact situation ... He even suggested that the only thing that might be agreed on was that the line went around the inlets, and that we might get that important thing decided in our favour and the Canadians nothing. He said that the Canadians attached great importance to the ownership of Pearse and Wales Islands. ... I left satisfied that he and Mr. Balfour would, if they had not already done so, tell Lord Alverstone what they thought as to the necessity of agreeing upon that line, and that the present chance of settling the controversy ought not to be lost.'[54]

After the interview, Lansdowne took the opportunity to converse intimately with Alverstone. 'I made no secret of our great desire for a settlement,' the Foreign Secretary told Balfour on October 16 'and I have no doubt he will do his level best not to let the tribunal separate without effecting one.'[55] It is clear, therefore, that, if Lansdowne and his colleagues did not actually force Alverstone into making the necessary concessions to the United States, they made sure that the British Commissioner fully appreciated the urgency of a successful settlement. Alverstone, subjected to such intense political pressure – the strength of which he fully acknowledged – had no alternative but to yield and, sadly, to abandon his Canadian colleagues.

On October 20, the Alaskan tribunal announced the results of its deliberations. The most important question, that of the coastal strip, was decided in favour of the United States. The Portland Channel was identified as the Tongas Passage; of the four islands in the Channel, Pearse and Wales were given to Canada, while the United States received Sitklan and Kannaghunut. The Award had, in effect, upheld the American contention and Alverstone was content that a settlement had been concluded. 'I have had a tremendous fight for six days,' he told Balfour, 'and it has been one of the hardest of many hard jobs I have had.' Nevertheless, he did not consider the result a bitter defeat for Canada, but rather blamed Jetté and Aylesworth for their intransigence. 'I have had to yield certain minor matters on which I pressed for a decision more favourable to Great Britain,' he explained, adding that 'had I not yielded I should not have got a settlement at all.'[56] Lansdowne was equally unprepared to give the Canadians much sympathy. Having taken very little interest in the details of the Canadian case, he considered the settlement perfectly fair and judicial. Accordingly, when the Foreign Office gave Balfour a copy of the Alaskan Award, Lansdowne explained that:

> 'Upon the main points, (the inlets), I expect the American contention was perfectly good. The 2nd point (position of the mountains parallel to the coast) the Award is a compromise and the Canadians saw a great extent of territory which they would have lost if the American line had

been accepted. The 3rd point (Portland Channel) is virtually decided in favour of Canada, but they are going to make a great grievance of the surrender of two tiny little islands west of Wales island, the value of which they have somewhat tardily discovered.'[57]

Naturally enough, opinion in Canada expressed a sharp sense of betrayal. While Jetté and Aylesworth had been disgusted at the Alaskan verdict, having refused to add their signatures to the Award, Laurier at first decided against giving an official statement. Nevertheless, there was no doubting his strength of feeling. In a dispatch to the Colonial Office, Minto remarked that Laurier 'is strongly impressed with the belief that the interests of Canada have been deliberately and intentionally sacrificed for the sake of United States' friendship.' The Governor-General continued by stressing that it

'is impossible to overrate the deep meaning of the expression of feeling the Alaskan Award has aroused throughout the Dominion. It would be an entire mistake to imagine that the impression produced is transient, or that time may obliterate the sure feeling so unfortunately created, for the supposed injury now done to Canada will undoubtedly be added to other supposed injuries inflicted upon her for the sake of United States' friendship'.[58]

Canadian journalists were equally clear in their explanation of the popular anger towards the Alaskan Award. 'This is not the first time that British Diplomacy has proved costly to Canada', the Toronto *World* remarked sadly. 'These easy triumphs of American diplomacy in the settlement of boundary disputes are full of dangerous possibilities.'[59] In his journal, Minto wrote that Alaska decision had produced a very bad effect, 'Canadian newspapers & public opinion having lost all reason!'[60] The strength of Canadian resentment was further emphasised when, on October 22, Aylesworth published his protest in *The Times*. Aylesworth's declaration that Alverstone had abandoned the Canadians for other than judicial reasons, was hard to ignore. As Minto wrote Lyttleton on October 25,

'owing to utterly unjustifiable communications to the press by the Canadian Commissioners, the Canadian public has assumed that instead of the judicial decision they were entitled by Treaty to expect, a compromise had been arrived at in deference to pressure from the United States, by which Canadian territory and interests have been inexcusably sacrificed.'[61]

Alverstone was more than ready to make an official rejoinder, but was dissuaded by the Foreign Secretary. 'I told him,' Lansdowne wrote, 'that, if I were him, I should not enter into a newspaper controversy.' However, after noting that the Canadian representatives had behaved badly during the negotiation, Lansdowne told the Prime Minister that 'I do not like the idea of allowing them to drag our

Chief Justice into a wrangle in the course of which each side will give the other the lie.' If the Canadian Parliament should make charges against Alverstone, a 'rejoinder may be inevitable.'[62]

Although such charges were indeed made, Lansdowne and the newly appointed Colonial Secretary, Alfred Lyttleton, came to an agreement in early December, not to send an official reply; it was better to allow the matter to drop, rather than create a public controversy with the Canadian Government that would question the imperial bond. '[A]ny statement by His Majesty's Government with regard to the charges made against the Lord Chief Justice,' Sir Francis Villiers wrote to the Colonial Office on December 21, 'would not serve any useful purpose, and ... in the circumstances it is neither necessary nor desirable to take any action in the matter for the present.'[63]

For the relatively quiet manner in which the Alaskan issue ended, Sir Wilfrid Laurier must take some credit. Like many Canadians, Laurier understood that the case had been lost and that there was little point in adding to Anglo-Canadian friction with further official and rather undignified protests. However much the defeated claims meant to the Canadian people, of far greater significance was the future of the imperial connection. On October 21, the Ottawa correspondent for *The Times* emphasised the prevalent sentiment in Canada: 'The dominant feeling may be summed up thus:– "We have been beaten and must accept the verdict like sensible people."'[64] Although Laurier refused to make a public denouncement of the Alaskan Award, the Canadian Premier considered himself duty bound to refute Alverstone's arguments. This he did in a private communication to the British representative himself.[65]

For their part, the Americans were naturally ecstatic. 'The President and the Cabinet regard the award as far and away the greatest diplomatic success which the United States have gained for a generation,' the Washington reporter for *The Times* explained on October 21, 'ensuring as it does for the country, for all time, the only spot on earth about which there was a question of relinquishing territory.'[66] In a celebratory state, American officials began a somewhat undignified fight to take the credit. John Hay hinted that success in the Alaskan issue had been, in no small part, due to his own efforts. Describing the result as 'one of the greatest transactions of my life,' Hay explained that it had justified 'a plan which I adopted and carried through against the misgivings of everybody, and the result will prove that I was right in relying upon the honor and conscience of an English Judge.'[67]

This was something of a delusion. While it is true that the Secretary of State had helped to bring about the Alaskan result, of far greater significance had been Roosevelt's constant interference. Indeed, it is manifestly clear that, without the President's brash diplomacy, the Alaskan Award would have been very different, and, perhaps, may not have arrived at all. Quick to declare that his strong diplomacy had been primarily responsible for the success, Roosevelt told his son on October 20 that 'I ... think that the clear understanding the British Government had as to what would follow a disagreement was very important and probably decisive'. On the very same day, in a letter to Oliver Wendell Holmes, Roosevelt happily remarked that 'I cannot help having a certain feeling that your showing that letter to Chamberlain and others was not without its indirect effect on the decision.'[68]

Britain's official reaction to the Alaska Award was delayed until February 1904 when the new session of Parliament began. During the King's speech on February 2, Edward VII maintained that, although much of the verdict was unsatisfactory, 'it must, nevertheless, be a matter of congratulation that the misunderstandings, in which ancient Boundary Treaties, made in ignorance of geographical facts, are so fertile, have in this case been finally removed from the field of controversy.' Others were quick to agree and similarly eager to stress the significance of the Alaskan verdict on the future of Anglo-American relations whilst playing down the abandonment of Canada. Lord Spencer gave his hearty congratulations to the Government and Lord Hylton pointed out that 'in Canada, as well as in this country, many will be found ready to acknowledge that it is for the benefit of all parties that this question, which might at any moment have given rise to serious international differences, should have been set at rest.'[69]

Lansdowne's official reply was by far the most significant, and deserves to be quoted at length:

'The result in the finding of the tribunal has no doubt not been entirely satisfactory to us, and in this respect I do not draw any distinction between the interests of the Dominion of Canada and our interests. The question at issue is a question not merely of the frontier of Canada, but of the frontier of the British Empire, for the defence and the integrity of which we are responsible. But, my Lords, I do not think that any one seriously expected that we should obtain a favourable verdict on all points; and I am inclined to find some consolation in the fact that our military and naval advisers tell us confidently that the two islands in the Portland Channel which, under the award were given to the United States, are of no strategical value whatever.'[70]

One historian has called this speech an 'astonishing performance', adding that the 'implication that if Britain lost some points she gained others of roughly equal importance was sheer dishonesty.'[71] Such an interpretation fails to explain Lansdowne's true meaning. The Foreign Secretary spoke not of British gains, but of a verdict that left the strategical position in North America unaltered. It was for this reason alone that Britain could take heart from the Alaskan verdict. If Lansdowne's speech was astonishing, it was due to the declaration, implicit yet nonetheless perfectly clear, that Britain would defend Canada's strategic position, but would not support dubious claims merely because of the imperial tie. Lansdowne had been acting not for Canada, but for the British Empire and only the former had suffered a setback.

Most importantly, the verdict had pleased the Americans and the British Government could now look forward to a greater friendship between the Foreign

Office and the State Department. From her desire to retain and further Anglo-American friendship, the British Government had never budged and this governed Lansdowne's Alaskan diplomacy throughout the Alaska affair. In July 1903, Balfour wrote to Andrew Carnegie about the Alaskan negotiation and explained that 'I have no wish, public or private, nearer my heart than of securing and preserving genuinely good relations with the U.S.A., who I do not in any sense regard as a foreign community.'[72]

At the moment of crisis, Britain recognised the vitality of retaining the 'special relationship' – more important even than the imperial bond with Canada – and took the necessary steps to ensure its survival. Naturally, then, it was with a sense of profound relief that British statesmen viewed the positive effect of the Alaska verdict on American opinion. 'Everyone I have seen both here [Washington] and in New York has been friendly and cordial', Sir Mortimer Durand, Britain's newly appointed Ambassador in Washington, told Lansdowne on December 4.[73] Now that the last great dispute between Britain and the United States had been settled, Lansdowne's ambition to bring about a 'clean slate' was practically realised – and without the necessity for significant concessions.

8

Alaskan Epilogue

Imperial Relations and Pelagic Sealing, 1903-1905

ONCE THE ALASKAN Tribunal made its decision public on October 20 1903, the Canadian press broke forth in angry and indignant protest. Canada had been '[s]acrificed on the altar of diplomacy to make Britain solid with the United States', the Toronto *World* fumed. She was, said the *Vancouver Province*, led 'like a lamb to the slaughter'.[1] It was, perhaps, natural that these immediate reactions should present a somewhat naive portrait of what had just occurred in London.[2] The combination of America's aggressive Alaskan policy and Britain's apparent wholesale desertion of the Canadian cause had left the Dominion reeling. As we have seen, Lord Alverstone suffered particular abuse. Many Canadian observers, however, suspected that Britain's betrayal had come from a higher level. In particular, they blamed Lansdowne and the Foreign Office for choosing American friendship over colonial loyalty. On October 24, the *Ottawa Citizen* sadly remarked that:

> 'The Foreign Office desired to have the controversy closed and pre-ferred compromise to long delay. The American Commissioners held out against Lord Alverstone's judgment [*sic*.]. His Lordship, against his own judgment, yielded for diplomatic reasons.'[3]

Lansdowne could do little either to refute these charges or to assuage Canadian hostility. Of influencing Alverstone, the Foreign Secretary had undoubtedly been at least indirectly guilty. Still more, an official defence of his actions would serve no useful purpose at a time when the Government wanted the Alaskan issue to fade from the public mind. Without doubt, the Foreign Office would have wel-comed a lengthy quiet period in Canadian-American relations but, while other major disputes remained unsettled, diplomacy could not stand still. Indeed, in February 1903, eight months before the Alaskan verdict was delivered, the long-running fur seal controversy came again before Congress and, as the months passed, Lansdowne was forced to consider his response.[4]

The sealing dispute had its origins in the mid nineteenth century. The United States, having purchased Alaska from the Russian Government in 1867, also acquired two Behring Sea islands, St. George and St. Paul, together comprising the Pribilof Islands. Hardly significant in themselves, they were inhabited in summer by a valuable fur seal colony and, by 1870, the Treasury had given to the Alaska Commercial Company a twenty-year concession that permitted an annual cull of 100,000 seals. Canadian sealers, equally dependent on the seal herd for their liveli-hood, refused to accept the monopoly, claiming that, outside the islands' three mile limit, international law guaranteed equal treatment for all nations. In 1886, the Treasury stepped in and authorised the seizure of foreign sealing vessels by American revenue cutters. Until 1891, this practice continued, despite protests by successive British Foreign Secretaries; a *modus vivendi*, established that year, tem-porarily eased the crisis.

Two years later, an Arbitral Tribunal met in Paris to consider the future of pelagic sealing in the Behring Sea. Broadly, its verdict went against the United States. While the seizures were held to be unlawful, however, the Tribunal agreed upon strict measures intended to preserve the seal colony. In particular, an annual close season was established from May until July and sealing was to be banned altogether within a sixty-mile zone around the islands.

This result satisfied neither side and, as a response to the continuing hostility in the North Pacific, the fur seal issue was raised during the meetings of the Joint High Commission of 1898. After much wrangling, the Commissioners appeared to have come close to a suitable compromise when Senator Charles Warren Fairbanks, heading the American delegation, offered Canada $500,000 and an annual percentage of the earnings of the Pribilof Islands in return for her aban-donment of pelagic sealing. To this arrangement, both sides were fully prepared to agree. In the latter stages of negotiation, however, the sharpest thorn in Canadian-American relations – the Alaska Boundary dispute – wrecked the chances of agreement and the Joint High Commission broke up in an atmosphere of outrage and hostility.[5]

Until 1903, the settlement of the Alaskan boundary remained the predomi-nant issue in Canadian-American relations and diplomatic moves for a pelagic set-tlement were effectively dropped. While a small number of communications between the State Department and the Foreign Office touched on the fur seal question, these tended to deal only with isolated incidents, particularly dwelling on the past seizures of fishing vessels and on resulting requests for compensation. On July 18 1901, Sir Francis Villiers wrote to the Colonial Office of the recent seizure of an American trawler by Canadian authorities off the New England coast. Canada, Villiers noted,

> 'was unable to entertain the claim of the United States' Government for compensation in respect of the alleged illegal forfeiture of the United States' fishing vessel "Frederick Gerring, Junior." With regard to the suggestion that advantage should be taken of the opportunity to remind the United States' Government that no compensation has yet been paid to the owners of the vessel "Coquitlan" for its illegal seizure in 1892, Lord Lansdowne is of the opinion that it would be more con-venient not to raise that question in the present connection but to leave

it for separate adjustment together with other claims of similar nature arising out of the Seal Fishery in the Behring Sea.'[6]

In June 1903, John Hay took advantage of a lull in the Alaskan negotiations to raise the possibility of a pelagic settlement. Spurred on by the bill passed by the House of Representatives on February 2 – which was subsequently opposed in the Senate – and by a visit to the Pribilof Islands by a Senate delegation that summer, Hay met Sir Michael Herbert to press for a quick and amicable agreement.[7] 'Hay is very anxious to sign a Convention in regard to the fur seal fishery,' Herbert reported on June 5. He would 'grant equitable compensation to the Canadian fishermen and he pretends that there will not [be] a seal left if pelagic sealing is not stopped.'[8] On July 27, Hay repeated the request, asking Herbert about the feasibility of an 'Anglo-American Convention for the prohibition of pelagic sealing by British and Americans in the North Pacific and Behring Sea.'[9]

Evidently encouraged by the meeting, Hay immediately instructed Joseph Choate to press ahead and discuss the terms of a possible agreement with Herbert, but the British Ambassador's sudden death forced Choate to turn instead to Lansdowne. On October 7, Choate found the Foreign Secretary fully willing to consider a new fur seal agreement, provided that he could first obtain official consent from Canada.[10]

The Alaskan verdict changed everything. Fearing a Canadian backlash against Britain, Lansdowne was pushed into a more careful and solicitous position on Canadian affairs. He was quick to recognise that the state of imperial relations after Alaska was a matter of grave concern and that Sir Wilfrid Laurier should not be asked, at least for a short time, even to consider further Canadian-American questions. For this reason, there would be no premature action on pelagic sealing, although the United States continued to urge fresh negotiations. On October 28, Lansdowne told Arthur Raikes, the Chargé d'Affairs at the Washington Embassy, that:

'The United States' Ambassador told me to-day that he had been informed by the Secretary of State that the United States' Government were anxious to arrive at an early settlement of the questions relating to pelagic sealing in the Northern Pacific. He trusted that I should find myself in a position to effect such a settlement.'

He continued:

'I repeated to Mr. Choate ... that the draft Treaty had been referred to the Canadian Government, and I ventured to express my opinion that having regard to the irritation which had been caused by the recent award of the Alaska Boundary Commission, it might be desirable not to press the Canadian Government at the present moment for an immediate statement of their views.'[11]

Alfred Lyttleton, who had succeeded Joseph Chamberlain at the Colonial Office, added his full support to the policy of non-intervention. H. Bertram Cox, an Assistant Under Secretary at the Colonial Office, wrote to the Foreign Office on November 11 of the Lyttleton's belief that,

> 'it will be expedient to defer, for a time, addressing any further communication to the Canadian Government in regard to the proposal to resume negotiations with the United States of America as to pelagic sealing.'[12]

Other issues received the same treatment. In early November, Villiers asked Sir Reginald Tower to write a memorandum on current Canadian questions. Tower's response was to suggest that, 'in view of the recent award of the Alaska Boundary Tribunal "the moment appears opportune for arranging the local question of bonding privileges."' '[A]re there not other outstanding questions which might also be taken up?' Lansdowne enquired on November 4; he referred particularly to pelagic sealing and the inclusion of bribery amongst extraditable offences and concluded that 'I doubt whether it would be wise to say anything to the Canadians about any of them for a time.'[13] When Villiers mentioned the subject at the Colonial Office nine days later, he found Sir Montagu Ommanney equally inclined to dismiss Tower's suggestion.

> 'As to bonding privileges and other questions now open between Canada and the U.S.,' he explained, 'I do not think we had better raise any of them at the present time. If Canada wishes for an early settlement of any of them, I should leave her to say so, but in her present temper we should get no thanks for having taken the initiative. Mr. Lyttleton agrees.'[14]

Choate dutifully relayed Lansdowne's opinion – that it would be 'wise to give Canada more time' – in his dispatch to Hay of November 25 and explained his belief that the Foreign Office would take no action on the fur seal matter in the immediate future.[15] Choate's view proved correct. Indeed, Lansdowne was yet further dissuaded from an active policy by a minute from the Canadian Government, forwarded by Minto on November 27. This note dealt with a previous American draft Convention on fur sealing and underlined Canada's belief in the inexpediency of pelagic negotiations. As Villiers noted on January 10 1904,

> 'The Dominion Government ... dwelt upon the fact that pelagic sealing was only one of the points brought before the High Commission, of which Lord Herschell was Chairman, and that the settlement of the Alaska Boundary as an isolated question had changed the position of affairs, and they expressed the hope that His Majesty's Government would decline to entertain the proposal or future proposals of a similar character.'[16]

In these circumstances, the question for the British Government was to protect Canadian sentiment by resisting diplomatic actions towards an immediate fur seal negotiation. This was a feasible goal for, unlike his active policy during the Alaskan affair, President Roosevelt took scant notice of the sealing issue, particularly at this time, when war threatened in the Far East (see chapters eleven and twelve).[17] The introduction of the Dillingham Bill on January 12, however, inevitably came as a significant blow to the Foreign Office. Senator William P. Dillingham's demand for suitable legislation to protect the seal herd on the Pribilof Islands advocated the mercy killing of almost the entire seal colony – to prevent its cruel and thoughtless extermination under existing conditions – should Britain refuse to enter into negotiations. On January 18, John Hay met Durand to discuss the basis for agreement, but immediately encountered difficulties.

> 'I explained to Mr. Hay your Lordship's views respecting the inexpediency at the present time of pressing Canada on this subject', Durand telegraphed that day, 'and he said that he especially wished you to understand that the United States Government had no wish to request that you should do anything which you consider inopportune.'[18]

Durand feared that the sealing controversy might wreck the burgeoning Anglo-American friendship, which had survived and indeed been strengthened by the Alaskan verdict, so he entered into long conversations with Henry W. Elliott, a consistent advocate of Anglo-American legislation on the seal issue. Elliott vehemently pressed his views upon the British Ambassador and found the latter willing to meet the Americans 'more than half-way'.[19]

Personally, Durand shared Elliott's desire that strong measures should be implemented for the purposes of seal preservation and, encouraged by these talks, Sir Mortimer now began sending urgent missives from the British Embassy. One such example was sent to Minto in early January, in turn inspiring a meeting between the Governor-General and Sir Wilfrid Laurier. Minto found the Canadian Premier 'inclined to sympathise with Sir Mortimer Durand in his apprehension of the total destruction of the seals', adding that he 'himself thinks that the Canadian system is most destructive to the herd as it so often causes the destruction of females heavy with young in the open sea.'[20]

Despite his personal dislike of Canadian sealing practice, however, there was little chance that either Laurier or his Government would accept the American proposal in the immediate wake of the Alaskan verdict. Certainly, this was the view sent by Minto to the Colonial Office.[21] Despite the urgent tone of Durand's letters to the Foreign Office, Lansdowne stood firmly with Canada. On March 31, he relayed the decision to the Washington Embassy, explaining the Dominion's attitude that,

> 'no sufficient ground had been adduced to justify the relinquishment by British subjects of their right of pelagic sealing. For this reason the Dominion considered that no good purpose would be served by resum-

ing negotiations, and expressed the hope that His Majesty's Government would decline to entertain the proposal of the United States' Government.'[22]

Durand continued to urge a settlement. While the Dillingham Bill had been blocked in Congress, Senator Joseph B. Foraker introduced a substitute Bill, providing for Anglo-American negotiations to amend the fur seal regulations. Less radical than its predecessor, there was every chance that it would be adopted and Durand fearfully reported that definite action was now a distinct possibility. Hay was under great pressure from partisan Senators to effect a settlement, he noted on March 24. On April 8, Roosevelt confirmed the Ambassador's reports by signing the Joint Resolution of Congress, 'requesting him to negotiate with His Majesty's Government for a revision of the Regulations which now govern the taking of fur seals'.[23]

At the same time, Laurier's obstruction left the Ambassador both frustrated and dispirited. Although the Canadian Premier's personal views on fur sealing have been noted, it was equally clear that Canada had no great interest in amending the pelagic regulations which, after all, would affect only a small part of her national economy and which meant further negotiations with the untrustworthy and aggressive Americans. The private correspondence between Durand and Minto thus became rather melancholy. On May 12, the Governor-General declared himself 'sorry' and 'disappointed' with Laurier's attitude and complained of the latter's,

> 'constant assertion that the United States were always trying to get the best of the bargain, and that the feeling against them in Canada at the present moment was most bitter – and he personally expressed more suspicion and dislike of them as bargainers than I had expected from him.'[24]

Five days later, Durand relayed this disappointing information to the Foreign Office. 'They [the Canadians] seem to be extraordinarily bitter against the United States', he noted simply.[25] In return, however, Durand received no tangible sympathy from a Foreign Secretary still steadfastly determined to act wholly in accordance with Canadian instructions. Lansdowne, whose opinion of American diplomacy after the Alaskan affair probably mirrored those held by Laurier, merely dispatched an official telegram to the British Embassy on May 30 asking the British Ambassador to inform Hay 'that the Government of the Dominion are not prepared to accept an arrangement based on the suspension of the killing of seals for a term of years both on land and at sea.'[26] Thus the Foraker Bill was summarily ignored.

The polite procrastination of the British Government led the United States reluctantly to let the issue lapse during the subsequent months of 1904. The attention of both State Department and Foreign Office was at that time focused on the Russian and Japanese struggle for supremacy in Eastern Asia and there was little time for the discussion of less immediately significant issues. By early 1905, however, American anger publicly resurfaced. On January 14, Senator Redfield Proctor, at Dillingham's request, introduced a further Bill in the Senate which revived the year-old threat of wholesale seal slaughter should the Foreign Office dismiss American calls to amend the pelagic regulations.[27] For his part, Lansdowne reacted with polite contempt. As he had dismissed the Davis Amendment to the Hay-Pauncefote Canal Convention for its unorthodox source and its blatantly threatening attitude, so he refused to admit the force of the Proctor Bill on the same ground and would not be bullied into premature action. On February 8, Ambassador Choate called upon Lansdowne at the Foreign Office to determine Britain's reaction to the news. Providing a detailed account of his position, Lansdowne explained that,

> 'a similar proposal had been contained in a Bill which was before the Senate in January of last year, but that the Bill had been superceded in April by a Joint Resolution ... The Resolution had not, so far as I was aware, led to any communication from the United States' Government, and the Resolution now before the Senate seemed to indicate an intention to revert to the more drastic measures of last year's Bill.'

He went on:

> 'Mr. Choate said that he had no recent information on the subject, but he doubted whether the proposal to reduce the herd would ever be carried. I did not pursue the matter beyond expressing my opinion that the question should be capable of settlement, and that the Canadian pelagic sealers had a strong claim to compensation.'[28]

This coldly polite interchange was to be the last significant event in the pelagic sealing controversy during Lansdowne's tenure at the Foreign Office. The Proctor Bill, pressed in the Senate by a small interest group with particular and precise interests, failed to gain significant political support and was quickly shelved.[29] In the meantime, the Canadian Government declared its continuing unwillingness 'to give a direct answer to United States' proposals' and, by September, the Canadian Minister of Marine and Fisheries simply stated that 'the present restrictions imposed upon pelagic sealing, as the result of the Paris Award, are a sufficient protection of the seals'.[30]

The Behring Sea question, from 1903 until 1905, thoroughly failed to arouse great interest either in Britain or in the United States. While strong American moves were indeed contemplated, they were suggested and supported only by a minority of partisan Congressmen. Still more, although Hay dutifully pressed the matter, his actions were restricted to a rather fragmentary series of enquiries at the British Embassy, enquires which the Secretary of State himself failed to carry through. Still, the question of fur seal preservation should not be regarded as a wholly insignificant part of Lansdowne's Western Hemispheric diplomacy. It is true that this stage of the dispute was of only slight significance in the busy world of Anglo-American relations. On the other hand, it served to underline the determination of the Foreign Office, in the wake of the unfortunate Alaskan verdict, to guarantee and support Canadian interests against her powerful southern neighbour. Roosevelt's inaction – due particularly to his preoccupation with Far Eastern affairs before and during the Russo-Japanese war – had been crucial in the formulation of Lansdowne's policy.

If the President's personal intervention in the Alaskan affair had spurred the Foreign Office into concessions, without similar interference regarding other Canadian-American concerns, Lansdowne would continue to lend the Laurier Government his firm support. There had, after all, been no real risk of a serious diplomatic conflict, and, for this reason alone, the Foreign Secretary used the opportunity to reassure both Laurier and the Canadian people that the Mother Country could still be relied upon to protect specific colonial interests. This was achieved without any significant harm to Anglo-American friendship.[31]

The Limits of Rapprochement

9

A Very Ugly Little Row

Reciprocity and Fisheries in Newfoundland, 1901-1905

IF, AT THE TURN of the century, Canada appeared to have a bright economic future, neighbouring Newfoundland was in a far poorer state. Whereas the great Dominion was rich in mineral deposits and abundant raw materials, Newfoundland's only significant source of wealth came from fish. Not only did her poor climate and infertile soils restrict agriculture, but a combination of thick fog and icebergs deterred foreign vessels from using Newfoundland as a convenient port-of-call. For these reasons, no major port had been constructed and the colony remained both geographically and economically isolated, with an uncertain and anxious future.[1] These hard to overcome obstacles were particularly detailed in a report sent to the Colonial Office in early 1905 by Governor Sir William MacGregor. In 1902-3, the fishing trade accounted for over 78 per cent of Newfoundland's exports and was as such, the 'staple export of this Colony'. For this reason, in a bad year like 1893 when the catch was low,[2] the whole economy suffered. In response, MacGregor advocated the establishment of a substantial reserve fund to bolster the local economy. 'Such precautions would be necessary under any circumstances in the face of such peturbations of income as are demonstrated in this report,' he maintained, 'but they are doubly necessary in a community that is dependent on other countries for its food, its clothing and its fuel.'[3]

The task of consolidating Newfoundland's future was left to Liberal Premier Sir Robert Bond. Bond had long publicised his belief that it was only by resolving the question of international fishery rights on the Treaty Shore – and by concluding a reciprocal trade arrangement with the United States – that the economic position of Newfoundland could be assured. In 1890, Bond, then Colonial Secretary, had discussed reciprocity with American Secretary of State James G. Blaine, and had come close to effecting a suitable arrangement.

Newfoundland's fish products would be admitted into the United States free of duty, while specific American goods including kerosene, gas engines and raw cotton would be received by the Colony in like manner. With the treaty's success apparently guaranteed, however, the Canadian Government led by Sir John Macdonald suddenly voiced its strong opposition. In Ottawa, Macdonald worried that the Bond-Blaine Convention would threaten Canadian trade, both with Newfoundland and the United States and successfully persuaded the British

Government to block the agreement. Accordingly, reciprocity discussions were dropped until August 1898, when the Joint High Commission convened in Washington to discuss all outstanding disputes between the United States and Britain's colonies in North America. While the members gave serious thought to reciprocity, however, they failed to deliver a result. Serious pressure from partisan interests in both Canada and the United States prevented a tariff reduction before the Commission was abandoned in February 1899.[4] Considering the acrimonious atmosphere of American-Canadian relations, Bond appreciated that a subsequent Commission would hardly be likely to conclude successful reciprocity negotiations. Because Newfoundland simply could not rely upon Sir Wilfrid Laurier to facilitate an agreement without ensuring significant concessions for Canada, the Newfoundland Premier determined to challenge Canada's control over colonial policy in North America and, preferring that his Government should deal directly with Washington, he attempted to exclude the Canadians altogether from the reciprocity issue.

The question of ending the international fishery rights on the Treaty Shore of Newfoundland presented an equally important challenge. French and American fishermen had long held the right to work in Newfoundland waters, thereby dividing the catch and damaging the potential prosperity of the local fishing trade. Signing the Treaty of Utrecht in 1713, the French Government agreed to cede its claim to the ownership of Newfoundland, but retained the right for her fishermen to work off the island's coast. The exact areas of coastline off which French trawlers could operate was further clarified in 1783, by the Treaty of Versailles. Under this agreement, the French Shore was to extend from Cape St. John in the North to Cape Ray on the south-west. At the same time, the United States upheld their legitimate interest in regional fishery matters and demanded extensive concessions. The final treaty gave American fishermen the right,

> 'to take fish of every kind on the Grand Bank, and on the other banks of Newfoundland', and the 'liberty to take fish of every kind on such parts of the coast of Newfoundland as British fishermen shall use (but not to dry or cure the same on that island) and also on the coasts, bays, and creeks of all other of His Britannic Majesty's dominions in America.'[5]

American fishery rights in British waters were partially curtailed in the wake of the Anglo-American war of 1812. A treaty signed on October 20 1818 restricted the areas open to American fishermen to the South, North and West coasts of Newfoundland, as well as parts of the Canadian coast and the scattered British islands. More importantly, American vessels were permitted to enter the ports of Nova Scotia and Newfoundland solely for the purposes of shelter and repair and were thereby obliged to obtain bait, and to dry and cure their catch on American soil.[6]

Forced to make long journeys for vital supplies, the Americans were left at a distinct disadvantage until, by the terms of the *modus vivendi* established on

February 15 1888, they were finally permitted to buy bait from the harbours of
Canada and Newfoundland, provided that they purchase an annual license at
$1.50 per ton.[7]

The *modus vivendi* proved only a short respite. It soon became clear that the
people of Newfoundland were no longer prepared to share their catch and had
determined to clear their waters of foreign competitors. On November 19 1900,
the prominent Newfoundlander Sir Ambrose Shea dispatched a letter to the
Foreign Office, insisting that the fishery issue should be brought to a quick conclusion. Shea informed Lansdowne that the issue was about to be raised once
more and added that,

> 'it would seem important, in the interests of Canada and
> Newfoundland, that there should be a definite record for purposes of
> record of the unselfish policy pursued for so many years in favour of
> American fishermen, as it should count for something more than mere
> sentiment in the course of future negotiations. It will not be disputed
> that ... Newfoundland has done its own good part in promoting the
> peaceful settlement of a controversy that has lived too long, but is now
> presumably destined to be finally set at rest.'[8]

For its part, the Conservative Government appreciated the need to support
Britain's oldest colony and to settle a dispute that concerned both Newfoundland
and Canada. As a result, in January 1901 Lansdowne began discussions with Paul
Cambon, the French Ambassador in London, to remove the French Treaty Shore
in return for territorial concessions elsewhere. The American Shore, on the other
hand, would be left for Bond to resolve, should Newfoundland enter negotiations
with Washington.

On January 11 1901, a secret and confidential telegram was dispatched from
the Colonial Office for Lord Minto's urgent attention. Sir Robert Bond 'is, I
understand, likely to press for permission to reopen negotiations with the United
States', Joseph Chamberlain explained, 'for [a] separate arrangement on [the]
lines discussed between Bond and Blaine in 1890.' The Colonial Office was content to give the colony a free hand in negotiations and Chamberlain concluded
that:

> 'No proposal for [the] resumption of the Joint High Commission has
> come from the United States' Government, and your Ministers appear
> to acquiesce in leaving it in abeyance. I presume that your Government
> would in these circumstances raise no objection for separate negotia-
> tions on [the] behalf of Newfoundland if pressed.'[9]

Laurier's response was both swift and critical. Inspired by his desire to effect the
incorporation of Newfoundland into the Dominion, he saw great dangers in
Bond's initiative: reciprocity with the United States would bring the two govern-

ments into greater accord, leaving Canada isolated and ruining the possibility of confederation. More importantly, negotiations for reciprocity would undoubtedly raise the Treaty Shore issue. Bond's willingness to give further privileges to the Americans – including the right to buy bait in the island's ports – would threaten the prosperity of the Canadian fishing trade.

In a state of extreme anxiety, Laurier raised objections. After relaying the substance of Chamberlain's dispatch to the Canadian Premier, Minto telegraphed the Colonial Office. 'It is the strong opinion of my Ministers', he explained, 'that [any] attempt by Newfoundland to enter into negotiations with the United States for a separate Treaty would be highly prejudicial to the interests of both Canada and Newfoundland.' Instead, he contended that united action 'by both Colonies is of supreme importance'.

Still more, in order to deter Bond from pressing his proposal, Laurier emphasised his strong hope that the Joint High Commission might reconvene in the spring, thereby enabling all outstanding questions between Canada, Newfoundland and the United States to be resolved. Although Laurier was perhaps excessively optimistic about the chances of reassembling the Commission, there is little doubt that he genuinely believed in its utility for both colonies. While Sir Julian Pauncefote was busily discussing the prospect with several prominent American officials, Laurier met Senator Charles Warren Fairbanks on January 16 and repeated his belief that the settlement of all American-Canadian disputes could best be resolved by that body.[10]

While the news undoubtedly surprised Chamberlain, it did not affect his decision to permit reciprocity discussions. Chamberlain 'would be glad to learn [the] nature of the communications with Senator Fairbanks', Minto was informed on January 18. However, the Colonial Secretary continued that 'it is not clear how [a] separate negotiation for Newfoundland would prevent the entry of the Colony into the Dominion.' Rather than dwell upon the objections to separate discussions, Chamberlain simply pointed out that 'it is probable that if His Majesty's Government were to allow such a negotiation, a settlement of the Treaty Shore difficulty would be greatly facilitated.'[11] The inference was clear: since Canada had a significant interest in settling the Treaty Shore question amicable negotiations between Bond and the State Department would actually benefit the Dominion and, therefore, should not be blocked.

Even if Laurier's interest had primarily concerned the Treaty Shore, it is unlikely that he would have given his assent to separate discussions. In fact, it soon became apparent that the anxieties of the Canadian Premier related, not to fishing questions, but to the threat, inherent in Bond's proposal, to confederation between Canada and Newfoundland. On January 19, Minto noted Laurier's deep sense of disappointment. '[H]e said that it appeared to him self-evident that separate negotiation on the part of Newfoundland would hinder chances of her entering confederation', the Governor-General explained. 'Sir Wilfrid Laurier is most strongly opposed to any separate negotiations ... on the ground that it would be quite contrary to [the] accepted policy to allow dealings by one of the North American Provinces or Colonies apart from the rest.'[12] To Minto, Laurier now wrote a lengthy dispatch, detailing earlier reciprocity proposals and defending Canada's legitimate interest in any negotiation between the United States and Newfoundland. Since Bond's primary aim was to obtain the free admission of Newfoundland's fish into the American market, Laurier worried that Bond would consent 'to grant to American fishermen the fishery rights and privileges in Newfoundland, from which they are excluded by the Convention of 1818.' Convinced that such concessions would threaten Canada's fishing trade, Laurier remarked that:

> 'All fishermen operating on the Grand Banks and in the waters of the North Atlantic require bait, they likewise require ice to preserve their fish and suitable places on shore to cure it. The Canadian and Newfoundland fishermen, if they fall short of any of these commodities, can have them in a few hours, in their own respective countries, whereas the American are denied access to the same.'

Should Bond grant concessions in the interests of reciprocity, Laurier continued, they would 'give at once, to American fishermen, a basis of operation in Newfoundland, and Canadian fishermen would thereby be seriously injured.' The threat that Bond's initiative would pose to further Canadian negotiations with Washington was a greater cause for alarm. If the authorities of Newfoundland allowed American vessels to buy bait on the island, Canada could hardly use identical concessions as a bargaining weapon and Canadian interests as a whole would suffer.

Finally, Laurier contended that the 1818 Treaty applied equally to Newfoundland and Canada and that both should have an equal say in its adjustment. '[F]rom the earliest times', he explained, 'the fishery rights of the British colonies have always been treated as one, and that, at no time, has there been any contemplation of separating them.'[13] Laurier had now done everything he could to prevent the proposed negotiation and Canada was obliged anxiously to await the next developments, hoping that the Colonial Office would stall Bond at least until the Joint High Commission could reconvene.

Bond was in no such mood for delay. On March 12, the Colonial Office sent Lansdowne news that the Newfoundland Premier had sent a formal request for permission to negotiate with Washington 'a separate arrangement on the lines of the Blaine-Bond Convention'. In order to apprise the Foreign Office of the situation fully, the Colonial Office enclosed a letter from the High Commissioner of Canada. Lord Strathcona's comments dealt mainly with the prevailing opinion in Canada. The 'Treaty, if it went into effect,' Strathcona reminded Chamberlain, 'would prejudicially affect the position of Canada in her relations with the United States regarding the Atlantic fisheries question.'[14]

Bond remained adamant that the discussions should proceed and informed Chamberlain in April that he would initiate talks with Laurier in order to lessen the friction between the Colonies.[15] Later that month, Bond travelled to Ottawa and held an interview with Laurier, strenuously urging the latter to remove his objections. While Laurier continued to stress that the Joint High Commission was the best means of achieving a satisfactory settlement, he knew that he must placate his colonial colleague or risk a breach in the imperial connection. For this reason, Laurier noted, albeit with some reluctance, that if negotiations for the Commission should fail, he might 'then be prepared to have the whole subject reconsidered.'[16] This was encouraging news, provided that the Dominion Premier could be kept to his word.

Simultaneous discussions to remove the French Shore were taking place at the Foreign Office, but had reached something of an impasse. Although there was no question that France could be persuaded to surrender her concessions on the Treaty Shore, the subject of territorial compensation had to be approached firmly, if tactfully, by British authorities. The removal of the Treaty Shore was vital to the people of Newfoundland, but was, in imperial terms, a matter of only marginal concern and the Foreign Office would not consider conceding significant territory to France simply to please Bond. On March 17, Joseph Chamberlain raised the possibility of giving the French land on the Sokoto boundary in Western Africa,[17] but quickly dropped the suggestion once the scale of French ambitions was clarified. It was not Sokoto the French wanted, but Morocco. Cambon urged Lansdowne to abandon British interests in Morocco, to allow the French to consolidate their position in that country.

On March 22, Sir Edmund Monson told the Foreign Secretary of the prevailing sentiment in Paris concerning discussions for the Treaty Shore. 'Cambon has the reputation here of being keenly ambitious of making diplomatic coups', the Ambassador explained, 'but his suggestion of obtaining compensation on the Moroccan frontier for a French abandonment of Treaty Rights in Newfoundland seems to my limited intelligence farfetched and impractical.'[18] Lansdowne had difficulty responding to this suggestion. Not only was Britain loath to relinquish her influence in Morocco, but there were no legal rights to abandon. 'I cannot believe that M. Delcassé can have suggested such a *quid pro quo* as a bargain over territory which England could never claim for herself', Monson noted, 'but which is, probably, the legitimate property of a friendly, if only half civilised Power.'[19]

Greatly disappointed, Lansdowne replied that the prospects of an agreement were 'not at all promising', concluding that 'the pretensions of each side were, it seemed to me, inadmissible.'[20] Chamberlain's response was quite different. Considering that whatever difficulties emerged could surely be overcome, he pushed for compromise. 'If we can agree on the territorial compensation,' he explained, 'I think we might settle the matter.' It was fundamentally important, Chamberlain concluded, that the Colonial and Foreign Offices come to an agreement concerning the territory they would abandon for the Treaty Shore.[21] In the meantime, Lansdowne awaited new proposals from the French Embassy. In October, he reported that Delcassé still 'had not been able to make any fresh suggestion with regard to the question of territorial compensation.' Later that month, a Foreign Office dispatch noted that there was still no 'guarantee of a satisfactory settlement to the Treaty Shore question.'[22] Negotiating a settlement would prove to be a lengthy and frustrating business.

On May 10, Pauncefote forwarded Hay's proposal for the resolution of the Alaska boundary and 'for the settlement of the majority of the other questions discussed by the Joint High commission [*sic*.], not however, including reciprocity and Atlantic fisheries.'[23] As we have seen, Laurier's strong disapproval caused a great delay in the Alaskan negotiations and played a significant part in increasing American-Canadian hostility. While Laurier resolved to wait for the Joint High Commission to settle the fishery question, Bond had become naturally eager that separate negotiations between the United States and Newfoundland should be effected without delay. Laurier still believed that the Joint High Commission had a future; the prevailing opinion suggested that the body would never reconvene. '[T]here is no chance for the re-assembling of the Washington Commission', Minto sadly informed Sir George Parkin on September 9. The reciprocity issue was in a critical state, Minto explained,

> 'the island itself has been flirting with the States re a possible fishery treaty independent of Canada – which the break-down of the Commission will almost certainly oblige the Dominion to object to – as long as there was a chance of the Commission meeting again there was also some chance of a fishery settlement – in which N'foundland might join. Now this chance is gone.'[24]

While there were sufficient grounds for scepticism concerning plans for the Joint High Commission, particularly during the troublesome Alaskan negotiation, Chamberlain made one last effort to determine whether it could be resurrected. A Commission, with the Colonial side headed by a British official, would be the best way to serve all the colonies. Moreover, simultaneous settlements for both Canada and Newfoundland would please the Colonial Office and limit inter-colonial tension; difficult as it was to envisage another sitting, the effort had to be made. In November, an impatient Chamberlain asked the Foreign Office to state 'whether any intimation, not necessarily official, has been received from Washington to the effect that the United States' Government would prefer that the Joint High Commission should not reassemble.' Lansdowne, who had heard nothing and who was vastly more interested in achieving quick settlements that would placate the State Department, simply replied that 'no intimation, official or otherwise, has reached this Office.'[25]

It was the worsening relations between Canada and the United States, caused by the Alaskan negotiations, that effectively extinguished the last hope for the Joint High Commission. By early 1902, Chamberlain and Lansdowne agreed that Bond's proposed reciprocity negotiations should proceed. Chamberlain explained that Newfoundland could 'no longer be reasonably opposed.' In reply, Sir Francis Villiers was directed to state 'that his Lordship [Lansdowne] agrees with the opinion expressed by Mr. Chamberlain ... and concurs in the proposed course of action.'[26] On April 17, the Colonial Office dispatched a confidential telegram to the Governor-General's office, stating that 'His Majesty's Government feel unable to continue to refuse permission for separate negotiation'.[27]

The Canadians, however, would not be beaten that easily. The impending Colonial Conference, due to convene in London in only two months, gave Laurier grounds for requesting further delay. Since 'ample opportunity has been given to discuss [the] matter in London,' Minto telegraphed, 'my responsible advisers submit that Newfoundland should not be allowed to take any such action as is now contemplated.'[28] Lansdowne, willing to leave the question open until the Colonial Conference, made no further approach to Laurier. However, the opinion of the State Department towards reciprocity discussions needed to be clarified. On June 4, the Foreign Secretary sent a dispatch to Chargé d'Affairs Arthur Raikes, stating that:

> 'His Majesty's Government feel unable [any] longer to refuse the application of Newfoundland, but the latter are willing that the matter shall stand over until the approaching Colonial Conference here if an assurance can be obtained from the United States Government that the question of the proposed separate arrangement will be taken up during the next session of Congress'.[29]

Raikes' response was not encouraging. Not only was the President disinclined to give any such promise, Raikes explained, but the Senate's hostility towards commercial reciprocity treaties had to be taken firmly into account. For these reasons, the Chargé d'Affairs thought it the wisest policy not to approach Roosevelt at that time, but rather to sit back and await developments.[30] Lansdowne seems to have agreed to this course of action. The risk of a clash between Bond and Laurier at the upcoming Colonial Conference was a matter of grave urgency and, before making another approach to the United States, this threat would first need to be resolved.

On June 6, Lord Minto sailed for London on the "Parisian" to attend the Colonial Conference and the King's coronation, the latter scheduled for June 26. In his journal entries, the Governor-General complained about the cold and the heavy seas, but was evidently pleased with his travel companions. Amongst the sizeable colonial contingent aboard the "Parisian" were several Dominion Premiers, including George H. Murray of Nova Scotia, Lemuel J. Tweedie of New Brunswick and, most importantly, Sir Robert Bond. 'He [Bond] is quiet & reserved', Minto noted, 'very pleasant, and I should say above the average of public men in Canada.' With ample opportunity to converse about the reciprocity proposal, Minto and Bond 'did not get on to any burning N'foundland questions' during the voyage, although Bond was quick to clarify his opposition to confederation with Canada.[31]

At his London home, Minto found a letter from Lansdowne, dated June 15, awaiting his attention. 'You will find me at my own house on Tuesday morning', the Foreign Secretary wrote, 'I am most anxious to talk to you about Alaska.'[32] Over the following days, indeed, the importance of settling the Alaskan boundary ensured that Newfoundland's scheme for reciprocity with the United States was hardly discussed until the Colonial Conference began.

In the event, it proved impossible for Laurier to destroy Bond's reciprocity proposal. The hope of another sitting of the Joint High Commission had been all but abandoned and Laurier's ongoing obstructive tactics – both to Hay's Alaskan proposal and to Bond's reciprocity scheme – no longer carried any tangible weight in the Foreign Office. While the two issues were in no way connected, Laurier's behaviour created an association in the official mind and, annoyed with Canada's long-term truculence, the Foreign Office determined to appease the United States in Alaska and proved equally unwilling to impose further delays on innocent Newfoundland. Accordingly, Bond was finally given permission to initiate a reciprocity treaty with the US.[33]

With reason, Canada could complain that her interests, yet again, had been summarily abandoned. Such, at least, was the opinion of Governor-General Minto, writing to Sir George Parkin on September 6: 'most sorry that H.M's Government have consented to separate negotiations between Newfoundland and the U.S.'. Minto then concluded that:

'He (Bond) says he means no discrimination against Canada, but, as a matter of fact, I do not see how he can avoid it, as his bargain will mean that U.S. fishermen will be put on better terms than Canadian fishermen. The advantage may be a slight one, but the pith of it is that the thin edge of the wedge will now be introduced towards a "rapprochement" between Newfoundland and the States.'[34]

On his return from the Colonial Conference, Bond wasted little time before approaching the United States Government. With Hay absent from the State Department, Bond was obliged to approach Acting Secretary of State Alvey Adee on September 12 1902. 'The interview was of a very pleasant and courteous character,' *The Times*' political reporter in Washington explained, 'but was not official, and nothing was done towards opening negotiations regarding a reciprocity treaty'.[35] *The Times* blamed the lack of progress on the Senate's prevailing hostility towards reciprocity, a view that was supported in an official dispatch from Raikes to Sir Francis Villiers, written that same day. Raikes noted that both Adee and Hay were behaving with extreme caution and concluded that Adee,

'used very much the same language as that employed by Mr. Hay on a previous occasion, viz. that the President and the Government were in favour of Reciprocity Treaties and had feelings of special kindness for Newfoundland, but that owing to the attitude of the Senate Hay had for some time given up the attempt to negotiate any new Reciprocity Conventions.'[36]

With Adee promising to inform Roosevelt of Bond's initiative and to await instructions, Bond left Washington on September 13. Upon his arrival in Newfoundland, he busily penned a draft treaty on the same lines as the Bond-Blaine Convention, to be given to Hay on his return. At the same time, Adee, evidently counselled by the President, sent official consent to the opening of negotiations between the two countries:

> 'Mr. Adee addressed a note to me on the 26th instant,' Raikes informed the Foreign Office on September 30, 'stating that the United States' Government would be glad to receive and consider any proposition Sir Robert Bond had to make. I, therefore, at Sir Robert Bond's request, have communicated to Mr. Adee a draft Convention ... for the improvement of commercial relations between the United States and His Britannic Majesty's Colony of Newfoundland.'[37]

Hay quickly approved Bond's draft, which, like the Blaine-Bond Convention, gave to American fishermen the right to buy bait and other supplies in Newfoundland and to buy and sell both fish and oil in that colony. Selected raw materials and manufacturing produce from the United States would also be admitted into Newfoundland free from duty. In return, no tariff would be imposed on Newfoundland's fishing and mining produce entering the United States.[38] Despite angry protests from the North-eastern States, Hay initially refused to yield. Opposition to reciprocity centred around the port of Gloucester in Massachusetts, whose advocate was Senator Robert Gardner, Lodge's son-in-law. Worried about the damage that a reciprocity treaty with Newfoundland would have on Gloucester's fishing trade, Lodge and Gardner spent the latter months of 1902 trying to persuade the Secretary of State to change his mind.[39] That there was powerful opposition in the United States to the draft treaty was not secret. On October 8, *The Times* explained that Bond was still in Washington pushing the treaty. 'Favourable action on the part of the Senate, however, is doubtful', the reporter sadly concluded.[40] Lodge's position would be crucial to the future of reciprocity, particularly since, as Herbert informed the Foreign Office in October, the American Government was likely to accept the treaty without delay.[41]

The provisional Hay-Bond Treaty was well received by British authorities, although it did not receive much attention compared to the ongoing Alaskan negotiation. Indeed, there is little evidence to suggest that either Chamberlain or Lansdowne, preoccupied and anxious about Alaska, gave the subject much attention. Accordingly, the reciprocity issue was allowed to run its course. 'Mr. Chamberlain sees no objection to the terms of this Convention', a Colonial Office clerk noted on October 17.[42] On the following day, Lansdowne gave official permission to the British Ambassador in Washington to sign the draft Convention, with a significant proviso:

> 'You should inform Sir R. Bond that His Majesty's Government have had much pleasure in authorising the completion of the Convention, as they rely upon the assurance given by him in his letter of the 25th April, 1901, that Great Britain and all British Colonies ... will receive the same treatment as the United States of America, both as regards bait and import duties.'[43]

Hay and Herbert signed the reciprocity treaty on November 8 1902 without much hope that it would satisfy anyone except Bond and his Government. 'I presume your Ministers do not approve of it,' Herbert told Minto the same day, 'but it will benefit Newfoundland if it passes the Senate, which is doubtful unless Lodge withdraws his opposition.'[44] Lodge's anger remained unabated: determined to bring an end to reciprocity, he ensured that the case for Gloucester and New England fisheries was presented to the Senate.[45] In the meantime, delegations from Maine and Massachusetts arrived at the State Department on December 17 to voice their strong criticism. Hay was overwhelmed. The 'Treaty has now no chance of passing the Senate,' he now told Herbert. 'I [Herbert] asked him whether any further concession on the part of Newfoundland would mend matters and he replied in the negative.'[46]

Suddenly, the significance of Lodge's opposition – and the impossibility of securing an agreement without his support – was fully appreciated. On December 20, Bond told Herbert that, rather than see Hay putting pressure on his Government to concede more to the Americans, he would prefer to see his treaty abandoned. In reply, the Secretary of State doggedly refused to give up all hope, but agreed to withdraw the treaty if it became necessary.[47] Until the issue reached the floor of the Senate, there was not much more that could be done.

Since October, no official dispatch had been written by the Foreign Office about the treaty's progress. While the Alaskan difficulty continued to preoccupy the Office's American Department, Lansdowne's silence suggests that he saw the reciprocity issue as a marginal concern and that he was quite willing to allow Bond a free hand. Still more, should the Hay-Bond Convention fail, the result would hardly be disastrous for Britain; rejection would do much to mollify Laurier at a time when Canada's consent to the proposed Alaskan tribunal was so vital. When the Foreign Secretary contacted the Washington Embassy on January 8 1903, it was only to question an unforeseen change in the wording of the final reciprocity Convention, a change that Herbert could not explain.[48] Months of inactivity followed. On April 2, an enquiry from Sir Montagu Ommanney at the Colonial Office asked the Foreign Office whether the Treaty might after all pass the Senate. Since 'no dispatch has been received from His Majesty's Ambassador at Washington on this subject', a Foreign Office clerk replied, 'it may be assumed that the Convention was not approved.'[49]

Now that the Alaskan settlement had reached its final stages, the reciprocity issue was all but forgotten. Only Bond continued to press for a settlement, asking Hay whether he was 'to regard the matter as having been finally dropped?' Hay's reply betrayed both his frustration and sense of futility. 'I regret very much that it is not in my power to predict what the Senate may do with the Convention at the coming Session', he explained on April 24. Herbert enclosed these two letters in a dispatch to the Foreign Office dated April 27, concluding that 'for your Lordship's attention, I venture to express the opinion that ... there is not the slightest chance of the Convention being ratified by the Senate.'[50] For Bond and Newfoundland, it seemed that the Hay-Bond Convention had, after all, been a barren and futile victory over Canada's determination to rule colonial affairs in North America.

With reciprocity at least temporarily halted, the resumption of discussions with France was both timely and increasingly necessary. The Treaty Shore issue was to be a minor part of a general settlement between the two countries and was largely a response to the increasing Russo-Japanese hostility in the Far East. As the respective allies of these aggressive Powers, France and Britain looked to reduce the necessity for intervention, best served by concluding their own agreement. It would be a far-reaching arrangement, designed to settle the position of the two Powers in Morocco, Egypt, Siam, the New Hebrides and Newfoundland.[51]

In the meantime, the arrival of King Edward in Paris on May 1, designed to promote friendly relations, was an unqualified success. Greeted by an unrestrained wave of enthusiasm from the people of Paris, the King spoke of his belief that there 'may have been misunderstandings and causes of dissension in the past, but all such differences are, I believe, happily removed and forgotten'.[52] While the mood of Monson's Foreign Office dispatches betrayed a newly found optimism, King Edward soon urged that the burgeoning friendship should be cemented by a return visit in July from French President Émile Loubet.[53]

In the same month, the Colonial Office drafted a memorandum on the French negotiation to be shown to the Cabinet. Giving his attention to the thorny question of the Treaty Shore, Chamberlain explained that the 'French would clear out if we give 1. Pecuniary compensation 2. Territorial compensation 3. Right to buy bait ... it might be considered in connection with an arrangement in regard to Morocco.' In the interests of a lasting settlement, Chamberlain concluded that the Hague Tribunal might consider pecuniary compensation and even approved a limited concession on bait.[54] However, his evident unwillingness to expand upon the matter of territorial compensation gave fair warning of future difficulty; only through such compensation would France declare herself satisfied and surrender her fishing rights off the Newfoundland coast. Months of diplomatic wrangling followed, without much prospect of success. On December 16, Lansdowne wrote of the serious obstacles to settlement in Newfoundland in a private letter to E. R. Moon, Member of Parliament for St. Pancras:

> 'The idea of bringing about a satisfactory settlement on the French Shore question has always attracted me,' he explained, 'and I have bestowed a good deal of thought upon it. Territorial compensation would no doubt be expected by the French Government, and the Gambia has been mentioned in this connection. I am afraid however that you will not find much support for the view that "it is of little value to us". I find the Colonial Office and the Admiralty would greatly object to surrendering it, and we must therefore look elsewhere. But I do not despair.'[55]

If Lansdowne had not quite given up hope on the Treaty Shore, there was a limit to the amount of territory he was prepared to abandon. A suggestion from Delcassé, that Britain might cede land on the right bank of the Niger was quickly labelled 'quite inadmissible.'[56] Still willing to give France part of Sokoto, this suggestion was quickly and summarily rejected, this time by Cambon.[57] By early 1904, the French Government's demand for significant territorial compensation threatened the very future of the Anglo-French *rapprochement* just when it seemed most valuable. This was unfortunate, since the major principles of the settlement had already been reached. France had pledged her non-interference in Egypt in return for an acknowledgement from the Foreign Office guaranteeing France's sphere of influence in Morocco. By January, the Newfoundland Shore had become the only outstanding issue and the apparent inability for either party to suggest a suitable compromise briefly halted discussions.[58] On January 15, Monson repeated his belief that the French would insist on significant territorial concessions. 'I am afraid from this letter that it will be difficult to acquire a satisfactory understanding', the King ruefully noted.[59] The Prime Minister was equally disappointed, even suggesting that the Treaty Shore question be temporarily abandoned to facilitate agreement:

> 'I am sorry, but not surprised, at the hitch which has occurred in the French negotiations', Balfour told Lansdowne on January 15, 'It would be an international misfortune if they broke down, and unsatisfactory as any negotiation must be which does not include the vexed question of Newfoundland, I would rather that we settled Egypt, Morocco and Siam, <u>without</u> Newfoundland than we settled nothing at all.'[60]

Matters were not quite that desperate. A compromise solution, giving France a selection of territorial concessions in the Gambia, Nigeria and the Îles de Los, was soon accepted by both Powers. In part, the Treaty Shore continued to exist, though officially relinquished; under the final agreement, French trawlers were given equal fishing rights off the Newfoundland shore during the summer season and the Colony's ports were to remain open for bait, shelter and supplies.[61] However, the agreement ensured the removal of French stations on the Treaty Shore and made French fishermen subject to Newfoundland's fishery laws and regulations. While D. J. Morgan's belief, that the 'settlement of the French Shore difficulty will be hailed with the greatest delight by all our friends there [Newfoundland]', was not quite accurate – Bond's acceptance in the St. John's legislature led to a vote of censure – Lansdowne regarded the compromise with distinct relief.[62] On the day preceding signature, the Foreign Secretary told Balfour that Britain was 'at last nearing the end of this interminable French negotiation', referring to 'the Newfoundland–Egypt–Morocco labyrinth' which had caused him so much trouble.[63]

In the final analysis, the long-running discussions had been more than worthwhile. If the Anglo-French Agreements, signed on April 8 1904, had not given Newfoundland everything she desired, they did much to secure Britain's colonial future, both in the Far East and in Africa. Most importantly, it would ensure that neither Britain nor France became embroiled in the Far Eastern war. Replying to Lord Alverstone's note of congratulation, Lansdowne agreed that the Newfoundland settlement had indeed satisfied the Foreign Office, although he concluded that '[w]e have been very near an explosion once or twice'.[64] With half of the fishery question at last resolved, and with the reciprocity question indefinitely delayed in the American Senate, the Foreign Office turned to more significant questions, primarily relating to the Far Eastern war.

The Hay-Bond Treaty still had not come before the Senate for ratification and this was largely due to the obstructive tactics pursued by Henry Cabot Lodge and the New England Senators. While John Hay felt impotent against the Senate and regretted the probable destruction of the Hay-Bond Convention, Roosevelt began to take a more active interest. His private letter to Lodge, written on November 12 1904, beseeched the Senator from Massachusetts to encourage moderation. Roosevelt explained that an 'effort ought to be made' to ensure ratification. 'Do not make the amendments any more drastic than you are absolutely obliged to, and of course remember that the Gloucester people cannot be trusted to establish the minimum they ought to receive.'[65]

Lodge had no such intention. In early February 1905, the Hay-Bond Treaty finally passed the Senate with such radical modifications to ensure Newfoundland's rejection. Everything Bond had asked for had been eliminated, Hay sadly noted on February 10, 'it seems to me as stupid a piece of bad manners as any country has ever been guilty of.'[66] Disappointed and disillusioned, the Newfoundland Government quickly ordered its Customs collectors to refuse bait licenses to all American vessels. Speaking at the opening of the St. John's legislature on April 2, Governor Sir William MacGregor announced further retaliatory measures:

'the Government had decided that it would be unwise under existing conditions and pending the ratification of the Bond-Hay Treaty to continue to grant to American fishermen the privileges conceded in past years, the scarcity of bait rendering it necessary that the interests of the Newfoundlanders should be first considered.'[67]

Bond's intention to end the concessions given to American fishermen by the Treaty of 1818 was soon clarified. On April 15, the Washington reporter for *The Times* explained Bond's proposal 'to substitute an export duty on herring conveyed from Colonial waters in American vessels for absolute exclusion'. Three days later, by a vote of thirteen to three, the Newfoundland Legislative Council approved a Bill barring American vessels from purchasing bait in the Colony.[68] As a final stroke, Bond decided that the long-standing special favours granted to American fishermen should altogether be abolished.

On June 15 1905, Newfoundland formally terminated the *modus vivendi*, which had enabled American vessels to buy bait and other fishery supplies in the Colony's ports. While the captains of these vessels were prohibited from employing native Newfoundlanders, colonial officials were authorised to board and examine the cargoes of American trawlers, and to confiscate both ship and cargo should evidence be found of bait purchase or wrongful employment.[69] Clearly, these reg-

ulations courted serious international complications with the United States. For
this reason, Elihu Root, appointed as Secretary of State on July 7 following John
Hay's death, visited Newfoundland that summer and returned advocating the use
of a 'small cruiser' to protect American interests. However, Roosevelt remained
cautious.[70] Newfoundland's anger was perfectly understandable, he noted on
August 19, 'it is ... mere common sense for us to try to show such patience and for-
bearance as is possible, until the exasperation caused by our very unfortunate
action has worn off.'[71] Similarly, the Foreign Office seemed content to let matters
rest, with MacGregor's assurance, given in mid October, that '[n]o attempt has
been made to stop American fishermen from fishing' in the colony's waters.[72]

Such complacency was both unfortunate and misplaced. On October 13,
Root relayed fresh and worrying information to the American Embassy in
London. The news came from Senator Robert Gardner, complaining that authorities in Newfoundland were forbidding American vessels from catching fish off the
colony's coast.[73] Immediately, the Foreign Office received a strongly worded
protest from Joseph Choate's successor, Whitelaw Reid. 'Your Lordship will, of
course, understand that my Government insist on the rights always enjoyed under
the Treaty of 1818', Reid explained, 'and feels bound to protect our fishermen
against an interference by the Newfoundland authorities'.

Lansdowne was not even aware that there might be a problem and, clearly
bemused, he simply responded by forwarding MacGregor's assurance and stating
his belief 'that the reports which reached the United States' Government are the
result of a misapprehension as to the facts of the case.'[74] A lengthy dispatch from
Root to Durand gave the counter case. The Secretary of State, reported to be
'looking very tired and worried', commented that, so far as his Government was
concerned, American vessels could ignore Bond's inflammatory proclamation and
continue to fish in Newfoundland's treaty waters:

> 'This is a proceeding which is not unlikely to lead to serious trouble',
> Durand worried on October 19, 'and it shows that the United States'
> Government intends to deal with the question in a very uncompromis-
> ing, not to say aggressive spirit. I have been told by more than one
> American that Massachusetts politics are at the bottom of the whole
> agitation, and that it is being deliberately fostered for election purposes.
> I have very little doubt that this is true.'[75]

Declaring his hope that a collision might still be prevented, Root nonetheless
emphasised the 'real and imminent' danger and urged Britain to act decisively to
control Newfoundland.[76] A simultaneous visit from Whitelaw Reid was enough to
persuade Lansdowne that he should look into the matter and consult his Colonial
Office colleagues.[77]

Together, Root and Durand appeared determined that the dispute would not
escalate into open hostility. The latter's desire to keep the State Department fully
informed was underlined on October 22 when a telegram from MacGregor, just
received by the Embassy, was quickly forwarded to Root. '[N]o Newfoundland

officer is preventing American vessels from fishing on the treaty coast', the Governor wired, 'and ... no distinction is being drawn between registered vessels and licensed vessels.'[78] This was encouraging news, appearing to disprove Gardner's evidence and supporting a view that Durand had expressed in his previous letter, that Massachusetts' Senators had mischievously spread the rumour.[79]

Root thanked Durand for his prompt action and declared that 'nothing could more promote the patience and good temper which we agree to be so important on the part of every one on the treaty coast than a knowledge of the spirit in which the subject is being dealt with by both governments.'[80] At the same time, Lansdowne told Reid that he could be relied upon to 'clear up any misunderstandings' relating to the American Shore.[81]

Misunderstandings or not, Lansdowne was quick to blame Bond for encouraging a crisis, even if one had not actually arisen. It was later acknowledged that, although American vessels had not been refused fishing rights in Newfoundland's territorial waters, they had indeed been ordered not to fish in Bonne Bay.[82] Two weeks earlier, the Foreign Secretary had been unaware that a significant threat existed. Now, Bond's impetuous behaviour threatened the fragile Anglo-American friendship, so painstakingly fostered by the Foreign Office over the last five years. On October 27, Lansdowne angrily voiced these complaints in a private note to Balfour, in which the former explained that there,

> 'is a very ugly little row going on between N'foundland and the U.S. about fishing on the Treaty shore – the former talk of arresting American fishermen. Bond is a very dangerous being. I have begged Ommanney to send the Governor a strongly worded deterrent telegram.'[83]

Colonial Secretary Alfred Lyttleton had already sent the telegram. On October 23, he wired a stern warning to the Governor's office at St. John's. Due to the 'risk of collision' between American and Newfoundland fishermen, Lyttleton looked 'to your Government to take steps to prevent such [a] deplorable occurrence.'[84] Once Bond had been prohibited from continuing his anti-American policy, Lansdowne finally began to relax.

On November 3, he reassured the American Ambassador that there were no real causes for concern. 'Sir William MacGregor has reported to the Secretary of State for the Colonies', Lansdowne remarked, 'that the action of the Colonial authorities would be confined to proceedings against the natives of the Colony, and that no arrests would be made on American ships.' In reply, Reid stated that his Government never had any intention of disputing Newfoundland's right 'to enforce their own municipal Regulations against the natives of the Colony.'[85] To Durand, Lansdowne wrote of the satisfaction with which he had viewed the recent events. It was, Lansdowne stated,

> 'most satisfactory that Root should have been so friendly in his attitude with regard to the Newfoundland Fishery question. I was seriously

alarmed about it. Bond is a very dangerous person, and when … fishermen get excited they are difficult to hold.'[86]

The consideration shown for American sentiment, both by the Foreign Office and the British Embassy, had done much to avert a diplomatic crisis and, provided that the Colonial Office could control Sir Robert Bond, there was every chance that peace would return to the fishery issue until a final agreement might be arranged. Such was the state of affairs when Sir Edward Grey replaced Lansdowne at the Foreign Office.

Over the following years, Grey's actions regarding North Atlantic fisheries underlined his strong desire for American friendship. On September 3 1906, the Foreign Secretary proposed that a *modus vivendi* should be re-established, guaranteeing an end to Bond's anti-American behaviour and cancelling Newfoundland's Act of June 15 1905. Dismissing a strong protest from Governor MacGregor, the Foreign Office went ahead and signed the *modus vivendi* with Secretary Root. Grey's behaviour, however, was strongly criticised in the House of Commons in November 1906 and at the Colonial Conference of 1907. To ensure an amicable end to the long-standing dispute, Roosevelt suggested a reference to arbitration at the Hague, and, on January 27 1909, an agreement for this purpose was drawn up by Root and James Bryce, Durand's successor.

The final award, delivered on September 7 1910, was, in effect, a compromise.[87] Concerning the times when American fishermen could take fish from the Treaty Shore, Great Britain would be enabled to 'make regulations without the consent of the United States whenever these regulations were necessary for the prevention of public order and good morals', but if the United States contested these regulations, the dispute would be settled by an 'impartial authority'; American vessels would be obliged to pay harbour dues, but no more than their Newfoundland counterparts.[88] With this decision accepted by both parties – and approved by both Bond and Lodge – the fishery dispute was finally concluded.

If Lansdowne was keen to settle the fisheries dispute, his diplomacy was essentially reactive and betrayed few indications of a definite policy. Permitting Sir Robert Bond to negotiate a reciprocity treaty, he paid little attention to its terms or its prospects. Preferring that the matter should stand or fall without British interference, the Foreign Secretary was clearly unwilling to support Bond and thereby risk causing offence to the United States.

That the sudden crisis of October 1905 had not been anticipated after Newfoundland's declaration of June 15 simply underlines Lansdowne's complete lack of interest. However, simultaneous approaches, by Lansdowne to Reid, and by Lyttleton to MacGregor, served well to rescue the situation; while the State Department was appeased, Colonial authorities were given stern notice that they must tow the imperial line. As the Foreign Secretary had chosen United States' friendship over Canadian loyalty during the Alaskan negotiation, so he was equally prepared to silence Newfoundland. American friendship was thus secured, but the cost was a significant weakening of the imperial tie. With good reason, Newfoundland could feel that her loyalty had been betrayed. If the adjustment of the French Shore had hardly satisfied the Government at St. John's, British diplomacy on the American reciprocity and fisheries issues served only to highlight her willingness to abandon colonial considerations for the sake of American friendship.

The trade figures outlined in MacGregor's 1905 report emphasised the trend away from Great Britain. In 1888, 44 per cent of Newfoundland's imports had come from the Mother Country while the combined imports from Canada and the United States totalled 48 per cent. By 1903-4, the tide had changed. Primarily, imports now came from Canada (36 per cent) and the United States (32 per cent); British goods now accounted for just over 26 per cent. As MacGregor ruefully noted, 'as regards imports the United Kingdom has come from the first position to occupy the third, and that, too, a bad third.'[89] Even without reciprocity, it seemed inevitable that this trend would continue.

10

Satisfying the Demands of Justice

The Hawaiian Claims Dispute, 1895-1905

IN THE FIELD OF Anglo-American historical research, the Hawaiian claims dispute has not yet found its place. This omission is understandable, if unfortunate. The preoccupation of statesmen and public (and subsequent historians) with the major and most publicised disputes, from the Isthmian Canal to the Alaska Boundary, inevitably reduced the Hawaiian issue to an irritating and frustrating private squabble. Still more, the claims made by British subjects for their ill-treatment after the 1895 uprising on Oahu involved, in diplomatic terms, only a trifling sum. There might have been no need for major reconsiderations of national policy, however, but an examination of the parts played by both Governments during the dispute reveals a significant clash of priorities, as the expansionist sensitivities of the United States frustrated the Foreign Office's determination to protect British subjects overseas. The Hawaiian affair was rare in another respect. For once, it was Britain that took the lead, pressing the Americans to assume their colonial responsibilities. As events proved – indeed, as each successive dispute served to underline – the popular *rapprochement* had no discernible effect on considerations of national interest.

On January 17 1893, Queen Liliuokalani of Hawaii was deposed in a quick and bloodless revolution. Over the preceding two years of her reign, her position had become increasingly perilous. Liliuokalani fought both consistently and angrily against the increasing American influence over her islands so eagerly welcomed by her brother, King Kalakaua. On January 12, in the latest of a long series of hostile actions, the Queen summarily removed the Cabinet – this had been imposed by the Hawaiian Legislature in November 1892 and was largely composed of wealthy men of American descent – and attempted to proclaim a new, anti-white constitution. The emerging revolutionary party, however, could count on American support, particularly in the shape of Minister John L. Stevens at the American Consulate.

As the crisis in Hawaii deepened, Stevens gave much needed encouragement while Captain G. S. Wiltse, commanding the warship "Boston" stationed at Honolulu sent American troops ashore ostensibly for the purposes of restoring order and securing American interests. With Wiltse's men swarming around the capital and surrounding both the Government offices and royal palace,

Liliuokalani had little choice but to direct her own soldiers to surrender and reluctantly accepted the establishment of a provisional government. Without delay, the newly appointed Administration sought the annexation of the Hawaiian islands by the United States. On January 19, a commission left for Washington to sound out the Americans and discovered President Benjamin Harrison and Secretary of State Foster more than ready to consider the matter. The treaty of annexation, concluded on February 14 was, however, withdrawn by the new President, Grover Cleveland, on March 9. Cleveland's abortive attempts to restore Queen Liliuokalani, together with Congressional doubt about the wisdom of annexation, left Hawaiian politics in a state of disarray.[1]

In July 1894, the Republic of Hawaii, headed by President Sandford Ballard Dole, officially replaced the provisional government. Its position, however, was far from secure and, in the following months, supporters of the ousted Royalist regime continued to trouble local authorities. On January 6 1895, a revolt suddenly erupted on the main island of Oahu, forcing Dole to pronounce Martial Law the following day.[2]

As it later emerged, the uprising had been both ill-timed and poorly managed. A group of Hawaiian police, searching for hidden arms on Waikiki Beach, six miles from Honolulu, had instead encountered a five hundred strong Royalist band led by Robert Wilcox and Sam Nowlein, who were even then preparing their surprise attack. After a quick skirmish, and with reinforcements busily marching from the capital, the conspirators quickly fled to the mountains, where they were either captured or dispersed.[3] The incident assumed international significance when, in the series of widespread arrests which followed over the following days, several British subjects found themselves implicated, imprisoned and subsequently deported from the Hawaiian islands. At a specially convened Military Commission at Honolulu from January 17, these prisoners were charged with:

'Treason by abetting, procuring, counselling, inciting and aiding others to commit treason and to engage in open rebellion against the Government of the Republic of Hawaii ... and by attempting by force and arms to overthrow and destroy the same, and by levying war against the same.'[4]

Britain's Consul at Honolulu, Albert G. S. Hawes, soon received a number of letters from angry and outraged British subjects, many of whom were then stranded in British Columbia. John Cranstoun, a shopkeeper, had been arrested and deported without trial. Another such claimant was Volney V. Ashford, who, although born in Ontario, had long practised law in Honolulu. To Hawes, Ashford wrote on May 2 that:

'The disastrous conditions enforced upon me by the Hawaiian Government, and the scandalous and brutal methods adopted by them in enforcing the same [involved] I believe the most gross violations of all law, domestic and international.'

He went on:

> 'The pretense [*sic.*] that the Government ever intended to give me a
> fair trial – indeed any chance, whatever, to defend my-self [*sic.*] – is
> substantially contradicted by all the facts in the history of the
> proceeding.'[5]

Hawaiian authorities, however, were unrepentant and, as order returned to Oahu,
President Dole's attention turned towards legislative defence. Recognising that a
series of claims for compensation would soon be pressed, an act guaranteeing
immunity was soon introduced in the Honolulu Legislature. As Hawes informed
Foreign Secretary Kimberley on March 7, the act would 'grant a retroactive
immunity to all persons who acted under the general authority of the Government
during the late and still pending reign of Martial law, in respect of all their acts
whether otherwise illegal or not.' Hawes feared a dangerous and unlawful precedent that might seriously endanger British interests in the region and anxiously
concluded that:

> 'If such legislation can stand may it not possibly mean that no man's
> liberty or property is secure from violation by an officer of
> Government acting with or without orders from his superiors and that
> no redress can be obtained for illegal acts committed in the name of
> the Government in connection with Martial Law.'[6]

In order to determine how it should respond, the Foreign Office quickly sought
legal advice from the Law Officers of the Crown. Although the 'Government of
any country has the right to request and compel an alien to leave the country', the
Law Officers' verdict went, it appeared clear from the evidence of this case that
the Hawaiian authorities had, in fact, proclaimed Martial Law 'not for the purposes of meeting immediate danger but for the purpose of harassing and compelling to leave the country residents who were known to hold pronounced
Royalist views.'[7]

Strengthened by the Law Officers' verdict, instructions were relayed to the
British Consulate at Honolulu, directing Hawes to present a firm and formal rep-
resentation to President Dole. The British Consul, however, was then suffering
from serious illness, which caused an unfortunate delay. Hawes was absent from
Hawaii at this critical juncture and died in the autumn of 1897. While his successor,
William R. Hoare, travelled to Oahu, Consulate affairs were left in the hands of
Mr. Keary. On February 2 1898, Keary received the defiant notice from the
Hawaiian Government,

> 'that they were unable to admit that any of the persons in question
> were subjected to punishment and for that reason saw no grounds for
> liability to compensate them for either loss of time, injury to business
> or personal feelings during their confinement.'[8]

William McKinley's succession to the White House, in March 1897, helped to solidify Dole's intransigence. The President's personal desire to see the United States annex Hawaii resulted in the immediate opening of negotiations. An annexation convention, signed on June 16, gave to the Hawaiian Republic hope of American protection and the treaty was unanimously approved in Honolulu on September 6 although it initially failed to achieve wholehearted American support.[9] The apparent imminence of annexation, though delayed by the Spanish-American war, gave Hawaii a good excuse for obstruction. As the crucial Senate vote of July 6 1898 narrowly achieved the necessary two-thirds majority by a vote of forty-two to twenty-one, annexation was formally approved and the islands became American property on August 12.[10] Now, in response to Britain's plea for arbitration by 'an international jurist of high standing', to be selected by the two governments or to be designated by the King of Sweden and Norway 'or by some other neutral personage of high distinction', the Hawaiian Minister for Foreign Affairs disingenuously replied on August 10 that,

> 'had the Hawaiian Government continued as a sovereign State it would undoubtedly have accepted the proposal of Her Majesty's Government but that the annexation of Hawaii by the United States having been consummated the Government held that it had no authority to go further in the matter.'[11]

As the Hawaiian Republic became an American territory, so the nature of the claims dispute shifted into the sphere of Anglo-American diplomacy. Although Britain could hope that Hay's influence might help to effect a settlement, this was tempered by the news that the obstructive Sandford B. Dole had been appointed Governor at Honolulu. If the Foreign Office expected quick results, it was to be disappointed. Hay's immediate actions underlined the reluctance of the United States' Government to force the issue so soon after annexation, thereby risking its popularity at a critical period in the political adjustment of the Hawaiian islands. Still more, for Americans still suspicious of Britain's imperialistic designs, it would be folly to aid a threatening competitor in the Pacific.[12]

While Dole duly notified the State Department of the existence of British claims against Hawaii, Sir Julian Pauncefote was directed to urge upon the State Department the pressing need for arbitration. In response, Hay advocated a further delay on October 20 1898, 'while the relation[s] of Hawaii and the U.S. were arranged by Congressional Legislation.'[13] The case was, however, given to the Attorney-General for legal consideration. To Reginald Tower at the British Embassy, Hay explained in October 1899 that,

> 'the Attorney-General had advised the [State] Department that the local Government of Hawaii is primarily responsible for the payment of any valid claims of the citizens or subjects of foreign Governments against the Republic of Hawaii at the time of its annexation to the United States'.[14]

Behind this action lay a set of very particular objectives. On the one hand, the US was clearly not prepared to assume liability for illegal actions committed by Hawaii before annexation. The danger of exposing the McKinley administration to criticism and outrage throughout Hawaii, however, led Hay to adopt a friendly and considerate attitude towards America's newest possession. The US therefore made no judgement on the validity of the claims and refused either to push for arbitration or even to impress upon Governor Dole the importance of a quick and amicable settlement. For this reason, the British claims, so recently dismissed by the Hawaiian Republic, were rather hopefully relayed back to Honolulu in early January 1900 for Dole's 'consideration and determination.'[15]

With the dispute already over five years old, a mood of exasperation and frustration began to pervade the Foreign Office, directed towards both Hawaiian and American authorities.[16] On one dispatch from Pauncefote, Arthur Larcom, Chief Clerk at the American Department, made the following statement:

'We know that the Hawaiian Government are endeavouring to whittle down the claims to an irreducible minimum but that they do not recognise any liability on their part to pay even that! We can only await a further communication from the U.S. Government.'[17]

Despite Foreign Office pessimism, Ambassador Pauncefote refused entirely to abandon the hope of receiving a decisive American initiative in the near future. As he informed Hay on August 14, 'the present status of these claims seem to me to indicate that little if any progress is being made with their settlement'. The prospect remained as unsettled as ever, while 'this long delay bears heavily on the British claimants'. In conclusion, Pauncefote hoped that the State Department might take an active interest and urge Dole to fix a definite date for adjustment and compensation to be resolved. Due to Hay's absence from the State Department, it was Acting Secretary David J. Hill who responded on September 11. Perhaps recognising that the claims would continue to be pressed unless something were done – and that the Hawaiian Government still strenuously upheld the legality of their actions – Hill notified the British Ambassador of a recent approach to Honolulu, that:

'the [State] Department would be pleased if a date could be fixed for the consideration and determination of the validity of all claims filed by subjects and citizens of foreign governments against the late government of Hawaii, with a view to their adjustment if they should prove to be well founded.'[18]

This rather limited and overly polite message represented the extent to which the United States was prepared to push the issue. In response, Sandford Dole was sufficiently impressed to present a formal reply, but nonetheless remained defiant; his report, sent by Pauncefote to the Foreign Office on December 21, detailed the cases separately and dismissed them in turn. '[T]he arrests were justifiable on common law principles, even though [the] complainants were innocent', the Governor insisted. Moreover, 'the greatest diligence was used in the preparation and prosecution of the cases presented to the Military Commission' while 'no sort of harsh or vigorous treatment was adopted. Such force as was necessary was used to make the arrests.' In any case, Dole concluded, a government could not be held at all culpable for actions committed under Martial Law.[19]

Dole's defence was circulated in the Foreign Office over the following weeks. From the busy correspondence that followed, it appears that British officials were taken by surprise and struggled initially to find an adequate response. Sir Francis Villiers raised the subject in a letter to Lord Lansdowne, dated January 12 1901,[20] while Arthur Larcom and William E. Davidson, the Legal Adviser to the Foreign Office, predicted a certain deadlock and agreed to refer the matter back to the Law Officers, to 'ask them whether they consider any further reply should be made to the U.S. Government with regard to all or any of these cases'.[21] When the Law Officers' verdict arrived three weeks later, it presented a strong defence on behalf of the British claimants. Attorney-General Sir Robert Finlay wrote to Lansdowne on February 6 that,

> 'there appears to be nothing in the papers now before me to modify the views expressed in the Law Officers' Report of 4th March 1896 ... Under these circumstances, I see no reason to modify the opinions already expressed upon these several individual cases. How far these claims should be pressed depends upon considerations of policy.'[22]

Finlay's inference, that Lansdowne's actions should primarily be determined by diplomatic considerations, gave to the Foreign Office all the encouragement it required. Armed with eminent legal support for the maltreated British subjects, Villiers now proposed that, as 'the U.S. Government have refused to admit the claims', Pauncefote should be directed to 'further press them diplomatically' and to repeat the appeal for arbitration. Lansdowne quickly signalled his consent, authorised Villiers to contact Pauncefote and, subsequently, wrote personally to the British Ambassador on February 26. In this dispatch, Lansdowne emphasised his determination to achieve either diplomatic satisfaction or international arbitration and concluded:

> 'In the event of your Excellency considering that it is useless further to press the claims through the diplomatic channel, and seeing no objection to this alternative course [arbitration], you should make a communication to the United States' Government accordingly.'[23]

In early 1901, however, negotiations concerning isthmian canal rights preoccupied Anglo-American affairs and it was not until April that Pauncefote was able to raise the Hawaiian issue with John Hay. As he explained on April 9, the members of His Majesty's Government were still 'unable to modify their views', and requested the United States either to grant compensation or to refer the matter to arbitration by an independent jurist.[24] Hay's response, simply forwarding a copy of the Ambassador's letter to Honolulu for Governor Dole's attention, was as predictable as it was disappointing.[25]

Claims made by several American citizens expelled from South Africa for their alleged complicity with the Boers changed the situation completely. First learning of the existence of the Hawaiian claims on January 12, Lansdowne had been quick to see the parallel and noted that the case, 'seems in many respects analogous to that of the S[outh] African "undesirables" our rôle being in this instance that of the claimants.' Accordingly, the Foreign Secretary hoped that 'we are not using any language which might be quoted against us in the S[outh] African controversy.'[26] In a significant memorandum, drawn up by David Hill and given to Ambassador Pauncefote on May 3, the two controversies were decisively linked. Hill provided the following suggestion:

> 'The British Government dissents from the report by Governor Dole of Hawaii of non-liability on account of the claims of British subjects for expulsion from Hawaii ... and proposes arbitration. Would His Majesty's Government be willing to submit to arbitration not only these claims, but the claims of American citizens recently expelled from South Africa by British authorities? The claims are of the same general character, and the common arbitration of both groups of claims would relieve both Governments of possible embarrassment, and at the same time satisfy the demands of justice.'[27]

It was for reasons of self-interest alone, then, that the United States took an active interest in the Hawaiian dispute. At last approving intervention, the Department of State began to exert strong pressure on Governor Dole and was pleased to inform the British Ambassador on June 14 that the Hawaiians had been brought to reason. It had 'now received the assent of the Hawaiian Government to the plan and awaits the reply of the British Embassy to the proposition to submit [the two issues] to a common arbitration.'[28]

In an apparently abrupt reversal, it was now Britain's turn to reject arbitration. While there was no particular reason to fear Anglo-American adjustment on valid claims emanating from the South African conflict, the precedent it would set might oblige Britain to enter into long and bitter arbitration with the many other Powers whose nationals had received similar treatment during the war. More to the point, a British Commission had already begun the process of deliberation upon a large selection of individual cases (and later gave the American claimants a lump sum of £6,000).[29] As one Foreign Office official noted, the American proposal 'comes too late to be of use.'[30]

Accordingly, Sir Francis Villiers directed Pauncefote to 'request that the question of the Hawaiian claims may be considered apart' and 'on its own merits'.[31] Without the hope of a reciprocal arrangement, however, the State Department immediately reverted to it policy of non-interference in Hawaiian affairs, thereby allowing Sandford Dole to relinquish his rather reluctant acceptance of arbitration. On July 31, Villiers explained the situation to William Hoare at the Honolulu Consulate and could only remark that the claims were 'still under their [the Americans] consideration'.[32] What little hope now existed for agreement soon vanished. The verdict delivered by the Commission into South African claims gave Pauncefote a suitable opportunity in January 1902 to repeat his hope that arbitration on the Hawaiian dispute 'might now receive the assent of the United States Government.' As an intermediary, unfortunately, the State Department was still proving to be rather unsatisfactory and its friendly suggestion to Dole, that he might take 'a similar course' and that 'a solution satisfactory to the Government of Hawaii and Great Britain might be reached', was far too easily repulsed.[33]

Dole's arrival in Washington in the spring of 1902 allowed Embassy officials a rare opportunity for direct negotiation. Pauncefote promised that he would speak with the Hawaiian Governor 'to renew [the Foreign Office's] proposal with a view to a prompt decision', but the Ambassador's ill-health left Chargé d'Affaires Arthur Raikes to conduct the interview.[34]

It was Raikes' intention to see Dole first, sort out some preliminary issues and then bring Hay into the discussion just when his weight were needed. While he succeeded in his first objective – the interview finally took place on April 22 – the Governor's rapid departure from Washington prevented a definite agreement between all three interested parties.[35] Yet more disappointing, the results of the solitary meeting were far from satisfactory. As Raikes later reported to Arthur Larcom, he had seen Dole,

> 'under the impression that something might be settled. I was disap-pointed to find that Mr. Dole entirely disclaimed any authority to give an answer. He said the decision must rest with Mr. Hay.'

Raikes continued:

> 'Personally he seemed to think that some American might be found in Washington or New York to whom our Government and the Hawaiian Government would be willing to refer the claim for settlement but he said that in any case the sanction of the Hawaiian Legislature would have to be first obtained and that it only met every other year, and would not meet for a considerable time. ... Governor Dole based his objections to arbitration on the ground of expense.'[36]

Who, then, controlled Hawaii's international responsibilities? Since 1899, Hay had maintained that the resolution of the outstanding claims was strictly a Hawaiian affair (although he was briefly prepared to take a more active role to support the South African claimants), while Dole's ardent refusal to acknowledge Hawaiian authority left the chances of settlement in considerable doubt.

It was not until January 1903 that the Foreign Office received the details of the interview between Raikes and Dole. The British Chargé d'Affaires, together with Pauncefote, considered that 'there was nothing to report' and it was only Lansdowne's enquiry to Sir Michael Herbert on November 29 that inspired Raikes to send an account of the meeting with Dole.[37]

By that time, the Hawaiian dispute had taken yet another predictably unpredictable turn. On February 17 1903, Herbert unexpectedly received some extremely promising information from the State Department, indicating that Governor Dole had approved the appointment of a judiciary Commission to resolve the long-standing claims once and for all. The Commission was to sit in Honolulu and would deliver a fully binding verdict, thereby ending the dispute with a single stroke.[38] From Hawaii five days later, William Hoare confirmed that the suggestion had indeed been made. To Herbert, the British Consul reported Dole's recommendation,

'providing for a Commission of three persons who shall have authority to hear and determine all political claims of citizens of foreign Powers arising under the status of martial law in the year 1895, ... the decision of a majority of such Commission to be final and obligatory on the parties.'

Hoare, left entirely without instructions, naturally concluded that Britain's consent to the proposal must already have been delivered.[39] Accordingly, he relayed detailed facts of the British claims to Dole on March 9 and announced that Britain would accept a total compensation sum of around £6,400.[40] In the meantime, however, the Foreign Office was continuing to act with considerable caution. On Herbert's dispatch of March 9, which relayed the news that the Hawaiian Governor's proposal had now been given to the Honolulu Legislature, Arthur Larcom noted that:

'H[is] M[ajesty's] Gov[ernment] have not concurred, nor been asked to concur, in the app[ointment] of a Commission. What they asked for was Arbitration. This should perhaps be pointed out for Consul Hoare's information.'[41]

In part, it was the nature of Dole's Commission that worried the Foreign Office. It should also be remembered that, in early March 1903, Britain was still reeling from the American appointments to the Alaska Tribunal that Theodore Roosevelt had announced on February 18. The Foreign Office, albeit reluctantly, was prepared to accept the appointments in order to resolve a dangerous source of Anglo-American friction, but similar action was not even contemplated to resolve the Hawaii issue. 'I think we should ask Sir M. Herbert to make enquiries as to the exact nature of the proposed Commission', Villiers noted on March 9. 'We could hardly agree to accept the decision of a majority of 3 Americans as "final and obligatory".'[42]

A dispatch with this aim was quickly sent to Washington and, meeting the Secretary of State the following month, Herbert subsequently received a lengthy note on April 20, which defended both Dole's proposal and United States' policy throughout the claims dispute. Hay argued that,

> 'a more full and satisfactory ascertainment of the facts can be gained on the ground where the claims arose, and the British Government or the claimants acting by counsel will be enabled to make [a] full presentation of the merits of their cases before the Commission, this probably leading to a satisfactory solution'.

More importantly, American support for Dole's initiative was based on the Attorney-General's decision,

> 'that these claims, so far as valid, were primarily a liability of Hawaii ... and it was the desire to avoid any complication which might arise by independent treatment of the matter by the United States Government, that the claims were referred to the insular government for adjustment'.[43]

Larcom, for one, was unimpressed with this argument. 'The reasons for the app[ointment] of a Commission appeal rather to the U.S. than to H[is] M[ajesty's] Gov[ernment], or the claimants', he remarked cynically, 'and the "probability" of "a satisfactory solution" is I fear remote.' Nonetheless, both Lansdowne and Sir Francis Villiers concurred with Larcom's suggestion that Britain should await Hawaii's next move before delivering her response.[44] In the meantime, Hoare's proposal, that Britain might request further compensation and interest for the long delay, was summarily rejected for the offence it would give the American Government.[45]

It was now time for the Foreign Office to determine whether it should accept the Hawaiian proposal or hold out for arbitration. Over the following weeks, Larcom and William Davidson drew up several notes on the subject. In the absence of a satisfactory assurance from Hawaii, that the Claims Commission would be both impartial and truly judicial, the Foreign Office was initially inclined to submit a formal protest against the provision guaranteeing finality.[46] Much discussion followed. 'If we accept the Commission as constituted', Larcom remarked on May 18, 'as a suitable means of adjusting these claims we must, I think, accept the provision – which is in itself reasonable – that its decision shall be final.'[47] In the last instant, it was a question of trust and, over the preceding eight years, Hawaiian authorities had done little to inspire confidence; the verdict of a purely Hawaiian Commission would, then, be at least open to question.

No doubt agreeing with Larcom's assessment, Davidson felt obliged to renew the parallel between the treatment of the Hawaiian and South African claims; as Britain had used national courts to adjust the latter cases, she could hardly complain if Hawaii undertook the same course. Rejecting Dole's scheme, which had wholehearted American backing, would thus smack of bad-faith whilst indefinitely delaying the possibilities of settlement. 'Can we object in view of the manner in which we dealt with S[outh] African claims?' Davidson enquired on May 26.[48] Preoccupied with the Alaskan negotiation and with Russian activities in Manchuria, neither Lansdowne nor Villiers had the opportunity to enter into the discussion, so the final decision was inevitably delayed. Had the Hawaiian Government pressed ahead with the proposed Commission however, the evidence suggests that it would have received reluctant British assent.

Unbeknownst to the Foreign Office, the Hawaiian Legislature had already decided the issue. Hoare ruefully reported to Sir Michael Herbert on May 13 that the House of Representatives had adopted a motion 'that the bill [sic.] ... be laid aside indefinitely', due both to 'the opposition the Bill had met with, and also on account of the pressure of other important business.' In conclusion, the British Consul gave the following accurate prediction.

> 'This will have the effect of postponing the consideration of any Bill in connection with the matter for two years, for the regular Session of the Legislature of sixty days, in which it might have been possible to pass a Bill, has expired'.[49]

Once the contents of Hoare's letter became known, British faith in Hawaii (and in the United States as an intermediary) fell yet further. Without much optimism about the chances of success, Larcom now asked whether further directions should be sent to the British Embassy 'to urge again the expediency of the claims "being referred to the arbitrament of an independent Jurist of high repute."' 'I think so', Villiers simply replied.[50] Probably aware that the same ineffectual moves were being played out, Arthur Raikes nonetheless dutifully penned the request on July 5 and, as expected, John Hay dodged the question of American responsibility eleven days later. 'I beg to say that a copy of your note has been forwarded to the Governor of Hawaii for his consideration', Hay explained.[51]

Diplomacy on the Hawaiian issue, although outwardly amicable, had become both awkward and strained and Larcom's despairing comment – written on the bottom of Raikes' dispatch – served as a suitable epitaph for the whole affair. 'The 'vicious circle' recommences with a further reference to Hawaii', he explained sadly. 'We can only wait.'[52]

The diplomacy of the Hawaiian claims dispute provides an alternative view of the condition of the Anglo-American relationship at the time of Lansdowne's tenure at the Foreign Office. This awkward incident, from which the United States consistently endeavoured to distance itself, reached its zenith during the final stages of the Alaskan negotiations and then summarily vanished from view. While it never threatened to impair Anglo-American relations, the Hawaiian dispute highlighted a clear set of international priorities. On the one hand, the Roosevelt Administration, although keen to force the issue in Alaska, was rather touchy on the subject of its own imperial possessions. Accordingly, it pursued a consistent policy of politely deflecting British enquiries and maintained a dignified, if friendly distance.[53] The motives of the Foreign Office were rather more complex.

Defending the interests of British subjects abroad was naturally a major concern and, while the claims themselves involved only a small sum, the Foreign Office regarded the Hawaiian dispute in an extremely serious light. Until mid 1903, Lansdowne steadily supported the claimants' right to compensation, without, however, strongly pressing the issue. Essentially reactive, the appeals to the United States were both infrequent and repetitive, while expressions of protest or indignation were carefully omitted: the very last thing the Foreign Secretary wanted was another acrimonious dispute with the United States at a time of increasing Anglo-American cordiality. As British diplomacy on the Behring Sea and Newfoundland issues also proved, the interests of the Empire – and of its subjects – were consistently upheld, provided that they posed no serious risk to the critical Anglo-American *rapprochement*.

In April 1905, the question of British claims briefly re-emerged in the Honolulu Legislature. A Senate resolution, as reported in the *Pacific Commercial Advertiser* of April 7, called for further information relative to the claims dispute. In response, D. P. Isenbery confirmed that there had been no progress since 1903.[54] If the opening of the 1905 legislative session brought a new opportunity to press the claims, there is no evidence that either Lansdowne, Sir Mortimer Durand or the newly appointed Consul, R. B. Layard, gave any thought to renewed appeals for arbitration.[55] Preoccupied with a complex and fearful situation in the Far East, British diplomacy in the Western Hemisphere became rather less significant after 1903. News of the international struggle for power in the Far East – and especially the dangerous Russo-Japanese rivalry – was received in both Britain and the United States with extreme disquiet and it is to Far Eastern matters that we shall now turn.

Side by Side on the World Stage

11

Diplomatic Duel

The China Issue, 1901-February 1904

LANSDOWNE'S AMERICAN DIPLOMACY gained added dimensions in the Far East. While his actions concerning Western Hemispheric issues had largely been an attempt to solidify Anglo-American friendship – the Foreign Secretary, to use his own phrase, wanted to 'give us [a] clean slate' – Britain's involvement with the United States in the East was inspired by a far grander aim. Fearful lest aggressive nations might turn their attentions towards Britain's scattered imperial possessions, affairs in the Orient became a prime international concern for the Salisbury and Balfour Administrations. Against the growing Russian shadow, Britain's special interests in Persia, Tibet and Afghanistan were hardly secure. 'My own *prima facie* apprehension is that Persia will certainly choose Russia rather than England to follow', Salisbury explained on September 30 1901, 'because Russia can do her the greatest amount of harm and that if ... Russia [starts] the diplomatic duel, (which is at all events very possible) and we do nothing, it will seem a lame and impotent conclusion.'[1] It was, however, Indian and Chinese affairs that would gain a predominant position in the Unionists' defensive strategy. Indian defence was an imponderable puzzle for, as Balfour explained to the Foreign Secretary on December 12 1901,

> 'The weakest spot in the Empire is probably the Indian frontier. In a war with Russia our military resources would be strained to the utmost to protect it, and while the progress of events strengthens the position of Russia for aggressive purposes in this part of the world, no corresponding gain is possible on the side of defence. A quarrel with Russia anywhere, about anything, means the invasion of India and, if England were without allies, I doubt whether it would be possible for the French to resist joining the fray. Our position would then be perilous.'[2]

The situation in China was more complex. Against the great Powers, this huge, yet weak nation sadly recognised its impotence and, in 1897 and 1898, Germany, Britain and Russia each gained control of a Chinese port: Kiao-Chow, Wei-hai-Wei and Port Arthur. The ensuing struggle to acquire concessions resulted in further losses to China's integrity. Widespread international hostility seemed inevitable as the apparent disintegration of China opened the door for a dangerous scramble for territory and the establishment of competing spheres of influence. In June 1900, a bloody, anti-foreign revolt sparked in Peking and quickly spread. Openly favoured by the Dowager Empress, a secret society known as the Boxers vented their anger by laying siege to the Legation sector, destroying foreign property and murdering the Chancellor of the Japanese Legation and the German Envoy. In response, an international contingent of over fifteen thousand men under the command of the German Field Marshall Count Alfred von Waldersee was sent to save the trapped foreign nationals. Its total success, however, did little to ease the situation. With the rapid re-establishment of order in Peking, the Powers were reluctant to abandon the stranglehold over China and, as the military contingents suspiciously faced one another, they began to consider their next moves.

Lord Salisbury had little interest in the further partition of China. In the summer of 1900, Britain attempted to consolidate her sphere of influence in the Yangtze Valley, but that region, coupled with commercial concessions, was considered a sufficient prize. Above all, it was vital to Britain's Eastern trade that the growing foreign influence in China should not result in her disintegration.[3] For this reason, Britain searched for allies who might join her in guaranteeing Chinese integrity. The Anglo-German agreement of October 17 1900 had this specific purpose. Both Powers pledged their support for open commerce in China without, however, committing themselves to the necessary defensive duties. The first Article contained a rather oblique promise that 'the two Governments agree on their part to uphold the same for all Chinese territory as far as they can exercise influence.'[4]

Whatever utility the arrangement actually possessed was soon thrown into doubt when, to prevent a conflict with Russia, Germany declared that the agreement could not apply to Manchuria; the inherent inadequacy of a Far Eastern agreement with Germany was thus made perfectly evident. Cynical of German designs and of her willingness to oppose the Tsar, Salisbury told the Indian Viceroy, Lord Curzon, that Germany 'is always rather inclined to curry favour with Russia by throwing us over ... my faith in her is infinitesimal.'[5]

Since both Germany and Russia were clearly either hostile or untrustworthy (and their respective allies – Italy, Austria and France – were no more approachable) and since Japan was still then largely an unknown factor, the Americans remained the only suitable ally. There were good reasons for optimism. Although traditionally shunning entanglement in Far Eastern politics, the State Department had recently assumed a more active interest in Chinese affairs. John Hay's 'open door' notes of September 6 1899 and July 3 1900, circulated to the major Powers, stressed the deep concern with which the United States regarded China's territorial and commercial future. In his second note, framed as an immediate response to the Boxer crisis, Hay outlined America's Chinese policy, which was,

'to seek a solution which may bring about permanent safety and peace to China, preserve Chinese territorial and administrative entity, protect all rights guaranteed to friendly powers by treaty and international law, and safeguard for the world the principle of equal and impartial trade with all parts of the Chinese Empire.'[6]

During the military operations of mid 1900, British and American forces temporarily had worked in harmony, together with the Japanese: one British official in Tientsin told Lansdowne that the detachments 'have worked as if they had been one army.'[7] No more than a temporary expedient, however, the State Department determined to stand alone once the troubles were over. Thus, the notion that the United States might continue to act in co-operation with other interested nations was barely considered in Washington and even Hay, a committed Anglophile, recommended that America should act 'singly and without the cooperation [*sic*.] of other powers.'[8] Hay realised that neither the Senate nor public opinion would approve wholehearted intervention, which might involve the United States in a costly Eastern conflict. To Whitelaw Reid, he remarked that,

> 'we are to limit as far as possible our military operations in China, to withdraw our troops at the earliest day consistent with our obligations, and in the final adjustment to do everything we can for the integrity and reform of China, and to hold on like grim death to the open door'.[9]

America's refusal to adopt a firm position in the Far East naturally disappointed both the Foreign Office and the Cabinet. In that region, British and American interests, so far as they could see, were identical and, more importantly, Anglo-American co-operation in China would deter even the most rapacious Powers from tearing the country apart. Lansdowne recognised the utility of an Anglo-American partnership in the Far East, while Britain's dreams of such an alliance gained momentum once Arthur Balfour succeeded Salisbury as Prime Minister. However, from the negotiations in Peking following the Boxer uprising to the conclusion of the Russo-Japanese war in September 1905, British and American actions would rarely follow the same path. Despite their similarity of outlook in the Far East, there were always good reasons against even temporary unity. As events would prove, it was one thing to clean the slate in the West, but an apparently impossible task to turn the burgeoning Anglo-American sympathy into a genuine and functional partnership. 'As to American policy in the Far East,' Sir Claude MacDonald, Britain's Minister in Japan, explained in February 1901, 'judging from my Chinese experiences there was a great deal of personal friendship but they left us to fight all the battles, and make ourselves generally disagreeable to the Chinese and they endeavoured to reap the benefits for themselves.'[10]

The international rivalries in China, from the aftermath of the Boxer rebellion to the outbreak of the Russo-Japanese war will be examined in this chapter. In particular, a number of proposed approaches to the United States' Government raised by Lansdowne and Balfour between April 1903 and February 1904 have hitherto received insufficient attention and will be considered in the light of Britain's strategic thinking and international anxieties.

In the wake of the Boxer uprising, diplomatic and political affairs in China were in a state of general chaos. The question of the indemnity that China should be obliged to pay did little to end the diplomatic tension. Instead, the discussions at Peking merely highlighted China's weakness and increased the desire for further concessions, while foreign armies remained stubbornly present. For his part, Lansdowne appreciated the dangers involved in the prolonged occupation of China. 'What we have to fear is not so much overt acts of aggression as insidious and gradual encroachments', he told Salisbury in July 1901.[11] Lansdowne's personal desire to facilitate withdrawal had been expressed as early as August 1900, immediately after news of the rebellion's demise reached the War Office. To Lord George Hamilton, Secretary of State for India, Lansdowne remarked on August 31 that '[m]y impression is that we ought to withdraw from Peking'. That same day, Lansdowne told Salisbury that he was 'anxious both for the present and the future'. It was 'obvious that international complications are likely to arise from the rivalries and jealousies of the Nationals of the different Powers.'[12]

As the stalemate continued, the Treasury strongly urged the evacuation of British troops to reduce military expenditure. Without the concurrent departure of the Russian, French and German troops, however, Lansdowne was not disposed to act. 'I am as anxious as you are to get away from China', he told Hicks Beach on April 7 1901, but Britain must 'bring about a situation which will enable us to withdraw without discredit.'[13] By September, Lansdowne conceded that at least some British forces would have to remain in China, until the 'outlook becomes better', holding little hope of a quick settlement. Adopting a policy of gradual withdrawal, the Foreign Secretary commented that 'Beach cannot really explain, because we have withdrawn almost with precipitation in deference to his wishes.'[14]

In the meantime, the progress of the indemnity negotiations had a demoralising effect on Britain's representative in Peking, Sir Ernest Satow. The Foreign Office soon received a number of angry dispatches, complaining about the unscrupulous designs of both Russia and Germany and of the inconsistent support of the United States. 'I wish ... that you should know that I thoroughly appreciate the immense difficulty of the task you had to undertake', Lansdowne wrote Satow on January 16 1901. 'The cross currents which affects the Govts. with which we have to deal here, flow not less strongly at Peking.'[15]

The problem was clear. Although the Powers had combined for the same purpose, their aims were vastly different. While Britain, the United States and Japan sought to limit forced concessions and uphold Chinese integrity, Russia and Germany took a less altruistic approach. From the moment discussions began, the Russians exerted strong pressure on China's representative, Li Hung-chang, to secure concessions in the North.[16] German activities were equally disturbing. As Sir Thomas Sanderson explained in March, the Germans were encouraging Japan into a war with Russia, promising Japan Britain's assistance: their 'attitude is apparently to be that of ... dancing round the combatants and ready to bleed whichever is first stunned'.[17]

At the same time, Satow busily detailed the erratic behaviour of his American colleague, Edwin H. Conger. In January, Satow reported that Conger would support him 'if his Government would let him.' Other reports were less glowing, and Conger's tendency to release confidential information to American journalists was a particular cause for concern. The American Minister had recently been offered a candidacy for the Governership of Iowa, and Satow reported that Conger was 'evidently bent on making friends of the American press', adding that 'I do not suppose much harm is really done by all these indiscretions, but it is not agreeable that the whole world should be invited to inspect us in the middle of our diplomatic toilette.' The 'leakiness [sic.] of these people is intolerable', Lansdowne replied, 'and we have to be extremely cautious how we tell them anything at this end. I have said this to Choate with the utmost frankness.'[18]

In all, a general lack of confidence in American Far Eastern diplomacy pervaded British official circles. In mid February, MacDonald wrote to Lansdowne of his fears concerning the imminent distribution of China among the great foreign Powers. '[T]he State Department have not moved a finger', he remarked sadly, 'although the interests – and most important ones, of their nationals are almost as much at stake as ours.'[19]

MacDonald's criticism was hardly fair. Serious, if impractical measures to effect a quick compromise were forwarded from Washington in early 1901. On September 12 1900, Hay had written to Alvey A. Adee, the Assistant Secretary of State that:

'We want to get out at the earliest possible moment. We do not want to have the appearance of being forced out, or frightened out, and we must not lose our proper influence in the final arrangement. If we leave Germany and England in Peking, and we retire with Russia, who has unquestionably made her bargain already with China, we will not only *seem* to have been beaten, but we run a risk of being *really* frozen out.'[20]

Anxious for a settlement, the State Department rather optimistically suggested in January that a Conference of Plenipotentiaries might be established at Washington to solve the indemnity issue.[21] In the meantime, Hay sent William Rockhill to Peking to assist Conger during the negotiations. Rockhill's deep knowledge of Chinese affairs had helped Hay draft his 'open door' notes; Satow welcomed his introduction as 'a great change for the better', a distinct improvement on the ambitious and indiscreet Conger.[22] However, Rockhill's efforts to lessen the indemnity amount to £40,000,000 was strenuously opposed by the German and Russian representatives and threatened indefinitely to delay the settlement. During a meeting on April 25, the total demand of the Powers was estimated at £67,000,000. With negotiations dragging, the threat of further international complications in China seemed inevitable.[23]

Reports received at the Foreign Office during 1901 detailed the aggressive threat to Chinese integrity posed by the Russian Empire. In January, Satow explained that Russia was attempting to gain control of China's railways.[24] Her designs upon Manchuria were yet more worrying. In August 1900, Russian troops took advantage of civil disturbances and seized much of Manchuria, including Niuchuang and Harbin.[25] A secret arrangement was then forced on China, giving Russia effective control over the region. The Tseng-Alekseyev draft agreement, signed on November 10 1900, was publicised by the Peking correspondent for *The Times*, Dr. George Ernest Morrison, on January 3 1901[26] and, although there remained much about the agreement that was not immediately understood, neither Britain nor the United States were prepared to let the matter go unnoticed. Motivated by some feelings of compassion towards the overwhelmed Chinese, both the Foreign Office and the State Department were primarily concerned with the restrictions on foreign commerce that the Russians would impose in Manchuria. Writing to Lansdowne in March, Balfour remarked that 'we could not view with indifference anything which interfered with our Treaty rights in Manchuria, as ... in China, to equal treatment in the matter of trade.'[27]

Four months earlier, Edwin Conger had dispatched a proposal for a joint protest by the Powers concerned to guarantee free trade in the province. 'Since the United States, England and Japan have a practical monopoly of foreign trade in Manchuria', he wrote, 'they might unite in warning Russia against endangering commercial interests that have resulted from treaty provisions.'[28] Hay soon rejected a joint note. Instead, he sent for the Chinese Minister in Washington on February 19 to warn China against concluding an arrangement with the Russians.[29] A copy of Hay's memorandum was given to Sir Julian Pauncefote, who duly transmitted its contents to the Foreign Office. Duly inspired by the American move, Lansdowne soon took the same line; he telegraphed Satow on March 1 with the news that he had,

> 'informed the [Chinese] Minister [in London] that the alleged Agreement had attracted our attention, that I considered it a matter of very serious importance and the description received by us suggested the idea that it involved nor only a temporary and provisional arrangement affecting a part of Manchuria, but the virtual establishment by Russia of a protectorate over the whole of Manchuria.'

Lansdowne was quick to appreciate that this was an issue on which Britain and the United States could unite. Handing a copy of the telegram to Joseph Choate at the American Embassy, the Foreign Secretary explained that '[t]he situation is becoming very difficult to understand. Perhaps you will allow me to discuss it with you at an early date?'[30]

Fortunately, the agitation with which Britain, the United States and Japan greeted the Manchurian agreement forced the Russians to yield. Count Lamsdorf, Russia's Foreign Minister announced on April 5 that the unpopular agreement would be abandoned, although Russia had no intention of immediately evacuating Manchuria.[31] To Sir Michael Hicks Beach, Lansdowne now wrote that 'I do not regard the incident as by any means disposing satisfactorily of the question. But it is something that they [the Russians] have been prevented from making a "back-stairs" agreement with China to our detriment.'[32]

The negotiations at Peking were now reaching a climax. On the indemnity issue, China agreed on May 26 to pay the Allied Powers over £67,000,000 for their expenses during and after the rebellion, to be paid within thirty-nine years. Until the final Award, Lansdowne remained intensely suspicious of the Russo-French combination, but hoped that a temporary coalition of friendly Powers might be created. On August 27, he wrote to Sir Francis Bertie from his Irish estate at Dereen that 'we shall not be able to keep out the French and Russians' and proceeded to recommend that the British representatives should act,

> 'together with the representatives of the Powers whose interests most resemble ours – Germany, Japan, the U.S. – and in all probability we should find that upon many points we were agreed and that a common platform could be constructed.'[33]

Under the terms of the Peking Protocol, signed on September 7 1901, the importation of arms and ammunition into China was prohibited for two years while membership of anti-foreign societies was outlawed and punishable by death.[34] The Manchurian question, however, was left undiscussed. Officially, the Boxer dispute had ended, yet those with an intimate knowledge of the real situation in China were less than optimistic about the restoration of order. A dispatch sent by Sir Ernest Satow to the Foreign Office on August 29 stressed his disappointment and general sense of pessimism:

> 'There is every indication that once the present negotiations are over the policy of demanding concessions from China, all of which tend in the direction of disintegration, will be reverted to ... I am convinced that the signature of the final protocol, so far from ending our troubles, will be but the signal for their commencement.'[35]

Satow's fears appeared justified as the scramble for China continued. At Canton and Shanghai, Satow reported in October, Russia, Germany and the United States were busily acquiring separate concessions. International, rather than separate agreements, the British Minister argued, would slow Chinese disintegration. 'The only way to stop all this "land grabbing"', Lansdowne agreed, 'will be to resort to international concessions'.[36] At the same time, Russian soldiers continued their occupation of Manchuria, although several towns in the province had been reluctantly returned to Chinese authorities. It was easy, in the face of Russia's continued presence, for Britain, the United States and Japan to fear the worst. At Niuchuang, British merchants complained of Russian behaviour and the gunboat "Algerine" was directed – with Lord Salisbury's personal approval – to remain at the port despite Russian hostility.[37] However, the information reaching Sir Charles Hardinge at the St. Petersburg Embassy tended to play down the Manchurian occupation. Convinced by Lamsdorf of Russia's good faith, Hardinge quickly dismissed the significance of the Russo-Chinese convention. 'The Russians want to get the bulk of their troops out of Manchuria, as the occupation is costing them too much money, and every kopeck has to be thought of at the present moment', he told Sir Francis Bertie on October 30. The treaty was 'the only means of an honourable retreat.'[38] Satow and Conger, however, remained anxious. The 'United States and Japanese colleagues have been actively trying to frighten the Chinese about the Manchurian convention', Satow explained. Conger had 'not such definite or strong instructions as I have, but he is disposed to do what he can.'[39]

Although Britain and the United States had pursued their own objectives in China, British officials attempted to create the impression that an Anglo-American joint policy had indeed existed and stressed its significance in the formulation of the final terms of the Peking Protocol. Cranborne spoke in the House of Commons on February 13 1902 of the common policy pursued by the two nations:

> 'All through the difficulties in China we have worked on the most cordial terms with the United States. I think I may say that in almost every crisis, and even in every small difficulty – which has arisen during the negotiations at Peking – the representatives of the United States and our representatives have been acting together.'[40]

Of course, this was mere diplomatic platitude. Although it was true that the United States shared Britain's desire to protect free commerce in China, that both Powers sought to reduce the indemnity and that Satow and Conger had acted closely together throughout the Peking negotiations, it was equally clearly understood that, should a Far Eastern crisis emerge, Britain could not and should not rely on the support of Washington. What 'with the obstruction of our opponents and the half hearted and inconsistent support of our friends', Lansdowne complained in August, 'we could not expect to get much more than we have obtained.'[41]

While he had not abandoned the hope that the Americans would eventually use their influence to restrain Russia's dangerous expansion and protect China, Lansdowne appreciated the need for more immediate support. Against the advice of many of his colleagues, he signed the Anglo-Japanese agreement on January 30 1902. Lansdowne and Viscount Hayashi, Japan's Ambassador in London, first discussed the possibility of a closer understanding with Japan in the summer of 1901; the Foreign Secretary doggedly pressed the scheme to success, despite serious opposition from Balfour, Hicks Beach and Joseph Chamberlain.[42] Balfour was particularly opposed to the Japanese agreement and strenuously voiced his reservation. To Lansdowne, on December 12, Balfour argued that, once the,

> 'momentous step has been taken, we may find ourselves fighting for our existence in every part of the Globe against Russia and France, because France has joined forces with her ally over some obscure Russian-Japanese quarrel in Corea [sic.].'[43]

Balfour's opposition came too late to prevent the agreement. The aged Lord Salisbury, no longer taking a great interest in foreign policy matters, allowed Lansdowne a free hand, while the Admiralty gave the alliance its wholehearted support. 'Such an agreement would, I believe add materially to the naval strength of this country all over the world', Selborne noted in September, 'and effectively diminish the prospect of war with France or Russia singly or in combination.'[44] During a crucial Cabinet meeting on November 6, Britain decided to go ahead.[45] Writing to MacDonald in March, Lansdowne explained that the agreement,

> 'has been criticised here upon the ground that it is much less advanta-geous to us than to the Japanese, and that we may be involved in war all over the world over come trivial incident and because the Japanese want, or may want, to have it out with Russia. I do not believe a word of it. Indeed I thought that in my conversations with [Marquis] Ito and Hayashi, I detected a desire to come to an understanding with Russia as well as with us.'[46]

The problem of Far Eastern isolation was only partly solved by the Japanese agreement. Japan's long-held determination to achieve a dominant position in Korea made her a major rival to Russia and, as such, hardly the ideal partner to ensure Far Eastern stability. In particular, the clauses ensuring the integrity of both China and Korea, forming a significant part of the overall agreement, could potentially throw the alliance into chaos. While Britain was not duty-bound to support Japan unless she was beset by two or more Powers, the dangerous implications of the treaty were not lost in the House of Commons. Campbell-Bannerman voiced his strong reservations while Sir Henry Norman, Liberal Member for Wolverhampton South, stressed that '[e]veryone knew that Japan and Russia have been preparing for war for a considerable period.' These were valid concerns, which Lansdowne personally tended to dismiss.[47]

The support given by the United States to the Japanese agreement, more-over, was greatly reassuring. From Peking, Satow reported that Conger 'thinks it is the most important political event that has taken place for a long time.' To Sir Julian Pauncefote, Lansdowne voiced his relief. 'I am glad the Anglo-Japanese agreement is well received in the U.S.', he wrote on February 25, 'I trust that we shall continue to push well together.'[48]

Despite her promise to evacuate Manchuria,[49] Russian troops continued to occupy the province long into 1903. Over preceding months, the international cries of outrage proved depressingly ineffectual and Russia, spurred by the appar-ently impotent resistance, began cementing her stranglehold in Manchuria. In April, news arrived at foreign capitals that Russia had made a fresh set of condi-tions. Conger reported the demands on April 23:

> 'No new treaty ports or foreign consuls allowed; no foreigners, except Russians, to be employed in the public service; status of administration

same as before; Niuchwang [*sic.*] customs receipts to be deposited in Russian-Chinese Bank; sanitary commission to be dominated by Russians; privilege of attaching wires to all telegraph poles; no territory ever to be alienated to any power.'[50]

Hay at once sent a discreet protest through Robert S. McCormick, America's Ambassador in St. Petersburg, while keeping the Japanese Ambassador fully informed. When Baron Komura saw Sir Claude MacDonald, he stressed the importance of American intervention. MacDonald agreed. '[I]t would be important if the American Government could be induced to stand in line on this question with the Japanese and British Governments,' he explained, 'for Russia seemed anxious not to alienate the sympathy of the American people'.[51]

The events of April 1903 seem to have caught Lansdowne off guard. The Foreign Office had recently entered into discussions with France for a wide-ranging arrangement on colonial concerns. At the same time, Lansdowne was engaged in tentative negotiations with Russia, from which he apparently received no indication of a forward policy. In his minute of April 12, he argued that Russia should not be regarded as an immediate threat:

'I doubt extremely whether the Russians wish to force the pace anywhere just at present – and I don't despair of finding a reasonable solution of the Russo-Afghan difficulty, and perhaps of other tiresome questions which concern Russia and us.'[52]

Within days, the Manchurian issue re-erupted. In the House of Lords on April 28, Earl Spencer politely called for an explanation of the Government's intentions. In reply, Lansdowne asked permission to delay his explanation, as negotiations were then in a particularly sensitive state. 'The matter is one which concerns several Powers', he explained, 'and it would be most inconvenient that while communications are passing any statement should be made, or any Papers laid upon the Table of the House.'[53]

In fact, an approach to the United States was even then under consideration, as Lansdowne sought to create a coalition strong enough to frighten St. Petersburg. On April 28, he sent an urgent telegram to Sir Michael Herbert. Lansdowne recognised that the Cabinet 'while strongly objecting to Russian action would probably refuse to go to war alone or with Japan only as an ally' and asked whether the United States would 'give assistance in certain eventualities.' In another dispatch, Lansdowne explained that if 'the United States Government should decide to press their claims even to the extremity of hostile actions, H[is] M[ajesty's] G[overnment] would take similar actions, although no previous agreement or alliance had been made with the United States Government.'[54] Herbert's replies, however, soon revealed the true state of American feeling.

'I do not believe that the U.S. Govt. would go to the extremity of hostile action over Manchuria', he explained on May 1. 'Hay will do his best to protect American Commerce and keep Russia to her promises, but neither he, the President, nor Congress are ... prepared to go to war if his efforts are unsuccessful. Rockhill ... is in favour of common action between England and the U.S. in China, and he thinks the President might go further than they do at present in this direction. But Rockhill is not in politics!'

A week later, the Ambassador continued,

'In my last letter I stated my opinion that the United States were not prepared to go to war with Russia over Manchuria at present. It is possible however that the people of this country may become educated as to a more vigorous policy in China in the next two or three years, especially if they begin to realise, what they do not at present, the large commercial interests they have at stake there.'[55]

In short, hopes for American interference in Manchuria were wholly unrealistic. Her commercial stake in China was not considered valuable enough to be protected. A letter, sent by Hay to President Roosevelt on April 28, reveals the Secretary of State's deep sense of frustration:

'I take it for granted that Russia knows as we do that we will not fight over Manchuria for the simple reason that we cannot. If our rights and interests in opposition to Russia in the Far East were as clear as noonday, we could never get a treaty through the Senate, the object of which was to check Russian aggression.'[56]

It has been suggested that this approach to the United States, which apparently never got beyond the British Embassy, was a 'fantastic scheme' and that Lansdowne and his colleagues 'woefully misread the situation.'[57] Indeed, if the Foreign Secretary really believed that his proposal might meet with success, he was being somewhat optimistic. While the Roosevelt Administration had shown a desire to involve itself in international issues, and although the President personally supported a strong line in the Far East (he wrote to Hay on May 22 that 'I wish, in Manchuria, to go to the very limit I think our people will stand')[58] an American war with Russia was simply out of the realm of practical politics. Lansdowne probably understood this, but the hostile atmosphere between Russia and Japan forced him to re-evaluate his options and, searching for allies, the United States was a natural choice. Should this fail, however, it would not embarrass the Foreign Office, but merely reaffirm Britain's desire to act jointly with Washington. Most importantly, Lansdowne wanted Roosevelt to understand his belief in Anglo-American co-operation. Should the latter consider that the time was right for intervention, he would have a firm and dependable ally.

The strength of anti-Russian sentiment in the United States was not ignored in Britain. On May 7, the New York correspondent for *The Times* noted that the

American people understood the gravity of the Far Eastern situation and remained steadfastly anti-Russian. 'Nor do I hear a single opinion expressed privately in favour of Russia', the reporter concluded four days later.[59] *The New York Times* took a similar view and suggested that American was strongly, though unofficially allied to Britain and Japan in the Far East. 'The recent and present performances of Russia give us a fair opportunity to 'underwrite' the [Anglo-Japanese] alliance', one article read, 'so to say, so that, for most practical purposes, Russia finds herself confronted with an Anglo-Japanese-American alliance.'[60]

In any case, the anxiety quickly diminished over Russia's presence in Manchuria, and with it the need for military operations in China. On April 30, following a further parliamentary request for clarification, Lansdowne adopted a reassuring tone. Britain had 'received from sources of authority of which we cannot question, information to the effect that the Russian Government has made an intimation that they disclaim all intention of seeking for exclusive privileges in Manchuria.' The next day, he informed the House that he had received a verbal statement from Count Benkendorff, Russia's Ambassador in London, that Russia had no desire permanently to occupy Manchuria. Her forces remained in the province merely in order to extract 'certain guarantees' from the Chinese Government after evacuation.

> 'As for measures which might tend to exclude foreign Consuls or obstruct foreign commerce and the use of ports', Benkendorff explained, 'such measures are far from entering into the intentions of the Imperial Government. They consider, on the contrary, that the development of foreign commerce is one of the main objectives for which the Russian Government have undertaken the construction of lines of railway in that part of the world.'[61]

This was encouraging news. Such comments were welcomed in Europe and in the United States, yet they were received with an equal measure of caution and cynicism. Although Hay took the opportunity to thank Russia for her 'satisfactory declaration' and express his regret 'that there should have been even a temporary misconception or doubt of Russia's position in the matter',[62] there would be no celebration until the Russian contingents were actually withdrawn. Further news of Russia's bad faith soon emerged. On May 9, reports reached foreign capitals that the Russian garrison at Niuchuang had actually been strengthened. Hay now informed journalists that he had been in urgent communication with Roosevelt, then in California 'with a view to further action – even, according to Washington dispatches, joint action, if necessary, with England and Japan.'[63] In the face of such pressure, Russian authorities re-evaluated the occupation, initiated a sharp reversal and began evacuation in May.

During the diplomatically quiet period that followed, the United States began to negotiate with China for a commercial treaty to establish free trade for American business and ensure the freedom of Chinese ports to American shipping. Signed on October 8, the treaty confirmed Roosevelt's fundamental interest in Far Eastern affairs.[64] At the same time, the State Department continued to press China not to yield to Russia in Manchuria. On September 24, Ernest Satow informed the Foreign Office that 'Conger's language to Prince Ch'ing about Manchuria ... was very explicit. He [Conger] has no doubt been pulled over the coals for expressing the opinion that his government is indifferent to the fate of Manchuria, provided they secure the open ports and commercial facilities they ask for.'[65]

The re-emergence of the Manchurian issue in October 1903, though not entirely unexpected, was nonetheless disappointing. On October 29, 1,500 Russian soldiers marched south and reoccupied the Manchurian capitol of Mukden. While Chinese forces in the area, which greatly outnumbered their Russian counterparts, were ordered not to resist the advance and thereby cause a crisis, the Chinese Foreign Office sent appeals to foreign Powers for aid.[66]

China's Ambassador in Washington, Chen-tung, hurried to the State Department to discuss the matter with Hay. The situation was indeed critical, Hay replied, but he was forced to consider the Senate's attitude and was therefore unable to be of any help. If Chen-tung left disappointed, he must have taken great pleasure from the uniformly anti-Russian attitude of the American people.[67] As one British reporter explained, the 'unofficial but authoritative opinion is freely expressed that the action of Russia is arrogant and indefensible.'[68] On December 11, *The New York Times* reported that eight Russian warships had sailed into Korean waters, although Russian authorities strenuously denied the rumour. 'The world had become altogether too well used to Russian diplomacy to disbelieve a creditable story simply because it is officially denied from St. Petersburg,' the article noted.[69]

Negotiations between Russia and Japan, meanwhile, had been taking place in Tokyo to settle their rivalry in Manchuria and Korea. Japan's proposal, that Russia might be given a free hand in Manchuria in return for Russia's recognition of Japanese preponderance in Korea, were submitted to St. Petersburg in August, but received no reply.[70] Such a slight, to a nation increasingly restless to see the matter resolved, inevitably led to talk of an imminent Russo-Japanese war and, with Russia rapidly strengthening her garrisons in Manchuria, Japan could not afford to wait indefinitely for an answer. On November 25, *The Times'* reporter in Tokyo relayed the prevalent anxiety that 'unless a basis of agreement is arranged before the opening of the Japanese Diet on December 6, the situation may possibly be carried beyond diplomatic control.'[71]

By the beginning of December, Japanese journals and business interests demanded a definite answer from Russia. When the reply eventually arrived, its high-handed and unsatisfactory contents merely served to confirm Japanese fears that only by war could the situation be satisfactorily resolved. In both countries, war plans were reaching maturity.

Despite American horror at Russia's bad faith in Manchuria, no aggressive action was contemplated by the State Department. Arthur Raikes, Britain's Chargé d'Affaires in Washington, met Rockhill on October 2 to discuss the worsening Far Eastern situation. 'Mr. Hay would not join in any more general protests or assertions,' Rockhill explained, 'but would prefer to deal with each separate point as it arose.'[72] Six days later, during an interview between Hay and the Chargé d'Affaires, Rockhill's opinion was confirmed. Hay,

> 'said he had been obliged to tell [Takahira] the Japanese Minister here that Japan must look for no help from this country in the event of war breaking out, as no special American interests were involved, and it was only from feelings of general decency that they were anxious to see Manchuria evacuated by Russia.'[73]

American journalists shared Hay's outlook. Traditionally, the United States had seen the Japanese as an uncultured and unsympathetic race. By 1903, however, they had begun to welcome her emergence as a significant protector of open trade in the Far East. 'England ... has contented herself with grumblings at the doings [of Russia]', *The New York Times* remarked on November 29 1903, 'confining herself, in fact, to a policy of pouting.' Japan, on the other hand, 'had so plainly been fighting the British battle of commercial freedom and commercial opportunity in China.'[74] Other reports praised Japan's initiative, but stressed that the China issue was relatively unimportant to the American people. In mid December, Japan increased her efforts to open Yongam-Pho, the main port of Seoul, to foreign trade. *The New York Times* welcomed Japan's Korean policy in the face of Russian obstruction and remarked that 'Japan will have the sympathy of all the trading Powers, particularly including ourselves, since our only actual or possible interest in the Far East is commercial.'[75]

In London, the gravity of the situation was fully understood. Government officials had been carefully watching developments in China and paid particular attention to the progress of the Russo-Japanese negotiations in Tokyo. Uncertain about Japan's military strength and her ability to defeat the mighty Russian Empire, a wave of fearful uncertainty swept through political circles. On September 10, Lord Salisbury – who, as Lord Cranborne, had been Under Secretary of State for Foreign Affairs before his father's death – told Lansdowne that '[i]t is evident that a War between Russia and Japan is on the cards; it is doubtful whether we could remain neutral. If we are to fight Russia in (say) six months, we shall want all the help we can get.' Balfour was in a similar state of anxiety. In October, he wrote to St. John Broderick at the War Office that 'if Japan goes to war, who is going to lay long odds that we are not at loggerheads with Russia within 6 months?'[76]

By December, British journalists insisted that Far Eastern affairs were in 'crisis'. *The Times* predicted on December 22 that the war might commence within days.[77] Naturally, such fears had great credence in official circles. 'What the Russian game is I cannot make out', Sir Charles Hardinge wrote to Sir Francis Bertie. 'I am very suspicious that it is only a game of bluff.' Nonetheless, according to Hardinge, the situation was both 'critical' and 'ominous', and war might be only weeks away.[78] Preparatory measures for a war in which Britain might find herself involved were discussed at the Committee of Imperial Defence in January 1904. In particular, the Committee asked for details of troop requirements and for confirmation of the time it would take British forces to reach the Indian garrisons from South Africa.[79] Those favouring British involvement, however, were in a distinct minority. From China, Sir Ernest Satow voiced his desire to see Britain give Japan her total support. As early as August 27 1903, Satow told Lansdowne that a Russo-Japanese conflict would result in the almost certain defeat of Japan and, more seriously, the irresistible predominance of Russia throughout the Far East. The Ambassador's concluding remarks were explicit:

> 'May I venture to say that to let Japan be crushed by Russia would be a disaster for us also? With our assistance she would have nothing to fear, even if the Russians were determined to provoke her to declare war ... if Russia is victorious over Japan then through we shall not have lost a ship or a man, we shall be powerless in the Far East.'[80]

Amongst Cabinet members, there was considerable disagreement about how best to meet the problem. Since the conclusion of the Anglo-Japanese agreement, Lansdowne had been inclined to support Japan as far as possible. His pro-Japanese sentiments were, however, rather more advanced than those of his colleagues, of whom the Prime Minister and Selborne were the most conspicuous. Anxious to prevent a return to Far Eastern isolation and convinced of the justice of Japan's demands, Lansdowne now advocated a strong line of support. On December 27, he explained that,

> 'we shall be wise to assume in good time the rôle of a protector, rather than wait for an opportunity of playing that of a deliverer. – By shielding Japan at the outset, we shall earn her gratitude, and find in her, when the time comes, an ally of the highest value, full of spirit and courage, and with intact resources.'[81]

December 1903 was to be a key month in the formulation of Britain's response to the Russo-Japanese crisis. Lansdowne continued to stress the importance of supporting Japan, even, as he told Balfour on Christmas Day, if 'such an effort morally obliges us to go further than the letter of the Anglo-Japanese Agreement obliges us.' It was hard to misunderstand such words. If Lansdowne received Cabinet approval, he would sanction armed intervention even if France refused to join the Russians.

In another note, the Foreign Secretary argued that, rather than see Japan crushed or crippled, Britain might 'make a determined effort even at the risk of war in order to prevent this from happening.'[82] The Cabinet, naturally, reacted with great caution. Britain was, even then, engaged in an abortive attempt to bring about an Anglo-Russian agreement[83] and Selborne, with the majority of his colleagues behind him, now sought to prevent Britain's involvement altogether. Japan was militarily weak, Selborne emphasised and, unless she could delay the conflict for a minimum period of three years, would certainly suffer a severe defeat. Worrying about offending Russia, he explained that,

> 'I mistrust the rôle of "deliverer" in this case, but see great dangers in that of a "mediator." You [Lansdowne] do not refer to France at all. Cannot you use France to put pressure on Russia? France must dread war more than we do. Otherwise, I do not differ from your view, but I would put forward France or the United States, and not ourselves.'[84]

Arnold-Forster, newly-appointed at the War Office, voiced his agreement. While Britain 'should help our Ally before she is disabled, rather than when she is crippled and consequently disheartened', he realised 'the weight of objections to this course, and assume for the moment that course of action is out of the question.'[85] Thus the general consensus held that the risks attached to intervention, or even to the active support of Japan, should be borne by other countries and that British diplomacy should remain essentially passive.

Searching for other nations that would be prepared to intervene was no easy matter, but Lansdowne was clearly optimistic that the United States could be induced to act as a peacekeeping Power. Roosevelt would quickly dismiss military intervention, but Lansdowne continued to believe in his diplomatic utility. Upon what grounds he held this hope, it is impossible to say. The United States had given no sign to suggest a contemplation of a more active Eastern policy. 'There is nothing to show that the U.S. contemplate more than a protest [against Russian activities in Manchuria]', one Foreign Office official noted in early November. Sir Francis Villiers added his personal comment. 'They will certainly not do more', he wrote, 'and may do less.'[86] Still more, such opinions were not confined to the Foreign Office. During the Cabinet discussions in December, Arnold-Forster argued that America's diplomacy was simply a matter of 'looking out for a profit on other people's failures.'[87]

Lansdowne's scheme for American involvement was first advanced on December 19. 'For the moment Japan apparently does not desire mediation', he wrote to Balfour, 'but I still think that we should be ready to mediate and that the idea of working through the United States is worth considering; but I should not recommend moving in the matter unless we have reason to know that the Japanese are favourable to the idea.'[88] Three days later, the Foreign Secretary gave to the Prime Minister a definite proposal: 'The U.S. will not take <u>joint</u> action, but it is conceivable that they might take the initiative in such a movement as I have suggested.' This idea was outlined in a draft telegram – which was never sent – to Britain's new Ambassador to Washington, Sir Mortimer Durand. Lansdowne began by explaining that:

> 'In our opinion [the] best solution would be that Japan should throw in her lot with [the] other Powers, and that Russia should be induced to place on record a formal engagement to respect all existing Treaty rights. Such a statement might be addressed, either to the Powers con-

cerned, or to China for communication to them. ... We have noticed
with satisfaction that [the] policy of [the] United States' Government
had from the first been favourable to [the] maintenance of Treaty
rights and equal opportunity for commerce throughout China.'

He went on:

'Communicate [the] substance of this telegram confidentially to Mr.
Hay and inquire whether [the] United States' Government would be
prepared to put forward a proposal calculated to lead to a general settlement on the above lines. If such a proposal were addressed to us, we
should gladly support it, and we should not be without hopes of inducing
the French Government to do so.'[89]

This arrangement was Lansdowne's sole chance of securing British interests in
China without offending either Japan or Russia. Still more, if Russia could be persuaded to acknowledge legitimate treaty rights, her continuing position in
Manchuria would be untenable. Should Britain officially initiate the proposal,
however, she would lay herself open to charges of unwanted and unwarranted
interference.

If, on the other hand, the idea was seen to come from Roosevelt, all such
problems would disappear. Lansdowne stressed, however, that the Japanese should
be sounded out before the telegram was sent, explaining to Balfour on December
22 that it 'would not do to approach the U.S. Gov[ernment] – perhaps successfully
– and then be thrown over by Japan.' At the same time, inspired by a distinct lack
of faith in Japan's military capabilities, Lansdowne still hoped that Japan might
still be brought to her senses and recognise the need for compromise. To Balfour,
he concluded that:

'If either through the U.S. or by any other means Russia could be persuaded to deal with the Manchurian point in the manner which I have
indicated, we should, I think, tell the Japanese distinctly that they must
be content with the best bargain they can get as to Korea.'[90]

The question that must be answered is why Lansdowne's proposed approach to
the United States did not receive Cabinet approval. Such a modest scheme would
probably have been approved six months earlier, yet both Balfour and Selborne
now voiced their strong opposition. In part, this was based on a prevalent belief
that, since Japan had evidently determined on war, Britain should not take any
kind of action, direct or otherwise, that might prove unacceptable to the Japanese
Government. On December 23, Balfour wrote of the suggestion to Selborne,

'that [if] we should get out of the Russians, with the help of the French
and the Americans, something which the Japanese could accept about
Manchuria, and that we should then "tell the Japanese distinctly that

they must be content with the best bargain they can get as to Corea"
[*sic*.] ... we should be giving diplomatic assistance to Russia in her
attempt to weaken Japan's position in Corea; we should profoundly
irritate the Japanese people ... In these circumstances I should let the
negotiations go on or break off as the parties principally interested see
fit. Corea is nothing to us except as far as it affects our ally, and there
is nothing in the letter or the spirit of our Treaty which requires us to
share in a contest with which we are not immediately concerned.'[91]

Selborne sent a similar note to Lansdowne. 'My difficulty in considering your draft
telegram to Sir M. Durand,' he explained in late December, 'is my old difficulty,
viz. that I really do not know what the views of the Japanese Government exactly
are.' Since Japan seemed as determined as Russia to fight, 'do we not run the risk
of gravely offending Japan by suggesting to the U.S.A. even this measure of interference, for Japan is sure to hear of the suggestion?'[92] Lansdowne clearly had not
expected such weighty Cabinet disapproval. Even Chancellor Austen
Chamberlain refused to lend his support to the proposal, remarking that,

'I should ... deprecate any intervention on our parts either directly or
through the United States' Government. If the latter acts ... we can
reconsider the position, but I do not believe that any engagements
about Manchuria made between Russia and China, or between Russia
and other Powers having Treaty rights in China, is of much value apart
from the material guarantees, and I should be sorry to see England
take any responsibility towards Japan for its due observance.'[93]

Considerations of Japanese susceptibilities only partially explain the Cabinet's
decision to take a passive role in the coming conflict. Of equal significance was the
increasing British willingness to see the Far Eastern crisis played out. Balfour listened to his colleagues' fears and promptly led a counter argument; he stressed
that a Russo-Japanese war might not necessarily damage British interests.
Indirectly, Britain might accrue serious gains in the Far East if Russian forces were
destroyed, or at least exhausted, in a long and costly war. In particular, the defence
of India would be a less pressing problem, while the potential defeat of the
Russian navy would allow Britain to reconsider her own naval strategy.

In reply to the King's private letter to the Prime Minister, dated December
25, in which Edward explained his fears that Britain might be drawn into the fight
– '[t]hat we should be engaged in another war so soon after the S. African War has
been brought to a close would be most disastrous' – Balfour countered that,

'a war between Japan and Russia, in which we were not actively concerned, and in which Japan did not suffer serious defeat, would not be
an unmixed curse. Russia ... would have created for herself an implaca-
ble and unsleeping enemy. ... Mr. Balfour concludes from all this that
she would be much easier to deal with, both in Asia and in Europe,

than she is at present. For these reasons, Mr. Balfour would do everything to maintain peace, *short* of wounding the susceptibilities of the
Japanese people.'[94]

The Anglo-French negotiations, then nearing a favourable conclusion, and a
simultaneous approach to Russia lessened the risk of British involvement.[95] Still
more, Balfour doggedly refused to admit the possibility of Japan's total defeat,
since the Russian navy was insufficiently prepared for an invasion on Japanese soil.
Only in Korea could Russia score a complete success. This would, Balfour maintained, be an expensive campaign, delivering little lasting reward.[96] 'Nor am I disposed, without further argument', he maintained, 'to admit that a defeat would
necessarily "deprive Japan for years" of her utility in the Far East.'[97] In a separate
letter to Selborne, he concluded that,

> 'I certainly would not thrust myself into a quarrel not my own, in
> which I am expected to aid an unfriendly Power, and to put pressure
> upon our ally, especially as I believe that if any way could be conceived
> as being advantageous to us, this is one.' It was likely 'to do wonders in
> making Russia amenable to sweet reason. For the present, therefore, I
> should hold my hand.'[98]

Selborne again acknowledged the strength of Balfour's reasoning:

> 'I agree with the Prime Minister that we should not put pressure upon
> Japan to abate her demands. Those demands are so modest and so rea-
> sonable and so necessary for her own welfare that I think we should do
> wrong to ask her to abate them.'[99]

Overwhelmingly outnumbered, Lansdowne had no choice but to abandon his
scheme and await further developments. This was a somewhat galling prospect,
particularly since he regarded the Anglo-Japanese agreement as an important,
even crucial part of Britain's global strategy and was anxious to prevent Japanese
cries of desertion. 'You were good enough to tell me that you thought Japan had
some reason for considering that we had not afforded her sufficient support since
the conclusion of the alliance,' Satow had explained in August.[100] After the
Cabinet discussions of December 1903, Lansdowne's hands were tied even more
firmly and, when Viscount Hayahi, Japan's Ambassador in London, saw
Lansdowne late that month, he encountered an unexpected evasion.[101]

The Cabinet's decision to reject any form of intervention led Lansdowne to
take a new position in line with his colleagues: Britain would not press any advice
upon her ally and neither would she urge Japan to compromise her demands.
While Lansdowne did not entirely abandon the idea that he might, at some later
date, initiate more forward action, he conceded that any efforts to prevent war had
now become useless. On January 7 1904, the Foreign Secretary admitted to
Balfour that the 'Japanese mean business, and I doubt whether anything which the

Russians could now say will stop them.'[102] Meanwhile, at the Committee of Imperial Defence meeting held on January 4, it was agreed that the Government 'could take no action at the present moment in the direction of a threat to Russia or a guarantee to Japan, but that certain preparatory measures, recommended by the War Office, should be adopted in view of the possibility of this country being involved in war.'[103]

On February 2, the new Parliamentary Session opened and preliminary speeches advocated active measures to prevent war. 'I cannot help thinking and hoping that the good and friendly offices of His Majesty's Government have been warmly and courteously given to both Powers', Earl Spencer remarked, 'and, possibly, more especially to the Power with whom we have a treaty – to induce them to come to amicable terms, and to prevent a war which would be so disastrous.'

In the Commons, Gibson Bowles argued that, once Britain signed the Anglo-Japanese agreement, 'if that State should come to extremity, it is impossible to abandon them.' Lansdowne refused to be drawn, simply stating his general and humanitarian feelings for peace. 'I believe it to be an axiom of diplomacy that it is not desirable to offer your good offices unless you have reason to know that they are desired', he explained. Instead, he would wait for a direct invitation from either Russia or Japan, concluding that 'if the opportunity of contributing to that end should present itself, we should be glad and ready to avail ourselves of it.'[104]

Although the Cabinet had already determined its policy, the fear that Russia, by defeating Japan, would achieve a yet more dominant position in the Far East and even facilitate the partition of China was still a widely held concern in the early weeks of 1904. The maintenance of China as an independent Power was, for Britain, of greater concern than a Japanese victory. In fact, British officials recognised that Russian encroachments in China would continue if she won the war against Japan, but also if no war was fought at all.

For this reason, even the prime exponent of non-intervention, Balfour, advocated a more active approach for the protection of Chinese integrity. Reports coming from the Peking Legation predicted that dire consequences would follow Russian success against Japan. Sir Ernest Satow had spoken to Conger, who believed that the 'victory of Russia will be followed by the partition of China. Manchuria will be gone for good'.[105] In the search for an adequate response, Balfour quickly returned to the old idea of American intervention. On February 11, he reverted to the somewhat naive Anglo-Saxon idealism that frequently coloured his thinking and wrote to Lansdowne:

> 'If the Americans would so far violate their traditions as to make any suggestion of an alliance for the purpose of preserving by arms, if necessary, the integrity of China, it would open a new era in the history of the world. It seems all important to induce them, however, to make the first move; if we start it the Senate are sure to upset the scheme.'[106]

This was the final proposal, but a previous draft seems to suggest that Balfour originally wanted Britain to make the first move. In this note, after his remark that the alliance would 'open a new era in the history of the world', the Prime Minister crossed out the fragment 'and we ought to do everything in our power [to bring the alliance about].'[107] Such remarks betray the strength of his belief in the importance of Anglo-American co-operation, yet there is no evidence that the suggestion was shown to anybody except Lansdowne or that it was even mentioned in the Cabinet.

Although Balfour had written that 'all American negotiations drag, so that the sooner we begin to feel our way, the better',[108] the lack of further correspondence on the matter and the absence of any instructions in this sense to Durand suggests that Balfour was content to let his idea lapse. Such a sudden change of heart can only be explained in the light of the war's early progress. The apparent destruction of the Russian fleet at Port Arthur on February 8, two days before Japan declared war, dispelled the spectre of Russian victory. Now more than ever determined to allow Japan a free hand, Britain would not risk foreign intervention that might end the war before Japan effected a decisive victory.

It was just at this moment when the United States raised the possibility of a joint undertaking in the Far East. On February 8, Joseph Choate sent to the Foreign Office a memorandum, penned by John Hay, outlining a fresh proposal. It enquired whether the neutral Powers would,

> 'concurrently using their good offices with Russia and Japan to induce them to respect the neutrality of China and her administrative entity, in all practicable ways to localise and limit as much as possible the area of hostilities, so that undue disturbance and excitement among the Chinese people may be prevented and the least possible injury to the commerce and peaceful intercourse of the world may be secured.'[109]

This was, in effect, the United States' third 'open door' note. It was far less than Britain had originally desired, neither offering a solution for averting the war – which was declared on February 10 – nor hinting at future American intervention. As British thinking stood in February, however, it was a welcome initiative, an encouraging sign of the continued American interest in Chinese affairs.[110] 'I see no reason for refusing our concurrence', Lansdowne told Balfour on February 9, '[i]t seems to me desirable that we should not discourage this overture from the U.S.' Balfour agreed. 'If this is for the purpose of "keeping the ring clear" I quite agree and I should like to please [the] U.S.A. and I understand Japan wishes it.'[111] Significantly, instead of grasping the chance for Anglo-American co-operation as they would have done six months before, Hay's note was meticulously examined. It was given to every Cabinet member for his approval. Even those with little business making foreign policy decisions were invited into the discussion, from Walter Long, President of the Local Government Board, to Irish Secretary George Wyndham.[112] Austen Chamberlain's remarks were particularly interesting.:

> 'I see no objection to this proposal', the Chancellor told Lansdowne, 'as the Japanese have already pressed the same advice on China; but I

venture to suggest that our answer should be that we will support any representations to this effect by the United States. I do not think we ought to act in advance of or without them. The more we can act with them, the better.'[113]

By February 10, Lansdowne had decided to accept the initiative. After conversing with Metternich, he wrote to Sir Frank Lascelles that, provided the belligerent Powers gave their consent, 'the proposal was one which would, I believed, be acceptable to His Majesty's Government.'[114] The unnecessarily cautious approach to the State Department's modest suggestion, however, revealed how timid Lansdowne's foreign policy in the Far East had become.

What became clear was the subordinate position which the desire to please the Americans took (although it was still prevalent throughout the Cabinet) to the maintenance of Japanese trust; the acceptance of Hay's proposal thus became contingent upon Japan's prior approval. As we shall see, Lansdowne's diplomacy during the Russo-Japanese war would further underline Britain's desperation to maintain and consolidate the Japanese alliance. Diplomatic actions during the Far Eastern conflict, therefore, were destined to receive intensive thought, to ensure the continuing friendship of both Japan and America. Personally, Lansdowne kept several crucial dispatches from Durand in a separate file, away from his usual Foreign Office correspondence. Judged too sensitive to broadcast, they 'have not gone through the office and they will not be printed.'[115] Only by such subterfuge could Lansdowne hope to bring Britain out of the Russo-Japanese crisis without offending Roosevelt or the American people and without risking a national outcry that Britain had thoughtlessly provoked American hostility.

12

This Wretched War

Diplomacy, Self-Interest and the Russo-Japanese War, 1904-April 1905

FOR ALL THE Balfour Administration's determination to support Japan through the Far Eastern war, there is no doubt that, in the early months of 1904, Britain was in a rather precarious and embarrassing position. Entirely apart from the gloomy predictions circulating in London that the Russian army would annihilate Japan,[1] the desire not unnecessarily to offend or anger the Tsarist Government was an equally vital concern. While a threat remained to the fragile Indian frontier – and to British interests in Persia and Afghanistan – Russian sensitivities could not be ignored.[2] With a million men in her regular army and two and a half million more in reserve, Russia could easily crush Britain's Eastern defences and overrun her distant possessions.[3] On January 18, Earl Percy, the Under Secretary of State for Foreign Affairs, insisted that the 'Anglo-Japanese Alliance must continue as long as the future war lasts'.[4] Such was the prevailing sentiment at the Foreign Office. During a public speech made at the Drill Hall, Manchester, on January 11, Balfour commented that,

> 'it is, I hope, unnecessary for me to say that Great Britain will to the full carry out all her engagements, all her treaty obligations, in regard to any of her allies, so I think I should do but little service to the cause of peace were I to bring into public discussion the topics of discussion between Japan on the one side and the Empire of Russia on the other.'[5]

In private, the Prime Minister confided to military journalist H. Spenser Wilkinson, 'I trust that, whatever be the course of events in the Far East, this country will not be dragged into hostilities.'[6] There was, however, a significant proviso: should Russia threaten British interests, or contravene international law, Britain reluctantly would be obliged to intervene. On January 11, Lansdowne raised one possible source of danger. If Russia's Black Sea Fleet attempted to sail through the Straits of the Dardanelles on route to the Far East, how would Britain react? Under the Convention of 1856 – to which the Turkish Sultan, Britain, France, Prussia, Austria and Russia had all adhered – foreign warships were prohibited from using the Dardanelles 'so long as the Porte is at peace'. 'On the merits', Lansdowne remarked, 'it would, I think, be impossible for us to overlook so serious a disregard of our Treaty rights. Nor, I think, would public opinion allow us to overlook it.' In conclusion, he forwarded the following suggestion. Britain might,

'(1.) Immediately after the declaration of war intimate to Russia that our neutrality would be conditional on her observance of the Treaties; or

(2.) Suggest to all the Signatory Powers that they should join us in making an intimation to the above effect; or

(3.) Say nothing, but act upon (1) when the case arose.'[7]

Selborne and Balfour shared Lansdowne's concern. 'To allow our ally to be crushed by an enemy by a breach of Treaty,' Selborne wrote on January 14, 'would be more, I think, than our people could stomach or ought to stomach.' A minute penned by Balfour four days later advocated strong naval measures to block the Russian fleet in the event of its approaching the Dardanelles. British warships should be gathered in the Eastern Mediterranean and prepare for attack, whilst Balfour would also let 'Russia know what course we should adopt in case the Black Sea Fleet attempted to force the Straits.' A definite plan was emerging. On January 19, Balfour wrote from Whittingehame that,

'Willie Selborne will have an adequate force in the Eastern Mediterranean; and I think he should prepare instructions to the Admiral of the Mediterranean Fleet, so that he also may know exactly what is expected of him.'[8]

There was, however, no indication that Russia actually intended to breach Treaty stipulations, so discussions at this time were largely theoretical. In the meantime, the Foreign Office continued its negotiations with France. With discussions then in their final stages, an Anglo-French agreement would serve as a further safeguard against intervention. Under the terms of the 1902 agreement, Japan could only call upon her ally should she be beset by two Powers and France, herself desperate to avoid a Russian plea for aid, seemed as anxious as Britain to conclude an agreement. Still more, the French *entente* was to have greater implications; it would either distance France from Russia, thereby isolating the latter Power, or it would push the Russian Government to conclude a similar agreement with Britain, something for which Balfour had long hoped.[9] From Paris, Ambassador Monson informed the Foreign Office on January 12 of the popular feeling against the war. There was, he said,

'every sign that it would take very exceptional reasons to drag this country into giving more aid to Russia in the Far East, and ... the Nationalists are charging into Government with the intention of behaving traitorously to France's ally. Although no-one really knows the exact obligation of the last [Russo-French] agreement ... public opinion is dead against any material participation in the Russo-Japanese dispute.'[10]

While Théophile Delcassé, France's Foreign Minister, remained doggedly optimistic that war could still be avoided,[11] intensive negotiations took place in London in January and February. As we have seen, talks stalled over the matter of suitable territorial compensation for France in return for her renunciation of fishery rights off the Newfoundland coast and Balfour briefly considered dropping the Treaty Shore issue altogether in order to facilitate an immediate agreement. In the meantime, the successful attack by Japanese warships against the Russian fleet stationed at Port Arthur signalled the beginning of hostilities on February 8 1904. Without the French agreement, British officials reacted nervously. A meeting of the Committee of Imperial Defence, held on the same day as the Japanese attack, discussed the chances of British military involvement and the readiness of the British navy to meet a possible Russo-French combination.[12]

When the House of Lords discussed the incident on February 12, Earl Spencer quickly asked the Government to explain a rumour that the Admiralty had given Japan use of Wei-hai-Wei and that this had been the base from which Admiral Togo has launched his attack on Port Arthur. In the face of such suspicion, Lansdowne became angrily defensive. His Government intended to retain its neutrality, he declared: the rumour was a 'mischievous suggestion'.[13] To counter Russian anger, King Edward sent for Benkendorff on February 18 and explained that Britain had 'maintained a scrupulously correct attitude' and had in no way encouraged or assisted Japan's attack on Port Arthur.[14]

Privately, British authorities reacted to Japan's victory with great enthusiasm and delight. Whatever the final result, several Russian warships had been sunk or disabled, whilst Japan had proved herself efficient and admirably daring, an eminently suitable Far Eastern ally. Still more, visions of Russian weakness appeared to take a significant pressure off Britain's stretched naval resources. 'The Japanese Alliance, coupled with the destruction of the Russian fleet in the Far East, has changed the balance of sea power in the Pacific', Esher happily noted.[15]

Earlier that month, when the House of Commons considered Britain's naval estimates, the Liberal M.P. Walter Runciman stressed that Britain need no longer press ahead with an immediate ship-building programme. '[W]e really should recognise the fact that the balance of power had been disturbed by the war in the Far East', he remarked on March 1, 'the fact was that Russia had been seriously crippled ... If the process went further he took it that there would be a still further diminution of those ships against which we were maintaining the two-Power standard.'[16] Ever eager to maintain the alliance, especially after Port Arthur, Lansdowne's dispatch to Marquis Ito was carefully worded, betraying an admiration for Japan's war capability and sympathising with her military endeavours. 'It is, I believe, a matter of common knowledge that you would yourself have been glad to avoid a conflict,' he wrote, 'had it been possible for your country to do so.'[17]

Events in the Far East moved rapidly. Japanese began to occupy Korea in February, initially meeting little resistance. At the Yalu river, the two armies came face to face and, in late April, Japan inflicted a significant and humiliating defeat upon a massive, but poorly prepared Russian force. Two further battles were fought over the ensuing months, at Nanshan Hill in May and at Telissu in mid June, during which the Japanese emerged overwhelmingly victorious. In their thousands, Russian troops were killed, routed or captured as Major-General Baron Kuroki and his Japanese army laid siege to Port Arthur.[18] Russia's military arrogance, her bad planning and inadequate communications, had been laid bare. At the same time, the Japanese endeavours were much admired by European spectators. One such witness was Ethel McCaul, an English nurse, who published her experiences at the Manchurian front in 1904. Describing the spirit of 'patriotism, which is carried almost to fanaticism', McCaul concluded that 'Japan is fast becoming, by using [her] ... mental power, the England of the Far East.'[19]

The British Government was equally impressed. A Japanese victory seemed assured and, with the Anglo-French *entente* concluded on April 8, the fear that Britain might be obliged to intervene all but vanished. The King's approaches to Russia in April and May, firstly to Alexander Isvolsky and then to the Tsar, had an equally calming effect. On April 17, Tsar Nicholas replied that 'there is not a man in the whole of Russia who would tolerate another country mixing in the affairs of ours and Japan's', explaining that '[n]o-one hindered England at the conclusion of her South African war.'[20]

At the same time, tentative steps were taken to achieve an eventual Anglo-Russian understanding. On May 4, the Foreign Secretary wrote to Sir Cecil Spring Rice of his interview with Ambassador Benkendorff. '[T]he Russian Government had never shown themselves averse to a sincere understanding', Lansdowne explained, 'provided that His Majesty's Government would formulate clearly the equitable conditions upon which they desired that it should be based.'[21] No longer anxious about a Japanese defeat or a Russo-French combination and with every indication that both Russia and Japan were keen to continue the fight, Lansdowne was perfectly willing to stand aside and await the first moves for peace.

When Sir Mortimer Durand arrived in New York at the end of November 1903 to assume his post at the Washington Embassy, he found the American people both kind and courteous. The Alaskan Award had been delivered only a month earlier and, in a spirit of renewed friendship for Britain, Durand soon found his diary filled up with invitations to dinners, private and official functions. 'Everyone I have seen both here [in Washington] and in New York has been friendly and cordial', he reported on December 4. 'The way Americans speak about England and their feelings towards her is as delightful as it is surprising.' In early January, Durand detailed the strength of American popular feeling:

> 'They constantly speak of the "Anglo Saxon" and contrast him with "foreigners"' ... It has evidently become the *mot d'ordre* not to speak of us as foreigners – as they used to do – for if the word slips out they pull themselves up and say that of course they don't regard Englishmen as foreigners.'

He continued that:

> 'All this is very pleasant. But of course, though it is pleasant, and of solid advantage also we must not expect too much from it. The Americans seem to me curiously emotional and touchy, and it would be very easy to rub the national sentiment the wrong way – particularly for us. They strike me as very simple and warm hearted in some ways, almost like children in their vanity and almost like children in their resentment of any criticism.'[22]

Britain's friendship with the United States, it then appeared, was dependent on Foreign Office acquiescence to the American line, whatever that might be. American friendship could not be relied upon, but must be carefully fostered. The Russo-Japanese war, as the main diplomatic concern of 1904, would be a testing ground for future Anglo-American relations and, in this respect, Roosevelt fortunately tended to share Britain's support for Japan. The President's correspondence during the first months of the war revealed his admiration for Japan's naval and military capabilities, while Russian diplomacy had long since exhausted his patience. To his son, Roosevelt remarked on February 10 that for 'several years Russia has behaved very badly in the far East, her attitude toward all nations, including us, but especially toward Japan, being grossly overbearing'. Confidentially, Roosevelt concluded that 'I was thoroughly pleased with the Japanese victory [at Port Arthur], for Japan is playing our game.'[23]

Broadly speaking, these views mirrored those held by British officials. However, there were crucial differences. Unlike Britain, Roosevelt wished to see Russia defeated, but not destroyed.'[I]f the Japanese win out, not only the Slav, but all of us will have to reckon with a new force in eastern Asia', he told his friend Spring Rice – then at the St. Petersburg Embassy – on March 19. Emphasising his hopes for the war, Roosevelt continued that it 'may be that the two powers will fight until both are fairly well exhausted, and that peace will come on terms which will not mean the creation of either a yellow peril or a Slav peril.'[24] During an interview with the President in May, Durand was left in no doubt that Roosevelt 'greatly admires the Japanese and wants them to win – but not in too crushing a manner.'[25] Victory for either Russia or Japan would drastically alter the balance of power in the Far East and threaten the territorial integrity and commerce of China. As Russian activities had restricted American trade in China, so Japanese preponderance could create an equally undesirable sphere of influence, limiting American enterprise in the Far East. Still more, although the President evidently admired the Japanese, there was no doubt that he feared the 'yellow peril', which might eventually threaten the American Pacific possessions. The President made sure that his views were understood. Lunching with the Japanese Minister in Washington and his guest, Baron Kaneko, Roosevelt explained,

> 'that I thought their chief danger was lest Japan might get the 'big head' and enter into a general career of insolence and aggression; that

such a career would undoubtedly be temporarily very unpleasant to the rest of the world, but that it would in the end be still more unpleasant for Japan.'

Somewhat carefully, the Japanese officials replied that,

'they did not believe there was any danger of Japan's becoming intoxicated with the victory, because they were convinced that the upper and influential class would not let them, and would show the same caution and decision which has made them so formidable in this war.'[26]

On August 10, Admiral Togo's warships again defeated the Russian fleet at Port Arthur; four days later, the Vladivostock squadron met a similar defeat at the hands of Admiral Kaimamura. 'I think the Japanese will whip them [the Russians] handsomely', Roosevelt now predicted. 'To judge from the Russians' attitude at present, if they were victorious they would be so intolerable as to force us to take action.'[27] To protect the US against either eventuality, Roosevelt suggested mediation to both Russia and Japan in late 1904. With both Powers still hoping for a complete victory, the American proposal for a Peace Conference was ignored,[28] while Roosevelt's efforts to obtain British aid were equally unsuccessful.

Ever since the intensive Cabinet discussions of December 1903, the Balfour Government had steadfastly maintained its refusal to promote peace, except at Japan's express direction. This came as a hard blow for Roosevelt and he reacted angrily. 'England has not a man I can deal with', he told German Ambassador Speck von Sternburg in September. 'I do not think much of Balfour and less of Lansdowne. Chamberlain is quite unreliable'.[29] Since the United States had approached the combatants and found them intractable, and had received little except friendly obstruction from the British Foreign Office, Roosevelt was forced, at least temporarily, to abandon his plans for peace.

On October 21, the lull in diplomatic activity suddenly ended when Admiral Rozhdestvensky's Baltic fleet, sailing through the North Sea on its way to the Far East, apparently mistook British fishing trawlers for Japanese vessels and opened fire. While one vessel was sunk on the Dogger Bank, several others were badly damaged, but received no assistance from the passing Russian fleet. 'What do you propose to do about the outrage in the North Sea?' Balfour immediately telegraphed Lansdowne, continuing that:

'My first thoughts are to stop the Russian Fleet at [the] first convenient place and exact explanation and reparation though granting this to be the best course we can only do it if we have [an] adequate force available on the spot. I should be sorry to see so gross and gratuitous a blunder left to the slow methods of diplomacy.'[30]

It was, as the King noted, a 'most dastardly outrage'; Lansdowne's dispatch to Sir Charles Hardinge, Britain's Ambassador in St. Petersburg, stressed that 'it is impossible to exaggerate the indignation which has been provoked.'[31] The apparent threat of an Anglo-Russian war, fortunately, was soon diffused. The Tsar, sending a private telegram to the King on October 25, apologised for the incident and hoped that 'no complications will arise between our countries owing to this occurrence.'[32] While Balfour pushed for compensation, an apology and the trial and punishment of the offending naval officers, the affair soon reached a satisfactory conclusion when, on October 28, Hardinge wired Lansdowne of Russia's offer to submit the dispute to 'an international commission of inquiry.'[33] Lansdowne immediately forwarded the news to Balfour, knowing that the latter was due to speak at Southampton later that day. '[I]t would be a great pity that you should pour too much ridicule upon them [the Russians] and their defence', he insisted.[34] Balfour's Southampton speech was generally reassuring. Although Benkendorff complained that the Prime Minister had been 'needlessly caustic and offensive', he admitted that 'he had not a word of complaint to make', and that 'it was better than he had ventured to expect.'[35] In all, the incident had been a most horrific mistake and was quickly recognised as such. Roosevelt later described it as an unintentional, but 'deplorable blunder'.[36] With an independent inquiry due to take place at the Hague, the sudden crisis had been just as suddenly averted.

In early November, President Roosevelt overwhelmingly secured his re-election to the White House, beating his Democratic opponent Judge Alton B. Parker by 336 electoral votes to 140.[37] The landslide vindicated Roosevelt and his aggressive approach to international affairs. During a public speech at the Guildhall, Roosevelt quoted some remarks that Hay had used at Boston: 'war is the most futile and the most ferocious of human follies'. Turning to the present conflict, he suggested that 'we have been able, by the observation of a strict neutrality and by wise international arrangements, to do something towards restricting the areas of hostilities [in Manchuria]'.[38]

Following the election and strengthened by its result, Roosevelt seemed ever more anxious to bring about the establishment of a Peace Conference that might end the Russo-Japanese war. At the same time, the Foreign Office had become increasingly anxious about the situation in the Far East, but regarded Roosevelt's proposal with great caution. 'We are having a trying time and the by-products of this wretched war do not add to our happiness', Lansdowne told Durand on December 11. 'Scarcely a day passes without some more or less awkward question arising, and we shall be lucky if we don't get into trouble both with our own people and the belligerents.' Turning to the proposal for mediation, the Foreign Secretary concluded that:

> 'I hope the President was satisfied with our reply as to the Peace Conference. We did not think it was for us to suggest difficulties, and if the President can get the Conference together we shall take part whenever things are ready. But the Russians will object.'[39]

The worsening relations between Roosevelt and Durand added to Lansdowne's troubles, preventing the ready flow of confidential information between the two

Governments. A rather stuffy and old-fashioned diplomat, Durand had long since lost Roosevelt's respect and, by late 1904, the two men hardly spoke. 'How am I to deal with this Ambassador?', Roosevelt asked Sternburg on September 27. 'If I had Spring Rice here, things might be different.'[40] At the same time, Spring Rice, who had maintained a busy correspondence with the President over the preceding months, noted:

> 'It is a curious fact that the U.S. Embassy in London doesn't seem to be consulted by Lansdowne, and our Embassy in Washington reports nothing from Roosevelt. And yet I know that both Roosevelt and Hay would like – not joint, but parallel action – and would be ready to co-operate in spirit if not in deed.'[41]

With Sir Mortimer at the Embassy, Roosevelt turned to Spring Rice as an unofficial mediator.[42] Not only was the arrangement somewhat unorthodox, but, with Spring Rice spending so much time in St. Petersburg, there were unacceptable delays in communication. Accordingly, in December, Roosevelt enquired whether Spring Rice would travel to Washington to converse intimately on the Far Eastern situation. '[U]nfortunately there is no one in your Embassy here to whom I can speak with even reasonable fullness', he explained. This would not be an idle visit and Roosevelt had 'very definitely concluded what I intend to do if circumstances permit, so far as this Far Eastern question is concerned', adding that 'I do not like to write my conclusions even to you'. At the same time, that Roosevelt doubted Britain's utility in the coming months was made perfectly clear. To Spring Rice, he voiced these strong worries about British diplomacy:

> 'I would hesitate upon the support of your Government and your people. I am not quite sure of their tenacity of purpose, of their fixity of conviction, of their willingness to take necessary risks and at need to endure heavy losses for a given end.'

However, Roosevelt hinted that the two countries should have a strong voice in the final settlement:

> 'Whether Russia wins or Japan wins, the victor will in the long run only yield either to England or to the United States substantially the respect which England or the United States is enabled to exact by power actual or potential ... When affairs come to the time of settlement in the Far East (even if previous to the peace no other nation gets embroiled beyond the present pair of combatants) we shall have to look sharply lest our interests be sacrificed.'[43]

Spring Rice was then on leave in London and, keen that he should accept the President's personal invitation to Washington, he soon handed Roosevelt's letter to the Foreign Office. The benefits of Spring Rice's long-standing friendship with the

President were obvious and Lansdowne quickly gave his consent.[44] Roosevelt's irritation, both with Embassy and Government, was a serious matter and the President clearly had important news to convey. However, Lansdowne could hardly give official approval to such informal diplomacy and his dispatches were necessarily vague. If the news got out, there would be a certain outcry from Ambassadorial circles. At the same time, if the Japanese learnt that an unofficial Ambassador had been sent to Washington to discuss terms for peace without her consent, the harmonious nature of Anglo-Japanese relations could be ruined. On January 2 1905, the Russian garrison at Port Arthur finally surrendered to the Japanese army led by General Nogi and, with total victory for Japan appearing to be ever more likely, it was vital to the continuance of the alliance that Britain should be seen to give her ally her wholehearted support. Consequently, when Sir Cecil met Foreign Office officials, he had a mixed reception. On January 14, Sir Francis Villiers wrote to Spring Rice that the latter had still not given him details of 'the object of your mission', and concluded that:

> 'Part of it is the initial steps in an attempt, of which I have heard something, to effect a new and most important combination. I quite understand your services being required, we have no one else on such good or intimate terms with the right people. As for our friends on the other side we know what they want and we cannot blame them for trying to have their friend.'[45]

Lansdowne, on the other hand, became assiduously formal. To Henry White, the Foreign Secretary pointed out that 'as Durand was the recognised Ambassador, he could not commission me [Spring Rice] to act behind his back, but that I could go on a private visit, if I wished.' When Lansdowne and Spring Rice met at the Foreign Office, the latter was left without instructions.[46]

Only to Balfour, who had also seen the Roosevelt letter, was Lansdowne forthcoming. 'I believe Spring Rice is going to spend part of his holidays in Washington', he told the Prime Minister on January 13, 'but it may be as well to say as little as possible about this.' In a separate letter written that day, Lansdowne remarked that Roosevelt,

> 'is to me a very attractive personality, but he is the kind of person who might be very awkward to handle in certain contingencies. Spring Rice is going to accept his invitation, but that is not a matter which concerns the F.O. and I am most anxious that we should know and say as little about it as possible.'[47]

'I was deeply impressed by Roosevelt's letter to Spring Rice', Balfour replied on January 17. 'I hear that the latter goes tomorrow to New York on a visit to the President, and no doubt he will find himself in a position of considerable delicacy and difficulty between the very unconventional Head of the Republic and the orthodox machinery of the Embassy.' Clearly appreciating the trip's importance,

Balfour was uneasy about sending Spring Rice across the Atlantic without any instructions, direct or otherwise:

> 'I think it very clear that we cannot leave the questions raised by the President where they are', he explained, 'and that, as he is feeling the ground in an unofficial way we ought to follow his example. If you agree, it may be more convenient perhaps that I should write to Spring Rice than that you should.'[48]

Accordingly, the Prime Minister drafted a lengthy note to Spring Rice. It was, in effect, a lengthy reprise of his earlier draft proposal to the Foreign Secretary, dated February 11 1904, and betrayed the Prime Minister's tendency to become rather idealistic when discussing Anglo-American affairs.[49] Dismissing the 'yellow peril' as 'altogether chimerical', Balfour stressed the 'very near and imminent peril of important fragments of China being dominated by more warlike and aggressive Powers' and continued that if,

> 'America and ourselves were to enter into a Treaty binding us jointly to resist such aggression, it would never, I believe, be attempted. Together we are too strong for any combination of Powers to fight us. I believe there would be no difficulty on this side of the Atlantic in the way of such a Treaty. The difficulty, I imagine, would be rather with the United States, whose traditions and whose Constitution conspire to make such arrangements hard to conclude.'[50]

It is impossible to determine whether Spring Rice sailed for New York with this missive in his possession. During his last discussion with the Foreign Secretary, taking place at the Foreign Office the day before he sailed, it seems that Lansdowne was already in possession of Balfour's draft. However, when reporting the meeting on January 18, he told Balfour that 'I see no objection whatever to your writing to Spring Rice. It is on the whole better that the F.O. should have as little to say to him as possible.'

From this, it is safe to assume that, when Spring Rice sailed that day, he had not seen Balfour's draft and there is no evidence that the Prime Minister ever sent a re-drafted message to the United States. This was no oversight; there were clear reasons for concealing official information from Spring Rice. While Roosevelt's confidences were naturally welcome, Britain had long since determined not to take an active role in the moves for peace. In effect, Spring Rice was to be little more than the President's courier. He was not, however, left entirely unguided. Describing their last interview, the Foreign Secretary explained that 'I said that, if the U.S. mean business, they must trust us and take us fully into their confidence, and in time.'[51] With only the barest of instruction, then, Spring Rice boarded the White Star Line steamship "Baltic" and sailed for New York.

The survival of the Anglo-Japanese bond, above all other policy considerations, governed Lansdowne's diplomacy and this precluded the possibility of serious and honest co-operation with the United States. Discussions now commenced for the renewal of the Japanese alliance, a suggestion that Earl Percy had proposed in early January. To Balfour, Percy wrote that he had approached Lansdowne, who found 'it a suggestion worth considering'; the agreement he now advocated with Japan would last a further five years. 'I feel doubtful of the prolonged existence of the present Government', Percy concluded, so 'I hope you won't mind my suggesting it to you.' When John Sandars, Balfour's Private Secretary, saw Lansdowne on January 17, he found the Foreign Secretary eager to renew the alliance. Indeed, Lansdowne had written to the Prime Minister a day earlier to suggest that the renewed alliance should last for fifteen years 'to show the Japanese that our affection is unabated.' At the same time, Balfour quickly concurred with Earl Percy that Campbell-Bannerman's Liberals were not to be trusted and once more raised the possibility of American involvement:

> 'If, indeed, we could bring in the Americans, that would be a new arrangement, and, as part of it, an extension of the Japanese Treaty would clearly be legitimate. Much, however, as I desire the Treaty with America, the difficulties – not on our side, but on theirs – are obviously immense.'[52]

At every available opportunity, it seemed, Balfour raised his great hope, that the United States would take a more active role in Far Eastern affairs. Although the Prime Minister dismissed the idea almost as soon as it had been proposed – as he had done on previous occasions – his desire to make America at least an implicit signatory to the new agreement was both clear and firm. In the meantime, with these discussions in their initial stages, Lansdowne kept a close watch on the military and diplomatic operations in the Far East. In particular, the Foreign Secretary maintained a close correspondence with Sir Francis Bertie, who had replaced Sir Edmund Monson at the French Embassy; as Russia's ally, French diplomatic circles were the most likely sphere of international activity. 'I am most anxious to know whether anything is going on at Paris about the terms for peace', Lansdowne wrote Bertie on January 18. According to Delcassé, Bertie remarked, nothing of any note was happening in France to end the war: 'it would be impossible for Russia to think of peace until she has had a military success.'[53]

Desperate for information, Lansdowne now worried that France had been secretly discussing the matter with Berlin. 'What really signifies is that the French Government, who wish to keep in line with us, should not commit themselves ... without previous consultation with us', the Foreign Secretary stressed on January 19.[54] Nevertheless, the Foreign Office was generally satisfied. While the surrender of the Russian garrison at Port Arthur was a natural cause for enthusiasm, the Russian Government seemed to have no reply. A popular uprising began in St. Petersburg in January and quickly spread. On January 22, Tsar Nicholas authorised the shooting of a petitioning crowd outside the Winter Palace. As the populace lost faith in the Tsarist Regime, disturbances quickly spread to Finland and Poland. Preoccupied with internal difficulties, Russia's chances of at least one military victory seemed to have vanished and, as Japanese troops left Port Arthur and travelled North to Mukden, the prospect of a total and humiliating defeat was imminent. A three-day battle began at Sandepu, just south of the Manchurian capital, on January 26. Despite initial success, the Russians once more were obliged to retreat and Russian General Grippenberg described his battle-weary men retiring 'unwillingly with tears in their eyes'. The Japanese army had finally reached Mukden.[55]

It was, perhaps, the clear disintegration of Russia as a fighting force that pushed Roosevelt suddenly to approach Durand on January 23. With Spring Rice still somewhere in the Atlantic and with the President determined quickly to elicit Britain's views, Durand was the natural and necessary choice. A secret and coded telegram, arriving at the Foreign Office that day, relayed the news that the Ambassador had been requested to attend an immediate interview at the White House. 'He [Roosevelt] said that he felt [the] time had come', Durand explained, 'when he should speak to me freely about [the] situation in the East.' This dispatch, revealing Roosevelt's intense sense of urgency, deserves to be quoted at length. Durand continued that,

> 'I think Y[our] L[ordship] should know [that the] President seems anx- ious lest [the] rapid development of [the] situation should force him to decide upon [a] line of action and that he evidently wants to know your views. I think he apprehends firstly that he may be asked to mediate and that Japan and Russia may show [themselves] inclined to come to terms. I believe he wishes to keep as far as possible in line with us and that there may be [an] opportunity for concerted action if desirable. ... He is strongly opposed to any interference by neutral Powers to deprive Japan of their conquests. He does not however think that [the] U.S. would seriously oppose [the] Russian claim to retain Northern Manchuria if not dispossessed by [the] Japanese ... It may be of great advantage if you could telegraph your views under any necessary reserve.'[56]

Lansdowne was clearly glad that official communications had been reopened and immediately wired his response. 'It is most satisfactory that the President has spoken so freely to you. I have always felt that the case was one in which a frank and timely interchange of ideas was most desirable.' This telegram was sent, as Lansdowne told Balfour, simply 'to keep the President quiet' while the Foreign Office considered its response. Still, the Foreign Secretary could not hide his satisfaction at the sudden and unexpected approach. 'It is satisfactory that Roosevelt has broken the ice with him', Lansdowne remarked, 'for I could not help feeling a little uneasy at the proposed extra-official communication between the President and Spring Rice at a moment when the former was keeping our Ambassador at arms length.'[57] Together, Foreign Secretary and Prime Minister began to draft their response. Roosevelt's initiative, as an official enquiry, demanded a lengthy and meaningful account of Britain's position: it was to be a careful and cautious reply. Lansdowne wrote that Russia would probably still resent mediation, so the discussions would be largely hypothetical. Secondly, Britain intended to support Japan's demand to retain Port Arthur and her paramount influence in Korea while Manchuria should be returned to China. On the other hand, Britain would not push for peace. Balfour privately explained to the Foreign Secretary on January 24 that he was not 'unduly afraid of hostilities'.

> 'I am, on broad moral grounds, very anxious, that we should do every-thing we can do to put an end to the war. But I have to admit that, from a narrowly national point of view the balance of advantage, I suspect, is on the side of continued hostilities.'[58]

Lansdowne could hardly print this. Instead, his remarks to Durand were broadly reassuring:

> 'We earnestly desire to remain in line with the United States, and we believe that in certain eventualities, concerted action between us might have the best results, and that it is therefore necessary that each Government should take the other fully into its confidence. We are confident that in all essential particulars there is not likely to be any divergence between the policy or conduct of the two Governments.'[59]

In Washington, Sir Mortimer suddenly found the President both approachable and forthcoming. Rather at a loss to explain the démarche, Durand stressed that Roosevelt had called the meeting and had declared his desire for a close Anglo-American working relationship until the war could be concluded. '"England and America must stand together"' he declared. 'He repeated these words two or three times, in his vehement way and I have no doubt that he meant what he said.' Having seen the British reply, the President thanked Durand and declared himself extremely pleased. Then, suggestively, Roosevelt went on:

> '"I shall have to speak to you [Durand] very freely from time to time about the doings of our German and other friends, and it is very important that nothing I ever say should get into a blue book." I reas-sured him about this ... I feel satisfied that things are going well. The President is impulsive and has a good deal of self assertion about him ... he is evidently at present thoroughly convinced that England is the best possible friend for America'.[60]

This dispatch, received at the Foreign Office on February 4, was naturally reas-suring. 'I am glad he [Roosevelt] has made this venture, and I am convinced that we were right in responding with alacrity', Lansdowne replied. 'He must be a strange being, but he is to me an attractive personality, altho' I should be sorry to have to deal with him if he happened to be in the wrong mood.' As for the

President's fears that his advances would be published in Britain, there was no cause for concern. Indeed, from January 13, Lansdowne had been keeping Durand's reports, and many of his own replies, in a separate file. '[T]hey have not gone through the office and they will not be printed', he explained. Too sensitive to broadcast, they had been shown only Balfour and the King, the latter being much satisfied with the turn of events.[61]

In the meantime, the Foreign Office asked Sir Claude MacDonald to obtain Japan's terms for peace and, on January 28, these were wired to the Washington Embassy in the strictest confidence; Port Arthur and Korea should go to Japan and control over Manchuria should be returned to the Chinese Government. 'These terms do not seem to us excessive', Lansdowne noted.[62] With the delivery of this note, Roosevelt had great reason to feel satisfied. Over the preceding months, the Foreign Office had refused to aid international efforts for a peace settlement. Now, through the President's intervention, Lansdowne had obtained from Japan a detailed list of the peace demands she considered to be acceptable. Roosevelt's use of the orthodox diplomatic machinery had paid off.

Such was the state of affairs when Spring Rice arrived in the United States. Sailing on January 18, he had doubtless envisaged a greater role than he was destined to play in Washington. When he landed in New York, on January 27, there was no longer much need for a confidential interview with Roosevelt; diplomatic intimacy has been restored between the President and Sir Mortimer Durand, and frank peace discussions were already underway.[63] A further interview between the two men on January 31 served to underline the new personal *rapprochement*. Once more, Roosevelt declared his cordiality: "'I desire and I intend for the future, so long as I am at the head of this Govt., [that] the U.S. shall keep in the closest touch with England. I consider that our interests in the East are identical.'"[64] Accordingly, in his dispatch to the Foreign Office – dated February 2 – Spring Rice had little additional information, and was obliged to explain that:

> 'Owing to difficulties of age and character Sir M. Durand was at a disadvantage in dealing with the President. But these difficulties appear to be overcome. Hay has a very high opinion of Durand: so has the President, personally, of his character, and specially his straightness and there is no doubt as to Durand's deep friendliness for the U.S. The longer he stays, he less should be the difficulty in communicating freely.'[65]

Although Roosevelt clearly appreciated Spring Rice's presence in Washington, the latter stayed only briefly and left for England on February 8 aboard the "Teutonic". While it now appears that Spring Rice had achieved little and that the increased cordiality between Roosevelt and the British Embassy pre-dated his arrival in the United States, his visit had been well publicised and, for this reason, assumed an unwarranted importance.[66] In some respect, Sir Cecil was rewarded. While Durand asked Lansdowne if Spring Rice could stay longer in Washington, his immediate return to Britain was Roosevelt's idea, keen that Lansdowne should hear a full and frank expression of his views.[67] Personally, Spring Rice appeared to have great weight in aiding the Anglo-American friendship. Henry White praised Spring Rice's achievements to Sir Francis Knollys, the King's Private Secretary. 'I rubbed into him, in all sincerity, the great work you have done in bringing the President and Durand together', White later told Spring Rice, 'which doubtless was duly transmitted to the Sovereign'.[68] Already impressed with his activities, King Edward allowed himself to be persuaded by Spring Rice to send the President an unofficial message of congratulation on his re-election to the White House. Such a letter, Spring Rice stressed, would not contravene historical precedent and would further encourage Anglo-American intimacy. On February 22, Lansdowne himself noted that the 'démarche has been mainly instigated by Spring Rice, and seems to me opportune at the present time.'[69]

Despite the renewed spirit of friendship between the two countries, there was little that could be done in January and February to end the war. Both Russia and Japan had their own reasons to continue the fight and they had made their objections to international pressure perfectly explicit.[70]

At the same time, Senate opposition to an overt Anglo-American policy prevented Roosevelt from advocating anything resembling an agreement, except in the most private and confidential terms. 'I hope that we are on the road to a concerted policy,' Durand wrote to Lansdowne on February 6, 'although the American Govt. must be very careful not to seem too much in with us. The Senate and people, though no longer unfriendly to us, are suspicious of any "entangling alliances" and watchful.'[71] Nonetheless, the President's dispatch to George von Lengerke Meyer, American Ambassador in St. Petersburg, revealed a new optimism:

'England's interest is exactly ours as regards this Oriental complication,' Roosevelt explained on February 6, 'and is likely to remain so ... it is important that without any talk whatever being made of it, there should be a thorough understanding between us and the English as to what is happening.'[72]

In the early months of 1905, official American diplomacy concerned itself largely with maintaining the integrity of China, so as at least to reduce the threat to international trade and protect the 'open door'. In this limited undertaking, the United States had Lansdowne's full support, although the Foreign Secretary was beginning to show signs of resentment at an apparent German-American collaboration for this end.[73] While Britain's support for Japan's military endeavours continued unabated, however, Lansdowne was hardly in a position to complain. At the opening of Parliament on February 14, he once more was obliged to pledge his resistance to unwanted mediation:

'His Majesty's Government would lose no opportunity of taking steps to bring that war to a close. I need not assure your Lordships that should the opportunity present itself we would avail ourselves of it with alacrity. On the other hand, I do not think your Lordships will differ from me when I say that ill-conceived intervention is likely to be fraught with the worst possible results.'[74]

Of Lansdowne's policy, there was no complaint. While Lord Spencer spoke solely of China's commercial affairs, the Marquis of Winchester gave his total support to the Government's actions. '[T]here never can be any question of mediation by the powers in this great struggle', he remarked, 'however much we may deplore the sacrifice and loss of life, so long as it is not desired by either of the belligerents.'[75] Knowing that Britain's apparent reticence would displease Roosevelt, Sir Cecil Spring Rice doggedly maintained an optimistic attitude to his American friends, stressing that, not only had the Foreign Office received Roosevelt's thoughts with gratitude and pleasure, but they intended to tow the American line. Once he returned to his post in St. Petersburg, Spring Rice wrote to the President's wife, 'I saw Lansdowne at once when I returned and found him very much delighted at the messages which had reached him from the President. He for his part is quite determined to play up.' On March 15, Spring Rice sent Hay a detailed account of his reception:

> 'In London I found Lord Lansdowne intensely interested at what he heard and very much rejoiced. Chamberlain spoke with the greatest earnestness – indeed his language was very striking. ... Lord Lansdowne was nervous as to outward manifestations which he was anxious to avoid. But he had absolute confidence in you, as to the diplomatic side of the question.'

His conclusion was mere wish-fulfilment and Hay must have known this. 'I should think you could be certain that we will follow your lead', Spring Rice explained, 'and that you will find us ready and anxious to take any action which you suggest beforehand.'[76] While Japan's army remained victorious, full co-operation with Washington was unlikely in the extreme and, only five days earlier, Japan had secured a significant victory at Mukden. The battle had commenced on February 23; once more, it was to be a long and bloody struggle with Japan's greater initiative baffling the increasingly desperate General Kuropatkin. Fought in sub-zero temperatures and in heavy snow, the struggle for Mukden ended with the dispirited Russian army in general retreat and the victorious Japanese occupying the Manchurian capital on March 10. Initially unknown to foreign diplomats and journalists, however, Mukden had a significant and sobering effect on Japan's war effort. Exhausted and unable to pursue the fleeing Russians, Japan's victory had been far from complete. Due to the immense strain on her diminishing military resources, she began to acknowledge the impossibility of securing total success and to understand the desirability of peace.[77]

With the news of the great Manchurian battle circulating in the international press, Japan's sudden approach to Roosevelt in early March surprised everyone. On March 15, Sir Mortimer Durand telegraphed that the President had been asked to suggest and to lead the efforts for international mediation. Roosevelt replied that 'he will do what he can if [the] Japanese Govt. really think him best fitted for the task.'[78]

Lansdowne was clearly shocked. After all, he had received no word from Tokyo that Japan had any thoughts towards mediation. Keen to get more precise information, the Foreign Secretary wired Sir Claude MacDonald on March 19. '[A]ll the information in my possession', MacDonald replied, 'was of a nature to make me believe that an appeal for mediation was the very last thing contemplated by the Japanese Government'.[79] Two days later, the Foreign Secretary wrote to Sir Francis Bertie of MacDonald's opinion that Japan still wished to fight. 'If this is their attitude we ought I think to be extremely careful how we take upon ourselves to suggest to them or for them that certain terms should be acceptable', he concluded. By early April, and with no further information, Lansdowne told Bertie that 'I do not think that, in spite of rumours to the contrary, either side is taking any serious steps [for peace].' Still more, the 'Japanese have, I think, been rendered extremely suspicious by reports that Roosevelt was about to offer mediation, or indeed had been asked by the Japanese Government to mediate.'[80] Was Durand's information, then, in fact only a mischievous rumour? Certainly, Takahira, Japan's Ambassador in Washington, had spoken to the President in March about possible American mediation. At the same time, Baron Kaneko was also discussing the matter with the President and with William H. Taft, who, due to Hay's illness, had been acting as Secretary of State. However, no definite proposals had been raised in late March, but merely cautious and hesitant advances. When Roosevelt wrote to his ailing Secretary of State on March 30, he remarked that:

'Cassini [the Russian Ambassador] and Takahira have been to see me about peace negotiations, but we do not make much progress as yet because neither side is willing to make the first advances. The Japanese say, quite rightly, that they will refuse to deal unless on the word of the Czar [sic.], because it is evident that no one minister has power to bind the government.'[81]

Despite their initial fears about international mediation, the Japanese Government decided in April to seek peace through Roosevelt. While this decision had been made during meetings on April 7 and 17, the Japanese Cabinet discussions on April 21 resolved upon fresh peace terms.[82] In the interests of settlement, Japan discarded her dispensable claims and concentrated on obtaining preponderance in Korea, the total military evacuation of Manchuria and retaining Port Arthur and the Port Arthur to Harbin railway.[83] At the same time, Tsar Nicholas had already made moves to secure peace through the assistance of French Foreign Minister Delcassé. The latter, asked in mid March to exchange ideas with the Japanese, was given a list of conditions acceptable and unacceptable to Russia; there could be no cession of territory, no indemnity, no surrender of the Manchurian railway and the Russian Pacific navy was to suffer no restrictions.[84] If the natural clash of interests appeared impossible to adjust, at least tentative talks had opened. Believing that the Far Eastern crisis might finally be resolved, Roosevelt left Washington in early April, travelling West on a six-week bear-hunting trip and leaving Taft in charge at Washington. On March 30, Durand wrote that:

> '[The] President assured me of his earnest desire to act with England, and told me that he had instructed Secretary Taft, who takes charge of the State Department during his absence, to regard England as on a footing wholly different from all other Powers, and to treat us with entire confidence.'[85]

Durand, also keen to leave the capital, prepared to return to Britain in late April. It appears that the President himself had suggested the timing of Durand's leave, designed to coincide with his own absence from Washington. On April 27, Lansdowne sent a telegram stating that 'there is no reason why you should postpone your leave.' The Ambassador duly set sail for England and, arriving in the first week of May, quickly met with the King and, later, the Foreign Secretary. 'He seemed to be entirely satisfied with the position in America', Durand noted. Lansdowne had 'evidently taken Roosevelt's measure.'[86]

With every indication that affairs were now proceeding well and that both Japan and Russia were intent upon peace, there now seemed little chance of a rupture in Anglo-American relations, while Britain had given her ally every possible support. This wholehearted support for Japan would continue until the final settlement. Over the ensuing months, Lansdowne would consistently refuse to put pressure on the Japanese Government to moderate their peace terms. However, if the Foreign Office's partisan diplomacy effectively ensured the solidity of the Anglo-Japanese agreement, it was destined to reawaken Roosevelt's anger towards Britain and her apparent impotence as a Far Eastern peacemaker.

13

Hats Off to Roosevelt

The 'Special Relationship' as Peacemaker,

April-September 1905

MONG THE DIPLOMATS it is universally agreed that President
Roosevelt has set himself an extremely difficult task', the St. Petersburg
correspondent for *The New York Times* remarked on June 22 1905, 'the
accomplishment of which would not only crown the triumphs he has already
achieved but would materially advance the chances of peace'.[1] Despite their initial
steps towards bringing the war to a welcome close, neither Russia nor Japan, in the
spring of 1905, were prepared to accept a humiliating or worthless settlement. On
the question of a financial indemnity, as on territorial loss, the Tsar would not
budge; without significant gains to ensure hegemony in Korea – and without
obtaining the leasehold of Port Arthur – the Japanese were equally obdurate. So
the conflict progressed. On April 11 Sir Charles Hardinge explained to
Lansdowne that, although the great majority of Russians were desperate to see the
war end, Tsar Nicholas refused to listen to his Ministers' counsel and 'accuses them
of a want of patriotism.' The military party in St. Petersburg at least found reasons
for optimism. An enormous army of four hundred thousand men still faced the
Japanese invaders, while Admiral Rozhdestvensky's fleet had been transferred
from the Baltic and, despite the unfortunate Dogger Bank incident, was eager for
the fight. In Russia's opinion, Hardinge noted, the Admiral had,

> 'a large squadron which he has trained and brought to such a state of
> perfection as to be able to defeat, or at least severely damage, the
> Japanese fleet which is persistently described as having leaking boilers,
> injured turrets, worn out guns and diminishing speed, while a decisive
> victory would entirely change the aspect of the campaign on land.'[2]

Delcassé presented a different picture. Pledged in March to aid the Tsar in achieving
a satisfactory peace settlement, the French Minister told the Japanese Ambassador
in mid April that 'the Russian Government desired peace, and would make it if
terms not too humiliating were put within her reach.'[3] During April and May,
however, all efforts to end the conflict were both fragmentary and ineffectual. The
impending naval battle, so anxiously anticipated by Russians and Japanese alike,
would determine the issue either way. To Henry Cabot Lodge on May 15,

Roosevelt explained that Japan was 'anxious to have me try to make peace.' There remained, however, significant and immediate obstacles to mediation:

> 'Takahira, and I think the Japanese Foreign Office, agreed with my position, but the war party, including the army and the navy, insisted upon an indemnity and cession of territory, and rather than accept such terms the Russians preferred to have another try with Rojestvensky's [*sic.*] fleet.'[4]

In this already fragile atmosphere, the Kaiser's sudden visit to Tangier on March 31 created a tangible panic. With Russia apparently crippled in the Far East, the German Emperor took the opportunity to challenge France's stake in Morocco, special interests recently recognised by the Anglo-French *entente* of 1904. His intention was to pose as the protector of Moorish interests and to stand against the widespread internal reforms proposed by France. In reality, he looked to sever the Anglo-French agreement and, in part, his plans succeeded. Diplomats in both Paris and London were thrown into a state of chaos. 'The Tangier incident was the most mischievous and uncalled for event which the German Emperor has ever been engaged in since he came to the Throne', King Edward fumed.[5] Lansdowne's outrage was more carefully expressed. To Bertie on April 3, he remarked that 'I am not surprised that Delcassé should be a little perturbed at the German Emperor's activity', to 'the best of my recollection, my conversations with Metternich when the negotiations were in progress last year with France ... made it quite clear that Germany knew what was going on.'[6]

Fearful of the Kaiser's apparent close co-operation with Roosevelt in the Far East, Lansdowne now nervously awaited America's reaction to the Moroccan incident. In early April, Durand promised that he would consult Taft who, with Hay ill and Roosevelt still out West hunting bears, was controlling the affairs of the State Department. On April 24, Durand telegraphed that 'Mr. Taft says that America does not care a cent about Morocco, and has no desire whatever to take sides between Germany and France.' Nevertheless, Taft expressed a keen desire to hear Britain's views.[7] Lansdowne, in turn, telegraphed a hasty reply, stressing that he had no intention of attacking Germany over Morocco. Privately, Lansdowne directed Durand to 'be careful to say nothing which could be interpreted as an invitation to the President to act as mediator between us and Germany.'[8]

Despite his belief in the potential utility of the United States as a strong diplomatic ally, Lansdowne clearly remained unconvinced about Roosevelt as a reliable supporter of British interests against Germany and feared that the President's brash approach to diplomatic affairs might serve only to exacerbate an already tense situation. Now the Foreign Secretary carefully explained his actions to Balfour, so that the latter might either voice his agreement or issue swift counter instructions to Durand. The Prime Minister, sent a copy of the telegram (which Lansdowne 'had to send without consulting you in order to catch Durand before his departure') was told that 'I think it is alright and hope you won't object, but Roosevelt terrifies me almost as much as the German Emperor.'[9]

Lansdowne need not have worried. Learning of Emperor William's inflammatory activities, both Roosevelt and the ailing Hay reacted with a combination of bemused amusement and horror. 'I wish to Heaven our excellent friend, the Kaiser, was not so jumpy and did not have so many pipe dreams', Roosevelt told Taft on April 8. From Nauheim, where he was receiving a water cure, Hay told Spring Rice, '[w]hat a cold-blooded calculator this seemingly reckless orator is!'[10] It was to Spring Rice on May 13 that the President fully expressed his views, dwelling not merely on Morocco, but on the entirety of German diplomacy. 'I suppose it is natural that my English friends generally, from the King down, should think I was under the influence of the Kaiser,' he explained, 'but you ought to know better, old man.' Believing William's policy to be 'one of such violent and often wholly irrational zigzags', he concluded that 'I should never dream of counting on his friendship for this country.'[11]

In the meantime, Lansdowne refused to promise France British military aid against Germany, and simply stated that,

> 'our two Governments should continue to treat one another with the most absolute confidence, should keep one another fully informed of everything which came to their knowledge, and should, as far as possible, discuss in advance any contingencies by which they might in the course of events find themselves confronted.'[12]

When Durand returned to Washington in early June, he found the President wholly in accordance with England, determined to discourage the Kaiser from further pressing ahead with his ill-advised Moroccan adventure. The Sultan's invitation to the Powers, on June 3, to attend a Conference that would discuss the future of Morocco, was welcomed by the United States, provided it was acceptable to Britain and to France. Delcassé had resigned and, deeply worried about the German threat, the resolve of several French diplomats and statesmen was wavering.[13] To Durand, Roosevelt explained that, even if the Germans won, 'they could get no good from it – that a French province would be to them what a piece of poisoned meat would be to a dog.'

Lansdowne declared himself 'extremely glad' at the news from Washington, knowing that, should France accept the Conference – and there was every indication that they would – the crisis would be over, with the United States wholeheartedly backing Britain, and France by association, in the coming negotiations.[14]

The long-expected naval battle between Russia and Japan occurred in the middle of the Moroccan crisis. On the morning of May 27 1905, Admiral Rozdestvensky's Baltic fleet, joined by several warships under Admiral Nebogatoff, engaged Togo's navy in the Tsushima Straits. By the end of the following day, Russia's prized fleet no longer existed. Four battleships had been destroyed. In all, Russia lost thirty-four warships while Japan had only three torpedo boats sunk. To add to the humiliation, both Nebogatoff and Rozdestvensky were forced to surrender to the Japanese, although the latter was badly wounded and unconscious when captured. What few Russian ships remained were scuttled, run aground or interned in neutral ports until the end of the war. Only three warships found refuge at Vladivostock; Russia's navy had suffered near total annihilation.[15] His last chance to turn the tide gone, the Tsar was forced to accept the necessity of peace negotiations, now wholeheartedly backed by the Kaiser. On June 3, the German Emperor wrote privately to Tsar Nicholas that:

> 'no doubt the Japanese have the highest regard for America before all other nations. Because this mighty rising Power with its tremendous fleet is next to them. If anybody in the world is able to influence the Japanese & to induce them to be reasonable in their proposals, it is President Roosevelt.'[16]

News of Tsushima spread quickly. A confidential telegram from Sir Claude MacDonald arrived at the Foreign Office on May 29, listing the Russian casualties and stating that Togo had sailed north to pursue the enemy's few surviving ships.[17] The battle's significance was not lost on Washington; the victory outshone both Trafalgar and the defeat of the Spanish Armada, Roosevelt told Baron Kaneko on May 31, '[n]o wonder you are happy!' While the President's congratulations no doubt were sincere, however, the prospect of Japanese naval supremacy in Far Eastern waters raised a new set of anxieties and seemed to present a very real threat to America's Pacific possessions. In consequence, once he had written to Kaneko, Roosevelt immediately penned a private letter to Secretary Taft, the latter then due to visit the Philippines. Subig Bay should be fortified against an attack, Roosevelt remarked:

> 'If we are not prepared to build and maintain a good-sized navy, each unit of which shall be at the highest point of efficiency, and if we are not prepared to establish a strong and suitable base for our navy in the Philippines, then we has better give up the Philippine Islands entirely.'[18]

Encouraged by Foreign Minister Komura's formal request on May 31 that he should mediate and more than ever determined to force a settlement any which way he could, Roosevelt contacted the British Embassy on June 2. Durand had returned to the United States, but was staying at Lenox before returning to his post at Washington, so the President approached Chargé d'Affaires Hugh O'Beirne. As O'Beirne reported to Sir Louis Mallet at the Foreign Office, Roosevelt tentatively sought British views, although he 'also said, and this he particularly wished me to report, that he was by no means anxious to be the medium of negotiation between Russia and Japan.'[19]

At Lenox, Durand also received notice of Roosevelt's wishes. '[The] President asks whether you are disposed to give him their [the Japanese] views confidentially', the Ambassador wired Lansdowne on June 2. Himself ignorant of Japan's demands and hardly anxious to facilitate peace at a time of great Japanese success, Lansdowne preferred to await 'the impression produced by [the] recent maritime catastrophe on [the] temper and expectations of both belligerents.'[20] As Britain had consistently held, Japan must take the initiative on her own terms and without interference.

O'Beirne informed Roosevelt of the substance of Lansdowne's dispatch on June 4, which the President 'said was just what he had expected.'[21] Such vague words could easily be misinterpreted and, although neither Lansdowne nor Durand appear to have appreciated it, the remarks betrayed a reawakening of American frustration, both towards Britain and her passive Far Eastern policy. The end of the temporary *rapprochement* between Roosevelt and Ambassador Durand can be dated to this period. On May 24, before the battle at Tsushima, Roosevelt had written to Henry Cabot Lodge that, as 'for Durand, unless we could have Springy I think he had better stay in Washington. I like him and get on with him.' A subsequent dispatch to Lodge, written on June 5, had an altogether different tone:

'I think I a little overstated the case about Durand', Roosevelt explained. 'He is a high-minded, conscientious public servant and I like him personally. But he is very slow. In this crisis he has been away at Lenox – which I have been glad of as O'Beirne is a really much more satisfactory man through whom to act.'[22]

To Whitelaw Reid, Joseph Choate's replacement as American Ambassador at the London Embassy, Roosevelt complained that 'Durand has come back, seen me in what was really a most perfunctory interview, and has gone back to Lenox'. Again, the President repeated that he had previously spoken too kindly of Sir Mortimer, and suggested that Spring Rice's name might be mentioned as a possible successor.[23] Unfortunately, Reid had already handed the Foreign Secretary an earlier Presidential message, stating that:

'The President had no reason to doubt that the diplomacy of the United States and that of Great Britain would be found moving upon parallel lines in the future.' As Lansdowne wrote to Durand on June 5, 'His Excellency added that the President's relations with yourself had been of the most confidential and satisfactory character.'[24]

It was O'Beirne, not Durand, whom Roosevelt called for an urgent interview on June 5. Durand, perhaps aware of the deliberate slight, simply reported Roosevelt's declared intention to make strenuous efforts to end the war. A message had been sent to George von Lengerke Meyer, America's Ambassador in St. Petersburg, 'to ask for an audience with the Czar, to urge [the] hopelessness of continuing the struggle and to press upon H[is] M[ajesty] the desirability of his consenting to [the] request of [the] President that Russian and Japanese plenipotentiaries should meet to confer as to whether it is not possible for them to agree as to terms of peace.'[25] Fortunately, Russia's resistance to mediation had, by early June, almost wholly evaporated. On June 8, welcome news arrived from St.

Petersburg, explaining that the Tsar had agreed to a meeting between Russian and Japanese representatives to discuss terms that might finally end the war.[26] With this information, Roosevelt wasted no time before authorising the formal proposal of mediation to both belligerent Powers. These were sent on June 8 by Acting Secretary of State Francis B. Loomis, to George Meyer and to Lloyd Griscom, United States' Ambassador in Japan. To the former, Loomis emphasised that:

> 'While the President does not feel that any intermediary should be called in in respect to the peace negotiations themselves, he is entirely willing to do what he properly can if the two powers concerned feel that his services will be of aid in arranging the preliminaries as to the time and place of meeting ... the President will be glad, as his sole purpose is to bring about a meeting which the whole civilized world will pray may result in peace.'[27]

Within four days, the official acceptance of Roosevelt's suggestion had been received from both Russia and Japan. Yet the latter, wary of abruptly ending hostilities without suitable compensation, showed little desire to compromise. 'Every section of the Japanese press is urging the Government not to be deceived by Russia,' Hardinge told Lansdowne on June 14, 'but to continue the war with the utmost vigour, until the plenipotentiaries have met.' Without a guarantee from Tsar Nicholas himself, Japan would fight on.[28] Frequently that month, the President called on the British Embassy, betraying the earnest desire that Britain pressure her ally to moderate her demands. Durand became increasingly evasive. 'I have avoided everything of the kind, supposing that H[is] M[ajesty's] G[overnment] would probably be reluctant to take any step which could embarrass [the] Japanese', he telegraphed. This attitude was 'quite in accordance with our view', Lansdowne wired back, 'and should be maintained'.[29]

The time for a decision had come and, whilst appreciating that American opinion might flare up against Britain, the Foreign Secretary continued wholeheartedly to back Japan. In mid June, no visible signs of such anger were evident to the British Ambassador, although his reports hinted that the President would not indefinitely maintain his friendly position. On June 16, Sir Mortimer explained that:

> 'The President rather to my relief seemed quite satisfied with our attitude. I had feared that he might think we had not backed him strongly enough, but he said our silence was wise and proper, and that if we advised mediation hereafter our advice would come with double force. ... The President is in the highest spirits, and perfectly confident of success. The Americans generally are rather proud of his performance, which they contrast with the timid and dilatory methods of Europe.'[30]

To Lansdowne, on the other hand, Roosevelt's impatience must have been easily apparent. American Ambassador Whitelaw Reid, visiting the Foreign Office on

June 16, voiced his concern that Britain might, through her total support for Japan, become an obstacle to peace. The Ambassador was to leave the meeting only partly reassured. Explaining his thoughts, Lansdowne maintained that 'it would in my opinion be inadvisable that we should take upon ourselves to tender such advice at a moment when we were not even aware of the terms for which she [Japan] intended to ask.' On the same day, Roosevelt wrote privately to Spring Rice, stating his earnest hope 'that your people take the same view [as that of the United States], and that they will not permit any feeling that they would like to see both combatants exhausted to prevent them doing all they can to bring about peace.'[31]

For purposes of consultation, Spring Rice was then staying in London. Receiving Roosevelt's letter on July 9, he wrote immediately to the Foreign Office, stressing that the President 'expresses the hope that England is sincerely desirous of peace and will use her influence at the proper time to prevent the Japanese from asking irresponsible terms.' Spring Rice consulted Lansdowne later that day and, on July 10, he described the interview at great length to the newly appointed Secretary of State, Elihu Root. 'English interests (apart from the general interests of humanity) suffered from the war', Lansdowne had explained. 'The object of England was to see peace established and above all a durable peace.' While his sentiments wholly coincided with Roosevelt's, however, Lansdowne could see no satisfactory way to exert pressure on Japan. In conclusion, Spring Rice told Root that, while the United States could always rely upon Britain's friendship,

> 'you yourself will be the first to recognise the claims of honour as the first interest of all nations; and honour commands us to abstain from putting any pressure whatever on Japan to abstain even from actions which may eventually entail very severe sacrifices from us under the Treaty. But Lord Lansdowne in reading your words repeated the phrase, 'I hope the English people will use their influence *at the proper time* ...' He thinks that the 'proper time' may come if and *when* it is apparent that Japan is asking 'impossible terms which make peace impossible.' Up to the present moment, he had no information which points to this.'[32]

Forced into this friendly obstruction, Lansdowne's policy simply reflected Britain's long-held determination to give Japan a free hand against Russia. If the Foreign Secretary's actions seemed to threaten Anglo-American friendship, they were consistent, apparent, and easily defensible. Nevertheless, the interview between Lansdowne and Spring Rice seems to have lifted the former from his state of complacency. Immediately after the interview, he recounted its contents in an urgent dispatch to the Washington Embassy. Thoroughly explaining the Foreign Office's attitude, this was an evident attempt to reassure American authorities:

> 'He [Spring Rice] told me that the President was certainly under the impression that we would like the war to continue,' Lansdowne

explained, 'I cannot help hoping from your letters that, if this suspicion has [entered] the President's mind, he does not entertain it with much conviction.'

Lansdowne continued that:

'This supposition is, I need not tell you, entirely erroneous. We should be glad to see peace concluded, first of all for reasons of humanity, which after all must be allowed to count for something, and in the next place because the war, with its reactions in other parts of the world, is a bad thing for us all. It is true that we have not lectured the Japanese or preached to them the virtues of moderation. They might, I think, justly have taken offence if we had assumed that their demands were likely to be unreasonable.'[33]

Evidence of the Foreign Secretary's unwillingness to admit the scale of Roosevelt's displeasure soon emerged. Writing to Balfour on July 12 from his London home in Berkeley Square, Lansdowne exhibited great faith in Durand and suggested that, from the tenor of the Ambassador's dispatches, there was little reason for anxiety: 'I doubt whether the President is very deeply convinced that we are obstructing the peace negotiations'. However, mentioning Spring Rice's letter to Roosevelt and his own to Durand, Lansdowne concluded that he would speak in the same sense when he saw Whitelaw Reid. Balfour, too, seemed content. On Lansdowne's letter, he added his own personal comment. Roosevelt 'can hardly doubt our desire for peace', he remarked happily.[34]

The Government's apparent inability to understand the strength of the President's displeasure betrayed a prevailing misconception, that mere protestations of friendship would deflect American anger; above all, British officials, including Lansdowne, Durand and even Spring Rice, had been slow to understand Roosevelt's character. Critical impressions of Roosevelt were even then circulating in British diplomatic circles. Lansdowne himself viewed the President's impulsive and brash style of diplomacy with a mixture of bemusement and irritation; Roosevelt's actions, he thought, were both ill-timed and indiscreet. Confusion and misapprehension prevailed; above all, Britain sincerely missed Hay. In April, Durand had bemoaned Hay's absence from the State Department: 'without Hay to keep him [Roosevelt] steady there is no saying what he might do', he commented. From Tokyo, Sir Claude MacDonald wrote on June 8 of the Secretary of State's 'chastening influence on the somewhat exuberant diplomacy of the President'. On the current moves for peace, MacDonald explained that Roosevelt 'has started the ball (not altogether I venture to think in a very adroit manner) to bring this about.'[35]

Adroit or otherwise, the ball was picking up speed. On July 2, an authorised statement from Roosevelt was printed in the international press. 'The Russian and Japanese Governments have notified the President that they have appointed plenipotentiaries, who will meet as soon as possible', the Washington reporter for

The Times explained. 'The representatives of both parties will have full powers to negotiate and conclude a treaty subject to the ratification of their respective Governments.'[36] On July 7, Lloyd Griscom listed Japan's chosen delegates and, four days later, George Meyer sent the State Department details of the Russian representatives.[37] By July 11, a location for negotiations had been published; the two sides would meet, sometime in August, at the Navy Yard in Portsmouth, New Hampshire.[38] During the intervening time, Roosevelt continued – through Baron Kaneko – to push for Japanese moderation at the coming Conference; at the same time Russia was pressed towards equal moderation. In the Far East, there was a fragile and unofficial armistice and the constant danger of renewed hostilities. A Japanese attack on the island of Sakhalin, north of Japan, was considered a very real threat and the uprising in Odessa in late June, culminating in a mutiny on the battleship "Potemkin" on June 27, had thrown the Russian Government once more into a state of despair. The sooner the settlement came, the greater were Russia's chances of emerging from the conflict, if not as an enduring great Eastern Power, then at least as one whole nation.[39] With these considerations in mind, Russia and Japan prepared for Portsmouth.

Despite the overwhelming nature of Russia's military defeat, an attack on the Northern frontier of India remained a significant concern in British official circles during the spring of 1905. This was more than paranoia. Through her alliance with Japan, Britain's relations with St. Petersburg had been strained and the Russian army, though defeated and dispirited, remained both vast and intact; the Russo-Japanese war had not destroyed, or even greatly diminished, the Russian threat. Military experts refused entirely to rule out a Russian move on India, in order to recover her military prestige and reassert her international position.[40]

On November 8 1904, G. F. Ellison at the War Office raised the subject of British reinforcements for India. If Britain sent enough troops to deter Russia in India, Ellison explained, 'the Artillery and Infantry units remaining in the United Kingdom would be little more than skeletons.' Secretary of State for War Arnold-Forster quickly voiced his own personal concern. In a memorandum prepared on January 19 1905, the old spectre returned of a powerful Russo-French combination marching on India. Arnold-Forster further explained that, because of 'the great and growing demands of India, all idea of providing such a force must be abandoned.'[41]

For this reason, the ongoing negotiations with Japan began to concentrate, not merely on the renewal of the 1902 alliance, but on its significant extension. On March 24, Lansdowne wrote to Sir Claude MacDonald of an interesting meeting with Viscount Hayashi, Japan's Ambassador in London. Replying to the Foreign Secretary's enquiry, Hayashi had maintained that the desire to renew the agreement 'was at present mainly a matter of sentiment [in Japan], although there was undoubtedly a general feeling in favour of making the alliance "more solid."' This was welcome news and soon inspired a number of suggestions for the practical extension of the alliance to incorporate India. A Committee of Imperial Defence meeting, held on April 12, thoroughly discussed questions relating to Indian defence and the renewal of the Japanese alliance. With Lansdowne in attendance, Balfour raised the issue, stressing that both Britain and Japan were looking to prolong the treaty; its scope might now be extended in the interests of both parties. However, the Prime Minister concluded that:

> 'In any extension, it is essential that the defensive character of the Treaty should be strictly maintained, and that the provisions should be so framed as neither to constitute a menace, in reality or appearance, to the position and interests of friendly Powers, such as France and the United States, nor to be regarded as an Anglo-Japanese Alliance against Europe.'[42]

Specific proposals were soon advanced. On May 4, Sir George Clarke suggested that 150,000 Japanese troops might be supplied by Japan to defend India in return for the protection given to Japan by the British navy.[43] When Balfour wrote to the King four weeks later, he explained that 'we have tried to frame Notes so as to make Japanese assistance in the defence of India bear a fixed relation to our efforts to send adequate forces to the front.'[44] Unfortunately, despite Hayashi's initial encouragement, Japanese diplomacy proved rather vacillatory on the subject of extension. Japan's diplomats, headed by Baron Komura, were evidently reluctant to sanction large-scale commitments to protecting Britain's Eastern Empire. On her decision not 'to develop or extend the alliance any way', Lord Selborne wrote to Lansdowne on April 26: 'I was, and am ... profoundly astonished. What can it mean?'[45]

Discussions between the Foreign Secretary and Viscount Hayashi in April and May served to quieten Japanese anxiety and, on May 26, the Ambassador forwarded an encouraging draft agreement to the Foreign Office. The draft acknowledged Japan's special rights and interests in Korea and stated that, should either country be attacked in Eastern Asia or India – whether by one or by several Powers – her ally would intervene.[46] Although many weeks of negotiation lay ahead, the fundamental nature of the new alliance had been laid. Accordingly, Lansdowne's counter draft, presented to Balfour and the Cabinet in June, received only the slightest of criticism.

> 'I am entirely in favour of retaining in the Treaty itself the vague phrase which is designed to include India proper, and those regions near it,' Balfour wrote to the Foreign Secretary on June 30, 'which, from a strategic point of view, are as important to us as India itself. But ought we not in an exchange of Notes to be a little more precise? Ought we not to enumerate what these regions are...?'[47]

The renewed Anglo-Japanese agreement was signed on August 12 1905, but would not be published until a successful settlement was concluded at Portsmouth. While both Powers stressed that the extensions to the treaty were essentially of a defensive character, it was also recognised that the horror and anxiety with which

Russia was expected to greet the news might disrupt, or even destroy, the ongoing peace discussions. Friendly nations, however, were quickly informed. Indeed, Ambassador Durand showed Roosevelt a draft copy of the agreement ten days before its formal signature. It was, as the President quickly told Whitelaw Reid on August 3, 'a good thing.'[48] The following day, Roosevelt met Durand and related the contents of a meeting that had just occurred between Taft and the Japanese Foreign Minister, Baron Komura. The latter, then in the United States as one of Japan's peace delegates, suggested to Taft,

> 'that [the] United States should join [the] Anglo-Japanese Alliance. Taft explained that no such arrangement could be made without [the] consent of Congress but stated [that the] views of [the] American Govt. regarding Eastern Asia were entirely in accordance with [the] views of England and Japan.'[49]

In a subsequent meeting, the British Ambassador travelled to Oyster Bay to show the President a revised article concerning Korea. During the interview Roosevelt voiced his wholehearted support for the renewed agreement:

> 'I had taken a copy of the Corean [sic.] article and read it over with him carefully – twice,' Durand recounted on August 10. 'He seemed entirely satisfied. He said that, in his opinion we were quite capable of repelling any attack upon India without a Japanese alliance, but that of course Russia would not see that such an attack was hopeless.'[50]

On August 12, after the news that the signature had taken place arrived in Washington, Durand telegraphed Lansdowne to enquire if he should inform the President. Lansdowne's reply was suggestive, both of the intense secrecy surrounding the agreement and of his personal reservations about the President's character. 'I am most anxious to show the President that we trust him completely', he remarked, 'but can we be quite sure that the secret would be kept[?]' In the event, the Foreign Secretary left Durand to decide whether Roosevelt could be relied upon not to broadcast the news, particularly to his international friends.[51]

Sir Mortimer chose silence. Equally, Lansdowne's subsequent dispatches entirely omitted the subject until September 4, by which time secrecy was no longer important. The Foreign Secretary, then staying at his Irish estate, had determined that both Russia and France should be given the text of the agreement to prevent a later outcry. These were sent through Hardinge and Bertie in early September.[52] The United States was the only other country to receive prior notification; in response to a private enquiry from Balfour, Lansdowne remarked on September 3 that 'I think America, France and Russia should certainly be taken into our confidence before the whole world is informed.'[53]

Lansdowne now instructed Durand to 'communicate [the] substance of [the] Anglo-Japanese Agreement privately to the President if you have not already done so.'[54] A friendly defence of the concealment was telegraphed to the Embassy six days later. '[W]e had supplied him [Roosevelt] with timely information as to the contents of the Agreement', Lansdowne explained, '[but] it was thought more convenient that, whilst the negotiations were proceeding, the fact of signature having taken place should remain undisclosed'.[55] Luckily, Roosevelt saw no reason for complaint.[56]

If Anglo-American diplomacy throughout the war had generally offended and disappointed the President, the extended Japanese agreement was welcomed with great enthusiasm. Not only had the alliance given Britain a greater authority over Japan – should Lansdowne chose to exert pressure on her peace demands – but the agreement linked Japan to a ten year agreement with a non-aggressive Power in the East and, consequently, served to dispel much of Roosevelt's anxiety about a dominant 'yellow peril' looking acquisitively at America's Pacific possessions.[57]

As the Russian and Japanese delegates made their way to Portsmouth in early August, Roosevelt again pressed upon Durand the necessity of British interference. However, the Ambassador proved stubbornly resistant when the two men met at Oyster Bay on August 2. 'I told him ... that if they [Britain] really wished peace, they would advise the Japs, in their own interest, to make it', the President told Whitelaw Reid the following day.[58]

Prominent Americans then in London, including Loomis and Lodge, pressed the same argument with as little success. Lansdowne, making no secret of his determination to protect the Japanese alliance, was prepared to endure Roosevelt's irritation, hoping it would quickly fade after the conclusion of peace. Explaining his actions, in what he believed was the best possible light, Lansdowne wrote to Spring Rice on August 7:

> 'I do not think that, after my conversations with Lodge and Loomis, the President can remain in any doubt as to our attitude ... You can say as strongly as you please that we yield to no-one in desiring that the negotiations should have a favourable result, but we have no reason for supposing that Japan is going to put forward unreasonable terms.'

The Foreign Secretary's subsequent remarks, betraying his personal desire to see peace concluded, were undoubtedly genuine. Pressed into accepting a passive attitude to the war by Balfour and the Cabinet in December 1903, Lansdowne had always favoured an amicable settlement. Nevertheless, Lansdowne recognised that encouraging words alone would do little to appease a President eager for direct action. He concluded by stating that:

> 'I shall watch the events of the next few days with intense interest, and with an earnest hope that I may be able, before I am much older, to offer to the President my best congratulations upon the conclusion of a peace which, if it is concluded, will be so largely due to his fearless efforts.'[59]

Preliminary consultations began at Portsmouth on August 9 and the Conference formally opened the following day. Stubbornly resisting Roosevelt's plea that Japan should compromise on the indemnity issue, Komura and the other Japanese delegates presented their formal list of demands on August 10. Firstly, the list stated that Japan's predominant interests in Korea should be fully recognised; while Russia must abandon her occupation of Manchuria, the leasehold of Port Arthur should be transferred to Japan, in addition to the island of Sakhalin and the Port Arthur to Harbin railway.

Furthermore, and perhaps most importantly, Russia should pay for Japan's 'actual expenses of the war.' Sergei Witte, heading the Russian delegation, quickly formulated a set of counter proposals. Broadly conciliatory, Witte nonetheless refused to sanction the abandonment of Sakhalin and wholeheartedly resisted the call for an indemnity payment; this, historically, had only been paid by 'a conquered country and we do not consider ourselves as such.'[60] In the face of an impending deadlock, Roosevelt strenuously continued to urge compromise on both Russia and Japan.[61] His efforts failing, the President turned once more to Japan's ally, believing in the persuasiveness of timely British interference that would induce the Japanese to moderate their demands.

Publicly, Britain backed the Conference and hoped for an amicable and enduring peace. In his speech in the House of Lords on August 11, King Edward spoke in the following sense:

'Negotiations due to the initiative of the President of the United States, are about to be entered into between the Russian and Japanese Governments for the purpose of terminating the deplorable conflict still proceeding in the Far East. It is my earnest hope that they may lead to a lasting and mutually honourable peace.'[62]

In private, no action to put pressure on Japan had been, or would be contemplated, although the Foreign Secretary did suggest to Hayashi on August 12 that arbitration might settle the indemnity issue. Unwilling to do anything to offend the Japanese, Lansdowne's meetings with Hayashi were further restricted due to the latter's evident reluctance to discuss Japan's intentions at Portsmouth. News of Komura's actions at the Conference primarily came from Sir Claude MacDonald, rather than from the Japanese Embassy.

Still, Lansdowne held firm. When, on August 23, Roosevelt wrote a confidential letter to Durand, pleading for British support, it was effectively ignored; while the Ambassador's remarks discouraged the President, they were welcomed at the Foreign Office. The Japanese were 'extraordinarily sensitive' about such pressure, Lansdowne noted. Roosevelt's suggestion centred on the indemnity issue; he wrote of his hope that every friend of Japan should tell her 'that the opinion of the civilised world will not support it in continuing the war merely for the purpose of extorting money from Russia'. Lansdowne's caution again resulted in inactivity. Were Britain to follow this course, the Foreign Secretary minuted, 'our advice would not be taken and would be resented.'[63]

Thus, while many continental European Powers joined America in exerting pressure on Japan, Britain stood aside. 'This means of course that she [the United States] will more or less resent our attitude', Durand astutely remarked on August 25, 'though there has been no manifestation of resentment as yet.'[64] Certainly, the President was angry. To Chargé d'Affairs Henry White, the President complained on August 23 that:

'The English government has been foolishly reluctant to advise Japan to be reasonable, and in this respect has not shown well compared to the attitude of the German and French governments in being willing to advise Russia. I have not much hope of a favourable result, but I will do what I can.'[65]

Since the rejection of compromise terms now endangered the future of the Peace Conference, Roosevelt stepped up his efforts for peace. Three urgent dispatches were sent to George Meyer, to be relayed immediately to the Tsar, between August 21 and August 25. In the same period, the President appealed twice to Baron Kaneko, whilst consistently informing the Kaiser of every development. As a final measure, Roosevelt wrote a lengthy message to Komura on August 28, strenuously advocating the advisability of an immediate compromise, for the sake of both warring parties.[66]

Concurrently, a re-evaluation of priorities had been taking place in both Tokyo and St. Petersburg. While partly bowing to American pressure, both Powers naturally recognised that, with their finances exhausted by the war, their interests would be safeguarded only by the early establishment of peace. It was during the formal session on August 29, when Japan proposed the eventual compromise. Sakhalin island would be split, with Japan receiving the Southern half and Russia retaining the North. Most importantly, the indemnity issue was dropped to ensure a quick settlement.

Even Japan's ally was unable to account for her unexpected compromise. 'Like you, I am a little puzzled by the suddenness of the Japanese climb-down,' Lansdowne told Balfour on September 3. 'They may have been to some extent convinced by Roosevelt's powerful argument, but I suspect that there is something more behind it.'[67] Evidently then, the poor state of Japan's economy, her war exhaustion and her fundamental need for peace were not understood at the Foreign Office. Now events moved rapidly. With every obstacle removed, the delegates were soon able to create a satisfactory compromise and, on September 5, they finally added their signatures to the Treaty of Portsmouth. So ended the Russo-Japanese war.[68]

However confused at Japan's sudden moderation, Lansdowne sent an immediate telegraph of thanks to the Washington Embassy on August 30. Durand was instructed to 'offer to [the] President [the] warmest congratulations of H[is] M[ajesty's] G[overnment] on the satisfactory conclusion of the labours of the Conference.' Britain recognised 'the immense service rendered by [the] President to the civilised world in bringing about, in circumstances of great difficulty, an honourable settlement between the belligerents.'[69] This was, of course, merely diplomatic courtesy. While Lansdowne struggled to understand the peace terms, several diplomats and officials, including MacDonald and Sir George Clarke, voiced their sorrow that Japan should have been bullied into unnecessary concessions by the American President.[70] At the same time, an exultant Roosevelt publicised his satisfaction. To Spring Rice, he wrote on September 1 that, while the 'Japanese gave up more than they need to have given up ... on the whole it is all right, and I think the peace is just to Russia and Japan, and also good for England and the United States.' Knowing that the letter would be shown to the Foreign Office, Roosevelt concluded by praising the Kaiser's efforts whilst saying nothing about Britain's diplomacy:

'In my letters to you I have sometimes spoken sharply of the Kaiser. I want to say that in these peace negotiations he has acted like a trump. He has done every thing he could to make the Czar [*sic.*] yield and has backed me up in every way, and I thoroughly appreciate how he has behaved.'

Lansdowne received Roosevelt's dispatch, through Spring Rice, in late September. The German Emperor had 'played his cards very astutely', he noted sadly. 'He shall find the U.S. much less critical of Germany than they were.'[71] In his reply, sent on September 30, the Foreign Secretary penned a rather graceless admission concerning the utility of Roosevelt's actions:

'I think he [Roosevelt] is entitled to assume that his letters to Komura did have the desired effect, or at any rate that they were a potent factor in determining the Japanese to give way. ... There may have been other reasons which we can only guess at. But Roosevelt may fairly take credit to himself for having done a big thing, and I for one take off my hat to him.'[72]

Given the President's evident frustration towards British and her recent diplomatic efforts, the Foreign Office anxiously awaited further signs of American anger, which might seriously endanger the precariously established 'special relationship'. For this reason, Durand's personal comments, sent in a secret and coded dispatch on October 22, were disappointing, but hardly surprising. Sir Mortimer recounted confidential information, received from 'an Englishman I can trust', stating that Roosevelt:

'spoke angrily about our refusal to support him in pressing Japan to abate peace terms. The President said that [the] German Emperor had helped him by putting pressure on [the] Tsar and was [a] far more satisfactory person to deal with. He also said that personally he had no desire for an alliance with England whose policy was always weak and vacillating. ... Mr. Hay's influence and the trend of public opinion and the working of his own cooler judgement have gradually led him to [the] conviction that American interests are to a great extent bound up with those of England and he has at times seemed really friendly. I hope and believe that this conviction will endure but his prejudices are all the other way and he is very impulsive.'

A copy of Durand's letter was circulated in the Foreign Office, where it was examined intensively. Searching for somebody to blame, Sir Louis Mallet focused his attentions on George Meyer, for the lack of information that Hardinge received from the American Embassy at St. Petersburg. Another Foreign Office clerk noted that at 'one time he [Roosevelt] said he quite understood our not wishing to put pressure on Japan but his vanity made him so desirous of securing peace on any terms that it may well be that he was annoyed with us for not playing up to his wishes.'

Finally, Lansdowne added his own personal comment. 'Sir M. Durand seems to me to have taken a very accurate measure of the President', he noted simply. 'He must see that it would have been out of the question for us to put pressure on Japan.'[73] Both unable and unwilling to justify his actions to the United States, Lansdowne could do nothing but regret Roosevelt's anger and hope it would evaporate when stability returned to the Far East.

Lansdowne's diplomacy throughout the Russo-Japanese war was, in the main, directed and controlled by Balfour and the Cabinet. Lansdowne had urged intervention in December 1903 to save Japan from a terrible destruction, but was overwhelmed by his colleagues, who enthusiastically predicted a Japanese victory and, more importantly, cherished the hope of Russia's total disintegration as a mighty Eastern Power. Once this decision had been made, there was no room left in which Lansdowne could manoeuvre. If Japan was to be given a free hand against Russia, both during the war and throughout the ensuing peace negotiations, however, the British Government would have to resist all unwanted moves for peace.

It is unnecessary to state that Lansdowne rued American displeasure. Throughout his tenure at the Foreign Office, his desire for cordial Anglo-American relations had been a constant diplomatic aim. Still more, the maintenance of Anglo-American friendship had become a crucial part of Britain's global strategy. For this reason, despite his determination not to authorise British intervention in the Far Eastern settlement, Lansdowne paid a great deal of attention to the President's anger and made every effort to minimise its effects. Through Durand and Spring Rice, he regularly explained his actions and, at every opportunity, repeated his sympathy for a policy he could not himself adopt. For his part, the President's ire soon cooled.

Welcoming the renewal of the Anglo-Japanese alliance, the terms of which he had received before its official publication on September 27, Roosevelt began to adopt a more sympathetic attitude. 'I did not get much direct assistance from the English government', he told Whitelaw Reid on September 11, 'but I did get indirect assistance.'[74] On November 1, Roosevelt sent a lengthy dispatch to Spring Rice, forwarded by the latter to the Foreign Office on November 23. The President's letter sounded a welcome and reassuring tone and must have been greeted in London with intense relief; it appeared, after all, that Britain's diplomacy during the Far Eastern crisis had done no lasting damage to the dream of Anglo-American harmony: the President wrote that:

> 'As for your own country I have never wavered. I feel that England and the United States, beyond any other two Powers, should be friendly with one another, and what I can legitimately do to increase this friendliness will be done.'[75]

During the Russo-Japanese war, the Unionist Government rather lost sight of its goal to achieve an Anglo-American understanding in the Far East. The prospect, either of an alliance or at least of a truly joint policy, was subordinated to the increasingly precious Anglo-Japanese relationship, the latter offering concrete advantages and drastically altering the Eastern balance of power in Britain's favour. Throughout Lansdowne's tenure at the Foreign Office, moreover, Far Eastern affairs had set a test for Great Britain and the United States.

If the Anglo-American bond had been more solid, a joint policy should have emerged. For reasons of self-interest alone, the two Powers – whose interests in the status quo and commercial freedom in China were so clearly similar – had much to gain from such co-operation. As it was, practical considerations wrecked the chances of agreement and, if American and British actions frequently took the same line, they were essentially concurrent, rather than co-operative. Such, unhappily, were the limits of friendship.

On December 4 1905, Arthur Balfour resigned his office. Since the resignations of such influential figures as Joseph Chamberlain and the Duke of Devonshire in late 1903, the Unionists had been fighting a losing battle to cling to power; Balfour, who struggled in the latter months of 1905 to hold his party together, finally realised that the game was up and handed over the political reins to Sir Henry Campbell-Bannerman's Liberals. Lansdowne's diplomacy, too, had come to an end. In the last exchange between Durand and the outgoing Foreign Secretary, Sir Mortimer ruefully stated that,

> 'I am more sorry than I can say that you have left us. I regret it much on my own account, as you will surely understand, but I regret it even more on public grounds. I hope it will not be long before the honour and interests of the country are again in your keeping, where everyone feels they are safe.'

Lansdowne, in reply, acknowledged that he had presided over a period of fundamental changes to the Anglo-American relationship. On January 2 1906, he asked whether Durand might relay his deep feelings of friendship and thanks to the President,

> '[to tell] him that I have very keenly appreciated his invariable courtesy, and the confidence which he has so constantly shown in us? Few things have given me more satisfaction than the knowledge that during my term of office the relations of G[rea]t Britain and the U[nited] S[tates] G[overnment] have been so cordial and intimate.'[76]

Conclusion

L ORD LANSDOWNE ASSUMED responsibility for the management of British foreign relations at a particularly critical moment in Anglo-American history. After more than a century of mutual antagonism, the events of the Spanish-American war initiated a cordial popular relationship, without, however, any guarantee of permanence. In the following years, the Canadian-American Joint High Commission broke up in acrimony over the Alaskan issue, while the American people clamoured for an isthmian canal and sympathised with the Boer republics during the South African conflict. Lansdowne's response had lasting repercussions on the future of the 'special relationship'. His willingness to settle the two major sources of Anglo-American dispute – the canal and Alaskan issues – did not quite cement an informal partnership, but, instead, provided a definite foundation for diplomatic harmony. Realising that the Empire no longer enjoyed the strategic and economic preponderance that it had so long taken for granted, the Unionist Government and the Lansdowne Foreign Office, appreciated the utility of Anglo-American friendship, and made sure that American affairs were handled with the utmost care. The task of defending and maintaining the Empire against foreign competition was the dominant objective of British foreign policy under Lansdowne.[1] This created an urgent need for powerful allies, and the emergence of the United States, for the first time, was viewed as a serious and important global phenomenon. The Americans ranked highly on the list of Britain's prospective friends; an Anglo-American understanding, after all, promised much-needed security for British colonies in the Western Hemisphere, whilst simultaneously offering tangible rewards in the Far East. For the remarkable transformation of the Anglo-American relationship in the opening years of the twentieth century, key figures in the political and diplomatic ranks of both nations were naturally responsible, but, without Lansdowne's adept and broadly sympathetic diplomacy (together with the strong encouragement of his Cabinet colleagues) the fragile *rapprochement* might rapidly have disintegrated.

Anglo-American diplomacy under Lansdowne may be divided roughly into two distinct periods, separated by the Alaskan verdict of October 1903. Of the two, the former period was, by far, the more productive. The Boer War, together with the bitter hostility of continental Europe, acted as the initial catalyst for greater international accommodation and inclined Lansdowne to approach the awkward canal negotiations in a firm, but conciliatory spirit. Above all, the legitimate right of the United States to build, and ultimately to control the canal, was quickly and absolutely admitted. As *The Times* explained on March 9 1900, Britain had 'no great interest in the Hay-Pauncefote treaty or in the Nicaraguan Canal question generally. The Foreign Office considers, and others consider, very naturally, that the concern of the United States in the matter is much greater than that of England.'[2]

If Lansdowne's personal desire to uphold diplomatic protocol temporarily stalled negotiations, Britain's willingness to accept necessary (and largely theoretical) concessions soon decided the issue. Still more, the Hay-Pauncefote Treaty of November 1901 was hardly what one historian has labelled a treaty of surrender, except, perhaps, in the narrowest sense.[3] Treaty rights were indeed abandoned, but these were rights that had little practical value, while contemporary British observers (and the policy-makers themselves) tended to view the canal convention as a landmark success in Anglo-American diplomatic relations. In a key dispatch already cited, penned on December 31 1901, Lansdowne told Sir Julian Pauncefote that,

> 'we should not delay much longer taking up the Alaska boundary and other questions dealt with by the Joint Commission. The conditions are favourable and indeed they may never be more so. How delightful it would be if you should be able, before you leave Washington, to give us that clean slate which we all so much desire.'[4]

Lansdowne's desire for a 'clean slate' became the governing consideration in his Alaskan diplomacy. Stoutly supported by Arthur Balfour, he ensured that the requirements of Anglo-American diplomacy over-rode Britain's imperial obligation to maintain and defend Canadian interests. Accordingly, the Foreign Office determined that Britain should not enter into a public controversy with the United States in February 1903, following President Roosevelt's overtly political appointments to the Alaska Tribunal.

Six months later, Balfour and Lansdowne pressed Lord Alverstone to accept diplomatic compromise for the sake of an amicable Anglo-American settlement: the arguments forwarded by Canada and the Colonial Office were thus summarily dismissed. If Roosevelt's rather brash use of the 'big stick' dictated specific concessions, the weakness of Canada's case simplified the issue, while the final Award owed a great deal to Lansdowne's long-sighted determination to clear the obstacles to Anglo-American harmony. The wisdom of British policy, in the event, was fully vindicated.

These were to be the Unionist Government's greatest Anglo-American achievements, producing an extraordinary change of attitude towards Britain in the United States. In this atmosphere, the Anglo-German blockade of Venezuela in the winter of 1902-3 passed with minimal danger. Had the incident occurred a few years earlier, the American reaction would undoubtedly have been very different and, even in 1902, needed delicate handling. The Lansdowne Foreign Office, fortunately, proved equal to the task. Through its public support for the Monroe Doctrine and quick acceptance of the principle of arbitration, Britain was able to reassure the United States of her friendly purpose, whilst steadfastly retaining the blockade until Castro's resistance crumbled.

British attempts to cultivate an Anglo-American joint policy in China, if unsuccessful, were rather half-hearted. On the surface, Britain and the United States were natural allies in the Far East. Equally horrified at the apparently inevitable disintegration of the Chinese Empire – and the resulting limitations on free commercial opportunity – there existed a definite opportunity for co-operation. That the two nations failed to arrive at an informal understanding, however, was hardly surprising.

The absence of critical American interests in China ensured a policy of general non-intervention, while the conclusion of the Anglo-Japanese agreement in January 1902 effectively ended British isolation and removed the urgent need for American assistance. Lansdowne's sudden approach to the United States of April 28 1903, suggesting the expediency of a possible Far Eastern partnership against Russia, was primarily a knee-jerk reaction to the depressing re-emergence of the Manchurian crisis and, once Sir Michael Herbert explained the true state of American feeling, Britain was content quickly to let the proposal drop. While Anglo-American relations in the Far East between 1900 and 1903 were generally cordial, the *rapprochement* remained a tangible factor only in the Western Hemisphere.

Once the Alaskan Tribunal delivered its verdict, Anglo-American relations underwent a noticeable transformation. Although the Unionist Government was to remain in power for a further two years, the Award proved to be the high point of its American diplomacy. In the aftermath of Alaska, widespread expressions of mutual sympathy and good will became increasingly prevalent and enthusiastic, itself a testament to the significance of the recent diplomatic achievements. In November 1904, John Hay spoke of Lansdowne to Sir Mortimer Durand and remarked that, 'I do not remember an instance in which anyone has established himself so rapidly and so firmly in the opinion of all alike as an international statesman of the fist rank.' More than ready to reciprocate, the Foreign Secretary replied: 'I have always had a sincere admiration for Hay, and there is no public man in the U.S. whose good opinion I should more highly prize.'[5] By 1905, American statesmen generally saw Britain as a staunch friend. Roosevelt spoke to Durand in January 1905,

'of the great change of feeling in the last few years. Nowadays he said no-one in America thinks of England as a possible enemy. Germany is the chosen foe of the Navy, and not only of the Navy. Since the Spanish war the feeling towards England is thoroughly friendly, and now that the Alaskan question is settled there is apparently nothing

which threatens to lead to any friction. The President spoke very cordially about this.'[6]

The Foreign Office received further notice of American friendship from Sir
Francis Mowatt, who, in the summer of 1905, headed the British delegation at the
Washington Railway Conference. After conversing intimately with both Roosevelt
and Taft, Mowatt sent Lansdowne the following remarks on June 10:

> 'It would be difficult to overstate the warmth of friendship with which
> each of those gentlemen spoke of this country, or to express a stronger
> conviction that the possibility of serious friction between the two
> Peoples has passed out of the range of practical politics so far as the
> present generation is concerned. In a private conversation with Mr.
> Taft, he used these words, 'I am confident that the time is at hand when
> you and we can speak to the nations with a common voice and a com-
> mon policy on all external questions'.'[7]

It might well have been assumed that, in this auspicious atmosphere, the lesser disputes would be quickly and easily resolved. In the post-Alaskan period of Anglo-
American diplomacy, however, the Lansdowne Foreign Office broadly chose the
opposite course. Thus, the efforts made between 1900 and 1903 to extract compensation from the Hawaiian Government (and the United States by association),
for the ill treatment of British subjects, were suddenly and completely abandoned.
Similarly, Lansdowne refused to negotiate on the future of pelagic sealing in the
Behring Sea and left Newfoundland to fight her own battles for reciprocity. This
ambivalent attitude to the residual Anglo-American issues transformed
Lansdowne, as far as Western Hemispheric affairs were concerned, into a reactive
and reluctant diplomat, whose actions were dictated by specific, and largely
unforeseen events.

It should be added that, on the two occasions when active interference was
urgently required, the Foreign Office responded swiftly and decisively. In August
1904, a warship was dispatched to the Venezuelan coast to protect British subjects
caught up in the New York and Bermudez Asphalt Company crisis. The dismay
with which Lansdowne reacted to the sudden re-emergence of the North Atlantic
Fisheries dispute in the autumn of 1905 inspired an equally strong policy and, by
preventing Sir Robert Bond from pursuing his anti-American behaviour whilst
simultaneously placating the anxieties of the State Department, Britain was able
effectively to minimise the danger of diplomatic friction.

After the Alaskan verdict, then, Lansdowne tended not to display much
interest in the settlement of outstanding Anglo-American disputes. While the poor
relationship between Theodore Roosevelt and Sir Mortimer Durand meant that
the Foreign Office was not always kept abreast of developments, Lansdowne was
determined not to risk renewed diplomatic hostility; negotiating the outstanding
issues only risked endangering the friendship, so painfully fostered during his first
three years as Foreign Secretary, without offering any tangible rewards. Still more,

in the light of the concurrent national instability of the Balfour Administration, and its mounting preoccupation with the Russo-Japanese crisis in the Far East, it was perhaps natural that this aspect of Lansdowne's diplomacy should suddenly lose its vitality.

The Anglo-American relationship in the Western Hemisphere, however, continued to undergo radical changes and this was particularly evident during the winter of 1904. When Roosevelt announced his Corollary to the Monroe Doctrine on December 6, it was not only welcomed in Britain, but coincided with her own fundamental reconsideration of naval and military strategy. As part of this process, British troops were withdrawn from Canadian and Caribbean garrisons, while similar reductions to the North Atlantic and Pacific squadrons effectively relinquished control of the hemisphere to the United States. 'The reported intention of the British Admiralty to withdraw most of its warships from American stations', the New York correspondent for *The Times* remarked on December 9, 'is described as a unique compliment to this country.'[8] These events, moreover, had been preceded in November by the successful negotiation of a general treaty of arbitration. Carefully formulated by Hay and Durand, it provided for the interpretation of treaties and the resolution of non vital legal differences, to be settled at the Hague Court. Although the strong opposition of the Senate forced Roosevelt reluctantly to abandon the arbitration treaty, its construction served further to underline the friendly spirit that now governed Anglo-American relations.[9]

After 1903, for very different reasons, Britain's diplomatic interaction with the United States underwent a similar transformation. In the formulation of Britain's response to the worsening situation in China, the Cabinet discussions of December 1903 proved critical and set the tone for a generally passive policy that would last throughout the Russo-Japanese conflict. Thus Lansdowne's efforts – firstly to persuade his colleagues actively to support Japan, and subsequently to induce the United States to lead the international appeal for a Far Eastern compromise – were quickly dismissed, most prominently, by the Prime Minister himself. In the event, Balfour's belief that British interests in the Far East might actually benefit from the war carried the day, and the signature of the Anglo-French agreements on April 8 1904 greatly strengthened his position.

Still more, the prevailing argument, that British security could best be maintained by ensuring firm ties with Japan and France naturally superseded the vague hope of American assistance and explain the diminishing interest with which Balfour and the Cabinet generally viewed Roosevelt's interventionist diplomacy. For this reason, while Balfour personally was susceptible to the rather naive dream of an Anglo-American partnership to protect the integrity of China, he voiced his wistful hopes only to close colleagues;[10] above all, he saw the Japanese alliance as the key stone of British Far Eastern diplomacy and, in 1905, wholeheartedly joined the effort to further its scope.

With the course of British policy dictated by the Cabinet, Lansdowne reluctantly was obliged to stand back. Given Roosevelt's determination to bring the war to a close, and to use the British Foreign Office as an intermediary, this course posed a tangible threat to the continuation of Anglo-American harmony. The execution of Lansdowne's diplomacy, however, successfully limited the danger. He used both Durand and Spring Rice to gauge the extent of Roosevelt's displeasure, whilst ensuring that important diplomatic dispatches – which, if published, might jeopardise relations either with the United States or Japan – were shown only to the King and to the inner circle of Cabinet policy makers. Above all, he consistently stressed his deep desire for intimate relations with the American Government. In some respects, Lansdowne was fortunate; although temporarily angered by Britain's stubborn refusal to press Japan for peace, Roosevelt never questioned her underlying motives nor lost his faith in the importance of Anglo-American harmony. That the Russo-Japanese war caused no lasting damage to the *rapprochement* was both a testament to its endurance and to Lansdowne's careful steering of British foreign policy.

To the Liberal Government, and to Foreign Secretary Sir Edward Grey, was left the task of resolving the final outstanding Western Hemispheric disputes. Grey fully shared his predecessor's belief in the utility of Anglo-American friendship[11] and, by working the ground prepared by the Lansdowne Foreign Office, encouraged fruitful negotiations. The North Atlantic fisheries dispute was resolved by the Hague Court on September 7 1910, while a pelagic settlement arrived at Washington ten months later.[12] Although further treaties for Anglo-American arbitration, so strenuously supported by President Taft in 1910 and 1911, failed to gain Senate approval,[13] and despite the diplomatic bitterness surrounding the Panama Tolls controversy of 1912,[14] there was little chance that the 'special relationship' would seriously be endangered. Clearly, a new era in Anglo-American history had begun.

The Unionist Government of 1900-1905 regarded the cultivation of a solid Anglo-American friendship as a critical diplomatic objective. In the event, Britain's struggle to find an adequate response to her apparent international weakness in the face of growing foreign competition had tangible results and Lansdowne's efforts to solidify the Anglo-American *rapprochement* constituted a substantive and impressive achievement. With both nations convinced of the urgency of agreement, this was broadly achieved by the end of 1903, ensuring both international cordiality and, more specifically, the protection of major British interests in the Western Hemisphere.

Although the brash style of American diplomacy, at times, offended and disappointed Lansdowne (particularly the Senate's unruly behaviour during the canal negotiation and Roosevelt's bullying attitude on the Alaska boundary question) he remained conscious of the larger objectives and, together with his Cabinet colleagues, carefully and steadily pursued solicitous diplomacy with the State Department until his departure from office in December 1905. In all, the major Anglo-American settlements, which set the diplomatic relationship on an entirely new path, owed a great deal to Britain's patience and her willingness to accept compromise.

Although diplomatic friction between Britain and the United States would occasionally re-emerge, the opening five years of the twentieth century transformed the bond between Britain and her 'brothers across the ocean' and paved the way for a firm, amicable 'special relationship', which would play an increasingly powerful role in world affairs and which has survived very much intact (for better or worse) to the present day.

More than a century after Lansdowne left the Foreign Office, the Anglo-American *rapprochement* has moved on, but remains clearly recognisable – from failed Far Eastern co-operation in 1905, a century of almost unbroken harmony led (albeit indirectly) to full-scale military partnership in the Middle East in 2005 and, in 2011, to continuing military operations in Afghanistan. Outdated race sentiment aside, the idealistic terminology used in 1900-1905 remain diplomatic buzz words today, while the relationship itself has solidified into the cornerstone of global strategic thinking in both London and Washington. Yet without the Unionists' achievements in the opening years of the twentieth century, the present-day 'special relationship' between President Barack Obama and Prime Minister Cameron might instead be one of hostility, distrust or, perhaps, simple indifference. That the world leaders of the two nations choose to stand shoulder to shoulder as the firmest of friends and the closest of allies, then, owes much to Lansdowne, a statesman who, somewhat ironically, has been relatively overlooked by historians and the general public on both sides of the Atlantic.

If Lansdowne was, to some extent, an old-style diplomat, whose formal and reserved nature clashed with Theodore Roosevelt's brash enthusiasm, his arrival at the Foreign Office gave British foreign policy a sudden new impetus. Lansdowne's willingness to remove unnecessary sources of international friction revealed a man of firm convictions, but fluid conceptions of Britain's global requirements. Moreover, although he did not claim personally to understand Roosevelt (at one moment during the Russo-Japanese war he labelled the President 'a strange being'),[15] it was his conception and execution of Anglo-American diplomacy that helped to bring about a lasting understanding, which, arguably, constituted his greatest and most enduring achievement.

Notes & References

Introduction

[1] France and Russia became allies in 1894, concluding the Dual Alliance. The Triple Alliance – Germany, Austria-Hungary and Italy – was renewed in 1891.

[2] Recent historians have rejected the traditional view that, under Salisbury, Britain pursued a policy of 'splendid isolation'; Lansdowne's willingness to embrace foreign allies, it is argued, should therefore not be considered a radical change of direction. See, for example, E. D. Steele, *Lord Salisbury: A Political Biography* (London, 1999).

[3] Works on Anglo-American relations in this period include L. M. Gelber, *The Rise of Anglo-American Friendship* (London, 1938); R. H. Heindel, *The American Impact on Great Britain, 1898-1914* (Philadelphia, 1940); H. S. Allen, *Great Britain and the United States* (London, 1954) and *The Anglo-American Special Relationship since 1783* (London, 1959); C. S. Campbell, *Anglo-American Understanding, 1898-1903* (Baltimore, 1957); A. E. Campbell, *Great Britain and the United States, 1895-1903* (London, 1960); K. Bourne, *Britain and the Balance of Power in North America, 1815-1908* (London, 1967); B. Perkins, *The Great Rapprochement: England and the United States, 1895-1914* (London, 1968); W. G. Kneer, *Great Britain and the Caribbean, 1901-1913: A Study in Anglo-American Relations* (New York, 1975).

The influence of Salisbury, Balfour, John Hay and Roosevelt has also received great attention. The most recent works on Salisbury are Steele, *Lord Salisbury* and A. Roberts, *Salisbury: Victorian Titan* (London, 1999). Also see J. A. S. Grenville, *Lord Salisbury and Foreign Policy: The Close of the Nineteenth Century* (London, 1964); C. H. D. Howard, *Splendid Isolation: A Study of Ideas Concerning Britain's International Position and Foreign Policy during the Later Years of the Third Marquis of Salisbury* (London, 1967); D. Judd, *Balfour and the British Empire* (London, 1968); J. Tomes, *Balfour and Foreign Policy: The International Thought of a Conservative Statesman* (London, 1997); K. L. Clymer, *John Hay: The Gentleman as Diplomat* (Michigan, 1975); W. N. Tilchin, *Theodore Roosevelt and the British Empire: A Study in Presidential Statescraft* (New York, 1997).

[4] The construction of the "Alabama", "Shenandoah" and "Florida", which subsequently waged a successful campaign against Union shipping, caused an indignant reaction in the United States. In 1871, a Joint High Commission convened in Washington and referred the claims to arbitration at Geneva. Its verdict favoured the United States' case. See C. S. Campbell, *The Transformation of American Foreign Relations, 1865-1900* (New York, 1976), pp. 9-12, 33-38, 44.

[5] Sackville-West to Lansdowne, 4 Feb. 1886. Lansdowne MSS BL L(5)7.

[6] J. Bryce, *The American Commonwealth* (London, 1895 ed.), vol. 2., p. 872.

[7] Quoted in R. B. Mowat, *The Life of Lord Pauncefote: First Ambassador to the United States* (London, 1929), p. 158.

[8] Note by Olney, 20 Jul. 1895., in A. S. Link and W. M. Leary (eds.), *The Diplomacy of World*

Power: The United States, 1889-1920 (London, 1970), pp. 44-60.

9 See Campbell, *Transformation of American Foreign Relations*, pp. 194-221.

10 Harcourt to Morley, 26 Jan. 1896, quoted in A. G. Gardiner, *The Life of Sir William Harcourt* (London, 1923), vol. 2., p. 399.

11 Anglo-American diplomacy during the war is covered in B. A. Reuter, *Anglo-American Relations During the Spanish-American War* (New York, 1924); R. G. Neale, *Great Britain and United States Expansion, 1898-1900* (New York, 1966); and G. Seed, "British Reactions to American Imperialism Reflected in Journals of Opinion, 1898-1900" *Political Science Quarterly* 73 (1958), pp. 254-272.

12 British and German warships looked on as Admiral Dewey destroyed the Spanish fleet at Manila Bay. A myth quickly arose that Captain Chichester prevented the Germans from unwarranted intervention. In fact, neither Britain nor Germany intended to intervene, and the squadrons fully obeyed their instructions. See Neale, *Great Britain and United States Expansion*, pp. 85-90 and R. Busetto, "Captain Edward Chichester and HMS Immortalité in Manila Bay during the Spanish-American War" in G. J. Milne (ed.), *New Researchers: Papers presented at the Fifth Annual New Researchers in Maritime History Conference* (Liverpool, 1997).

13 See Tilchin, *Theodore Roosevelt and the British Empire*, pp. 7-8.

14 W. P. Trent, *Progress of the United States of America in the Century* (London, 1903 ed.), p. 412

15 A. Gorren, *Anglo-Saxons and Others* (Boston, 1900), pp. 8-9.

16 Speech by Balfour at Manchester, 15 Jan. 1896, quoted in B. E. C. Dugdale, *Arthur James Balfour: First Earl of Balfour, K.G., O.M., F.R.S., Etc.* (London, 1936), vol. 1., p. 226.

17 Balfour to White, 12 Dec. 1900. Balfour MSS Add. 49742.

18 Speech by Chamberlain at Birmingham, 13 May, 1898, quoted in Campbell, *Anglo-American Understanding*, p. 47.

19 See ibid., pp. 88-137.

20 A young Franklin D. Roosevelt wrote to his parents in 1901 that 'I cannot help feeling convinced that the Boers have the side of right ... [but] it will be best from the humanitarian standpoint for the British to win speedily and civilization will be hurried on.' Roosevelt to his parents, 21 Jan. 1901., in E. Roosevelt (ed.), *The Roosevelt Letters, being the Personal Correspondence of Franklin Delano Roosevelt* (London, 1949), vol. 1., pp. 327-8. See also S. Anderson, "Racial Anglo-Saxonism and the American Response to the Boer War" *Diplomatic History* 2 (1978), pp. 219-236; R. B. Mulanax, *The Boer War in American Politics and Diplomacy* (Lanham, Maryland, 1994); and W. N. Tilchin, "The United States and the Boer War", in K. M. Wilson (ed.), *The International Impact of the Boer War* (Chesham, 2001), pp. 107-122 .

21 The Kaiser sent a personal message of congratulation to Paul Kruger, President of the Transvaal, on January 3 1896, thus offending Britain. He wrote that 'without appealing for the help of friendly Powers, you have succeeded ... against armed bands which invaded your country ... and have thus been enabled to restore peace'. Quoted in J. A. Spender, *Great Britain; Empire and Commonwealth, 1886-1935* (London, no date), p. 91.

22 Admiral Tirpitz initiated his program of naval expansion that same year, placing a further strain on the already out-dated two-Power standard. See Z. S. Steiner, *Britain and the Origins of the First World War* (London, 1977), pp. 24-27.

23 A detailed analysis of the global reaction to the Boer war is given in Wilson (ed.), *The International Impact of the Boer War*.

24 The defence of India became an obsession of the Salisbury and Balfour administrations. From the Admiralty, Sir John Fisher penned several letters of complaint. To Balfour's Private Secretary, he explained that 'That d[amne]d N[orth] W[estern] Frontier of India is what your Master [Balfour] is suffering from! For God's sake ask him to drop it!' Fisher to Sandars, 18 Jun. 1904. Balfour MSS Add. 49710.

25 Selborne to Hicks Beach, 29 Dec. 1900., in D. G. Boyce (ed.), *The Crisis of British Power: The Imperial and Naval Papers of the Second Earl of Selborne, 1895-1910* (London, 1990), pp. 105-106.

[26] Amongst the recommendations of the Report on War Office Reconstitution, delivered in the spring of 1904, was the establishment of an Army Council on the lines of the Board of Admiralty. See Sir S. Lee, *King Edward VII: A Biography* (London, 1927), vol. 2., pp. 194-197.

[27] Dugdale, *Arthur James Balfour*, vol. 1., pp. 335-336.

[28] Lansdowne to his mother, 18 May. 1883., quoted in Lord Newton, *Lord Lansdowne: A Biography* (London, 1929), p. 25.

[29] See Campbell, *Anglo-American Understanding*, p. 4.

[30] Undated notes by Lansdowne. Lansdowne MSS BL 'Canadian Notes', p. 5.

[31] Newton, *Lord Lansdowne*, pp. 47-48.

[32] Lansdowne to his mother, 8 Feb. 1888. ibid., p. 50.

[33] Esher's journal entry, 9 Nov. 1900., in M. V. Brett (ed.), *Journals and Letters of Reginald, Viscount Esher* (London, 1934), vol. 1., pp. 267-268.

[34] Lucy's diary entry, 13 Jul. 1897., in H. W. Lucy, *A Diary of the Unionist Parliament, 1895-1900* (London, 1901), p. 172.

[35] For the failure of British forces in South Africa, Lansdowne was hardly to blame. In August, Lansdowne wrote that the 'I do not see that anyone, let alone Beach, c[oul]d expect us to keep full transport in readiness for an operation of such magnitude in this particular theatre of war.' Lansdowne to Wyndham, 15 Aug. 1899. Lansdowne MSS BL L(5)40. Charles Beresford agreed. 'The navy is now in a very good condition', he told Balfour, 'but not equal to its needs in many details. We shall never be adequately or economically defended as long as the present system holds. The Naval and Military advisers are in no way responsible ... The defences of the Empire are not made out on exigencies of defence but on Budget exigencies.' Beresford to Balfour, 25 Dec. 1899. Balfour MSS Add. 49713.

[36] Lansdowne to Victoria, 29 Oct. 1900., in Newton, *Lord Lansdowne*, p. 190.

[37] See Grenville, *Lord Salisbury and Foreign Policy*, p. 325.

[38] Lansdowne to Hamilton, 31 Aug. 1900. Lansdowne MSS BL L(5)28.

[39] See, for example, E. W. Edwards, "The Prime Minister and Foreign Policy: The Balfour Government, 1902-1905", in H. Hearder and H. R. Loyn (eds.), *British Government and Administration: Studies Presented to S. B. Chrimes* (Cardiff, 1974), pp. 202-214. John Sandars recalled that 'Lansdowne liked to be fortified by his leader's judgement in nearly every step of importance he took in that department [the Foreign Office]. ... no dispatch of any real importance was ever sent without the draft being submitted to the Prime Minister'. Undated letter by Sandars, in M. Egremont, *Balfour: A Life of Arthur James Balfour* (London, 1980), p. 163. Austen Chamberlain backs this view: 'Lansdowne took no important step and sent no important dispatch without first consulting him [Balfour]. It does not detract from Lansdowne's services as Foreign Secretary to say that his chief accomplishments would never have been achieved but for the constructive mind of Balfour'. A. Chamberlain, *Down the Years* (London, 1935), p. 209.

[40] Lansdowne's French ancestry provided an initial impetus to Anglo-French diplomatic cordiality. Monson wrote that Delcassé 'begged me to tell you that he and all the members of the [French] Govt. would cooperate [sic.] most earnestly with you in maintaining good relations; and that they were much interested in fact of your family connection with France.' Monson to Lansdowne, 14 Nov. 1900. Lansdowne MSS F.O. 800/125.

[41] "Lord Lansdowne at Darlington" *The Times*, 28 Nov. 1901., p, 10; "Lord Lansdowne on Foreign Affairs" *The Times*, 13 Dec. 1902., p. 8.

[42] Balfour to Lansdowne, 11 Feb. 1904. Balfour MSS Add. 49728

[43] Viscount Cecil of Chelwood, however, remembered that Lansdowne 'who doubted the wisdom of Preference or Protection, [was] favourable to Retaliation.' Viscount Cecil, *All the Way* (London, 1949), p. 86. See also R. A. Rempel, *Unionists Divided: Arthur Balfour, Joseph Chamberlain and the Unionist Free Traders* (Newton Abbot, 1972).

[44] Lansdowne to Lascelles, 11 Nov. 1900. Lansdowne MSS F.O. 800/128.

[45] Lansdowne to Monson, 12 Nov. 1900. Lansdowne MSS F.O. 800/125.
[46] Lansdowne to Pauncefote, 11 Nov. 1900. Lansdowne soon asked the Ambassador to 'remain at Washington for a further period of a year.' Lansdowne to Pauncefote, 14 Dec. 1900. Lansdowne MSS F.O. 800/144.

1: No Apology, No Explanation

[1] Balfour to White, 12 Dec. 1900. Balfour MSS Add. 49742.
[2] See, for example, A. E. Campbell, *Great Britain and the United States, 1895-1903* (London, 1960), p. 68; J. A. S. Grenville, "Great Britain and the Isthmian Canal" *The American Historical Review* 61 (1955-6), p. 65; C. S. Campbell, *Anglo-American Understanding, 1898-1903* (Baltimore, 1957), pp. 213-7.
[3] Article I of the Clayton-Bulwer Treaty, 19 Apr. 1850, printed in *Papers Relating to the Foreign Relations of the United States 1901* (Washington, 1902), p. 238.
[4] Part of Article II of the Hay-Pauncefote Treaty, 5 Feb. 1900, ibid., p. 242.
[5] Adams to Hay, 16 Dec. 1900, in J. Levenson, E. Samuels, C. Vandersee and V. H. Winner (eds.), *The Letters of Henry Adams* (Cambridge, Mass., 1988), vol. 5., pp. 180-1.
[6] Pauncefote to Salisbury, 9 Jun. 1900. F.O. 5/2428.
[7] "Favors Nicaragua Route" *The New York Times*, 4 Dec. 1900, p. 2. The treaty stated that neither country should 'take advantage of any intimacy, or use any alliance, connection, or influence that either may possess with any state or government through whose territory the said canal may pass, for the purpose of acquiring ... any rights or advantages in regard to commerce or navigation through the said canal'. Clayton-Bulwer Treaty, April19 1850, in *Foreign Relations of the United States 1901*, p. 238.
[8] "President's Message to Congress" *The New York Times*, 4 Dec. 1900, p. 6.
[9] Pauncefote to Lansdowne, 23 Nov. 1900. Lansdowne MSS F.O. 800/144.
[10] Pauncefote to Lansdowne, 21 Dec. 1900. ibid.
[11] Part of Article II of the Hay-Pauncefote Treaty as ratified by the Senate, 16 Dec. 1900, printed in *Foreign Relations of the United States 1901*, p. 243.
[12] Hay to McCook, 22 Apr. 1900, in M. R. Hay (ed.), *Letters of John Hay and Extracts from Diary* (Washington, 1908 [printed but not published]), vol. 3., p. 176.
[13] Hay to Balfour, 12 Jan. in White to Balfour, 12 Jan. 1901. Balfour MSS Add. 49742
[14] Report by Acting-Governor Sir C. Boyle [British Guiana] to the Colonial Office, 24 Dec. 1900. *British Parliamentary Papers, Accounts and Papers 1901*, vol. XLV. (London, 1901).
[15] Report by Acting-Governor S. Olivier [Jamaica], sent to the Colonial Office, 31 Oct. 1900. ibid.
[16] Chamberlain to Minto, 30 Jan., in C.O to F.O., 31 Jan. 1900. F.O. 420/197.
[17] Salisbury to Victoria, 2 Feb. 1900. *Prime Minister's Letters to the Monarch, Reporting on Meetings of the Cabinet, 1895-1914*, vol. 2. Royal Archives, Windsor [copies of these letters (printed in 1974) are available in the Brotherton Library, University of Leeds].
[18] Salisbury to Victoria, 2 Feb. 1900. ibid.
[19] "Opinion in Great Britain" *The New York Times*, 16 Dec. 1900, p. 1.
[20] "The Hay-Pauncefote Treaty" *The Manchester Guardian*, 15 Dec. 1900, p. 7; "The Nicaragua Canal" *The Times*, 16 Jan. 1901, p. 3.
[21] Pauncefote to Lansdowne, tel., 9 Dec. 1900. F.O. 420/197.
[22] Cabinet Memorandum by Lansdowne, 13 Dec. 1900, in J. A. S. Grenville, *Lord Salisbury and Foreign Policy: The Close of the Nineteenth Century* (London, 1964), p. 383.
[23] Salisbury to Victoria, 14 Dec. 1900. *Prime Minister's Letters*, vol. 2.
[24] Lansdowne to Pauncefote, 14 Dec. 1900. Lansdowne MSS F.O. 800/144.
[25] Admiralty to F.O., 5 Jan. 1900. F.O. 420/200.
[26] Pauncefote argued that, should the notification of rejection come before the end of the session, the Senate would surely pass a resolution abrogating the Clayton-Bulwer Treaty altogether. Pauncefote to Lansdowne 'secret' tel., 8 Feb. 1901. F.O. 420/200.
[27] Memorandum by Lansdowne, dated Sep. 1912. Lansdowne MSS BL Lab 4/10.

[28] Lansdowne to Pauncefote, 'secret', 19 Feb. 1901. Lansdowne MSS F.O. 800/144.
[29] "The Hay-Pauncefote Treaty" *The New York Times*, 9 Dec. 1900, p. 1.
[30] Lansdowne to Pauncefote, 'secret', 19 Feb. 1901. Lansdowne MSS F.O. 800/144.
[31] Lansdowne to Pauncefote, 14 Jan. 1901. F.O. 420/200.
[32] ibid.
[33] ibid.
[34] "Hay Canal Treaty may be Killed" *The New York Times*, 8 Dec. 1900, p. 1.
[35] Pauncefote to Lansdowne, 18 Dec. 1900. F.O. 420/197.
[36] "Hay-Pauncefote Treaty" *The New York Times*, 25 Dec. 1900, p. 4.
[37] Hay to Balfour, 12 Jan. in White to Balfour, 12 Jan. 1901. Balfour MSS Add. 49742.
[38] White to Balfour, 12 Jan. 1901. ibid.
[39] Lansdowne to Pauncefote, 17 Jan. 1901. Lansdowne MSS F.O. 800/144.
[40] Lansdowne to Pauncefote 'secret', 19 Feb. 1901. ibid.
[41] Lansdowne's Cabinet Memorandum, 15 Jan. 1901., in Grenville, *Lord Salisbury and Foreign Policy*, p. 386.
[42] Lansdowne to Pauncefote, 8 Jan. 1901. F.O. 420/200.
[43] Lansdowne to Pauncefote, 19 Feb. 1901. ibid.
[44] Lansdowne to Pauncefote, 'confidential', 14 Jan. 1901. ibid.
[45] Lansdowne to Pauncefote, 'confidential', 27 Feb. 1901. ibid.
[46] "Another Defeat for Morgan", 2 Mar. 1901, p. 3, and "Morgan Pleads for the Canal Bill" *The New York Times*, 7 Mar. 1901, p. 5.
[47] "Hay-Pauncefote Treaty Dead" *The New York Times*, 6 Mar. 1901, p. 5.
[48] Memorandum by Lansdowne, 22 Feb., quoted in Hay to Pauncefote, 25 Mar., in Pauncefote to Lansdowne, 26 Mar. 1901. F.O. 420/200.
[49] Pauncefote to Lansdowne, 1 Mar. 1901 Lansdowne MSS F.O. 800/144 and Pauncefote to Lansdowne, 11 Mar. 1901. ibid.
[50] "The Nicaragua Canal" *The Times*, 13 Mar. 1901, p. 5; "Canal Agreement Fails" *The New York Times*, 12 Mar. 1901, p. 1.
[51] Quoted in B. Perkins, *The Great Rapprochement: England and the United States, 1895-1914* (London, 1968), p. 182. Adams to Cameron, 25 Feb. 1901. *Letters of Henry Adams*, vol. 5., p. 204.
[52] *Hansard* XC col. 1558, 14 Mar. 1901.
[53] Pauncefote to Lansdowne, 26 Mar. 1901. F.O. 420/200.
[54] Pauncefote to Lansdowne, 24 Apr. 1901. Lansdowne MSS F.O. 800/144.
[55] Lansdowne to Pauncefote, 7 May. 1901. ibid.
[56] Pauncefote to Lansdowne, 7 Jul. 1901. ibid.
[57] Cabinet Memorandum by Lansdowne, 8 Jul. 1901. Lansdowne MSS BL L(5)77.
[58] ibid.
[59] Lansdowne to Lowther, 'confidential', 16 Jul. 1901. F.O. 420/200.
[60] "Lord Pauncefote on Anglo-American Relations" *The Times*, 19 Jul. 1901, p. 5.
[61] Hay to King, 27 Oct. 1901. *Letters of John Hay and Extracts from Diary*, vol. 3., p. 244.
[62] H. C. Lodge, "The Treaty-Making Powers of the Senate", in Lodge to Lansdowne, 9 Sep. 1901. Lansdowne MSS F.O. 800/144.
[63] Pauncefote to Lansdowne, 'confidential', 10 Jan. 1901. F.O. 420/200.
[64] Lansdowne to Lodge, 12 Sep. 1901. Lansdowne MSS F.O. 800/144.
[65] Hay to Pauncefote, 2 Sep. 1901. ibid.
[66] Salisbury to Lansdowne, 7 Oct. 1901. Lansdowne MSS BL L(5)34.
[67] Cabinet Memorandum by Lansdowne, 16 Oct. 1901. Lansdowne MSS BL L(5)77.
[68] Hicks-Beach to Lansdowne, 17 Oct. 1901. Lansdowne MSS BL 'Private Letters', vol. 6.
[69] White to Balfour, 5 Oct. 1901. Balfour MSS Add. 49742.
[70] Lansdowne to Pauncefote, 13 Sep. 1901. Lansdowne MSS F.O. 800/144.
[71] Article III of the Hay-Pauncefote Treaty, Dec. 1901., in *Foreign Relations of the United States 1901*, p. 245.
[72] Lansdowne, in his Memorandum of July 8, wrote that the 'omission of the words "in

time of war as in time of peace," … is the alteration which we shall find most difficult in justifying.' The United States had 'always stressed they should be able to secure the safety of the canal in wartime: even temporarily deneutralisation of the canal.' Lansdowne did not object, because he thought the change was if 'no practical value.' Cabinet Memorandum by Lansdowne, 8 Jul. 1901. Lansdowne MSS BL L(5)77.

[73] "Lord Lansdowne at Darlington" *The Times*, 28 Nov. 1901., p. 10.
[74] Pauncefote to Lansdowne, 19 Dec. 1901. Lansdowne MSS F.O. 800/144.
[75] *Hansard*, XCIII, cols. 10 & 20, 16 Jan. 1902.
[76] Pauncefote to Lansdowne, 22 Nov. 1901. F.O. 5/2458.
[77] Pauncefote to Dilke, 30 Jan. 1902. Dilke MSS Add. 43882.
[78] Lansdowne to Pauncefote, 31 Dec. 1901. Lansdowne MSS F.O. 800/144..
[79] Pauncefote to Lansdowne, 19 Dec. 1901. ibid.
[80] Lansdowne to Pauncefote, 31 Dec. 1901. ibid.
[81] Goldwin Smith to Dilke, 2 Nov. 1901. Dilke MSS Add. 43917.

2: That Disreputable Little Republic

[1] Lord Charles William de la Poer Beresford, Second-in-Command of the Mediterranean Fleet, 1900-1902, M.P. for Woolwich, 1902-3.
[2] *Hansard's Parliamentary Debates* (4th ser.) CXVI cols. 1250, 1278 and 1280, 15 Dec. 1902.
[3] See C. S. Campbell, *Anglo-American Understanding, 1898-1903* (Baltimore, 1957), p. 270, W. G. Kneer, *Great Britain and the Caribbean, 1901-1913: A Study in Anglo-American Relations* (New York, 1975), p. xiv, and B. Perkins, *The Great Rapprochement: England and the United States, 1895-1914* (London, 1968), p. 187.
[4] E. Halévy, *Imperialism and the Rise of Labour* (London, 1951), p. 134.
[5] Herbert to Lansdowne, 19 Dec. 1902. Lansdowne MSS F.O. 800/144.
[6] Moore to Pauncefote, 21 Apr., in Pauncefote to Salisbury, 24 Apr. 1900. F.O. 420/195.
[7] Sendall to Chamberlain, 6 Nov. 1899, and Chamberlain to Sendall, 23 Jan. 1900, in C.O.to F.O., 24 Jan. 1900. ibid.
[8] In an undated note, Larcom noted the grievances between Britain and Venezuela, including 'the illegal imposition of a 30 per cent. preferential duty on goods from Trinidad and the other West Indian Islands', illegal activities committed by Venezuelan soldiers in Guiria and Patos Island, and offences on British shipping. "Memo by Mr. Larcom on existing causes of complaint against Venezuela", in "Confidential Correspondence respecting Causes of Complaint against Venezuela", 10 Oct. 1902. Lansdowne MSS BL 'Private Letters', vol. 5.
[9] C.O. to F.O., 16 Mar. 1901. F.O. 420/206.
[10] Maloney to Chamberlain, 14 Apr. 1901, in C.O. to F.O., 2 May. ibid.
[11] Haggard to Lansdowne, 'confidential', 30 Apr. 1901. ibid.
[12] Haggard to Lansdowne, 13 Jun. 1902. ibid.
[13] H. H. Herwig, *Germany's Vision of Empire in Venezuela, 1871-1914* (Princeton, 1986), p. 93.
[14] Haggard to Lansdowne, 'confidential', 27 Oct. 1901. F.O. 420/206.
[15] Bertie to C.O., 30 Nov. and Villiers to C.O., 28 Dec. 1901. ibid. The ownership of Patos was hardly clear-cut; Britain hoisted the Union Jack over the island only in the summer of 1902. As one historian puts it, 'the British were staking a territorial claim and therefore skirting dangerously close to the Monroe Doctrine.' See N. Mitchell, "The Height of the German Challenge: The Venezuela Blockade, 1902-3" *Diplomatic History* 20 (1996), p. 191.
[16] Haggard to Lansdowne, 'confidential', 30 Jun. 1902. F.O. 420/206.
[17] Haggard to Lansdowne, 'confidential', 16 May. 1902. ibid.
[18] Quoted in Herwig, *Germany's Vision of Empire*, pp. 86-7.
[19] See Kneer, *Great Britain and the Caribbean*, pp. 11-13.
[20] The Treaty of Vereeniging, signed on May 31 1902, ended the Boer War.

[21] MacGregor to Cranborne, 11 Feb. 1902. F.O. 58/339.
[22] Note by Villiers, 11 Feb. and Villiers to Admiralty, 24 Feb. 1902. ibid.
[23] MacGregor to Cranborne, 6 Mar., and Bertie to Admiralty, 12 Mar. 1902. ibid.
[24] Villiers to C.O., 1 Jul. 1902. F.O. 420/206.
[25] Quoted in Kneer, *Great Britain and the Caribbean*, p. 16,
[26] Lansdowne to Haggard, tel., 29 Jul. and Villiers to Admiralty, 'very confidential'. 8 Aug. 1902. F.O. 420/206.
[27] Salisbury waited for the South African peace and resigned on July 10. It appears that Balfour first learnt of the pending Venezuelan dispute from Lansdowne on October 12: 'We have consulted the Adm[iralt]y who are prepared for a naval demonstration in November. A blockade will be better than the alternative of seizing the Venezuelan gun boats.' Lansdowne was quickly dissuaded from this course. In his Cabinet memorandum of October 21, he wrote that 'We should ... in the first instance, address a final warning to the Venezuelans, and ... if it is disregarded [inform them that] we are prepared to go in with them [the Germans] in measures of coercion ... [that is,] the seizure of the gunboats.' Lansdowne to Balfour, 12 Oct. 1902. Lansdowne MSS BL 'Private Letters', vol. 5., Memorandum by Lansdowne, 21 Oct. 1902., in Mitchell, "Height of the German Challenge", pp. 195-196.
[28] Lansdowne to Lascelles, 22 Oct. 1902, quoted in G. P. Gooch and H. Temperley (eds.), *British Documents on the Origins of the War, 1898-1914* (London, 1927), vol. 2., p. 154.
[29] Balfour to the King, 21 Oct. 1902. *Prime Minister's Letters to the Monarch, Reporting on Meetings of the Cabinet, 1895-1914* vol. 2. Edward's Private Secretary, Sir Francis Knollys, replied that the King 'entirely agrees with you in thinking that a Blockade would be very unsatisfactory, and that the proposal to seize on the gun boats an excellent one.' Knollys to Balfour, 22 Oct. 1902. Balfour MSS Add. 49683.
[30] Memorandum by Lansdowne, printed 24 Nov. 1902. Lansdowne MSS BL L(5)77.
[31] The blockade, imposed on December 20, was belligerent, rather than pacific. This decision was reached after discussions with Germany, and correspondence with the United States. Henry White wrote on December 13 that 'The United States ... does not acquiesce in any extending of the doctrine of pacific blockade which may adversely affect the right of States not parties to the controversy or discriminate against the commerce of neutral nations, and my Government reserves all of its rights in the premises.' White to Lansdowne, 13 Dec. 1902. F.O. 420/206. Also see Mitchell, "Height of the German Challenge", p. 196.
[32] Pauncefote to Lansdowne, 28 Feb. 1902. Lansdowne MSS F.O. 800/144.
[33] Chamberlain to Lansdowne, 25 Feb. 1902. Lansdowne MSS BL 'Private Letters', vol. 1.
[34] See Campbell, *Anglo-American Understanding*, pp. 244-252. Also F. R. Bridge, "Great Britain, Austria-Hungary, and the Concert of Europe on the Eve of the Spanish-American War", pp. 87-108.
[35] Sanderson to Lascelles, private, 2 Jun. 1902. Lascelles MSS F.O. 800/11.
[36] Lowther to Lansdowne, 17 Jun. 1901. F.O. 5/2457; "President Roosevelt and the Monroe Doctrine" *The Times*, 2 Sep. 1902, p. 3.
[37] Quoted in Campbell, *Anglo-American Understanding*, p. 270.
[38] "Editorial Comment: Coercing Venezuela" *The New York Times*, 5 Dec. 1902, p. 8.
[39] Quoted in Perkins, *The Great Rapprochement*, p. 188.
[40] Pauncefote to Larcom, 2 Dec. 1901. F.O. 5/2458.
[41] Selborne to Lansdowne, 6 Feb. 1901. Lansdowne MSS BL 'Private Letters', vol. 1.
[42] Quoted in Kneer, *Great Britain and the Caribbean*, p. 6.
[43] ibid., p. 5.
[44] Pauncefote to Hay, 9 Apr., in Pauncefote to Lansdowne, 13 Apr. 1901. F.O. 5/2457.
[45] Pauncefote to Lansdowne, 10 Feb, 1902. F.O. 5/2485.
[46] Washington Post article, 8 Oct., in Herbert to Lansdowne, 8 Oct. 1902. F.O. 5/2487.
[47] Raikes to Lansdowne, 5 Oct. 1902. ibid.
[48] Raikes to Lansdowne, 3 Aug. 1902. ibid.

[49] "Venezuela" *The Times*, 21 Nov. 1902, p. 3.
[50] "The Orinoco Blockade" *The New York Times*, 1 Dec. 1902, p. 9.
[51] "Venezuela" *The Times*, 26 Nov. 1902, p. 7, and "Venezuela and the Monroe Doctrine" *The Times*, 27 Nov. 1902., p. 5.
[52] Lansdowne to Buchanan, 11 Nov. 1902. *British Documents*, vol. 2., p. 157; Herbert to Lansdowne, 19 Nov. 1902. Lansdowne MSS F.O. 800/144.
[53] Herbert to Lansdowne, 13 Nov. 1902. F.O. 420/206.
[54] Herbert to Lansdowne, 4 Dec. 1902. ibid.
[55] Campbell, *Anglo-American Understanding*, pp. 274-5.
[56] Memorandum by Lansdowne, 2 Dec. 1902. *British Documents*, vol. 2., p. 160.
[57] *Hansard*, CXVI, cols. 1105 and 1106, 15 Dec. 1902.
[58] "Lord Lansdowne on Foreign Affairs" *The Times*, 13 Dec. 1902, p. 8.
[59] *Hansard*, CXVI, cols. 1105 and 1106, 15 Dec. 1902.
[60] "Lord Lansdowne on Foreign Affairs" *The Times*, 13 Dec. 1902, p. 8.
[61] *Hansard*, CXVI, col. 1107, 15 Dec. 1902.
[62] Herbert to Lansdowne, 19 Nov. 1902. Lansdowne MSS F.O. 800/144.
[63] In April 1902, the Kaiser sounded out Roosevelt 'as to whether, in case of annexation of Holland by Germany, U.S. would object to acquisition of Dutch colonies in America by Germany'. Pauncefote to Lansdowne, tel., 28 Apr. 1902. Lansdowne MSS F.O. 800/144.
[64] Memorandum by Arnold-Forster, 15 Sep. 1902. Arnold-Forster MSS Add. 50294.
[65] Lansdowne to Herbert, 4 Dec. 1902. Lansdowne MSS F.O. 800/144.
[66] Metternich to Balfour, 17 Dec. 1902. Balfour MSS Add. 49747.
[67] "Venezuelan Ships Sunk: British and Germans Released: Attitude of the United States" *The Times*, 12 Dec. 1902, p. 3.
[68] "Editorial Comment: The British and German Policy" *The New York Times*, 12 Dec. 1902, p. 8.
[69] Arnold-Forster to Cranborne, 12 Dec. 1902. Arnold-Forster MSS Add. 50294.
[70] "Editorial Comment: A Pacific Settlement", *The New York Times*, 16 Dec. 1902, p. 8.
[71] Herbert to Lansdowne, 19 Dec. 1902. Quoted in Lord Newton, *Lord Lansdowne: A Biography* (London, 1929), p. 256.
[72] Herbert to Lansdowne, tel., 16 Dec. F.O. 420/206.
[73] "Editorial Comment: The British and German Policy" *The New York Times*, 12 Dec. 1902, p. 8.
[74] Balfour to Edward VII, 15 Dec. 1902. *Prime Minister's Letters*, vol. 2.
[75] Herbert to Lansdowne, 19 Dec. 1902. Lansdowne MSS F.O. 800/144.
[76] *Hansard*, CXVI, col. 1489, 17 Dec. 1902.

3: Difficult Money Matters

[1] *Hansard's Parliamentary Debates* (4th ser.) CXVI col. 1107, 15 Dec. 1902.
[2] Lansdowne to Buchanan, 15 Dec. 1902. F.O. 420/206.
[3] Lansdowne to Herbert, 15 Dec. 1902. ibid.
[4] Lansdowne to Lascelles, 18 Dec. 1902. ibid.
[5] White to Hay, 17 Dec. 1902., in *Papers Relating to the Foreign Relations of the United States 1903* (Washington, 1904), p. 454. A similar message was given to the Germans on the same day. See Lascelles to Lansdowne, 18 Dec. 1902. F.O. 420/206.
[6] Devonshire to Lansdowne, 30 Dec. 1902. Lansdowne MSS BL 'Private Letters', vol. 6.
[7] Balfour to Edward VII, 18 Dec. 1902. *Prime Minister's Letters to the Monarch, Reporting on Meetings of the Cabinet, 1895-1914.*, vol. 2.
[8] Balfour to Carnegie, 18 Dec. 1902. Balfour MSS Add. 49742.
[9] 'The British abandoned their efforts in Venezuela at the murmur of American disapproval and accepted such terms as the United States chose to offer.' A. J. P. Taylor, *The Struggle for Mastery in Europe, 1848-1918* (Oxford, 1954), p. 410. Also see B. Perkins, *The*

Great Rapprochement: England and the United States, 1895-1914 (London, 1968), p. 187.

[10] Lansdowne to Herbert, 18 Dec. 1902. F.O. 420/206.

[11] Balfour to Edward VII, 18 Dec. 1902. *Prime Minister's Letters*. vol. 2.

[12] 'Memorandum Communicated to Mr. White', 23 Dec. 1902. F.O. 420/206.

[13] Quoted in *Hansard* CXVI col. 1253, 15 Dec. 1902.

[14] Memorandum by Lansdowne, 24 Nov. 1902. Lansdowne MSS BL L(5)77.

[15] White to Hay, 18 Dec. 1902. *Foreign Relations of the United States 1903*, p. 456.

[16] Lansdowne to White, 18 Dec. 1902. Lansdowne MSS F.O. 800/144.

[17] Roosevelt to Shaw, 26 Dec. 1902. in E. E. Morison (ed.), *The Letters of Theodore Roosevelt* (Cambridge, Mass., 1951), vol. 3., pp. 396-7.

[18] "Venezuela: Attitude of the United States" *The Times*, 17 Dec. 1902, p. 5.

[19] Lansdowne wrote to Herbert on December 22 that Britain 'would greatly regret the President's inability to give us the benefit of his assistance.' Lansdowne to Herbert, 22 Dec. 1902. F.O. 420/206.

[20] "Venezuela: Mr Roosevelt and Arbitration" ibid., 22 Dec. 1902, p. 5.

[21] Lansdowne to Herbert, 27 Dec 1902 and 2 Jan. 1903. Lansdowne MSS F.O. 800/144.

[22] Haggard to Lansdowne, tel., 17 Dec. 1903. F.O. 420/206.

[23] Lansdowne to Herbert, 13 Jan. 1903. Lansdowne MSS F.O. 800/144.

[24] Lansdowne to Metternich, 2 Jan. 1903. Lansdowne MSS F.O. 800/128.

[25] Lansdowne to Devonshire, 23 Dec. 1902. Lansdowne MSS BL 'Private Letters', vol. 6.

[26] Herbert to Lansdowne, 29 Dec. 1902. in G. P. Gooch and H. Temperley (eds.), *British Documents on the Origins of the War, 1898-1914* (London, 1927), vol. 2., pp. 163-4.

[27] Devonshire to Lansdowne, 30 Dec. 1902 and Lansdowne to Devonshire, 1 Jan. 1903. Lansdowne MSS BL 'Private Letters' vol. 6.

[28] Lansdowne to Balfour, 1 Jan. 1903. Lansdowne MSS BL 'Private Letters' vol. 5.

[29] Lansdowne to Herbert, 13 Jan. 1903. Lansdowne MSS F.O. 800/144.

[30] Lansdowne to Balfour, 2 Jan. 1903. Balfour MSS Add. 49728.

[31] Lansdowne to Herbert, 12 Jan. 1903. F.O. 420/212.

[32] Villiers to Admiralty, 9 Jan. 1903 and Lansdowne to White, 9 Jan. 1903. ibid.

[33] Lansdowne to Herbert, 13 Jan. 1903. Lansdowne MSS F.O. 800/144.

[34] White to Lansdowne, 22 Jan. 1903. F.O. 420/212.

[35] On January 16, the German warship "Vineta" fired a single shell into Fort Salano, on the spurious pretext that Venezuelan soldiers were illegally camped inside. Three days later, German ships fired on San Carlos. See *The Manchester Guardian*, 17 Jan, p. 7 and 20 Jan. 1903, p. 7.

[36] Quoted in G. E. Mowry, *The Era of Theodore Roosevelt, 1900-1912* (London, 1958), p. 157.

[37] "Venezuelan Claims" *The Manchester Guardian*, 26 Jan. 1903., p. 5.

[38] Herbert to Lansdowne, secret tel., 26 Jan. 1903. F.O. 420/212.

[39] For the conversation between Henry White and Balfour, see C. S. Campbell, *Anglo-American Understanding, 1898-1903* (Baltimore, 1957), p. 293.

[40] Admiralty to Vice-Admiral Douglas, tel., 24 Jan., in Admiralty to F.O., 24 Jan. 1903. F.O. 420/212.

[41] Lansdowne to Lascelles, 27 Jan. 1903. ibid.

[42] Lansdowne to Lascelles, 15 Jan. 1903. ibid.

[43] Herbert to Lansdowne, 30 Jan. 1903. ibid.

[44] Herbert to Lansdowne, 30 Jan. 1903. Lansdowne MSS F.O. 800/144.

[45] Lansdowne to Lascelles, 27 Jan. 1903. *British Documents*, vol. 2., p. 167.

[46] Devonshire to Lansdowne, 29 Jan. 1903. Lansdowne MSS BL 'Private Letters', vol. 6.

[47] Lascelles to Lansdowne, 30 Jan. and Lansdowne to Lascelles, 3 Feb. 1903. Lansdowne MSS F.O. 800/128.

[48] Herbert to Lansdowne, 30 Jan. and 10 Feb. 1903. Lansdowne MSS F.O. 800/144.

[49] Bowen wrote that 'I think it is unjust, unfair, and illegal to tie the hands of the said other nations for the period of five or six years that it would take to pay the claims of the allied Powers.' The blockading Powers should have demanded preferential treatment at the

outset, he noted; giving in to them now would mean submitting to brute force and set a dangerous precedent. Herbert to Lansdowne, 29 Jan. 1903. F. O. 420/212.

[50] Lansdowne to Herbert, tel., 24 Jan. 1903. ibid.

[51] Lansdowne to Balfour, 4 Feb. 1903. Balfour MSS Add. 49728.

[52] "Venezuelan Trouble: The Delayed Settlement" *The Manchester Guardian*, 30 Jan. 1903, p. 5.

[53] Lansdowne to Lascelles, 3 Feb. 1903. Lansdowne MSS F.O. 800/128.

[54] Lansdowne to Herbert, 20 Feb. 1903. Lansdowne MSS F.O. 800/144.

[55] Lansdowne to Balfour, 29 Jan. 1903. Lansdowne MSS BL 'Private Letters', vol. 5. The same letter, albeit with slightly different wording, appears in the Balfour MSS Add. 49728.

[56] Adams to E. Cameron, 8 Feb. 1903, in J. Levenson, E, Samuels, C. Vandersee and V. H. Winner (eds.), *The Letters of Henry Adams* (Cambridge, Mass., 1988), vol. 5., p. 452.

[57] Lansdowne explained that his agitation had affected his health. He wrote, on January 29: 'I devoutly hope the next few hours may bring us an acceptable offer from Washington. I am so vexed at having collapsed when there is so much to do.' Lansdowne to Balfour, 29 Jan. Later, he confessed that 'My brain is reeling'. Lansdowne to Balfour, 4 Feb. 1903. Balfour MSS Add. 49728.

[58] Captain de Chair's report in Herbert to Lansdowne, 6 Feb. 1903. F.O. 5/2522.

[59] Herbert to Lansdowne, secret tel. 7 Feb. 1903. F.O. 420/213.

[60] Lansdowne to Herbert, tel., 2 Feb. 1903. F.O. 420/213.

[61] Lansdowne to Herbert, 3 Feb. 1903. Lansdowne MSS F.O. 800/144, and Lansdowne to Herbert, secret tel., 7 Feb. 1903. F.O. 420/213.

[62] "Viscount Cranborne on Foreign Politics" *The Manchester Guardian*, 31 Jan. 1903, p. 6.

[63] "Austen Chamberlain on Venezuela", ibid., 2 Feb. 1903, p. 10.

[64] Sanderson to Herbert, 5 Feb. 1903. F.O. 5/2531.

[65] Lansdowne to Herbert, confidential tel., 9 Feb. 1903. *British Documents*, vol. 2., pp. 172-3. See also Lansdowne to Lascelles, 9 Feb. 1903. F.O. 420/213.

[66] Herbert to Lansdowne, 13 Feb. 1903. Lansdowne MSS F.O. 800/144.

[67] *Hansard* CXVIII, col. 68, 17 Feb. 1903.

[68] ibid., col.1044, 2 Mar. 1903.

[69] "The Venezuelan Debate: America and Anglo-German Co-operation" *The Times*, 4 Mar. 1903, p. 5.

[70] Smalley's comments were made in *The Times*, 4 Mar. 1903., quoted in Campbell, *Anglo-American Understanding*, p. 300.

[71] *Hansard* CXVIII col. 97, 17 Feb. 1903.

[72] A. S. T. Griffith-Boscawen, *Fourteen Years in Parliament* (London, 1907), p. 250.

[73] Lord Newton, *Lord Lansdowne: A Biography* (London, 1929), p. 255.

[74] "Sir H. Campbell-Bannerman: Speech at Stirling" *The Manchester Guardian*, 9 Jan. 1903, p. 7.

[75] "Viscount Cranborne on Foreign Politics" ibid., 31 Jan. 1903, p. 6.

[76] Herbert to Hamilton, 29 Mar. 1903. Hamilton MSS Add. 48620.

[77] Bertie to Lansdowne, 14 Feb. 1903. Bertie MSS Add. 63015.

[78] Lansdowne to Herbert, 20 Feb. 1903. Lansdowne MSS F.O. 800/144.

[79] *Hansard* (4th ser.) CXVIII col. 1059, 2 Mar. 1903.

[80] Esher to M. V. B., 7 Apr. 1903. In M. V. Brett (ed.), *Journals and Letters of Reginald, Viscount Esher* (London, 1934), vol. 1., p. 397.

[81] "Venezuela: San Carlos Again Shelled" *The Manchester Guardian*, 23 Jan. 1903, p. 5.

[82] Herbert to Hamilton, 29 Mar. 1903. Hamilton MSS Add. 48620.

[83] White to Hay, 14 Feb. 1903. *Foreign Relations of the United States 1903*, p. 476.

[84] See Perkins, *The Great Rapprochement*, p. 190.

[85] Lansdowne to Herbert, 20 Feb. 1903. Lansdowne MSS F. O. 800/144.

4: A Marvellously Elastic Doctrine

[1] Carnegie to Balfour, 23 Jul. 1903. Balfour MSS Add. 49742.
[2] *Hansard's Parliamentary Debates*, (4th ser.) CXXVI, col. 126, 23 Jul. 1903.
[3] Speech by Greville in the House of Commons, in B. Perkins, *The Great Rapprochement: England and the United States, 1895-1914* (London, 1968), p. 193.
[4] Balfour's speech at Liverpool, 14 Feb. 1903, quoted in W. G. Kneer, *Great Britain and the Caribbean, 1901-1913: A Study in Anglo-American Relations* (Michigan, 1975), pp. 61-2.
[5] Memorandum by the Argentine Ministry of Foreign Affairs, 29 Dec. 1902. *Papers Relating to the Foreign Relations of the United States 1903* (Washington, 1904), pp. 3-4.
[6] Hay to Mérou, 17 Feb. 1903. ibid.
[7] Herbert to Lansdowne, 13 Mar. 1903. and note by Larcom on the same. F.O. 5/2522.
[8] Herbert to Lansdowne, confidential, 26 Mar. 1903. ibid.
[9] ibid.
[10] Roosevelt to Hay, confidential, 13 Mar. 1903., in E. E. Morison (ed.), *The Letters of Theodore Roosevelt* (Cambridge, Mass., 1951), vol. 3., p. 446.
[11] Editorial comment, Correio de Manha, 30 Mar. 1903. in *Foreign Relations of the United States 1903*, p. 24.
[12] Ames to Hay, 6 May., enclosing the President's Message to Congress, 5 May. 1903. ibid., p. 9.
[13] Herbert to Lansdowne, 'very confidential', 25 Feb. 1903. F.O. 420/214.
[14] Lansdowne to Herbert, tel., 16 Mar. 1903. ibid.
[15] Lansdowne to Herbert, tel., 21 Mar. 1903. ibid.
[16] Choate to Lansdowne, 16 May. 1903. F.O. 420/216.
[17] Admiralty to F.O., 30 Mar. and Lansdowne to Herbert, tel., 1 Apr. 1903. F.O. 420/215.
[18] Lansdowne to Lascelles, 2 Apr. 1903. ibid.
[19] Lansdowne to Herbert, tel., 6 Apr. 1903. ibid.
[20] Herbert to Lansdowne, tel., 9 Apr. 1903. ibid.
[21] Lansdowne to Herbert, tel., 1 May., Lansdowne to Herbert, tel., 6 May. and Herbert to Lansdowne, 7 May. F.O. 420/216.
[22] Lansdowne to Herbert, 2 Sep. 1903. Lansdowne MSS F.O. 800/144. Spring Rice, too, placed the blame squarely on Germany. 'Venezuela has not allowed its sweet name to be forgotten', he wrote. 'The Germans were plainly anxious at one time to have no arbitration.' Spring Rice to Villiers, 17 Sep. 1903. Villiers MSS F.O. 800/23.
[23] Lansdowne to Herbert, tel., 5 Jun. and Herbert to Lansdowne, tel., 6 Jun. 1903. F.O. 420/216.
[24] Lansdowne to Bax-Ironside, tel, 3 Jul. 1903. F.O. 420/218.
[25] Bax-Ironside to Lansdowne, 18 Sep. 1903. F.O. 420/219.
[26] Bax-Ironside to Lansdowne, 25 Sep. 1903. ibid.
[27] Lansdowne to Bax-Ironside, 3 Nov. 1903. ibid.
[28] C.O. to F.O., 12 Dec. and Lansdowne to Bax-Ironside, 29 Dec. 1903. ibid.
[29] Larcom to Lansdowne, 22 Feb., Lansdowne to Cohen, 4 Mar. and Lascelles to Lansdowne, 25 Feb. 1904. F.O. 420/224.
[30] Larcom to Lansdowne, 13 Nov. 1903. F.O. 420/219.
[31] See Perkins, *The Great Rapprochement*, p. 193.
[32] Bax-Ironside to Lansdowne, confidential, 18 Jun., received 14 Jul. 1904. F.O. 420/226.
[33] Bax-Ironside to Lansdowne, 25 Feb. 1904. F.O. 420/224.
[34] Lansdowne to Bax-Ironside, 19 May. 1904. F.O. 420/225.
[35] Durand to Lansdowne, 19 Jul. 1904. Lansdowne MSS F.O. 800/144.
[36] Durand to Lansdowne, 13 Sep. 1904. F.O. 5/2550.
[37] See J. Ewell, *Venezuela and the United States: From Monroe's Hemisphere to Petroleum's Empire* (Athens, Georgia, 1996), pp. 73, 100-102.
[38] Hay to Bowen, 16 Apr. and Bowen to Hay, 22 Jul. 1904. *Papers Relating to the Foreign Relations of the United States 1905* (Washington, 1906), pp. 919-920.

39 Wright to Bax-Ironside, 22 Jul. and Bax-Ironside to Lansdowne, 23 Jul. 1904. F.O. 420/226.
40 Bax-Ironside to Lansdowne, tel., 27 Jul. and Bax-Ironside to Lansdowne, 22 Aug. 1904. ibid.
41 Bax-Ironside to Lansdowne, tel., 20 Aug. 1904. ibid.
42 Bax-Ironside to Lansdowne, 20 Aug. 1904. ibid.
43 Roosevelt to Hay, 30 Aug. 1904. in *Letters of Theodore Roosevelt* vol. 4., p. 914.
44 Lansdowne to Bax-Ironside, tel., 25 Jul. 1904. F.O. 420/226.
45 *Port of Spain Gazette*, 3 Aug., in Bax-Ironside to Lansdowne, confidential, 6 Aug. 1904. ibid.
46 Lansdowne to Bax-Ironside, tel., 6 Aug., Villiers to Admiralty, 9 Aug. and Admiralty to F.O., 'confidential', 11 Aug. 1904. ibid.
47 Bax-Ironside to Lansdowne, 21 Aug. 1904. ibid.
48 Lansdowne to Bax-Ironside, 23 Aug. 1904. ibid.
49 Bax-Ironside to Lansdowne, tel., 17 Aug. and Lansdowne to Durand, 31 Aug. 1904. ibid.
50 Swettenham to Lyttleton, 21 Sep. in C.O. to F.O., 10 Oct. 1904. F.O. 420/220.
51 Lansdowne to Bax-Ironside, tel., 19 Oct. 1904. ibid.
52 Hodgson to Lyttleton, 19 Oct. in C.O. to F.O., 5 Nov. 1904. ibid.
53 Hodgson to Bax-Ironside, 21 Oct. in C.O. to F.O., 19 Nov. 1904. ibid.
54 Lansdowne to Bax-Ironside, 24 Nov. 1904. ibid.
55 Hodgson to Lyttleton, 13 Dec. in C.O. to F.O., 30 Dec. 1904. ibid.
56 See Perkins, *The Great Rapprochement*, pp. 157-8.
57 24th Meeting of the C.I.D., 25 Nov. 1903. Privy Council Committee of Imperial Defence Minutes. Cab 2/1494.
58 48th Meeting, 8 Jul. and 58th Meeting, 22 Nov. 1904. ibid.
59 Hutchinson to Hay, 14 Oct., enclosing Decision of the Court, 4 Oct. 1904. *Foreign Relations of the United States 1905*, pp. 960-962.
60 Bax-Ironside to Lansdowne, 29 Oct. 1904. F.O. 420/228.
61 Bax-Ironside to Lansdowne, confidential, 6 Dec. 1904. ibid.
62 Roosevelt Corollary, in A. S. Link and W. M. Leary, *The Diplomacy of World Power: The United States, 1889-1911* (Edinburgh, 1970), pp. 72-76.
63 Quoted in Perkins, *The Great Rapprochement*, p. 194.
64 See *Foreign Relations of the United States 1905*, pp. 978-1003.
65 Roosevelt to Hay, 2 Apr. 1905. *Letters of Theodore Roosevelt* vol. 4., p. 1156.
66 Root to Russell, 10 Nov. 1905. *Foreign Relations of the United States 1905*, p. 1002.
67 "Sir H. Campbell-Bannerman at Stirling" *The Manchester Guardian*, 9 Jan. 1903, p. 7.

5: Responsibility, Strategy & Paranoia

1 See, for example, R. F. Mackay, "The Admiralty, The German Navy, and the Redistribution of the British Fleet, 1904-1905" *The Mariner's Mirror* 56 (1970), pp. 341-346.
2 Balfour to Mahan, 20 Dec. 1899. Balfour MSS Add. 49742.
3 Selborne to Lansdowne, 6 Sep. 1901. Lansdowne MSS BL 'Private Letters', vol. 1.
4 Laurier Speech at Massey Hall, Toronto, 20 May. 1902., in H. L. Keenleyside, *Canada and the United States: Some Aspects of their Historical Relations* (New York, 1952), p. 263.
5 Memorandum by Chamberlain, undated, in R. A. Shields, "Imperial Policy and Canadian-American Commercial Relations, 1880-1911" *Bulletin of the Institute of Historical Research* 59 (1986), p. 118.
6 See Keenleyside, *Canada and the United States*, p. 279.
7 Minto to Lansdowne, 25 Aug. 1898. Lansdowne MSS BL L(5)32.
8 Undated notes by Lansdowne, Lansdowne MSS BL 'Canadian Notes', pp. 72-3.
9 Memorandum prepared by Mr. Tilley, "Relations between Germany and Great Britain,

1892-1904" Lansdowne MSS BL L(5)77, and J. A. Colvin, "Sir Wilfrid Laurier and the British Preferential Tariff System" in C. Berger (ed.), *Imperial Relations in the Age of Laurier* (Toronto, 1969), pp. 34-39.

[10] See, for example, R. A. Rempel, *Unionists Divided: Arthur Balfour, Joseph Chamberlain and the Unionist Free Traders* (Newton Abbot, 1972), pp. 18-20.

[11] C. W. Dilke, *The British Empire* (London, 1899), pp. 36 & 33.

[12] Borden to Lansdowne, 10 Nov. and Lansdowne to Borden, 24 Nov. 1899. Lansdowne MSS BL L(5)40.

[13] Minto to Parkin, 30 Oct. 1901. in P. Stevens and J. T. Saywell (eds.), *Lord Minto's Canadian Papers: A Selection of the Public and Private Papers of the Fourth Earl of Minto, 1898-1904* (Toronto, 1983), vol. 2., p. 82.

[14] See C. Miller, "Sir Frederick Borden and Military Reform, 1896-1911", in B. D. Hunt and R. G. Haycock (eds.), *Canada's Defence: Perspectives on Policy in the Twentieth Century* (Toronto, 1993), p. 10.

[15] Lansdowne to Chamberlain, 28 Feb. 1896. Lansdowne MSS BL L(5)20.

[16] Notes on the Hutton-Lansdowne interview, 3 Aug. 1898. Hutton MSS Add. 50085.

[17] See, for example, Dilke, *The British Empire*, p. 130.

[18] Memorandum by Arnold-Forster, 12 Feb. 1902. Arnold-Forster MSS Add. 50294.

[19] Hay to White, 3 Dec. 1898, in B. Perkins, *The Great Rapprochement: England and the United States, 1895-1914* (London, 1968), p. 163.

[20] For a detailed history of the proceedings of the Joint High Commission, see C. C. Tansill, *Canadian-American Relations, 1875-1911* (Toronto, 1943).

[21] Goldwin Smith to Dilke, 2 Nov. 1901. Dilke MSS Add. 43917.

[22] Minto to Roberts, 2 Jul. and 'Memo. Re Offer of Troops for South Africa', 18 Nov. 1901. *Lord Minto's Canadian Papers*, vol. 2, pp. 50-51 & 90.

[23] See J. A. S. Grenville, "Lansdowne's Abortive Project of 12 March 1901 for a Secret Agreement with Germany" *Bulletin of the Institute of Historical Research* 27 (1954), pp. 201-213. For a thorough exposition of Britain's naval worries, see J. T. Sumida, *In Defence of Naval Supremacy: Finance, Technology and British Naval Policy, 1889-1914* (London, 1993).

[24] Selborne, "Balance of Naval Power in the Far East", 4 Sep. 1901., in D. G. Boyce (ed.), *The Crisis of British Power: The Imperial and Naval Papers of the Second Earl of Selborne, 1895-1910* (London, 1990), pp. 123-124.

[25] Selborne to Balfour, 'confidential', 4 Apr. 1902. Balfour MSS Add. 49707. Balfour replied that 'I shall be very glad to discuss your naval subjects with you whenever you choose to fix a time. I find it extremely difficult to believe that we have, as you seem to suppose, much to fear from Germany – in the immediate future at all events. It seems to me so clear that, broadly speaking, her interests and ours are identical.' Balfour to Selborne, 5 Apr. 1902. *The Crisis of British Power*, p. 142.

[26] Lansdowne to Lascelles, 22 Apr. 1902. Lascelles MSS F.O. 800/11; Lascelles to Lansdowne, 25 Apr. 1902. Lansdowne MSS F.O. 800/129.

[27] Selborne to Lansdowne, 2 May. 1902. Lansdowne MSS BL 'Private Letters', vol. 1.

[28] See D. Judd, *Balfour and the British Empire: A Study in Imperial Evolution, 1874-1932* (London, 1968), pp. 36-7.

[29] "Papers Relating to a Conference between the Secretary of State for the Colonies and the Prime Ministers of Self-Governing Colonies, June to August 1902" in *British Parliamentary Papers, Accounts and Papers 1902*, vol LXVI (London, 1902), p. 459.

[30] ibid., pp. 459-484.

[31] See R. Shannon, *The Crisis of Imperialism, 1865-1915* (London, 1976), pp. 312-3.

[32] "A Demand for Inquiry", Chamberlain at Birmingham, 15 May. 1903. in C. W. Boyd (ed.), *Mr. Chamberlain's Speeches* (London, 1914), vol. 2., pp. 127-8 & 131.

[33] Chamberlain to Halsbury, 18 May. 1903. Halsbury MSS Add. 56372.

[34] For a thorough discussion of the tariff crisis of 1903, see, for example, Rempel, *Unionists Divided* and B. E. C. Dugdale, *Arthur James Balfour: First Earl of Balfour, K.G., O.M., F.R.S., Etc.* (London, 1936), vol. 1., pp. 333-363.

[35] Diary entry, 20 Aug. 1903. in J. A. Spender (ed.), *A Modern Journal, being the Diary of Greville Minor for the Year of Agitation, 1903-1904* (London, 1904), p. 39.

[36] Note by Balfour, Jun. 1903. Balfour MSS. Add. 49855. Dugdale cites this letter as Balfour to Devonshire, Aug. 1903. Dugdale, *Balfour*, p. 338.

[37] Memorandum by Tilley, "Relations between Germany and Great Britain, 1892-1904" Lansdowne MSS BL L(5)77.

[38] Undated Memorandum by Lansdowne. Underlining by Lansdowne. Lansdowne MSS BL Lab 4/25.

[39] Sandars to Balfour, 18 Aug. 1903. Balfour MSS Add. 49761.

[40] Devonshire to Lansdowne, 19 Jun. 1903. Lansdowne MSS BL 'Private Letters', vol. 6.

[41] 'Conversation with Laurier', 30 Jun. 1903. *Lord Minto's Canadian Papers*, vol. 2., p. 312.

[42] Minto to Elliott, 5 Jul. 1903. ibid., p. 316.

[43] H. George, *Protection or Free Trade: An Examination of the Tariff Question with Especial Regard to the Interests of Labour* (London, 1903), pp. 353-354.

[44] Minto to Willison, 4 Jul. 1903. *Lord Minto's Canadian Papers*, vol. 2., p. 314.

[45] Willison to Minto, 18 Jul. and 'Conversation with Fielding', 10 Jul. 1903. ibid., pp. 326 & 318.

[46] Minto to Chamberlain, 14 Dec. 1903. ibid., p. 392.

[47] Herbert to Lansdowne, 27 Feb., enclosing "Looks Towards Acquiring Canada" *New York Tribune*, 26 Feb. 1903., and Lansdowne's note on the same. F.O. 5/2522.

[48] See H. K. Beale, *Theodore Roosevelt and the Rise of America to World Power* (Baltimore, 1956), pp. 40-41.

[49] Herbert to Lansdowne, secret, 18 Jun. 1903., and Lansdowne's note on the same. F.O. 5/2523.

[50] Note by Villiers on the above. ibid.

[51] 29th Meeting of the C.I.D., 25 Nov. 1903. Privy Council Committee of Imperial Defence Minutes. Cab 2/1494.

[52] Minto to Broderick, 10 Apr. and Broderick to Minto, 18 Jul. 1903. *Lord Minto's Canadian Papers*, vol. 2., pp. 282 & 327.

[53] See Perkins, *The Great Rapprochement*, pp. 157-8.

[54] Arnold-Forster Diary Entry, 8 Dec. 1903. Arnold-Forster MSS Add. 50335.

[55] 26th Meeting of the C.I.D., 11 Dec. 1903. C.I.D. Minutes.

[56] Memorandum by Balfour, Feb. 1904. Balfour MSS Add. 49698.

[57] 48th Meeting of the C.I.D., 8 Jul., and Secret Addendum, 13 Jul. 1904. C.I.D. Minutes.

[58] 58th Meeting of the C.I.D., 22 Nov. 1904. ibid.

[59] Selborne to Balfour, 26 Dec. 1904., and Balfour to Selborne, 1 Jan. 1905. Underlining by Balfour. Balfour MSS Add. 49708.

[60] 61st Meeting of the C.I.D., 9 Dec. 1904. C.I.D. Minutes.

[61] Minute by Arnold-Forster, 27 Jan. 1905. Arnold-Forster MSS Add. 50318.

[62] 73rd Meeting of the C.I.D., 28 Jun. 1905. C.I.D. Minutes.

[63] 69th Meeting of the C.I.D., 4 Apr. 1905. ibid.

[64] Minto to Parkin, 26 Sep. 1904. *Lord Minto's Canadian Papers*, vol. 2., p. 542.

[65] Chamberlain to Balfour, 19 Apr. 1905. Balfour MSS Add. 49774.

[66] "The Alaska Boundary: Treaty Signed" *The Times*, 26 Jan. 1903, p. 5.

[67] Minto to Lansdowne, 8 Mar. 1903. Lansdowne MSS BL 'Private Letters', vol. 6.

6: Last of the Great Disputes

[1] Fourth Congress of Chambers of Commerce of the Empire to Salisbury, Jun. 1900. F.O. 5/2479.

[2] Pauncefote to Lansdowne, 25 Dec. 1900. Lansdowne MSS F.O. 800/144.

[3] Article IV of the Anglo-Russian Treaty, 28 Feb. 1825., in H. L. Keenleyside, *Canada and the United States: Some Aspects of their Historical Relations* (New York, 1952), p. 173.

[4]   Choate to Salisbury, 22 Jan. 1900. F.O. 414/165.

[5]   F.O. to C.O., 27 Jan. 1900. F.O. 5/2479.

[6]   Note on Choate to Salisbury, 22 Jan. 1900. ibid.

[7]   The position taken by the Canadian Government had long irritated British officials, who believed that Canada's arguments were both weak and unrealistic. See C. S. Campbell, *Anglo-American Understanding, 1898-1903* (Baltimore, 1957), pp. 145-6.

[8]   Pauncefote to Lansdowne, 10 May. 1901. F.O. 414/169.

[9]   Memorandum by Larcom, 13 Jul. 1900. ibid.

[10]   Memorandum by Pauncefote, 15 Jul. 1901. F.O. 5/2479.

[11]   Note by Lansdowne on the above. ibid.

[12]   Minto to Chamberlain, 3 Aug. 1901. in P. Stevens and J. T. Saywell (eds.), *Lord Minto's Canadian Papers: A Selection of the Public and Private Letters of the Fourth Earl of Minto, 1898-1904* (Toronto, 1983), vol. 2., p. 53.

[13]   Minto to Chamberlain, tel., 7 Aug. 1901. F.O. 414/169.

[14]   Minto to Chamberlain, secret tel., 24 Aug., in C.O. to F.O., 14 Sep. 1901. ibid.

[15]   Minto to Chamberlain, tel., 7 Aug., in C.O. to F.O., 10 Aug. 1901. ibid.

[16]   Chamberlain to Minto, tel., 8 Oct., in C.O to F.O., 8 Oct. 1901. F.O. 414/169.

[17]   Chamberlain to Minto, 30 Jan., in C.O. to F.O., 31 Jan. 1900. F.O.420/197.

[18]   Villiers to C.O., 19 Sep. 1901. F.O. 414/169.

[19]   Minto to Chamberlain, tel., 15 Oct., in C.O. to F.O., 21 Oct. 1901. ibid.

[20]   C.O. to F.O., 4 Jan. 1902. F.O. 414/173.

[21]   Note by Larcom on the above. F.O. 5/1510.

[22]   Minto to Chamberlain, secret tel., 20 Nov., in C.O. to F.O., 'secret', 22 Nov. 1901. F.O 414/169.

[23]   Pauncefote to Lansdowne, 19 Dec. 1901. Lansdowne MSS F.O. 800/144.

[24]   Lansdowne to Pauncefote, 31 Dec. 1901. ibid.

[25]   Pauncefote to Lansdowne, confidential, 28 Mar. 1902. F.O. 5/2510.

[26]   ibid.

[27]   C.O. to F.O., 23 Apr. 1902. F.O. 414/173.

[28]   Raikes to Lansdowne, 23 May. 1902. Lansdowne MSS BL L(5)20.

[29]   ibid.

[30]   Lansdowne to Spring Rice, 6 Jun. 1902. Lansdowne MSS F.O. 800/144.

[31]   Lansdowne to Raikes, 25 Jun. 1902. F.O. 414/173.

[32]   Lansdowne to Raikes, 16 Jul. 1902. ibid.

[33]   Lansdowne to Raikes, 18 Aug. 1902. ibid.

[34]   In September 1901, Lansdowne received a letter from Moreton Frewen, who had spent much of his life in the United States, and who thoroughly understood American affairs. Frewen described Herbert as 'the closest ally of both Roosevelt and Lodge', adding that 'there is nothing ... that Roosevelt will not do for Herbert.' Frewen to Lansdowne, 16 Sep. in Lansdowne to Balfour, 22 Sep. 1901. Balfour MSS Add. 49727.

[35]   Herbert to Lansdowne, 24 Oct. 1902. Lansdowne MSS F.O. 800/144.

[36]   Lansdowne to Herbert, 3 Nov. 1902. ibid.

[37]   Minto to Chamberlain, tel., 18 Nov., in C.O. to F.O., 24 Nov. 1902. F.O. 414/177.

[38]   Lansdowne to Herbert, tel., 6 Dec. 1902. ibid.

[39]   Herbert to Lansdowne, private, 9 Dec. 1902. F.O. 5/2510.

[40]   Note by Lansdowne on the above. ibid.

[41]   Lansdowne to Herbert, 10 Dec. 1902. ibid.

[42]   Lansdowne to Herbert, 27 Dec. 1902. Lansdowne MSS F.O. 800/144.

[43]   Herbert to Lansdowne, 12 Dec. 1902. ibid.

[44]   Ommanney to Lansdowne, 6 Jan. 1903. Lansdowne MSS BL 'Private Letters', vol. 1.

[45]   Ommanney to Minto, tel., 12 Jan. 1903. Lansdowne noted that the Canadians should be allowed to 'make their own suggestion for a compromise if they don't like Herbert's scheme.' Lansdowne note on Ommanney to Villiers, 7 Jan. 1903. C.O. 42/892.

[46]   Roosevelt to Hay, 14 Jan. 1903. in E. E. Morison (ed.), *The Letters of Theodore Roosevelt*

(Cambridge, Mass., 1951), vol. 3., p. 405.

[47] Lansdowne to Herbert, 13 Jan. 1903. Lansdowne MSS F.O. 800/144.

[48] Herbert to Lansdowne, tel., 15 Jan. 1903. and Lansdowne's note on the same. ibid.

[49] Lansdowne to Herbert, 15 Jan. 1903. ibid.

[50] Herbert to Lansdowne, tel., 18 Jan. 1903. F.O. 414/177.

[51] 'Conversation with Laurier', 19 Jan. 1903. *Lord Minto's Canadian Papers*, vol. 2., p. 248.

[52] On January 22, Minto wrote that, as 'for the composition of the Tribunal my Ministers are of [the] opinion that it is premature to adopt any final arrangement. They regard it as sufficient now to have it clearly understood that the members of the Court to be appointed by His Majesty's Government shall be jurists of repute and British subjects.' Minto to C.O., paraphrase tel., 22 Jan. 1903. C.O. 42/892.

[53] Knollys to Lansdowne, tel., 23 Jan. 1903. F.O. 5/2542.

[54] Terms of the Hay-Herbert Convention, 24 Jan. 1903. printed in *Papers Relating to the Foreign Relations of the United States 1903* (Washington, 1904), pp. 488-493.

[55] "The Alaska Boundary Treaty" *The Times*, 6 Feb. 1903, p. 3.

[56] Notes by Villiers and Lansdowne on Herbert to Lansdowne, 4 Feb. 1903. F.O. 5/2542.

[57] *Hansard's Parliamentary Debates* (4th ser.) CXVIII cols. 6, 15, 74 & 63, 17 Feb. 1903.

[58] "The Alaska Boundary; Treaty Signed" *The Times*, 26 Jan., p. 5. and "The Alaska Treaty" *The Times*, 28 Jan. 1903., p. 5.

[59] Herbert to Lansdowne, tel., 12 Feb. and Lansdowne's note on the same, 13 Feb. 1903. Lansdowne MSS F.O. 800/144.

7: Alaskan Settlement

[1] The New York correspondent for *The Manchester Guardian* remarked that 'The complaints to which expression is given in Canada ... are not regarded here as well founded. It would have been impossible to name any Commissioner of repute who did not believe thoroughly in the American case. ... If the Commissioners chosen by the other party prove to be as apparently committed in advance there will be no protest here. Our counsel profess themselves able to convince any man not judicially blinded.' "The Alaskan Boundary" *The Manchester Guardian*, 26 Feb. 1903, p. 5.

[2] "The Alaska Boundary Commission" *The Times*, 21 Feb. 1903, p. 8.

[3] Herbert to Lansdowne, tel., 19 Feb. and Herbert to Lansdowne, 24 Feb. 1903. Lansdowne MSS F.O. 800/144.

[4] Minto to Lansdowne, 19 Feb. 1903. Lansdowne MSS BL 'Private Letters', vol. 6. To Lord Onslow, Minto explained that his 'Ministers respectfully but strongly represent that Mr. Root as a member of the United States Government directly concerned is therefore one of the disputants in the case, and further that Senators Lodge and Turner cannot be accepted as of the class of impartial jurists provided for in the Treaty, as both have already emphatically declared themselves against the Canadian side of the case. My ministers would regard the proposed appointments as a violation of an important article of the Treaty.' Minto to Onslow, paraphrase tel., 20 Feb. 1903. C.O. 42/892.

[5] Lansdowne note on Herbert to Lansdowne, secret tel., 14 Feb. 1903. F.O. 5/2542. Herbert's information came directly from John Hay, who saw the British Ambassador on the 14th. See C. C. Tansill, *Canadian-American Relations, 1875-1911* (Toronto, 1943), p. 232.

[6] Note by Lansdowne on the above, 19 Feb. 1903. ibid.

[7] Lansdowne to Herbert, 20 Feb. 1903. Lansdowne MSS F.O. 800/144.

[8] Lansdowne to Minto, 21 Feb. 1903. Lansdowne MSS BL 'Private Letters', vol. 6.

[9] Ommanney to F.O., secret, 20 Feb. 1903. F.O. 414/177.

[10] Note by Villiers, 19 Feb. 1903. F.O. 5/2542.

[11] Second note by Villiers, 19 Feb. 1903. ibid.

[12] Herbert to Lansdowne, 24 Feb. 1903. Lansdowne MSS F.O. 800/144.

[13] Herbert to Laurier, 23 Feb. 1903. ibid.

[14] Memorandum by Lansdowne to Villiers, 25 Feb. 1903. F.O. 5/2542.

[15] ibid.

[16] Villiers to C.O., 25 Feb. 1903. F.O. 414/177.

[17] Onslow to Lansdowne, 26 Feb. 1903. Lansdowne MSS BL 'Private Letters', vol. 1.

[18] Onslow to Minto, 26 Feb. 1903., in P. Stevens and J. T. Saywell (eds.), *Lord Minto's Canadian Papers: A Selection of the Public Letters of the Fourth Earl of Minto, 1898-1904* (Toronto, 1983), vol. 2., pp. 261-2.

[19] Minto to C.O, secret and personal, 27 Feb. 1903. ibid, p. 262.

[20] Note by Lansdowne, 3 Mar. F.O. 5/2542. and Lansdowne to Minto, 5 Mar. 1903. Lansdowne MSS BL 'Private Letters', vol. 6.

[21] *Hansard's Parliamentary Debates* (4th ser.) CXIX col. 1098, 18 Mar. 1903.

[22] Minto to Lansdowne, 8 Mar. 1903. Lansdowne MSS BL 'Private Letters', vol. 6. Minto wrote to Chamberlain the following day that 'Sir W. Laurier called upon me yesterday entirely annoyed at the exchange of ratifications of the Treaty before my Government had sent an official reply to your telegram of the 26th of February. He considers it a "slap in the face for Canada." Hitherto, while regretting the President's action, he has in conversation with me taken a calm view and had personally quite decided to accept the President's nominations, but the announcement of the final ratifications of the Treaty has had the most unfortunate effect.' Minto to Chamberlain, paraphrased tel., 9 Mar. 1903. C.O. 42/892.

[23] Note by Villiers, 8 Mar. 1903. and Lansdowne's note on the same. F.O. 5/2542.

[24] Villiers to C.O., 10 Mar. 1903. F.O. 414/177.

[25] Minto to Chamberlain, secret, 9 Mar. 1903. Lord Minto's Canadian Papers, vol. 2., p. 273.

[26] Extract of Fielding to Chamberlain, in Chamberlain to Lansdowne, 30 Mar. 1903. Lansdowne MSS BL 'Private Letters', vol. 1.

[27] Lansdowne to Villiers, 9 Apr. 1903. underlining by Lansdowne. F.O. 5/2542. Lansdowne was responding to a recent note from Chamberlain. On April 14, Sandars told Balfour that 'Mr. Chamberlain, I understand, is overworked, and suffering from the consequences of overwork! His paper is a mere exposition of the Canadian grievances: he neither asks for not suggests that anything can be done now in the matter; and I should have thought the F.O. might have been content to let the matter rest ... But Ld. L[ansdowne] now sends a memorandum which in part defends the action of the Govt and in the main is argumentative'. Sandars to Balfour, 14 Apr. 1903. Balfour MSS Add, 49761.

[28] Sifton, believing that Britain intended to abandon Canada, nonetheless mailed an article to the Manitoba Free Press, the Toronto Globe, and the Montreal Herald before leaving for London, in which he stated that the inlets question had 'been to some extent compromised by official neglect and indifference and also by acts of jurisdiction and occupation on the part of the United States. It will unquestionably be most difficult to secure recognition of our view of this claim'. Article by Sifton, 23 Mar. 1903. See D. J. Hall, *Clifford Sifton*, vol. 2. (Vancouver, 1985), pp. 114-115.

[29] Herbert to Loomis, 13 Mar. and Herbert to Hay, 23 Mar. 1903. in *Papers Relating to the Foreign Relations of the United States 1903* (Washington, 1904), p. 495.

[30] Lansdowne to Herbert, tel., 26 May. and Herbert to Lansdowne, tel., 27 May. 1903. F.O. 414/177.

[31] Herbert to Lansdowne, tel., 5 Jun. 1903. ibid.

[32] Lansdowne to Herbert, tel., 16 Jun. 1903. ibid.

[33] Roosevelt to Hay, 29 Jun. 1903., in E. E. Morison (ed.), *The Letters of Theodore Roosevelt* (Cambridge, Mass., 1951), vol. 3., p. 507.

[34] Choate to Lansdowne, 5 Aug. 1903. F.O. 414/177.

[35] Lansdowne to Lodge, 3 Aug. 1903. Lansdowne MSS F.O. 800/144.

[36] Lansdowne to Raikes, 13 Aug. 1903. F.O. 414/177.

[37] Carnegie to Balfour, 23 Jul. 1903. Balfour MSS Add. 49742.

[38] Hay to White, 22 May. 1903., in M. R. Hay (ed.), *Letters of John Hay and Extracts from Diary* (Washington, 1908 [printed but not published]), vol. 3., p. 271.

[39] Roosevelt to Holmes, 25 Jul. 1903. in C. S. Campbell, *Anglo-American Understanding, 1898-1903* (Baltimore, 1957), p. 324.

[40] Chamberlain to Balfour, 8 Aug. 1903. Balfour MSS Add. 49774.

[41] Roosevelt to Root, 3 Oct. 1903. *Letters of Theodore Roosevelt*, vol. 3., p. 613

[42] Herbert to Lansdowne, 10 Sep. 1903. Lansdowne MSS F.O. 800/144.

[43] Lansdowne to Herbert, 14 Sep. 1903. ibid.

[44] When Lodge arrived in London at the end of July, he was approached by several prominent British officials, determined to bring about an Alaskan settlement. Lodge held meetings with Alverstone, and met Lord Halsbury and Sir Henry Campbell-Bannerman. At the same time, both Chamberlain and Balfour promised to exert pressure on the Canadians; unfortunately, these efforts resulted in failure, and Lodge told C. L. Gardner that the English 'are as timid about the Canadians as they can possibly be; they are so afraid of injuring their sensibilities that they hardly dare to say anything.' Lodge to Gardner, 30 Jul. 1903. See J. A. Garraty, *Henry Cabot Lodge: A Biography* (New York, 1953), pp. 246-248.

[45] Chamberlain to Alverstone, 7 Oct. 1903. Alverstone MSS Add. 61738.

[46] Sandars to Balfour, 14 Oct. 1903. Balfour MSS Add. 49761. In a letter to Hay, Henry White remarked that, when Balfour came to see him on October 9, he had already personally made his determination for a settlement known to Lord Alverstone. White to Hay, 20 Oct. 1903., in Garraty, *Lodge*, p. 253.

[47] Balfour to Sandars, 15 Oct. 1903. ibid.

[48] Chamberlain to Balfour, 8 Aug. 1903. Balfour MSS Add. 49774.

[49] Minto to Elliot, 18 Oct. 1903. *Lord Minto's Canadian Papers*, vol. 2., p. 348.

[50] Choate to Hay, 20 Oct. 1903., in Campbell, *Anglo-American Relations*, p. 337.

[51] See ibid., p. 338.

[52] Lodge to Gardner, 19 Oct. 1903., in Garraty, *Lodge*, p. 253.

[53] Lansdowne to Balfour, 16 Oct. 1903. Balfour MSS Add. 49728.

[54] Choate to Hay, 20 Oct. 1903, quoted in Tansill, *Canadian-American Relations*, pp. 258-259n.

[55] Lansdowne to Balfour, 16 Oct. 1903. Balfour MSS Add. 49728.

[56] Alverstone to Balfour, 20 Oct. 1903. ibid.

[57] Lansdowne to Balfour, 20 Oct. 1903. ibid.

[58] Minto to Lyttleton, 18 Nov. in C.O. to F.O., 18 Nov. 1903. ibid.

[59] Quoted in "The Alaska Boundary Arbitration" *The Times*, 20. Oct. 1903., p. 5.

[60] Entry in Minto's Journal, 22 Oct. 1903. *Lord Minto's Canadian Papers*, vol. 2., p. 351.

[61] Minto to Lyttleton, paraphrased tel., 25 Oct. 1903. C.O. 42/893.

[62] Lansdowne to Balfour, 23 Oct. 1903. underlining by Lansdowne. Balfour MSS Add. 49728.

[63] Villiers to C.O., secret, 21 Dec. 1903. F.O. 414/177.

[64] "The Alaska Boundary Award: Canadian and American Opinion" *The Times*, 21 Oct. 1903, p. 5.

[65] Laurier to Minto, 23 Dec. and Minto to Alverstone, 24 Dec. 1903. *Lord Minto's Canadian Papers*, vol. 2., pp. 397-401.

[66] "The Alaska Boundary Award: Canadian and American Opinion" *The Times*, 21 Oct. 1903, p. 5.

[67] Hay to Whitney, 19 Oct. 1903. *Letters of John Hay and Extracts from Diary*, vol. 3., p. 282.

[68] Roosevelt to T. Roosevelt Jnr, 20 Oct. and Roosevelt to Holmes, 20 Oct. 1903. *Letters of Theodore Roosevelt*, vol. 3., pp. 634-5.

[69] *Hansard* CXXIX cols. 2, 23 &16, 2 Feb. 1904.

[70] ibid., cols 39 & 40, 2 Feb. 1903.

[71] A. E. Campbell, *Great Britain and the United States, 1895-1903* (London, 1960), p. 121.

[72] Balfour to Carnegie, 28 Jul. 1903. Balfour MSS Add. 49742.
[73] Durand to Lansdowne, 4 Dec. 1903. Lansdowne MSS F.O. 800/144.

8: Alaskan Epilogue

[1] These quotes, along with many similar expressions of hostility and regret, are quoted in H. F. Angus (ed.), *Canada and Her Great Neighbor: Sociological Surveys of Opinions and Attitudes in Canada Concerning the United States* (Toronto, 1938), pp. 78-80.
[2] Certainly, the Canadians had been, at times, equally guilty of bad faith during the Alaskan negotiations. The immediate journalistic interpretations after October 20, moreover, tended to ignore the inherent weakness of Canada's territorial contention. In his memoirs, Colonel George T. Denison explained that 'I felt confidence that we had a very weak case for our contentions, in fact I thought we had none at all. ... The award was better than I expected and gave us two islands, which the United States had held for years.' G. T. Denison, *The Struggle for Imperial Unity: Recollections & Experiences* (London, 1909), pp. 347-348.
[3] Comment in the *Ottawa Citizen*, 24 Oct. 1903., in Angus, *Canada and her Great Neighbor*, p. 79.
[4] See C. C. Tansill, *Canadian-American Relations, 1875-1911* (Toronto, 1943), p. 364.
[5] A full description of the history of the pelagic sealing dispute is given in C. S. Campbell, *Anglo-American Understanding, 1898-1903* (Baltimore, 1957), pp. 80-94, and Tansill, *Canadian-American Relations*, pp. 267-371.
[6] Villiers to C.O., 18 Jul. 1901. F.O. 414/170.
[7] Roosevelt published his Alaskan nominations on February 18 and the Alaska treaty was ratified in early March. The Tribunal did not begin deliberating until September 1903. The Senate delegation found the seals in a desperate state, with sealers illegally culling female seals and yearlings. For details, see Tansill, *Canadian-American Relations*, p. 364.
[8] Herbert to Lansdowne, 5 Jun. 1903. Lansdowne MSS F.O. 800/144.
[9] Hay to Herbert, 17 Jul. 1903. F.O. 414/176.
[10] See Tansill, *Canadian-American Relations*, p. 365 and Lansdowne to Raikes, 7 Oct. 1903. F.O. 414/176.
[11] Lansdowne to Raikes, 28 Oct. 1903. ibid.
[12] Cox to F.O., 11 Nov. 1903. F.O. ibid.
[13] Villiers to Lansdowne, 4 Nov., and Lansdowne's note on the same. Underlining by Lansdowne. Also Villiers to Lansdowne, 13 Nov. 1903. F.O. 5/2608.
[14] Comments by Ommanney in Villiers to Lansdowne, 13 Nov. 1903. ibid.
[15] Choate to Hay 25 Nov. 1903., quoted in Tansill, *Canadian-American Relations*, p. 365.
[16] Memorandum by Villiers, 10 Jan. 1904. F.O. 414/180.
[17] There had been great presidential interest in fur seal preservation before the Joint High Commission of 1898. In 1897, McKinley told Hay, then at the American Embassy in London, that 'I do not need to be reassured that you are using untiring energy and tact to held along two of the Administration's greatest efforts – Bimetalism and Behring Sea Negotiations'. Roosevelt's interference only really began in 1906. In his Annual Message of that year, he suggested exterminating the seals 'to put an end to the hideous cruelty now incident to pelagic sealing.' See S. F. Bemis (ed.), *The American Secretaries of State and their Diplomacy* (New York, 1958), vol. 9., pp. 120 &343.
[18] Durand to Lansdowne, tel., 18 Jan. 1904. ibid.
[19] See Tansill, *Canadian-American Relations*, pp. 366-367.
[20] 'Conversation with Laurier, 9 Jan. 1904., in P. Stevens and J. T. Saywell (eds.), *Lord Minto's Canadian Papers: A Selection of the Public and Private Letters of the Fourth Earl of Minto, 1898-1904* (Toronto, 1983), vol. 2., pp. 411-412.
[21] C.O. to F.O., 3 Mar. 1904. F.O. 414/180.
[22] Lansdowne to Durand, 31 Mar. 1904. ibid.

[23] Durand to Lansdowne, 24 Mar. and 12 Apr. 1904. ibid.
[24] Minto to Durand, private, 12 May. in C.O. to F.O., secret, 11 Jun. 1904. ibid.
[25] Durand to Lansdowne, 17 May. 1904. Lansdowne MSS F.O. 800/144.
[26] Lansdowne to Durand, tel., 30 May. 1904. F.O. 414/180.
[27] See Tansill, *Canadian-American Relations*, p. 367. A copy of this resolution was sent by Durand to the Foreign Office on January 17 1904. F.O. 414/185.
[28] Lansdowne to Durand, 8 Feb. 1904. ibid.
[29] See Tansill, *Canadian-American Relations*, p. 368.
[30] Lansdowne to Durand, tel., 5 Apr. and Lansdowne to Durand, 14 Sep. 1905. F.O. 414/185.
[31] The sealing dispute was settled by a joint treaty signed at Washington in 1911 to which Great Britain, the US, Russia and Japan all adhered. Britain was to be given fifteen per cent of Pribilof fur skins and an immediate payment of $200,000; the other signatory Powers were given similar terms. In return, pelagic sealing was effectively prohibited in the Behring Sea. See Tansill, *Canadian-American Relations*, p. 371.

9. A Very Ugly Little Row

[1] See C. B. Fawcett, *A Political Geography of the British Empire* (Westport, Conn., 1970), pp. 146-149.
[2] See C. C. Tansill, *Canadian-American Relations, 1875-1911* (New Haven, 1943), p. 88.
[3] W. MacGregor, "Report on the Foreign Trade and Commerce of Newfoundland", presented to Parliament, May. 1905. British Parliamentary Papers, *Accounts and Papers* 1905, vol. LIV (London, 1905), pp. 463-478.
[4] See C. S. Campbell, *Anglo-American Understanding, 1898-1903* (Baltimore, 1957), pp. 96-97.
[5] Quoted in P. Neary, "The French and American Shore Questions as Factors in Newfoundland History" in J. Hiller and P. Neary (eds.), *Newfoundland in the Nineteenth and Twentieth Centuries: Essays in Interpretation* (Toronto, 1980), p. 114.
[6] ibid., p. 115.
[7] See H. A. Innes, *The Cod Fisheries: The History of an International Economy* (New Haven, 1940), p. 450 and Tansill, *Canadian-American Relations*, pp. 85-88.
[8] Shea to Lansdowne, 19 Nov. 1900. F.O. 414/166.
[9] Chamberlain to Minto, 'secret and confidential' tel., 11 Jan. in C.O. to F.O. 11 Jan. 1901. F.O. 414/170.
[10] Minto to Chamberlain, tel., 12 Jan. and Minto to Chamberlain, 16 Jan. in C.O. to F.O., 21 Jan. 1901. ibid.
[11] Chamberlain to Minto, 18 Jan. in C.O. to F.O., 21 Jan. F.O. 414/167.
[12] Memorandum by Minto, 19 Jan. 1901., in P. Stevens and J. T. Saywell (eds.), *Lord Minto's Canadian Papers: A Selection of the Public and Private Papers of the Fourth Earl of Minto, 1898-1904* (Toronto, 1983), vol. 2., pp. 5-6.
[13] Laurier to Minto, 16 Feb. 1901. ibid., pp. 24-26.
[14] C.O. to F.O., 12 Mar., enclosing Strathcona to Chamberlain, 1 Mar. 1901. F.O. 414/170.
[15] Bond to C.O., 25 Apr. in C.O. to F.O., 29 Apr. 1901. ibid.
[16] Quoted in Campbell, *Anglo-American Understanding*, p. 263.
[17] Chamberlain to Lansdowne, 17 Mar. 1901. Lansdowne MSS BL 'Private Letters', vol. 1.
[18] Monson to Lansdowne, 22 Mar. 1901. Underlining by Monson. Lansdowne MSS F.O. 800/125.
[19] Monson to Lansdowne, 21 Mar. 1901. F.O. 414/170.
[20] Lansdowne to Monson, 2 Apr. 1901. ibid.
[21] Chamberlain to Lansdowne, 24 Jul. 1901. Lansdowne MSS BL 'Private Letters', vol. 1.
[22] Lansdowne to Monson, 23 Oct. and F.O. to C.O., 29 Oct. 1901. F.O. 414/170.
[23] Hay's proposal, quoted in Laurier to Minto, secret, 14 Aug. 1901. *Lord Minto's Canadian Papers*, vol. 2., p. 59.

[24] Minto to Parkin, 9 Sep. 1901. ibid., p. 71.

[25] F.O. to C.O., 15 Nov. 1901. F.O. 414/170.

[26] C.O. to F.O., 12 Apr. 1902., in Campbell, *Anglo-American Understanding*, p. 263, and Villiers to C.O., 17 Apr. 1902. F.O. 414/171.

[27] Chamberlain to Minto, 'confidential' tel., 17 Apr., in C.O. to F.O., 1 May. 1902. ibid.

[28] Minto to Chamberlain, 23 Apr., in C.O. to F.O., 1 May. 1902. ibid.

[29] Lansdowne to Raikes, tel., 4 Jun. 1902. F.O. 5/2608.

[30] Raikes to Lansdowne, 'very confidential' tel., 5 Jun. 1902. F.O. 414/171.

[31] Minto's journal entries, 6 Jun., 9 Jun. & 19 Jun. 1902. *Lord Minto's Canadian Papers*, vol. 2., p. 169.

[32] Lansdowne to Minto, 15 Jun. 1902. ibid., p. 170.

[33] See Campbell, *Anglo-American Understanding*, pp. 263-265.

[34] Minto to Parkin, 6 Sep. 1902. *Lord Minto's Canadian Papers*, vol. 2., p. 187.

[35] "Newfoundland and the United States" *The Times*, 15 Sep. 1902, p. 3.

[36] Raikes to Villiers, 15 Sep. 1902. F.O. 5/2487.

[37] Raikes to Lansdowne, 30 Sep. 1902. F.O. 414/171.

[38] See Tansill, *Canadian-American Relations*, p. 94.

[39] See Campbell, *Anglo-American Understanding*, pp. 265-267.

[40] "Newfoundland" *The Times*, 8 Oct. 1902, p. 3.

[41] F.O. to C.O., 13 Oct. 1902. F.O. 414/171.

[42] Antrobus to F.O., 17 Oct. 1902. ibid.

[43] Lansdowne to Herbert, tel., 18 Oct. 1902. F.O. 414/174. Lansdowne's dispatch follows, almost word for word, the advised telegram to Herbert suggested by R. A. Antrobus, in his dispatch to the Foreign Office. Antrobus to F.O., 17 Oct. 1902. F.O. 414/171.

[44] Herbert to Minto, 8 Nov. 1902. *Lord Minto's Canadian Papers*, vol. 2., p. 219.

[45] Herbert to Lansdowne, 17 Dec. 1902. F.O. 5/2608.

[46] Herbert to F.O., tel., 18 Dec. 1902., in Campbell, *Anglo-American Understanding*, p. 267.

[47] Bond to Herbert, 20 Dec. and Herbert to Bond, 31 Dec. 1902. Lansdowne MSS F.O. 800/144.

[48] Lansdowne to Herbert, tel., 8 Jan. and Herbert to Lansdowne, tel., 9 Jan. 1903. F.O. 414/175.

[49] Ommanney to F.O., 2 Apr. and F.O. to C.O., 15 Apr. 1903. ibid.

[50] Herbert to Lansdowne, 27 Apr., enclosing Bond to Herbert, 18 Apr. and Hay to Herbert, 24 Apr. 1903. ibid.

[51] See Z. S. Steiner, *Great Britain and the Origins of the First World War* (London, 1977), pp. 29-30.

[52] Quoted in Sir S. Lee, *King Edward VII: A Biography* (London, 1927), vol. 2., p. 237.

[53] Monson to Lansdowne, 15 May. and Lansdowne to Monson, 19 May. 1903. Lansdowne MSS F.O. 800/125.

[54] Memorandum by Chamberlain, Jul. 1903. Balfour MSS Add. 49774.

[55] Lansdowne to Moon, 16 Dec. 1903. Lansdowne MSS BL L(5)32.

[56] Lansdowne to Monson, 5 Jan. 1904. Lansdowne MSS F.O. 800/125.

[57] Lansdowne to Balfour, 14 Jan. and Lansdowne to Balfour, 18 Jan. 1904. Balfour MSS Add. 49728.

[58] See E. W. Edwards, "The Japanese Alliance and the Anglo-French Agreements of 1904" *History* (1957), p. 26.

[59] Monson to Lansdowne, 15 Jan. 1904., and the King's note on the same. Lansdowne MSS F.O. 800/125.

[60] Balfour to Lansdowne, 15 Jan. 1904. Underlining by Balfour. Lansdowne MSS BL 'Private Letters' vol. 5.

[61] See Neary, "French and American Shore Questions", pp. 113-4.

[62] Morgan to Barrington, 24 Mar. 1904. Lansdowne MSS BL L(5)32 and Neary, "French and American Shore Questions", p. 114. Lord Minto approved the agreement. 'I ... must now send you my heartiest congrats. for it really is a splendid success after all your hard

work.' Minto to Lansdowne, 7 May. 1904. *Lord Minto's Canadian Papers*, vol. 2., p. 457.

[63] Lansdowne to Balfour, 7 Apr. 1904. Balfour MSS Add. 49728.

[64] Lansdowne to Alverstone, 12 Apr. 1904. Alverstone MSS Add. 61738.

[65] Roosevelt to Lodge, 12 Nov. 1904., in E. E. Morison (ed.), *The Letters of Theodore Roosevelt*, (Cambridge, Mass., 1951), vol. 4., p. 1031.

[66] Hay to Choate, 10 Feb. 1905. Quoted in Tansill, *Canadian-American Relations*, p. 95.

[67] "Newfoundland and the United States", *The Times*, 24 Mar., p. 3. and "Newfoundland", *The Times*, 3 Apr. 1905, p. 4.

[68] "Newfoundland and American Fishermen" *The Times*, 15 Apr., p. 7. and "Newfoundland" *The Times*, 19 Apr. 1905, p. 5.

[69] See Tansill, *Canadian-American Relations*, p. 97.

[70] ibid., pp. 97-8.

[71] Roosevelt to Lodge, 19 Aug. 1905., in Sir P. Sykes, *The Right Honourable Sir Mortimer Durand: A Biography* (London, 1926), p. 294.

[72] Lansdowne to Durand, tel., 16 Oct. 1905. F.O. 414/187.

[73] Root to Reid, 13 Oct. 1905., in *Papers Relating to the Foreign Relations of the United States 1905* (Washington, 1906), p. 489.

[74] Reid to Lansdowne, 16 Oct. and Lansdowne to Reid, 19 Oct. 1905. F.O. 414/187. Lansdowne spent the preceding days at Bowood, and it was Sir Thomas Sanderson, not Lansdowne, who received the American Ambassador. Impressed with the gravity of the situation, Sanderson promised to lay the fishery question before the Foreign Secretary on his return. Lansdowne's declaration that the reports were due to a misapprehension can thus be explained as a knee-jerk reaction to a sudden and unexpected crisis. See Reid to Root, 20 Oct. 1905. *Foreign Relations of the United States 1905*, p. 495.

[75] Durand to Lansdowne, 19 Oct. 1905. F.O. 414/187.

[76] Root to Durand, 19 Oct. 1905. in *Foreign Relations of the United States 1905*, pp. 490-494.

[77] Lansdowne to Durand, 21 Oct. 1905. F.O. 414/187.

[78] Durand to Root, 22 Oct. 1905. *Foreign Relations of the United States 1905*, p. 496.

[79] Durand to Lansdowne, 19 Oct. 1905. F.O. 414/187.

[80] Root to Durand, 25 Oct. 1905. *Foreign Relations of the United States 1905*, p. 497.

[81] Lansdowne to Reid, 25 Oct. 1905. F.O. 414/187.

[82] See J. B. Scott, "Elihu Root" in S. F. Bemis (ed.), *The American Secretaries of State and their Diplomacy*, (New York, 1958); vol. 9., pp. 231-233.

[83] Lansdowne to Balfour, 27 Oct. 1905. Underlining by Lansdowne. Balfour MSS Add. 49729.

[84] Lyttleton to MacGregor, tel., 23 Oct. 1905. F.O. 414/188.

[85] Lansdowne to Durand, 3 Nov. 1905. F.O. 414/187.

[86] Lansdowne to Durand, 13 Nov. 1905. Lansdowne MSS F.O. 800/144.

[87] For a more detailed account of Sir Edward Grey's actions, see Tansill, *Canadian-American Relations*, pp. 103-120, Scott, "Elihu Root", pp. 235-237 and B. Perkins, *The Great Rapprochement: England and the United States, 1895-1914* (London, 1968), pp. 257-8.

[88] See Tansill, *Canadian-American Relations*, pp. 119-120n.

[89] MacGregor, "Report of the Foreign Trade and Commerce of Newfoundland" 1905, p. 472.

10: Satisfying the Demands of Justice

[1] Thorough accounts of the Hawaiian revolution and the attitude of the United States are given in C. S. Campbell, *The Transformation of America's Foreign Relations, 1865-1900* (New York, 1976), pp. 178-193; J. A. S. Grenville and G. B. Young, Politics, *Strategy, and American Diplomacy: Studies in Foreign Policy, 1873-1917* (New Haven, 1966), pp. 102-116; and J. W. Pratt, *Expansionists of 1898: the Acquisition of Hawaii and the Spanish Islands* (Baltimore, 1936), pp. 34-110.

2   Dole, "Proclamation", 7 Jan. in C. W. Ashford to Hawes, 4 Mar. 1895. F.O. 331/63.

3   This information comes from "An Uprising in Hawaii" *The New York Times*, 19 Jan., p. 1, "The Uprising in Hawaii" *The New York Times*, 20 Jan. 1895, p. 1. Also Pratt, *Expansionists of 1898*, pp. 197-200.

4   Report by G. C. Potters, 22 Mar. 1895., p. 3. F.O. 331/62.

5   V. V. Ashford to Hawes, 2 May. 1895. Volney's brother, Clarence, suffered similar treatment and complained that 'despite our innocence of any complicity ... we were by order of the Government, and without warrant from any court or Magistrate, arrested ... and thrust into prison, and from thence to the present time neither of us has been charged or arraigned before any civil court in respect of the causes of such imprisonment.' C. W. Ashford to Hawes, 4 Mar. 1895. Other claimants included E. B. Thomas, G. C. Kenyon, and F. Harrison. Hoare to Dole, 9 Mar. 1903. F.O. 331/63. John Cranstoun's claim was doubtful: he claimed initially that he was American, and not British. "Exiled From Honolulu" *The New York Times*, 11 Feb. 1895, p. 1.

6   Hawes to Kimberley, 7 Mar. 1895. F.O. 331/62. Hawes' first action was to fight against capital punishment. Willis to Gresham, 20 Jan., in "Information for House: Hawaiian Correspondence Submitted by Secretary Gresham" *The New York Times*, 5 Feb. 1895, p. 9.

7   Law Officers' verdict of 4 Mar. 1896, paraphrased in Larcom to the Law Officers, 19 Jan. 1901. F.O. 58/335.

8   Hawaiian reply, 2 Feb. 1898, paraphrased in the above. ibid.

9   See L. B. Shippee and R. B. Way, "William Rufus Day" in S. F. Bemis (ed.), *The American Secretaries of State and their Diplomacy* (New York, 1958), vol. 9., pp. 33-37; Campbell, *Transformation of American Foreign Relations*, pp. 232-238.

10 See Campbell, *Transformation of American Foreign Relations*, p. 294.

11 Hawaiian reply, 10 Aug. 1898, paraphrased in Larcom to the Law Officers, 19 Jan. 1901. F.O. 58/335.

12 American fears of British designs on Hawaii can be seen in "The Uprising in Hawaii", *The New York Times*, 20 Jan. 1895, p. 1. Also D. Healy, *US Expansionism: the Imperialist Urge in the 1890s* (Madison, Wis., 1970), pp. 24-25.

13 Cited in Larcom to the Law Officers, 19 Jan. 1901. F.O. 58/335.

14 Hay to Tower, Oct. 1899, quoted in Hay to Pauncefote, 4 Jan. 1900. F.O. 5/2426.

15 Hay to Pauncefote, 4 Jan. 1900. ibid.

16 One claimant, G. Carson Kenyon, asked the Foreign Office whether any progress has been made in obtaining compensation. Villiers responded that 'your claim, together with others of a like nature, is still before the U.S.G. and that the latter's decision in regard to them must be awaited.' Kenyon to F.O., 20 Jun. and Villiers to Kenyon, 26 Jul. 1900. F.O. 58/335.

17 Note by Larcom on Pauncefote to Salisbury, 15 May. 1900. F.O. 5/2428.

18 Pauncefote to Hay, 14 Aug. and Hill to Pauncefote, 11 Sep. 1900. F.O. 5/2428.

19 "Extract of the Report of the Governor of Hawaii", in Pauncefote to Lansdowne, 21 Dec. 1900. F.O. 5/2429. This report is also included in. F.O. 313/64.

20 This dispatch, it appears, first brought the Hawaiian affair to Lansdowne's attention. Villiers to Lansdowne, 12 Jan. 1901. ibid.

21 Notes by Larcom and Davidson on Pauncefote to Lansdowne, 21 Dec. 1900. Davidson explained that 'I didn't think we were likely to get much out of our representations.' F.O. 5/2429. Larcom to the Law Officers, 19 Jan. 1901. F.O. 58/335.

22 Finlay to Lansdowne, 6 Feb. 1901. In a previous dispatch, however, Finlay found significant difficulties in John Cranstoun's claim: 'there appears to be a residuum of facts showing that Mr. Cranstoun was engaged in projects of a revolutionary nature ... It is possible that Mr. Cranstoun may have explanations to offer which put a different aspect on the case. This however does not appear to me to be very probable.' In response, Larcom suggested that the claim should not be pressed, and wrote in this sense to Cranstoun on February 26. Finlay to F.O., 4 Feb., note by Larcom, 9 Feb. and Larcom

to Cranstoun, 26 Feb. 1901. F.O. 58/337.

[23] Undated notes by Villiers and Lansdowne on Finlay to Lansdowne, 6 Feb. ibid. Lansdowne to Pauncefote, 26 Feb. 1901. F.O. 331/64.

[24] Pauncefote to Hay, 9 Apr. 1901. F.O. 5/2457.

[25] Hay to Pauncefote, 15 Apr. 1901. ibid.

[26] Note by Lansdowne on Villiers to Lansdowne, 12 Jan. 1901. F.O. 58/335.

[27] Memorandum by Hill, enclosed in Pauncefote to Lansdowne, 7 May. 1901. F.O. 5/2457.

[28] Memorandum by the State Department, 14 Jun., enclosed in Pauncefote to Lansdowne, 17 Jun. 1901. ibid.

[29] Extract from the London Gazette, 9 Apr. 1901. ibid., Pauncefote to Lansdowne, 2 Jan. 1902. F.O. 5/2485.

[30] Note by Fainall, 7 May. 1901. F.O. 5/2457.

[31] Note by Villiers on Pauncefote to Lansdowne, 7 May., note by Larcom on Pauncefote to Lansdowne, 17 Jun, 1901. ibid.

[32] Villiers to Hoare, 31 Jul. 1901. F.O. 331/64.

[33] Pauncefote to Lansdowne, 2 Jan. 1902., and Hay to Pauncefote, undated. F.O. 5/2485.

[34] Pauncefote to Lansdowne, 3 Apr. 1902. F.O. 5/2486.

[35] Raikes to Villiers, 8 Feb. 1903. F.O. 5/2488.

[36] Raikes to Larcom, 10 Jan. 1903. F.O. 5/2531.

[37] Herbert to Lansdowne, 23 Dec. 1902. F.O. 5/2488. This was the response to Lansdowne's enquiry of November 29. Raikes left no record of the interview in the British Embassy and Herbert accordingly recommended that Lansdowne should contact Raikes personally. Raikes replied, firstly to Larcom and then to Villiers. Raikes to Larcom, 10 Jan. 1903. F.O. 5/2531 and Raikes to Villiers, 8 Feb. 1903. F.O. 5/2488.

[38] Herbert to Lansdowne, 18 Feb., enclosing Hay to Herbert, 17 Feb. 1903. F.O. 5/2522.

[39] Hoare to Herbert, 23 Feb. 1903. ibid.

[40] One Honolulu newspaper had listed the requested compensation in dollars, rather than pounds. "Foreigner's Claims" Pacific Commercial Advertiser, 6 Mar., Hoare to Dole, 9 Mar. and "Pounds, Not Dollars" *Pacific Commercial Advertiser*, 11 Mar. 1903. After the cases had been fully scrutinised, only nine claimants would be supported. Of these, Clarence Ashford, for example, claimed £1,400 while G. Carson Kenyon called for £900. F.O. 331/62.

[41] Note by Larcom on Herbert to Lansdowne, 9 Mar. 1903. F.O. 5/2522.

[42] Note by Villiers on the above. ibid., Villiers to Herbert, 2 Apr. 1903. F.O. 331/62.

[43] Herbert to Lansdowne, 16 Apr. 1903. F.O. 5/2522., Hay to Herbert, 20 Apr., enclosed in Herbert to Hoare, 21 Apr. 1903. F.O. 331/62.

[44] Notes by Larcom, Villiers and Lansdowne on Herbert to Lansdowne, 21 Apr. 1903. F.O. 5/2522.

[45] Hoare to Herbert, paraphrased tel., 15 Apr., enclosed in Herbert to Lansdowne, 16 Apr. 1903. ibid. On this, Larcom noted that Villiers 'thinks that if we were to ask for interest on those claims it might provoke, or at any rate suggest to the US to ask for interest against us in some other outstanding matters and that on the balance we should lose by the transaction ... it is rather late in the day to start the question of interest for the first time and I think we should do better probably to complain of the delay as being unreasonably prolonged in the hope of this hurrying a settlement.' Lansdowne noted, 'I agree'. Herbert wired Hoare not to request interest. Herbert to Lansdowne, 2 May. 1903. ibid.

[46] Foreign Office note on Hay to Herbert, 20 Apr. 1903. ibid.

[47] Note by Larcom, 18 May., on the above. ibid.

[48] Note by Davidson, 26 May., on the above. Davidson appreciated the parallel between Hawaiian and South African claims. The latter 'have been referred to purely British Courts, with the single exception of the claims founded on the arrest of the "Bundesrath" and other German ships. But the joint commission appointed in this case had merely to assess the damages, after it had decided that damages were due – the law involved and the facts were no longer in dispute. Unnecessary hardship connected

with deportation appears to be no longer a subject of claim in the Hawaiian claim, although it is mentioned in the earlier references to the Law Officers.' Davidson to Herbert, 2 May. 1903. ibid.

49 Hoare to Herbert, 13 May., in Herbert to Lansdowne, 28 May. 1903. F.O. 5/2523.

50 Notes by Larcom and Villiers on the above. ibid.

51 Raikes to Lansdowne, 18 Jul., enclosing Hay to Raikes, 16 Jul. 1903. ibid.

52 Note by Larcom on the above. ibid.

53 In 1899, Roosevelt asserted that '[w]e cannot avoid the responsibilities that confront us in Hawaii, Cuba, Porto Rico [*sic*.], and the Philippines. All we can decide is whether we shall meet them in a way that will redound [sic.] to the national credit, or whether we shall make of our dealings with these new problems a dark and shameful page in our history.' T. Roosevelt, *The Strenuous Life: Essays and Addresses* (London, 1902), pp. 6-7.

54 Extract from the *Pacific Commercial Advertiser*, 7 Apr. and "British Claims", *Pacific Commercial Advertiser*, 14 Apr. 1905. F.O. 331/62.

55 A small amount of correspondence continued until 1920. On several occasions, it seemed that the United States would consider the claims. In 1913, Barclay at the British Embassy wrote to Consul John B. Reuters that the 'cases have been included on the first schedule of the claims to be submitted to the American and British Claims Tribunal and will therefore presumably be held next year.' Barclay to Reuters, 15 Dec. 1903. In 1920, the British Embassy wrote to Consul W. M. Royds of another proposal, made to the United States on August 11 of that year, 'that a session of the Claims Convention should be held either in London or Paris on October 1 next at which awards of cases argued in 1914 would be pronounced.' Embassy to Royds, 14 Sep. 1920. ibid.

11: Diplomatic Duel

1 Salisbury to Lansdowne, 30 Sep. 1901. Lansdowne MSS BL L(5)34.

2 Balfour to Lansdowne, 12 Dec. 1901., quoted in S. Mahajan, "The Defence of India and the End of Isolation: A Study in the Foreign Policy of the Conservative Government, 1900-1905" *Journal of Imperial and Commonwealth History* 10 (1981-2), p. 169.

3 See J. D. Hargreaves, "Lord Salisbury, British Isolation and the Yangtze Valley, June-September, 1900" *Bulletin of the Institute of Historical Research* 30 (1957), pp. 62.75, and Hu Bin, "Contradictions and Conflicts Among the Imperial Powers in China at the Time of the Boxer Movement" in D. D. Buck (ed.), *Recent Chinese Studies of the Boxer Movement* (New York, 1987), pp. 156-174.

4 Quoted in Hu Bin, "Contradictions and Conflicts", pp. 162-163.

5 Salisbury to Curzon, 17 Oct. 1900., in K. M. Wilson, "The Boer War in the Context of Britain's Imperial Problems" in K. M. Wilson (ed.), *The International Impact of the Boer War* (Chesham, 2001), p. 161.

6 Hay's second Open Door Note, 3 Jul. 1900., in A. S. Link and W. M. Leary (eds.), *The Diplomacy of World Power: The United States 1889-1920* (London, 1970), pp. 95-96.

7 Unidentified to Lansdowne, 7 Aug. 1900. Lansdowne MSS BL L(5)40. Impressions of the Russians were critical. They 'have behaved like wild beasts', MacDonald explained, 'killing and slaying, ravishing the ladies, and generally getting themselves severely dis liked.' MacDonald to Bertie, 4 Sep. 1900. Bertie MSS F.O. 800/163.

8 Conger to Hay, 22 Mar. 1900., in E. H. Zabriskie, *American-Russian Rivalry in the Far East: A Study in Diplomacy and Power Politics, 1895-1914* (Westport, Conn., 1976), p. 61.

9 Hay to Reid, 20 Sep. 1900., in M. R. Hay (ed.), *Letters of John Hay and Extracts from Diary* (Washington, 1908 [printed but not published]), vol. 3., p. 193.

10 MacDonald to Lansdowne, 17 Feb. 1901. Lansdowne MSS F.O. 800/134.

11 Memorandum by Lansdowne, 24 Jul. 1901. Lansdowne MSS BL L(5)78

12 Lansdowne to Hamilton, 31 Aug. Lansdowne MSS BL L(5)28. and Lansdowne to Salisbury, 31 Aug. 1900, with a crossed-out note on the same. Lansdowne MSS BL L(5)63.

[13] Lansdowne to Hicks Beach, 7 Apr. 1901. Lansdowne MSS BL 'Private Letters', vol. 6.

[14] Lansdowne to Hamilton, 9 Sep. 1901. Lansdowne MSS BL L(5)28.

[15] Lansdowne to Satow, 16 Jan. 1901. On December 13 1900, Salisbury wrote: 'I think Satow has behaved very badly. I am ashamed of having nominated him.' Lansdowne replied that Satow 'has not kept us fully informed as to the action of the powers throughout these negotiations. Lansdowne MSS F.O. 800/119.

[16] See I. H. Nish, The Origins of the Russo-Japanese War (London, 1985), pp. 80-81.

[17] Sanderson to Lansdowne, 10 Mar. 1901. Lansdowne MSS F.O. 800/119.

[18] Satow to Lansdowne, 17 Jan. and 8 Feb., Lansdowne to Satow, 9 Apr. 1901. ibid.

[19] MacDonald to Lansdowne, 17 Feb. 1901. Lansdowne MSS F.O. 800/134.

[20] Hay to Adee, 14 Sep. 1900., in P. A. Varg, The Making of a Myth: The United States and China, 1897-1912 (East Lansing, 1968), p. 28.

[21] Choate to Lansdowne, 4 Jan. and a note by Lansdowne, 6 Jan. 1901. F.O. 5/2471. Lansdowne, clearly optimistic, wrote that the 'selection of Washington would be agree able to the U.S., but I should have thought Paris or Berlin more convenient. I should be inclined to defer to the wishes of the other Powers upon this point.' Lansdowne to Salisbury, 6 Jan. 1901. Lansdowne MSS F.O. 800/144.

[22] Satow to Lansdowne, 8 Feb. 1901. Lansdowne MSS F.O. 800/119.

[23] Satow to Lansdowne, 24 May. 1901. Ibid. Also see C. C. Tan, The Boxer Catastrophe (New York, 1975), p. 225.

[24] Satow to Lansdowne, 30 Jan. 1901. Lansdowne MSS F.O. 800/119.

[25] See P. H. Clyde, International Rivalries in Manchuria, 1689-1922 (New York, 1966), pp. 85-85.

[26] See Nish, Origins of the Russo-Japanese War, pp. 91-93. Satow sent Lansdowne a copy of the Russo-Chinese agreement on January 2. I. C. Ruxton (ed.), The Diaries and Letters of Sir Ernest Mason Satow (1843-1929), A Scholar-Diplomat in East Asia (New York, 1998), pp. 302-303.

[27] Balfour to Lansdowne, 30 Mar. 1901. Lansdowne MSS F.O. 800/119.

[28] Conger to Hay, 9 Nov. 1900., in Zabriskie, American-Russian Rivalry, p. 78.

[29] Memorandum by the State Department, 19 Feb. 1901. F.O. 5/2471.

[30] Lansdowne to Satow, tel., 1 Mar., in Lansdowne to Choate, 2 Mar. 1901. ibid.

[31] See Nish, Russo-Japanese War, pp. 103-104.

[32] Lansdowne to Hicks Beach, 7 Apr. 1901. Lansdowne MSS BL 'Private Letters', vol. 6.

[33] Lansdowne to Bertie, 27 Aug. 1901. Bertie MSS F.O. 800/163.

[34] See Tan, Boxer Catastrophe, pp. 215-236.

[35] Satow to Lansdowne, 29 Aug. 1901. Lansdowne MSS F.O. 800/119.

[36] Satow to Lansdowne, 23 Oct. and Lansdowne to Satow, 10 Dec. 1901. ibid.

[37] See Nish, Russo-Japanese War, pp. 112-113.

[38] Hardinge to Bertie, 30 Oct. 1901. Bertie was then an Assistant Under Secretary in charge of the Far Eastern Department at the Foreign Office. Bertie MSS Add. 63014.

[39] Satow to Lansdowne, 29 Jan. and 27 Feb. 1902. Lansdowne MSS F.O. 800/119.

[40] Hansard's Parliamentary Debates (4th ser.) CIII col. 1287. 12 Feb. 1902. Cranborne's statement was also a response to the German allegations against Lord Pauncefote.

[41] Lansdowne to Satow, 25 Aug. 1901. Lansdowne MSS F.O. 800/119.

[42] Lansdowne to Satow, 25 Aug. 1901. ibid. Hicks Beach wrote that the gains were out weighed by the objections: 'you will have noticed that Balfour, who would have to defend it in the H. Of C., and Chamberlain are inclined to the same opinion.' Hicks Beach to Lansdowne, 2 Jan. 1902. Lansdowne MSS F.O. 800/134.

[43] Balfour to Lansdowne, 12 Dec. 1901. Balfour MSS Add. 49727.

[44] Memorandum by Lord Selborne, 4 Sep. 1901., in Z. S. Steiner, "Great Britain and the Creation of the Anglo-Japanese Alliance" Journal of Modern History 31 (1959), pp. 29-31.

[45] Lansdowne to MacDonald, 9 Jan. 1902. Lansdowne MSS F.O. 800/134.

[46] Lansdowne to MacDonald, 31 Mar. 1903. ibid.

[47] See D. Walder, The Short Victorious War: The Russo-Japanese Conflict 1904-5 (London, 1973),

pp. 27-29. Also Nish, *Russo-Japanese War*, pp. 129-130.

[48] Satow to Lansdowne, 13 Feb. 1902. Lansdowne MSS F.O. 800/119. and Lansdowne to Pauncefote, 25 Feb. 1902. Lansdowne MSS F.O. 800/144.

[49] A Russo-Chinese agreement was signed for this purpose on April 8 1902. Niuchuang should have been evacuated in October but Russian forces remained. See Nish, *Russo-Japanese War*, pp. 140-141.

[50] Conger to State Department, 23 Apr. 1903., in P. J. Treat, *Diplomatic Relations between the United States and Japan, 1895-1905* (Gloucester, Mass., 1963), pp. 173-174. The news was also reported by Satow and the Japanese Minister.

[51] MacDonald to Lansdowne, 27 Apr. 1903. ibid., p. 174.

[52] Minute by Lansdowne, 12 Apr. 1903. Balfour MSS Add. 49728.

[53] *Hansard* CXXI col. 639, 28 Apr. 1903.

[54] Lansdowne to Herbert, tel., 28 Apr. Lansdowne MSS F.O. 800/144 and Lansdowne to Herbert, 28 Apr. 1903., in G. W. Monger, *The End of Isolation: British Foreign Policy, 1900-1907* (London, 1963), p. 124.

[55] Herbert to Lansdowne, 1 May and 8 May. 1903. Lansdowne MSS F.O. 800/144.

[56] Hay to Roosevelt, 28 Apr. 1903., in Zabriskie, *American-Russian Rivalry*, p. 89.

[57] B. Perkins, *The Great Rapprochement: England and the United States, 1895-1914* (London, 1968), p. 220.

[58] Roosevelt to Hay, 22 May. 1903., in G. E. Mowry, *The Era of Theodore Roosevelt, 1900-1912* (London, 1958), pp. 182-183.

[59] "Russia and Manchuria: American Expressions of Opinion", *The Times*, 7 May., p. 7; "Russia and Manchuria: Attitude of the United States" *The Times*, 11 May. 1903, p. 5.

[60] Article in *The New York Times*, in "The Manchurian Question" ibid., 9 May. 1903, p. 7.

[61] *Hansard*, CXXI, col. 917, 30 Apr. and col. 1067, 1 May. 1903.

[62] "The Manchurian Question" *The Times*, 2 May. 1903, p. 7.

[63] "The Manchurian Question" ibid., 9 May. 1903, p. 7.

[64] See P. H. Clyde (ed.), *United States Policy toward China: Diplomatic and Public Documents, 1839-1939* (New York, 1964), pp. 222-230.

[65] Satow to Lansdowne, 24 Sep. 1903. Lansdowne MSS F.O. 800/119.

[66] "Russia and the Far East: The Re-Occupation of Mukden" *The Times*, 2 Nov. 1903, p. 5.

[67] "Russia and the Far East: The Re-Occupation of Mukden" ibid., 3 Nov. 1903, p. 3.

[68] ibid.

[69] "Russia in Korean Waters" *The New York Times*, 11 Dec. 1903, p. 8.

[70] Minister Kurino gave the draft agreement to Count Lamsdorf on August 12, For a full description of the agreement, see Nish, *Russo-Japanese War*, pp. 183-185.

[71] Report from Tokyo, 25 Nov,.in "The Situation in the Far East: Russian Military Strength" *The Times*, 26 Nov. 1903, p. 3.

[72] Raikes to Lansdowne, 'confidential', 2 Oct. 1903. F.O. 5/2524.

[73] Raikes to Lansdowne, 'confidential', 8 Oct. ibid. Raikes telegraphed the news the same day. Raikes to Lansdowne, 'very confidential' tel., 8 Oct. 1903. F.O. 405/139.

[74] "England and Russia in Asia" *The New York Times*, 29 Nov. 1903, p. 6.

[75] "Russia in Korean Waters" ibid., 11 Dec. 1903, p. 8.

[76] Salisbury to Lansdowne, 10 Sep. Lansdowne MSS BL L(5)34 and Balfour to Broderick, 28 Oct. Balfour MSS Add. 49720. Sanderson saw no immediate threat of war. To Spring Rice he wrote: 'for the Japanese there are no signs as yet that they will let their temper over ride their judgment [*sic*.]. If they eventually do anything I should say that it would most probably be some action in Corea [*sic*.] as a counter poise to the Russian position in Manchuria. It would then be for the Russians to consider whether they would stand this or fight. There are several reasons why they should prefer not to go to war at present. But all this is mere conjecture. We have not got to the turning point yet.' Sanderson to Spring Rice, 21 Oct. 1903. Spring Rice MSS F.O. 800/241.

[77] "The Crisis in the Far East: Japan and the Russian Reply" *The Times*, 22 Dec. 1903, p. 3.

[78] Hardinge to Bertie, 18 Dec. 1903. Bertie MSS Add. 63015.

79 29th Meeting of the C.I.D., 4 Jan. 1904. Privy Council Committee of Imperial Defence Minutes. Cab 2/1494.
80 Satow to Lansdowne, 27 Aug. 1903. Lansdowne MSS F.O. 800/119.
81 Note by Lansdowne for the Cabinet, 27 Dec. 1903. Lansdowne MSS BL Lab 4/34.
82 Lansdowne to Balfour, 25 Dec. and Lansdowne's Cabinet Note, 27 Dec. 1903. ibid. Lansdowne refused to commit himself. Britain had 'in no wise changed their opinion in regard to the maintenance of the integrity of the Chinese Empire', he commented, 'and that they gave no encouragement to the idea of its partition. I said that I found it difficult to express an opinion as to the course which China should adopt with regard to the reoccupation of Mukden by Russian troops'. Lansdowne to Satow, 4 Nov. 1903. F.O. 405/139.
83 'We are endeavouring to negotiate with Russia, but as each day somebody introduces some new problem it is gradually becoming complicated and too unwieldy to inspire confidence. They are losing the substance in order to secure the shadow of Parliamentary success.' Hardinge to Bertie, 18 Dec. 1903. Bertie MSS F.O. 800/163.
84 Selborne, "Confidential Notes on Lord Lansdowne's Comments on Mr. Balfour's Memorandum on the Crisis between Japan and Russia", 25 Dec. 1903. Lansdowne MSS BL Lab 4/34..
85 Arnold-Forster to Lansdowne, 27 Dec. and 23 Dec. 1903. Balfour MSS Add. 49722.
86 Notes by an unknown official and Villiers on Raikes to Lansdowne, 3 Nov. 1903. F.O. 5/2524.
87 Arnold-Forster to Lansdowne, 25 Dec. 1903. Lansdowne MSS BL Lab 4/34.
88 Lansdowne to Balfour, 19 Dec. 1903. ibid.
89 Lansdowne to Durand, draft tel., 22 Dec. 1903. ibid.
90 Lansdowne to Balfour, 22 Dec. 1903. Balfour MSS Add. 49728.
91 Balfour to Selborne, 23 Dec. 1903. Balfour MSS Add. 49707.
92 Selborne to Lansdowne, 29 Dec. 1903. Lansdowne MSS BL 'Private Letters', vol. 1.
93 Chamberlain to Lansdowne, 'confidential', 25 Dec. 1903. Lansdowne MSS BL Lab 4/34.
94 Edward to Balfour, 25 Dec. 1903. Balfour MSS Add. 49683 and Balfour to Edward, 28 Dec. 1903., in B. E. C. Dugdale, *Arthur James Balfour: First Earl of Balfour, K.G., O.M., F.R.S., Etc.* (London, 1936), vol. 1., p. 378.
95 See E. Halévy, *Imperialism and the Rise of Labour* (London, 1951), pp. 416-417.
96 Balfour to Lansdowne, "Japan and Russia", 22 Dec. 1903, in Dugdale, *Balfour*, vol. 1., p. 377.
97 Balfour to Lansdowne, 31 Dec. 1903. Balfour MSS Add. 49728.
98 Balfour to Selborne, 23 Dec. 1903. Balfour MSS Add. 49707.
99 Selborne to Lansdowne, not dated, but late December 1903. Lansdowne MSS BL Lab 4/34. The Lord Chancellor, similarly, dismissed Lansdowne's suggestion: 'if, as seems highly probable, Russia and Japan are unable to come to terms, I doubt whether it will be expedient, or worth while to follow up these proposals for the present; they are not of a kind which could be taken up, with much promise of success, by a Power engaged in so formidable a struggle'. Halsbury to Lansdowne, 11 Jan. 1904. Halsbury MSS Add. 56372.
100 Satow to Lansdowne, 27 Aug. 1903. Lansdowne MSS F.O. 800/119.
101 Sanderson to Balfour, 28 Dec. 1903. Balfour MSS Add. 49739.
102 Lansdowne to Balfour, 7 Jan. 1904. Lansdowne MSS BL 'Private Letters', vol. 5.
103 29th Meeting of the C.I.D., 4 Jan. 1904. C.I.D. Minutes.
104 *Hansard* CXXIX, cols. 24, 172 & 41, 2 Feb. 1904.
105 Satow to Lansdowne, 27 Jan. 1904. Lansdowne MSS F.O. 800/119.
106 Balfour to Lansdowne, 11 Feb. 1904. Balfour MSS Add. 49728.
107 Balfour's draft letter to Lansdowne, not dated. ibid.
108 Balfour to Lansdowne, 11 Feb. 1904. ibid.
109 Memorandum by Choate, 8 Feb. 1904. Lansdowne MSS BL Lab 4/34.

[110] The proposal was suggested, not by the United States, but by Germany. Choate ruefully acknowledged this fact in a confidential addendum to his memorandum. ibid.

[111] Lansdowne to Balfour, 9 Feb. 1904. and a note by Balfour enclosed. ibid.

[112] Eric Barrington, a Foreign Office clerk, noted that 'Mr. Lyttleton and Mr. Long also agree.' Note by Barrington. Also note by Wyndham, enclosed in Lansdowne to Balfour, 9 Feb. 1904. ibid. George Wyndham gave his approval to the scheme, but raised objections based on his suspicions of Germany. 'Might it not create a precedent', he noted, 'which would make it harder to resist overtures from Powers, other than the U.S. for intervening, or offers of mediation of an objectionable character?'

[113] Note by Chamberlain, not dated. ibid.

[114] Lansdowne to Lascelles, 10 Feb. 1904, in G. P. Gooch and H. Temperley (eds.), *British Documents on the Origins of the War, 1898-1914* (London, 1929), vol. 4., p. 252.

[115] Lansdowne to Durand, 4 Feb. 1905. Lansdowne MSS F.O. 800/144.

12: This Wretched War

[1] Admiral Sir John Fisher is said to have shown Lansdowne the exact location where Japanese forces would meet a crushing defeat. See Lord Newton, *Lord Lansdowne: A Biography* (London, 1929), p. 307.

[2] Selborne, writing to Sir Walter Kerr, remarked that 'We all on the C.I.D. must be impressed with the great weakness which accrues to the British Empire from the fact that, whereas Russia can strike at us when she pleases through Afghanistan, we apparently can hit back at her nowhere.' Selborne to Kerr, 1 Apr. 1904. Balfour MSS Add. 49707.

[3] These figures come from D. Walder, *The Short Victorious War: The Russo-Japanese Conflict, 1904-5* (London, 1973), p. 78. An Anglo-Russian agreement was not dismissed. On June 3, Hardinge chastised Sir Valentine Chiriol of *The Times* for the paper's anti-Russian attitude: 'our policy is to maintain friendly relations with the Russian Government during the present war which is not at all incompatible with our alliance with Japan, and I believe that our Government hope soon after the conclusion of the war to arrive at a friendly agreement with Russia on many of the thorny questions at issue between the two Governments.' Hardinge to Chiriol, 3 Jun. 1904. Sanderson MSS F.O. 800/2.

[4] Percy to Balfour, 18 Jan. 1904. Balfour MSS Add. 49747.

[5] "The Prime Minister at Manchester" *The Times*, 12 Jan. 1904, p. 9.

[6] Balfour to Wilkinson, 3 Jan. 1904. Balfour MSS Add. 49747.

[7] "Memorandum by the Marquess of Lansdowne respecting the Russian Black Sea Fleet", 11 Jan. 1904. Cabinet and Committee of Imperial Defence Series CAB 37/roll 68, vol. 11.

[8] Selborne to Lansdowne, 14 Jan., "Memorandum by Mr. Balfour respecting the Russian Black Sea Fleet and the Passage of the Dardanelles", 18 Jan., and Balfour to Lansdowne, 19 Jan. 1904. ibid.

[9] Balfour wrote that there 'is I believe no British Government that would not gladly make a permanent arrangement with Russia in Central Asia and the Far East, and Russian Statesmen and diplomatists have from time to time expressed a desire to see some such arrangement carried into effect. Why then, with this good-will, or at least the appearance of good-will, on both sides, has no such arrangement yet been found practicable?' Balfour to Lansdowne, 21 Dec. 1903. Balfour MSS Add. 49728.

[10] Monson to Lansdowne, 12 Jan. 1904. Lansdowne MSS F.O. 800/125.

[11] Monson to Lansdowne, 15 Jan. 1904. ibid.

[12] 31st Meeting of the C.I.D., 8 Feb. 1904. Privy Council Committee of Imperial Defence Minutes. Cab 2/2494.

[13] *Hansard's Parliamentary Debates* (4th ser.) CXXIX col. 1139, 12 Feb. Lord Selborne later labelled the rumour 'a most wicked falsehood'. *Hansard* CXXX cols. 940-941, 25 Feb. 1904.

[14] See Sir S. Lee, *King Edward VII: A Biography* (London, 1927), vol. 2., p. 283.

[15] Esher, "National Strategy", 27 Mar., in Esher to Sandars, 29 Mar. 1904. Balfour MSS Add. 49718.

[16] *Hansard* CXXX cols. 1415-1416, 1 Mar. 1904. Runciman, an 'economist' welcomed anything that reduced British spending. Selborne, however, rejected the immediate reduction of British naval expenditure. In a Cabinet memorandum, dated February 26, he reviewed calls for a reduction of the Navy Estimates for 1904-5. 'We are only at the commencement of a war,' he explained, ' the scope of which we earnestly desire to con fine. Every one knows that there is a grave danger of such a conflagration spreading, and that if this conflagration did spread it might easily involve us. Under these circumstances it does not appear to me to be a moment at which it would be possible to defend the suggested reduction.' Memorandum by Selborne, 26 Feb. 1904., in D. G. Boyce (ed.), *The Crisis of British Power: the Imperial and Naval Papers of the Second Earl of Selborne, 1895-1910* (London, 1990), p. 170.

[17] Lansdowne to Ito, 18 Mar. 1904. Lansdowne MSS F.O. 800/134.

[18] For a more detailed account, see Walder, *The Short Victorious War*, pp. 84-111. Lord Brooke, an observer with the Russians, noted the 'stupendous task of maintaining an army in the field six thousand miles from its base and dependent for almost everything on the smooth working of the railway.' However, the Russian defeat was largely self-inflicted. Her army had been supplied with poor maps 'because the Russian plans did not contemplate the possibility of the Japanese getting north of Liao-Yang!' Lord Brooke, *An Eye-Witness in Manchuria* (London, 1905), pp. 3 & 138.

[19] E. McCaul, *Under the Care of the Japanese War Office* (London, 1904), p. 217.

[20] Nicholas II to Edward VII, 17 Apr. 1904., in Lee, *Edward VII*, vol. 2., pp. 278-288.

[21] Lansdowne to Spring Rice, 4 May. 1904., in G. P. Gooch and H. Temperley (eds.), *British Documents on the Origins of the War, 1898-1914* (London, 1929), vol. 4., p. 189. Britain became angry with Russia in mid 1904, due to Russian seizures of British vessels. The "Hopsang" was actually sunk by Russian ships. See S. Gwynn, *The Letters and Friendships of Sir Cecil Spring Rice: A Record* (London, 1929), vol. 1., p. 389.

[22] Durand to Lansdowne, 4 Dec. 1903 and 8 Jan. 1904. Lansdowne MSS F.O. 800/144. Also see Sir P. Sykes, *The Right Honourable Sir Mortimer Durand: A Biography* (London, 1926), pp. 265-278.

[23] Roosevelt to Roosevelt Jnr, 10 Feb. 1904., in E. E. Morison (ed.), *The Letters of Theodore Roosevelt* (Cambridge, Mass., 1951), vol. 4., p. 724.

[24] Roosevelt to Spring Rice, 19 Mar. 1904. in Gwynn, *Spring Rice*, vol. 1.,p. 398.

[25] Durand to Lansdowne, 17 May. 1904. Lansdowne MSS F.O. 800/144.

[26] Roosevelt to Spring Rice, 12 Jun. 1904. in Gwynn, *Spring Rice*, vol. 1., p. 417. Ito sent Kaneko to Washington to foster American-Japanese goodwill, knowing that, when Japan desired peace, Roosevelt would be a suitable mediator. See J. A. White, *The Diplomacy of the Russo-Japanese War* (Princeton, 1964), pp. 156-157.

[27] Roosevelt to Hay, 29 Aug. 1904. *Letters of Theodore Roosevelt*, vol. 4., p. 913.

[28] See G. E. Mowry, *The Era of Theodore Roosevelt, 1900-1912* (London, 1958), p. 184.

[29] Sternburg to the German Foreign Office, 27 Sep. 1904., in B. Perkins, *The Great Rapprochement: England and the United States, 1895-1904* (London, 1968), p. 223.

[30] Balfour to Lansdowne, tel., 21 Oct. 1904. Lansdowne MSS BL 'Private Letters', vol. 5.

[31] Edward VII's note on Jackson & Co. to Lansdowne, 23 Oct., and Lansdowne to Hardinge, 24 Oct. 1904. *British Documents*, vol. 4., pp. 5-6.

[32] Nicholas II to Edward VII, tel., 25 Oct. 1904. in Lee, *Edward VII*, vol. 2., p. 301.

[33] Memorandum by Balfour, 26 Oct. Balfour MSS Add. 49698, and Hardinge to Lansdowne, tel., 28 Oct. 1904. *British Documents*, vol. 4., p. 18.

[34] Lansdowne to Balfour, private, 28 Oct. 1904. Balfour MSS Add. 49729.

[35] See A. S. T. Griffith-Boscawen, *Fourteen Years in Parliament* (London, 1907), p. 321., and Lansdowne to Hardinge, 29 Oct. 1904. *British Documents*, vol. 4., p. 23.

[36] "The Presidential Election: Mr. Roosevelt's Victory" *The Times*, 10 Nov. 1904, p. 6.

[37] *Letters of Theodore Roosevelt*, vol 4., p. 1017n.

[38] "The Presidential Election: Mr. Roosevelt's Victory" *The Times*, 10 Nov. 1904, p. 6. Choate gave Lansdowne a copy of Hay's address. 'The description of war as 'the most futile and ferocious of human follies' is not to be forgotten' Lansdowne replied. Lansdowne MSS BL L(5)18.

[39] Lansdowne to Durand, 11 Dec. 1904. Underlining by Lansdowne. Lansdowne MSS F.O. 800/144. Durand replied: 'Our answer about the Peace Conference gave much satisfaction ... A question much discussed here just now is what England and America are going to do if Russia offers Japan reasonable terms ... Roosevelt, I think is personally inclined to back Japan, and to insist on the restoration of Manchuria to China, and the open door. Whether this mood will last, and whether if so he could get the country to fight, or threaten to fight on such an issue, is another matter'. Durand to Lansdowne, 13 Jan. 1905. Lansdowne MSS F.O. 800/116 (S.F.).

[40] Roosevelt to Sternburg, 27 Sep. 1904. in Gwynn, *Spring Rice*, vol. 1., p. 443n.

[41] Spring Rice to Ferguson, 10 Nov. 1904. ibid, pp. 432-433.

[42] Roosevelt had a high opinion of Spring Rice. In a letter to George Meyer, leaving for Russia as American Ambassador, Roosevelt explained that 'There is at St. Petersburg, in the English Embassy, an Englishman ... whom I shall ask to call on you ... I have gained the most valuable information from him – better information than I have ever gained from any of our own people abroad, save only Harry White.' Roosevelt to Meyer, 26 Dec. 1904. *Letters of Theodore Roosevelt*, vol. 4., p. 1079.

[43] Roosevelt to Spring Rice, 17 Dec. 1904. ibid., pp. 441-446.

[44] However, hearing from White on January 13 that Spring Rice was coming, Roosevelt's reaction was somewhat light-hearted. 'Won't you ask Henry [Adams] if his can put up this distinguished member of the kitchen ambassadorial circle – if there are members of the kitchen Cabinet, why cannot there be kitchen ambassadors?' he told John Hay. Roosevelt to Hay, 13 Jan. 1905. *Letters of Theodore Roosevelt*, vol. 4., p. 1102.

[45] Villiers to Spring Rice, 14 Jan. 1905. Villiers MSS F.O. 800/23.

[46] Spring Rice to his wife [no date], Gwynn, *Spring Rice*, pp. 447-448.

[47] Lansdowne to Balfour, 13 Jan. and 13 Jan. 1905. Balfour MSS Add. 49729.

[48] Balfour to Lansdowne, 17 Jan. 1905. Underlining by Balfour. Lansdowne MSS BL 'Private Letters', vol. 5.

[49] See, for example, pp. 12-13.

[50] Balfour to Spring Rice, draft, 17 Jan. 1905. Balfour MSS Add. 49729. The letter is quoted in full in B. E. C. Dugdale, *Arthur James Balfour: First Earl of Balfour, K.G., O.M., F.R.S., Etc.* (London, 1936), vol 1., pp. 386-388.

[51] Lansdowne to Balfour, 18 Jan. 1905. Underlining by Lansdowne. Balfour MSS Add. 49729. There is no evidence – in the Spring Rice, Balfour, Lansdowne or Villiers papers – that Balfour actually sent his letter to Spring Rice.

[52] Percy to Balfour, 13 Jan. and Balfour to Percy, 15 Jan. 1905. Balfour MSS Add. 49747. Sandars to Balfour, 17 Jan. 1905. Balfour MSS Add. 49763. Lansdowne to Balfour, 16 Jan. 1905. Balfour MSS Add, 49729.

[53] Lansdowne to Bertie, 18 Jan. and Bertie to Lansdowne, 16 Jan. 1905. Lansdowne MSS F.O. 800/125.

[54] Lansdowne to Bertie, 19 Jan. 1905. ibid.

[55] See Walder, *The Short Victorious War*, pp. 248-261.

[56] Durand to Lansdowne, tel., 23 Jan. 1905. Lansdowne MSS F.O. 800/116 (S.F.).

[57] Lansdowne to Durand, tel., 23 Jan. ibid., and Lansdowne to Balfour, 23 Jan. 1905. Balfour MSS Add. 49729.

[58] Balfour to Lansdowne, 24 Jan. 1905. ibid.

[59] Lansdowne to Durand, tel., 25 Jan. 1905. Lansdowne MSS F.O. 800/144.

[60] Durand to Lansdowne, 26 Jan. 1905. Lansdowne MSS F.O. 800/116 (S.F.).

[61] Lansdowne to Durand, 4 Feb. 1905. ibid. Documents removed to the separate file [F.O. 800/116] are labelled (S.F.) in these endnotes.

[62] Lansdowne to Durand, tel., 28 Jan. 1905. ibid., (S.F.). On January 25, MacDonald stressed 'that the war party is still in the ascendant and likely to remain so, the influence of Count Lamsdorff being absolutely nil. Proposals emanating from the peace party at the present juncture would be [a] waste of time, and could not be considered.' MacDonald to Lansdowne, 'secret' tel., 25 Jan. 1905. Bertie MSS F.O. 800/163.

[63] See "Ships Arriving from Europe" Morton Allan Directory.

[64] Durand to Lansdowne, tel., 31 Jan. 1905. Lansdowne MSS F.O. 800/116 (S.F.).

[65] Memorandum by Spring Rice, 2 Feb. 1905. ibid., (S.F).

[66] After his visit to the White House on February 5, Spring Rice's visit could hardly be concealed, and was much publicised on the 6th. See Gwynn, *Spring Rice*, vol. 1., p. 449.

[67] Durand to Lansdowne, 5 Feb. and 6 Feb. 1905. Lansdowne MSS F.O. 800/116 (S.F.).

[68] White to Spring Rice, no date, but late Feb. 1905. Gwynn, *Spring Rice*, vol. 1., p. 451.

[69] The King's message, sent on February 20, is described in Lee, *Edward VII*, vol. 2., pp. 429-431. Lansdowne to Durand, 22 Feb. 1905. Lansdowne MSS F.O. 800/144.

[70] See J. A. White, *The Diplomacy of the Russo-Japanese War* (Princeton, 1964), pp. 195-196.

[71] Durand to Lansdowne, 6 Feb. Spring Rice had told Lansdowne four days earlier that the 'President has great personal prestige but the professional politicians and especially the Senate are opposed to him. A conflict with the Senate is probable and has in fact begun ... a written convention would not pass the Senate and a verbal agreement, if known, would excite great opposition All indications of an agreement should be avoided.' Memorandum by Spring Rice, 2 Feb. 1905. Lansdowne MSS F.O. 800/116 (S.F.).

[72] Roosevelt to Meyer, 6 Feb. 1905. *Letters of Theodore Roosevelt*, vol. 4., pp. 1115-1116.

[73] See Lansdowne to Durand, 14 Jan. and Durand to Lansdowne, 27 Jan. 1905. *British Documents*, vol. 4., pp. 69-70. Sandars to Lansdowne, 17 Jan. 1905. Balfour MSS Add. 49763.

[74] *Hansard* CXLI col. 28, 14 Feb. 1905.

[75] ibid., cols. 20 & 6, 14 Feb. 1905.

[76] Spring Rice to Mrs. Roosevelt, 13 Mar. and Spring Rice to Hay, 15 Mar. 1905. Gwynn, *Spring Rice*, vol 1, pp. 453, 462-463.

[77] See Walder, *The Short Victorious War*, pp. 266-272.

[78] Durand to Lansdowne, tel., 15 Mar. 1905. Lansdowne MSS F.O. 800/116 (S.F.).

[79] MacDonald to Lansdowne, 24 Mar. 1905. *British Documents*, vol. 4., p. 71.

[80] Lansdowne to Bertie, 21 Mar. and 2 Apr. 1905. Lansdowne MSS F.O. 800/125.

[81] Roosevelt to Hay, 30 Mar. 1905. *Letters of Theodore Roosevelt*, vol. 4., p. 1150.

[82] See White, *Diplomacy of the Russo-Japanese War*, p. 203.

[83] See R. A. Esthus, *Double Eagle and Rising Sun: The Russians and Japanese at Portsmouth in 1905* (London, 1988), p. 32.

[84] ibid., pp. 28-29.

[85] Durand to Lansdowne, 30 Mar. 1905. Lansdowne MSS F.O. 800/116 (S.F.).

[86] See Sykes, *Durand*, pp. 279-282. Lansdowne to Durand, tel., 27 Apr. 1905. Lansdowne MSS F.O. 800/144.

13: Hats Off to Roosevelt

[1] "Far East Committee Abolished by Czar: Roosevelt Seeks a Truce" *The New York Times*, 22 Jun. 1905, p. 5.

[2] Hardinge to Lansdowne, 11 Apr. 1905., in G. P. Gooch and H. Temperley (eds.), *British Documents on the Origins of the War, 1898-1914* (London, 1929), vol. 4., pp. 75-76.

[3] Lansdowne to MacDonald, 19 Apr. 1905. ibid., p. 76.

[4] Roosevelt to Lodge, 15 May. 1905., in E. E. Morison (ed.), *The Letters of Theodore Roosevelt* (Cambridge, Mass., 1951), vol. 4., p. 1180.

[5] Edward to Lansdowne, 15 Apr. 1905., in Sir S. Lee, *King Edward VII: A Biography* (London, 1927), vol. 2., p. 340.

[6] Lansdowne to Bertie, 3 Apr. 1905. Lansdowne MSS F.O. 800/125.

[7] Durand to Lansdowne, 7 Apr. and tel., 24 Apr. 1905. Lansdowne MSS F.O. 800/116 (S.F.).

[8] Lansdowne to Durand, tel., 27 Apr. 1905. Lansdowne MSS F.O. 800/144.

[9] Lansdowne to Balfour, 27 Apr. 1905. Balfour MSS Add. 49729.

[10] Roosevelt to Taft, 8 Apr. *Letters of Theodore Roosevelt*, vol. 4., p. 1159. Hay to Spring Rice, 1 May. 1905. in S. Gwynn, *The Letters and Friendships of Sir Cecil Spring Rice: A Record* (London, 1929), vol. 1., p. 465.

[11] Roosevelt to Spring Rice, 13 May. 1905. *Letters of Theodore Roosevelt*, vol. 4., pp. 1177-1178.

[12] Memorandum by Lansdowne, 17 May. 1905., in Z. S. Steiner, *Britain and the Origins of the First World War* (London, 1977), p. 33.

[13] Delcassé claimed that he had achieved an English alliance and that war should be declared against Germany. The French Cabinet wholeheartedly blocked Delcassé's ambitious, provocative scheme. In a minority of one, Delcassé's position was untenable.

[14] Durand to Lansdowne, tel., 27 Jun. Lansdowne MSS F.O. 800/116 (S.F.), and Lansdowne to Durand, tel., 28 Jun. 1905. Lansdowne MSS F.O. 800/144.

[15] See D. Walder, *The Short Victorious War: The Russo-Japanese Conflict 1904-5* (London, 1973), pp. 277-288.

[16] William to Nicholas, 3 Jun. 1905., in N. F. Grant (ed.), *The Kaiser's Letters to the Tsar* (London, 1920), p. 189.

[17] The Foreign Office heard the news by telegram from MacDonald. MacDonald to Lansdowne, tel., 29 May. 1905. *British Documents*, vol. 4., p. 78.

[18] Roosevelt to Kaneko, 31 May. and Roosevelt to Taft, 31 May. 1905. *Letters of Theodore Roosevelt*, vol. 4., p. 1198.

[19] See J. A. White, *The Diplomacy of the Russo-Japanese War* (Princeton, 1964), p. 208. O'Beirne to Mallet, 2 Jun. 1905. Lansdowne MSS F.O. 800/116 (S.F.).

[20] Durand to Lansdowne, tel., 2 Jun. and Lansdowne to Durand, 3 Jun. 1905. *British Documents*, vol. 4., pp. 78-79.

[21] Durand to Lansdowne, tel., 5 Jun. 1905. ibid., p. 79.

[22] Roosevelt to Lodge, 24 May. and 5 Jun. 1905. *Letters of Theodore Roosevelt*, vol. 4., pp. 1191 & 1204. Roosevelt and Lodge pushed for Spring Rice as early as December 1903. When 'Senator Lodge was here for the Alaska Boundary business', Villiers told Spring Rice, 'he urged both Ld. Lansdowne and Mr. Balfour that you should be transferred to Washington as Sec. of [the British] Embassy. Ld. L. ... was unable to entertain the idea because he could not spare you from St. Petersburg.' Spring Rice, in reply, explained that 'I should of course enjoy it, though I [fear] Durand would make it rather warm for me.' Villiers to Spring Rice, 2 Dec. and Spring Rice to Villiers, 9 Dec. 1903. Villiers MSS F.O. 800/23.

[23] Roosevelt to Reid, 5 Jun. 1905. ibid., p. 1206.

[24] Lansdowne to Durand, 5 Jun. 1905. *British Documents*, vol. 4., p. 82.

[25] Durand to Lansdowne, tel., 5 Jun. 1905. ibid., pp. 80-81. O'Beirne also reported the meeting with Roosevelt, and knew Takahira's views. Japan was now disposed to consider peace on advantageous terms, he remarked, but were prepared to continue the war rather than sacrifice their interests. 'Referring to the attitude of the neutral Powers the Japanese Minister had said that Great Britain and the United States had acted generously ... but that there was some reason to suspect that the German Emperor desired to obtain some territorial advantage for himself in the Far East. Memorandum by O'Beirne, 6 Jun. 1905. F.O. 5/2579.

[26] Durand to Lansdowne, tel., 8 Jun. 1905. *British Documents*, vol. 4., p. 85.

[27] Loomis to Meyer, 8 Jun. and Loomis to Griscom, 8 Jun. 1905., in *Papers Relating to the Foreign Relations of the United States 1905* (Washington, 1906), pp. 807-808.

[28] Hardinge to Lansdowne, 14 Jun. 1905. *British Documents*, vol. 4., pp. 86-87.

[29] Durand to Lansdowne, tel., 13 Jun. and Lansdowne to Durand, tel., 13 Jun. 1905. ibid., p. 86.

[30] Durand to Lansdowne, 16 Jun. 1905. Lansdowne MSS F.O. 800/116 (S.F.).

[31] Lansdowne to Durand, 16 Jun. 1905. *British Documents*, vol. 4., p. 89. Roosevelt to Spring Rice, Gwynn, *Spring Rice*, vol. 1., p. 474.

[32] Spring Rice to Root, 10 Jul. Underlining by Spring Rice. Roosevelt presented a lengthy counter case. See Roosevelt to Spring Rice, 24 Jul. 1905. ibid., pp. 474-475, 478.

[33] Lansdowne to Durand, 10 Jul. 1905. Lansdowne MSS F.O. 800/144.

[34] Lansdowne to Balfour, 12 Jul. 1905. and Balfour's note on the same. Lansdowne MSS F.O. 800/116 (S.F.). Lansdowne saw Reid on July 12, and stressed Britain's desire for peace. Reid replied 'that he did not believe that the President entertained this view, although it was one which might possibly have been suggested to him by interested parties.' Lansdowne to Durand, 12 Jul. 1905. *British Documents*, vol. 4., p. 91.

[35] See R. A. Esthus, *Double Eagle and Rising Sun: The Russians and Japanese at Portsmouth in 1905* (London, 1988), p. 50. Durand to Lansdowne, 7 Apr. 1905. Lansdowne MSS F.O. 800/116 (S.F.). and MacDonald to Lansdowne, 8 Jun. 1905. Lansdowne MSS F.O. 800/134.

[36] "The Peace Negotiations: Plenipotentiaries Appointed" *The Times*, 2 Jul. 1905, p. 5.

[37] Griscom to Root, 7 Jul. and Meyer to Root, tel., 11 Jul. 1905. *Foreign Relations of the United States 1905*, pp. 817 & 819.

[38] "The Peace Negotiations: Meeting Place of the Delegates" *The Times*, 11 Jul. 1905, p. 5.

[39] See Esthus, *Double Eagle and Rising Sun*, pp. 51-57.

[40] See S. Mahajan, "The Defence of India and the End of Isolation: A Study of the Foreign Policy of the Conservative Government" *Journal of Imperial and Commonwealth History* 10 (1981-2), pp. 187-188.

[41] G. F. Ellison, "Indian Re-inforcements", 8 Nov. 1904. and Arnold-Forster, "The Secretary of State's Remarks on Mr. Balfour's Paper (No. 25A). Secret. Supplementary Note on the Military Needs of the Empire (No. 28A), 19 Jan. 1905. Arnold-Forster MSS Add. 50317.

[42] 70th Meeting of the C.I.D., 12 Apr. 1905. Privy Council Committee of Imperial Defence Minutes. Cab 2/1494.

[43] G. S. Clarke, "Note on Future Relations of Great Britain and Japan", 4 May. 1905., quoted in Mahajan, "The Defence of India", p. 188.

[44] Balfour to Edward, 9 Jun. 1905., in K. M. Wilson, "The Anglo-Japanese Alliance of August 1905 and the Defending of India: A Case of the Worst Scenario" *Journal of Imperial and Commonwealth History* 21 (1993), p. 336.

[45] Selborne to Lansdowne, 26 Apr. According to Barrington, Hardinge hoped that the Russians would be asked to adhere to the agreement. 'I think it would rob the alliance of half its terrors', Barrington noted. '[T]here is much to be said in its favour – that it would prevent Russia from throwing herself into Germany's arms.' Note by Barrington, 25 May. 1905. Lansdowne MSS BL Lab 4/13.

[46] See *British Documents*, vol. 4., pp. 122-169.

[47] Balfour to Lansdowne, 30 Jun. 1905. Lansdowne MSS BL Lab 4/13

[48] Roosevelt to Reid, 2 Aug. 1905. *Letters of Theodore Roosevelt*, vol. 4., p. 1298.

[49] Durand to Lansdowne, secret tel., 4 Aug. 1905. Lansdowne MSS F.O. 800/134.

[50] Durand to Lansdowne, 10 Aug. 1905. Lansdowne MSS F.O. 800/144.

[51] Durand to Lansdowne, tel., 12 Aug. and Lansdowne to Durand, tel., 16 Aug. 1905. *British Documents*, vol. 4., p. 170.

[52] Lansdowne to Barrington, 2 Sep., Lansdowne to Hardinge, tel., 4 Sep., Lansdowne to Bertie, 6 Sep. and Hardinge to Lansdowne, 8 Sep. 1905. ibid., pp. 171-176. Lansdowne informed Cambon personally on September 4. Lansdowne to Cambon, 4 Sep. 1905. Lansdowne MSS F.O. 800/125. 'I am glad Rouvier's mind is not disturbed by the new Anglo-Japanese Agreement', Lansdowne told Bertie on September 12. 'The Russians have, so far, made the best of it.' Lansdowne to Bertie, 12 Sep. 1905. Bertie MSS F.O. 800/163.

[53] Balfour to Lansdowne, 1 Sep. and Lansdowne to Balfour, 3 Sep. 1905. Balfour MSS Add. 49729.

[54] Lansdowne to Durand, tel., 4 Sep. 1905. Lansdowne MSS F.O. 800/144.

[55] Lansdowne to Durand, tel., 10 Sep. 1905. *British Documents*, vol. 4., pp. 179-180.

[56] Roosevelt to Durand, 8 Sep. and Durand to Lansdowne, 22 Sep. 1905. Lansdowne MSS F.O. 800/116 (S.F.).

[57] Roosevelt to Reid, 11 Sep. 1905. *Letters of Theodore Roosevelt*, vol. 5., p. 18.

[58] Roosevelt to Reid, 3 Aug. 1905. ibid., vol. 4., p. 1298.

[59] Lansdowne to Spring Rice, 7 Aug. 1905. Lansdowne MSS F.O. 800/116 (S.F.). As early as March 1905, Lodge had attempted to influence Britain. To Balfour, he wrote that 'all that is necessary is for the United States and England to take the same tone and the same position to ... secure a peace which is obviously in our common interest.' Balfour replied that 'I agree with you in thinking that the interests of the United States and of ourselves are absolutely identical in the Far East and that the more closely we can work together, the better it will be for us and the world at large.' Lodge to Balfour, 29 Mar. and Balfour to Lodge, 11 Apr. 1905. Balfour MSS Add. 49742.

[60] Details of the initial peace talks are presented in Esthus, *Double Eagle and Rising Sun*, pp. 82-89; White, *Diplomacy of the Russo-Japanese War*, pp. 269-281.

[61] See, for example, Roosevelt to Meyer, 21 Aug., in Roosevelt to Sternburg, 21 Aug. 1905. *Letters of Theodore Roosevelt*, vol. 4., pp. 1306-1307.

[62] *Hansard's Parliamentary Debates* (4th ser.) CLI col. 991, 11 Aug. 1905.

[63] Lansdowne to Durand, 22 Aug. Lansdowne MSS F.O. 800/144. Roosevelt to Durand, 23 Aug., in Durand to Lansdowne, 24 Aug. 1905, and Lansdowne's minute on the same. *British Documents*, vol. 4., pp. 104-105.

[64] Durand to Lansdowne, 25 Aug. 1905. Lansdowne MSS F.O. 800/116 (S.F.).

[65] Roosevelt to White, 23 Aug. 1905. *Letters of Theodore Roosevelt*, vol. 4., p. 1313.

[66] See ibid., pp 1306-1323.

[67] Lansdowne to Balfour, 3 Sep. 1905. Balfour MSS Add. 49729. After peace had been effected, Hayashi explained to Lansdowne that Japan 'could not be quite sure of winning the next battle, and after their ... series of successes, a reverse or an indecisive conflict might have seriously prejudiced their position.' Lansdowne to Spring Rice, 30 Sep. 1905. Lansdowne MSS F.O. 800/144.

[68] See Esthus, *Double Eagle and Rising Sun*, pp. 90-163.

[69] Lansdowne to Durand, tel., 30 Aug. 1905. Lansdowne MSS BL Lab 4/34.

[70] See Esthus, *Double Eagle and Rising Sun*, pp. 171-172.

[71] Roosevelt to Spring Rice, 1 Sep., in Spring Rice to Lansdowne, 27 Sep. 1905. Balfour MSS Add. 49729.

[72] Lansdowne to Spring Rice, 30 Sep. 1905. Lansdowne MSS F.O. 800/144. Spring Rice forwarded the letter's contents to Mrs. Roosevelt on October 10. See Gwynn, *Spring Rice*, pp. 498-501.

[73] Durand to Lansdowne, secret tel., 22 Oct. 1905., and comments by Mallet, an unknown Foreign Office clerk, and Lansdowne. Two copies of this dispatch exist, one in Lansdowne's regular Foreign Office correspondence regarding the United States, and the other in the separate file which he had kept since January. Lansdowne MSS F.O. 800/144 & F.O. 800/116 (S.F.).

[74] Roosevelt to Reid, 11 Sep. 1905., in B. Perkins, *The Great Rapprochement: England and the United States, 1895-1914* (London, 1968), p. 227.

[75] Roosevelt to Spring Rice, 1 Nov., in Spring Rice to Lansdowne, 23 Nov. 1905. Lansdowne MSS F.O. 800/116 (S.F.).

[76] Durand to Lansdowne, 15 Dec. 1905., and Lansdowne to Durand, 2 Jan. 1906. Lansdowne MSS F.O. 800/144.

Conclusion

[1] 'For the last century', Harold Nicolson wrote in July 1920, 'the policy of His Majesty's Government has been inductive, intuitive and quite deliberately opportunistic, but through it all has run the dominant impulse of the defence of India. If this impulse is to be maintained during the next generation, it can only be maintained by vastly increased commitments, [and] by a concentration of Imperial activity upon this central object'. Memorandum by Nicolson, C.I.D. Paper 25/B, 10 Jul. 1920. CAB 4/7.

[2] "Anglo-American Relations" *The Times*, 9 Mar. 1900, p. 3.

[3] A. E. Campbell, *Great Britain and the United States, 1895-1903* (London, 1960), p. 193.

[4] Lansdowne to Pauncefote, 31 Dec. 1901. Lansdowne MSS F.O. 800/144.

[5] Durand to Lansdowne, 29 Nov., and Lansdowne to Durand, 11 Dec. 1904. ibid.

[6] Durand to Lansdowne, 26 Jan. 1905. Lansdowne MSS F.O. 800/116 (S.F.).

[7] Mowatt to Lansdowne, 10 Jun. 'Many thanks for your impressions de voyage!', Lansdowne replied three days later, 'They are most interesting and will be found so by (all) of my colleagues to whom I am passing them out.' Lansdowne to Mowatt, 13 Jun. 1905. Lansdowne MSS BL L(5)32.

[8] "Anglo-American Relations" *The Times*, 9 Dec. 1904., p. 5.

[9] In January 1904, Durand reported that 'enthusiastic meetings have been held, and I am informed that the feeling in Congress is decidedly in favour of an Arbitration Treaty. ... I have been told by several leading Senators that the feeling towards England through out the United States is now more friendly than it has ever been. Perhaps therefore some thing may come of this movement, but I am not sanguine about it. Mr. Barclay tells me it is fully understood here that if any Arbitration Treaty is to be concluded, the proposal must come from the United States and must be of such a nature as to commit Congress.' Durand to Lansdowne, 14 Jan. 1904. F.O. 5/2549.
News that the treaty had been announced was published in *The Times* in November. See "An Anglo-American Arbitration Treaty" *The Times*, 26 Nov., p. 5, and "Anglo-American Arbitration" *The Times*, 13 Dec. 1904, p. 3. See also W. N. Tilchin, *Theodore Roosevelt and the British Empire: A Study in Presidential Statescraft* (New York, 1997), pp. 260n.8, and B. Perkins, *The Great Rapprochement: England and the United States, 1895-1914* (London, 1968), p. 252.

[10] Consistently, Balfour continued to express his strident Anglo-Saxonism to American friends. In June 1905, he wrote to outgoing Ambassador Choate that he had 'never concealed the strength of the convictions which have all of my life animated me, even in the now far-distant days before I entered Parliament and was a student, and not an actor, in the sphere of politics. But I have always been careful to make my words, strong through they have been, less strong than my convictions; for (as it seems to me) the feeling that the two great co-heirs of Anglo-Saxon freedom and civilization have a common mission, has more quickly developed on this side of the Atlantic than on the other ... and that there is therefore some danger lest phrases which are suitable enough in Great Britain might seem excessive in America, and may excite, not sympathy, but suspicion or ridicule.' Balfour to Choate, 1 Jun. 1905. Balfour MSS Add. 49742.

[11] Even before he arrived at the Foreign Office, Grey acknowledged the significance of the United States' emergence as a major factor in global diplomacy. In 1901, he told Andrew Carnegie that 'I have always felt that it was folly for us to argue about the Monroe Doctrine. The Monroe Doctrine is, whatever the United States says it is, and what we have to consider is how far we can meet it.' On September 9 1903, during the Alaskan negotiation, Grey admitted that 'if the U.S. Govt. had met the Alaska question with a simple defiance [it] is a very awkward one [question] and a real one. If the U.S. Govt. choose, they can make a great difficulty between us & Canada by picking quarrels with Canada, which we should be reluctant to fight for'. See K. Robbins, *Sir Edward Grey: A Biography of Lord Grey of Fallodon* (London, 1971), pp. 129-130

[12] By the Treaty of Washington of July 7 1911, negotiated between the United States,

Britain, Japan and Russia.

[13] See G. E. Mowry, *The Era of Theodore Roosevelt, 1900-1912* (London, 1958), pp. 278-279.

[14] The Taft Administration aimed to charge foreign vessels a toll for using the Panama Canal, whilst exempting American ships. Regulations for this result were repealed by Woodrow Wilson in 1914. See Perkins, *The Great Rapprochement*, pp. 301-305. In September 1912, Lansdowne wrote a lengthy memorandum on the dispute, focusing on the canal negotiations of 1900-1901. He criticised the tolls legislation on the grounds that the Hay-Pauncefote treaty, which was honourable and satisfactory to both nations, was of a definite and unambiguous character, and did not admit recriminatory tariffs. Memorandum by Lansdowne, dated Sep. 1912. Lansdowne MSS BL Lab 4/10.

[15] Lansdowne to Durand, 4 Feb. 1905. Lansdowne MSS F.O. 800/144.

Bibliography

PRIMARY SOURCES

A. Unpublished Papers

ALVERSTONE MSS. Papers of Sir Richard Everard Webster, Viscount Alverstone. British Library.

ARNOLD-FORSTER MSS. Papers of Hugh Oakley Arnold-Forster. British Library.

BALFOUR MSS. Papers of Arthur James Balfour. British Library.

BERTIE MSS. Papers of Sir Francis Leveson Bertie. British Library.

BERTIE MSS. Foreign Office and diplomatic papers of the above. Public Record Office.

DILKE MSS. Papers of Sir Charles Wentworth Dilke. British Library.

HALSBURY MSS. Papers of Hardinge Stanely Giffard, Earl Halsbury. British Library.

HAMILTON MSS. Papers of Sir Edward Hamilton. British Library.

HUTTON MSS. Papers of Colonel Edward Hutton. British Library.

LANSDOWNE MSS. Foreign Office papers of Henry Charles Keith Petty-Fitzmaurice, Fifth Marquis of Lansdowne. Public Record Office.

LANSDOWNE MSS. General correspondence of the above, transferred from Bowood House in 1995. British Library.

LASCELLES MSS. Papers of Sir Frank Cavendish Lascelles. Public Record Office.

SANDERSON MSS. Papers of Sir Thomas Henry Sanderson. Public Record Office.

SPRING RICE MSS. Papers of Sir Cecil Arthur Spring Rice. Public Record Office.

VILLIERS MSS. Papers of Sir Francis Hyde Villiers. Public Record Office.

B. Foreign and Colonial Office Series

F.O. 414 America, North: Confidential Print.

F.O. 5   America, North: General Correspondence.

F.O. 420 America, South and Central: Confidential Print.

C.O. 42   Canada: General Correspondence.

F.O. 405 China: Confidential Print.

F.O. 58   Pacific Islands: General Correspondence.
F.O. 313   United States of America, Honolulu: Embassy and Consular Archives.

C. Miscellaneous

British Parliamentary Papers, *Accounts and Papers*, 1901-1905 (London, 1901-1905).
Cabinet and Committee of Imperial Defence Papers. Public Record Office
Hansard's Parliamentary Debates: Fourth Series.
Papers Relating to the Foreign Relations of the United States 1900-1905 (Washington, 1901-1906).
Prime Minister's Letters to the Monarch, Reporting on Meetings of the Cabinet, 1895-1914. Originals in the Royal Archives, Windsor; copies available in the Brotherton Library, University of Leeds.
Privy Council Committee of Imperial Defence Minutes. PRO CAB 2/1494.
The Manchester Guardian.
The New York Times.
The Times.

D. Published Papers

M. V. Brett (ed.), *Journals and Letters of Reginald, Viscount Esher*, 3 vols. (London, 1934).
D. G. Boyce (ed.), *The Crisis of British Power: The Imperial and Naval Papers of the Second Earl of Selborne, 1895-1910* (London, 1990).
P. H. Clyde (ed.) *United States Policy Toward China: Diplomatic and Public Documents, 1839-1939* (New York, 1964).
G. P. Gooch and H. Temperley (eds.), *British Documents on the Origin of the War*, 11 vols. (London, 1926-38).
N. F. Grant (ed.), *The Kaiser's Letters to the Tsar* (London, 1920).
M. R. Hay (ed.), *Letters of John Hay and Extracts from Diary*, 3 vols. (Washington, 1908 [printed but not published]).
J. C. Levenson, Ernest Samuels, C. Vandersee and V. H. Winner (eds.), *The Letters of Henry Adams*, 6 vols. (Cambridge, Mass., 1982-1988).
A. S. Link and W. M. Leary, *The Diplomacy of World Power: The United States, 1889-1920* (Edinburgh, 1970).
E. E. Morison (ed.), *The Letters of Theodore Roosevelt*, 8 vols. (Cambridge, Mass., 1951-54).
N. Rich & M. H. Fisher (eds.), *The Holstein Papers: The Memoirs, Diaries and Correspondence of Friedrich Von Holstein, 1837-1909*, 4 vols. (Cambridge, 1963).
J. Ridley and C. Percy, *The Letters of Arthur Balfour and Lady Elcho, 1885-1917* (London, 1992).
I. C. Ruxton, *The Diaries and Letters of Sir Ernest Mason Satow (1843-1929), A Scholar-Diplomat in East Asia* (New York, 1998).
P. Stevens and J. T. Saywell (eds.), *Lord Minto's Canadian Papers: A Selection of the Public and Private Papers of the Fourth Earl of Minto, 1898-1904*, 2 vols. (Toronto, 1981-83).

E. Memoirs and Other Contemporary Publications

A. J. Balfour, *Chapters of Autobiography*, (ed.), E. Dugdale (London, 1930).

C. W. Boyd (ed.), *Mr. Chamberlain's Speeches*, 2 vols. (London, 1914).

Lord Brooks, *An Eye-Witness in Manchuria* (London, 1905).

B. Von Bülow, *Imperial Germany* (London, 1914).

Viscount Cecil, *All the Way* (London, 1949).

A. Chamberlain, *Down the Years* (London, 1935).

V. Corbett, *Reminiscences, Autobiographical and Diplomatic* (London, 1927).

G. T. Denison, *The Struggle for Imperial Unity: Recollections and Experiences* (London, 1909).

C. W. Dilke, *The British Empire* (London, 1899).

Baron Von Eckardstein, *Ten Years at the Court of St. James', 1895-1905* (London, 1921).

Viscount Esher, *Cloud-Capp'd Towers* (London, 1927).

Lord Fisher, *Memories* (London, 1919).

J. Fiske, *American Political Ideas, Viewed from the Standpoint of Universal History* (London, 1885).

A. Fitzroy, *Memoirs*, 2 vols. (London, 1925).

M. Frewen, *Melton Mowbray and Other Memories* (London, 1939).

H. George, *Protection or Free Trade: An Examination of the Tariff Question with Especial Regard to the Interests of Labour* (London, 1903).

A. Gorren, *Anglo-Saxons and Others* (Boston, 1900).

A. S. T. Griffith-Boscawen, *Fourteen Years in Parliament* (London, 1907).

H. W. Lucy, *A Diary of the Unionist Parliament, 1895-1900* (London, 1901).

G. Lynch, *The War of the Civilisations, being a Record of a "Foreign Devil's" Experiences with the Allies in China* (London, 1901).

W. A. P. Martin, *The Siege in Peking: China Against the World, by an Eye Witness* (London, 1900).

E. McCaul, *Under the Care of the Japanese War Office* (London, 1904).

Lord Newton, *Retrospection* (London, 1941).

F. Oppenheimer, *Stranger Within: Autobiographical Pages* (London, 1960).

T. Roosevelt, *Fear God and Take Your Own Part* (London, 1916).

     - *The Rough Riders* (New York, 1990).

     - *The Strenuous Life: Essays and Addresses* (London, 1902).

J. A. Spender (ed.), *A Modern Journal, Being the Diary of Greville Minor for the Year of Agitation, 1903-1904* (London, 1904).

C. Tupper, *Recollections of Sixty Years* (London, 1914).

H. S. Wilkinson, *Thirty-Five Years, 1874-1909* (London, 1933).

SECONDARY SOURCES

A. Books

H. C. Allen, *Great Britain and the United States* (London, 1954).

     - *The Anglo-Saxon Special Relationship Since 1783* (London, 1959).

H. F. Angus, *Canada and her Great Neighbor: Sociological Surveys of Opinions and Attitudes in*

Canada concerning the United States (Toronto, 1938).

K. A. Asakawa, *The Russo-Japanese Conflict: Its Causes and Issues* (Shannon, 1972, c. 1905).

P. S. Bagwell and G. E. Mingay, *Britain and America, 1850-1939: A Study of Economic Change* (London, 1970).

H. K. Beale, *Theodore Roosevelt and the Rise of America to World Power* (Baltimore, 1956).

C. Berger (ed.), *Imperial Relations in the Age of Laurier* (Toronto, 1969).

H. Bingham, *The Monroe Doctrine: An Obsolete Shibboleth* (New Haven, 1913).

D. G. Bishop, *The Administration of British Foreign Relations* (Westport, Conn., 1974).

J. M. Blum, *The Republican Roosevelt* (Cambridge, Mass., 1954).

K. Bourne, *Britain and the Balance of Power in North America, 1815-1908* (London, 1967).

E. Brandenburg, *From Bismarck to the Great War: A History of German Foreign Policy, 1870-1914* (trans.), A. E. Adams (London, 1933).

C. Brinton, *The United States and Britain* (Cambridge, Mass., 1948).

O. Brox, *Newfoundland Fishermen in the Age of Industry: A Sociology of Economic Dualism* (Toronto, 1972).

J. M. Callahan, *American Foreign Policy in Canadian Relations* (New York, 1937).

A. E. Campbell, *Great Britain and the United States, 1895-1903* (London, 1960).

C. S. Campbell, *Anglo-American Understanding, 1898-1903* (Baltimore, 1957).

     - *The Transformation of American Foreign Relations, 1865-1900* (New York, 1976).

A. Cecil, *Queen Victoria and her Prime Ministers* (London, 1953).

R. D. Challener, *Admirals, Generals, and American Foreign Policy, 1898-1914* (Princeton, 1973).

W. S. Churchill, *Great Contemporaries* (London, 1941).

P. H. Clyde, *International Rivalries in Manchuria, 1689-1922* (New York, 1966).

K. L. Clymer, *John Hay, The Gentleman as Diplomat* (Michigan, 1975).

L. Creswicke, *The Life of the Right Honourable Joseph Chamberlain*, 4 vols. (London, 1904).

C. R. M. F. Cruttwell, *A History of Peaceful Change in the Modern World* (Oxford, 1937).

V. Cowles, *Edward VII and his Circle* (London, 1956).

Lord Crewe, *Lord Rosebery*, 2 vols. (London, 1931).

J. W. Dafoe, *Laurier: A Study in Canadian Politics* (Toronto, 1978).

B. E. C. Dugdale, *Arthur James Balfour: First Earl of Balfour, K.G., O.M., F.R.S., Etc.*, 2 vols. (London, 1936).

F. R. Dulles, *America's Rise to World Power, 1898-1954* (New York, 1955).

W. A. Dunning, *The British Empire and the United States: A Review of their Relations during the Century of Peace Following the Treaty of Ghent* (New York, 1914).

E. W. Edwards, *British Diplomacy and Finance in China, 1895-1914* (Oxford, 1987).

M. Egremont, *Balfour: A Life of Arthur James Balfour* (London, 1980).

D. E. Elletson, *The Chamberlains* (London, 1966).

R. A. Esthus, *Double Eagle and Rising Sun: The Russians and Japanese at Portsmouth in 1905* (London, 1988).

J. Ewell, *Venezuela: A Century of Change* (London, 1984).

     - *Venezuela and the United States: From Monroe's Hemisphere to Petroleum's Empire* (Athens, Georgia, 1996).

J. K. Fairbank, *The United States and China* (Cambridge, Mass., 1948).

H. U. Faulkner, *Politics, Reform and Expansion, 1890-1900* (London, 1959).

J. A. Ferguson, *American Diplomacy and the Boer War* (Philadelphia, 1939).

H. A. L. Fisher, *James Bryce: Viscount Bryce of Dechmont*, 2 vols. (New York, 1917).

P. Fleming, *The Siege of Peking* (London, 1960).

W. Franke, *A Century of Chinese Revolution, 1851-1949* (Oxford, 1970).

A. G. Gardiner, *The Life of Sir William Harcourt*, 2 vols. (London, 1923).

J. A. Garraty, *Henry Cabot Lodge: A Biography* (New York, 1953).

J. L. Garvin, *The Life of Joseph Chamberlain*, 4 vols. (London, 1932-51).

I. Geiss, *German Foreign Policy, 1871-1914* (London, 1976).

L. M. Gelber, *The Rise of Anglo-American Friendship* (London, 1938).

G. P. Gooch and J. H. B. Masterman, *A Century of British Foreign Policy* (London, 1917).

J. A. S. Grenville, *Lord Salisbury and Foreign Policy: The Close of the Nineteenth Century* (London, 1964).

J. A. S. Grenville and G. B. Young, *Politics, Strategy and American Diplomacy: Studies in Foreign Policy, 1873-1917* (New Haven, 1966).

F. Gribble, *What America Owes Europe* (London, 1932).

S. Gwynn (ed.), *The Letters and Friendships of Sir Cecil Spring Rice: A Record*, 2 vols. (London, 1929).

E. Halévy, *Imperialism and the Rise of Labour* (London, 1951).

D. J. Hall, *Clifford Sifton*, 2 vols. (Vancouver, 1985).

J. B. Hattendorf and R. S. Jordan (eds.), *Maritime Strategy and the Balance of Power: Britain and America in the Twentieth Century* (London, 1989).

D. Healy, *US Expansionism: The Imperialist Urge in the 1890s* (Madison, Wis., 1970).

R. H. Heindel, *The American Impact on Great Britain, 1898-1914* (Philadelphia, 1940).

H. H. Herwig, *Germany's Vision of Empire in Venezuela, 1871-1914* (Princeton, 1986).

C. Hibbert, *Edward VII: A Portrait* (London, 1976).

H. C. Hill, *Roosevelt and the Caribbean* (New York, 1965).

J. Hiller and P. Neary, *Newfoundland in the Nineteenth and Twentieth Centuries: Essays in Interpretation* (Toronto, 1980).

C. H. D. Howard, *Splendid Isolation: A Study of Ideas Concerning Britain's International Position and Foreign Policy during the Later Years of the Third Marquis of Salisbury* (London, 1967).

B. D. Hunt and R. G. Haycock, *Canada's Defence:Perspectives on Policy in the Twentieth Century* (Toronto, 1993).

H. A. Innes, *The Cod Fisheries:The History of an International Economy* (New Haven, 1940).

R. J. Jensen, *The Alaska Purchase and Russian-American Relations* (Seattle, 1975).

D. Judd, *Balfour and the British Empire: A Study in Imperial Evolution, 1874-1932* (London, 1968).

W. Karp, *The Politics of War: The Story of Two Wars Which Altered Forever the Political Life of the American Republic (1890-1920)* (New York, 1979).

H. L. Keenleyside, *Canada and the United States: Some Aspects of their Historical Relations* (New York, 1952).

J. E. Kendle, *The Colonial and Imperial Conferences 1887-1911: A Study in Imperial Organization* (London, 1967).

G. F. Kennan, *American Diplomacy, 1900-1950* (New York, 1951).

P. Kennedy (ed.), *The Rise and Fall of British Naval Mastery* (London, 1983).

W. G. Kneer, *Great Britain and the Caribbean, 1901-1913: A Study in Anglo-American Relations* (New York, 1975).

R. V. Kubicek, *The Administration of Imperialism: Joseph Chamberlain at the Colonial Office*

(Durham, N.C., 1969).

M. Kullnick, *From Rough Rider to President* (trans.) F. Von Reithdorf (London, 1911).

W. LaFeber, *The American Age: United States Foreign Policy at Home and Abroad, 1750 to the Present* (New York, 1994).

W. L. Langer, *The Diplomacy of Imperialism*, 2 vols. (New York, 1935).

S. Lee, *King Edward VII: A Biography*, 2 vols. (London, 1925-27).

W. Lippmann, *Public Opinion and Foreign Policy in the United States* (London, 1952).

J. V. Lombardi, *Venezuela: the Search for Order, the Dream of Progress* (New York, 1982).

W. Lord, *The Good Years: From 1900 to the First World War* (London, 1960).

R. F. Mackay, *Fisher of Kilverstone* (Oxford, 1973).

    - *Balfour: Intellectual Statesman* (London, 1985).

A. J. Marder, *Fear God and Dread Nought: the Correspondence of Admiral of the Fleet Lord Fisher of Kilverstone*, 2 vols. (London, 1952-59).

L. Martin, *The Presidents and the Prime Ministers: Washington and Ottawa Face to Face, the Myth of Bilateral Bliss, 1867-1982* (Toronto, 1982).

E. R. May, *Imperial Democracy: The Emergence of America as a Great Power* (New York, 1961).

G. W. Monger, *The End of Isolation: British Foreign Policy, 1900-1907* (London, 1963).

L. Mosley, *Curzon: The End of an Epoch* (London, 1961).

R. B. Mowat, *The Diplomatic Relations of Great Britain and the United States* (London, 1925).

    - *The Life of Lord Pauncefote: First Ambassador to the United States* (London, 1929).

G. E. Mowry, *The Era of Theodore Roosevelt, 1900-1912* (London, 1958).

R. B. Mulanax, *The Boer War in American Politics and Diplomacy* (Lanham, Maryland, 1994).

J. A. Munroe (ed.), *The Alaska Boundary Dispute* (Toronto, 1970).

R. G. Neale, *Great Britain and United States Expansion, 1898-1900* (New York, 1966).

A. Nevins, *Henry White: Thirty Years of American Diplomacy* (New York, 1930).

Lord Newton, *Lord Lansdowne: A Biography* (London, 1929).

H. G. Nicholas, *The United States and Britain* (Chicago, 1975).

I. H. Nish, *The Anglo-Japanese Alliance: The Diplomacy of Two Island Empires, 1894-1907* (London, 1966).

    - *The Origins of the Russo-Japanese War* (London, 1985).

R. E. Osgood, *Ideals and Self-Interest in America's Foreign Relations: The Great Transformation of the Twentieth Century* (Chicago, 1965).

T. Pakenham, *The Boer War* (London, 1966).

N. Penlington, *Canada and Imperialism, 1896-1899* (Toronto, 1965).

    - *The Alaska Boundary Dispute: A Critical Reappraisal* (Toronto, 1972).

B. Perkins, *The Great Rapprochement: England and the United States, 1895-1914* (New York, 1968).

D. Perkins, *The Monroe Doctrine, 1867-1907* (Baltimore, 1937).

J. W. Pratt, *Expansionists of 1898: The Acquisition of Hawaii and the Spanish Islands* (Baltimore, 1936).

R. Price, *An Imperial War and the British Working-Class: Working-Class Attitudes and Reactions to the Boer War, 1899-1902* (London, 1972).

H. G. Rawlinson, *The British Achievement in India* (London, 1948).

E. T. Raymond, *Portraits of the Nineties* (London, 1922).

R. A. Rempel, *Unionists Divided: Arthur Balfour, Joseph Chamberlain and the Unionist Free Traders* (Newton Abbot, 1972).

B. A. Reuter, *Anglo-American Relations During the Spanish-American War* (New York, 1924).

K. Robbins, *Sir Edward Grey: A Biography of Lord Grey of Fallodon* (London, 1971).

A. Roberts, *Salisbury: Victorian Titan* (London, 1999).

N. Roosevelt, *America and England?* (London, 1930).

S. B. Saul, *Studies in British Overseas Trade, 1870-1914* (Liverpool, 1960).

R. Shannon, *The Crisis of Imperialism, 1865-1915* (London, 1979).

O. D. Skelton, *Life and Letters of Sir Wilfrid Laurier*, 2 vols. (Toronto, 1971).

J. A. Spender, *The Public Life*, 2 vols. (London, 1925).

     - *Great Britain: Empire and Commonwealth, 1886-1935* (London, n.d.).

E. D. Steele, *Lord Salisbury: A Political Biography* (London, 1999).

Z. S. Steiner, *The Foreign Office and Foreign Policy, 1898-1914* (Cambridge, 1969).

     - *Britain and the Origins of the First World War* (London, 1977).

C. Strout, *The American Image of the Old World* (New York, 1963).

J. T. Sumida, *In Defence of Naval Supremacy: Finance, Technology, and British Naval Policy, 1889-1914* (London, 1993).

P. Sykes, *Sir Mortimer Durand: A Biography* (London, 1926).

C. C. Tan, *The Boxer Catastrophe* (New York, 1975).

C. C. Tansill, *Canadian-American Relations, 1875-1911* (New Haven, 1943).

A. J. P. Taylor, *The Struggle for Mastery in Europe, 1848-1918* (Oxford, 1987).

R. Taylor, *Lord Salisbury* (London, 1975).

W. R. Thayer, *The Life and Letters of John Hay*, 2 vols. (Boston, 1915).

W. N. Tilchin, *Theodore Roosevelt and the British Empire: A Study in Presidential Statescraft* (New York, 1997).

P. J. Treat, *Diplomatic Relations between the United States and Japan, 1895-1905* (Gloucester, Mass., 1963).

W. P. Trent, *Progress of the United States in the Century* (London, 1903).

J. Tomes, *Balfour and Foreign Policy: The International Thought of a Conservative Statesman* (London, 1997).

B. Turner, *Free Trade and Protection* (London, 1971).

R. W. Van Alstyne, *The Rising American Empire* (Oxford, 1960).

P. A. Varg, *The Making of a Myth: The United States and China, 1897-1912* (East Lansing, 1968).

D. Walder, *The Short Victorious War: The Russo-Japanese Conflict, 1904-5* (London, 1973).

A. J. Ward, *Ireland and Anglo-American Relations, 1899-1921* (London, 1969).

A Ward and G. P. Gooch (eds.), *The Cambridge History of British Foreign Policy, 1783-1919*, 3 vols. (Cambridge, 1923).

J. A. White, *The Diplomacy of the Russo-Japanese War* (Princeton, 1964).

     - *Transition to global rivalry: Alliance Diplomacy and the Quadruple Entente, 1895-1907* (Cambridge, 1995).

W. C. Widenor, *Henry Cabot Lodge and the Search for an American Foreign Policy* (Berkeley, 1980).

K. M. Wilson (ed.), *British Foreign Secretaries and Foreign Policy: From Crimean War to First World War* (London, 1987).

     - (ed.), *The International Impact of the Boer War* (Chesham, 2001).

E. H. Zabriskie, *Anglo-Russian Rivalry in the Far East: A Study in Diplomacy and Power Politics, 1895-1914* (Westport, 1976).

S. H. Zebel, *Balfour: A Political Biography* (Cambridge, 1973).

B. Articles

S. Anderson, "Racial Anglo-Saxonism and the American Response to the Boer War" *Diplomatic History* 2 (1978).

T. A. Bailey, "Was the Presidental Election of 1900 a Mandate on Imperialism?" *Mississippi Valley Historical Review* 24 (1937-38).

- "The United States and Hawaii during the Spanish-American War" *American Historical Review* 36 (1930-31)

- "Theodore Roosevelt and the Alaska Boundary Settlement" *Canadian Historical Review* 18 (1937).

- "Dewey and the Germans at Manila Bay" *American Historical Review* 65 (1939-40).

M. Beloff, "Is there an Anglo-American Political Tradition?" *History* 36 (1951).

- "Theodore Roosevelt and the British Empire" in *The Great Powers: Essays in Twentieth Century Politics* (London, 1959).

- "The Special Relationship: an Anglo-American Myth" in M. Gilbert (ed.), *A Century of Conflict: Essays for A. J. P. Taylor* (London, 1966).

N. M. Blake, "The Olney-Pauncefote Treaty of 1897" *American Historical Review* 50 (1944-5).

- "Ambassadors at the Court of Theodore Roosevelt" *Mississippi Valley Historical Review* 42 (1955-56).

F. R. Bridge, "Great Britain, Austria-Hungary, and the Concert of Europe on the Eve of the Spanish-American War".

D. H. Burton, "Theodore Roosevelt and the 'Special Relationship' with Britain" *History Today* 23 (1973).

R. Busetto, "Captain Edward Chichester and HMS Immortalité in Manila Bay during the Spanish-American War" in G. J. Milne (ed.), *New Researchers: Papers presented at the Fifth Annual New Researchers in Maritime History Conference* (Liverpool, 1997).

A. E. Campbell, "Great Britain and the United States in the Far East, 1895-1903" *Historical Journal* 1 (1958).

A. L. P. Dennis, "John Hay" in S. F. Bemis (ed.), *The American Secretaries of State and their Diplomacy*, vol. 9. (New York, 1958).

E. W. Edwards, "The Japanese Alliance and the Anglo-French Agreement of 1904" *History* (1957).

- "The Prime Minister and Foreign Policy: The Balfour Government, 1902-1905" in Hearder and Loyn (eds.), *British Government and Administration: Studies Presented to S. B. Chrimes* (Cardiff, 1974).

R. A. Esthus, "The Changing Concept of the Open Door, 1899-1910" *Mississippi Valley Historical Review* 46 (1959-60).

J. A. S. Grenville, "Lansdowne's Abortive Project of 12 March 1901 for a Secret Agreement with Germany" *Bulletin of the Institute of Historical Research* 27 (1954).

- "Great Britain and the Isthmian Canal, 1898-1901" *American Historical Review* 61 (1955-6).

J. D. Hargreaves, "Lord Salisbury, British Isolation and the Yangtze Valley, June-September, 1900" *Bulletin of the Institute of Historical Research* 30 (1957).

F. H. Harrington, "The Anti-Imperialist Movement in the United States, 1898-1900" *Mississippi Valley Historical Review* 22 (1935-6).

Hu Bin, "Contradictions and Conflicts Among the Imperialist Powers in China at the Time of the Boxer Movement" in D. D. Buck (ed.), *Recent Chinese Studies of the Boxer Movement* (New York, 1987).

S. E. Knee, "Anglo-American Understanding and the Boer War" *Australian Journal of Politics and History*, 30 (1973).

H. W. Koch, "The Anglo-German Alliance Negotiations: Missed Opportunity or Myth?" *History* 54 (1969).

W. E. Leuchtenburg, "Progressivism and Imperialism: The Progressive Movement and American Foreign Policy, 1898-1916" *Mississippi Valley Historical Review* 39 (1952-3).

S. W. Livemore, "Theodore Roosevelt, the American Navy, and the Venezuelan Crisis of 1902-1903" *American Historical Review* 51 (1945-6).

B. J. C. McKercher, "Diplomatic Equipoise: The Lansdowne Foreign Office, the Russo-Japanese War of 1904-5, and the Global Balance of Power" *Canadian Journal of History* 24 (1989).

R. F. Mackay, "The Admiralty, The German Navy, and the Redistribution of the British Fleet, 1904-1905" *Mariner's Mirror* 56 (1970).

J. P. Mackintosh, "The Role of the Committee of Imperial Defence before 1914" *The English Historical Review* 77 (1962).

S. Mahajan, "The Defence of India and the End of Isolation: A Study in the Foreign Policy of the Conservative Government, 1900-1905" *Journal of Imperial and Commonwealth History* 10 (1981-2).

N. Mitchell, "The Height of the German Challenge: The Venezuela Blockade, 1902-3" *Diplomatic History* 20 (1996).

W. M. Morgan, "The Anti-Japanese Origins of the Hawaiian Annexation Treaty of 1897" *Diplomatic History* 6 (1982).

I. T. Naamani, "The 'Anglo-Saxon' Idea and British Public Opinion" *Canadian Historical Review* (1951).

I. Nish, "British Foreign Secretaries and Japan, 1892-1905" in B. J. C. McKercher and D. J. Moss (eds.), *Shadow and Substance in British Foreign Policy: Memorial Essays Honouring C. J. Lowe* (Edmonton, 1984).

L. M. Penson, "Obligations by Treaty: their Place in British Foreign Policy, 1898-1914" in A. O. Sarkissian (ed.), *Studies in Diplomatic History and Historiography* (London, 1961).

G. Seed, "British Reactions to American Imperialism Reflected in Journals of Opinion, 1898-1900" *Political Science Quarterly* 73 (1958).

R. A. Shields, "Imperial Policy and Canadian-American Commercial Relations, 1880-1911" *Bulletin of the Institute of Historical Research* 59 (1986).

E. D. Steele, "The Place of Germany in Salisbury's Foreign Policy, 1878-1902" in A. M. Birke, M. Brechtken and A. Searle (eds.), *An Anglo-German Dialogue: The Munich Lectures on the History of International Relations* (Munich, 2000).

Z. S. Steiner, "Great Britain and the Creation of the Anglo-Japanese Alliance" *Journal of Modern History* 31 (1959).

- "The Last Years of the Old Foreign Office, 1898-1905" *The Historical Journal* 6 (1963).

A. Vagts, "Hopes and Fears of an American-German War, 1870-1915" *Political Science Quarterly* 54 (1939).
H. Weinroth, "The British Radicals and the Balance of Power, 1902-1914" *The Historical Journal* 13 (1970).
K. M. Wilson, "The Anglo-Japanese Alliance of August 1905 and the Defending of India: A Case of the Worst Scenario" *Journal of Imperial and Commonwealth History* 21 (1993).

Index

Adams, Henry, 22, 31, 58
Adee, Alvey A., 141-142, 169
Aliotti, Baron, 70
Allison, William B., 10
Alverstone, Lord, 110, 114-120, 123, 145, 224
Armour, Judge J. Douglas, 110
Arnold-Forster, Sir Hugh O., 47-48; campaigns for a colonial contribution, 82, 89-90; on the prospects of a Russo-Japanese war, 180; on British reinforcements for Indian defence, 213
Ashford, Volney V., 152-153
Aylesworth, Allen B., 110, 115-116, 118-119

Balfour, Arthur J., 10, 12-13, 15, 28, 83, 89-91, 148, 227; and Anglo-American relations, 21, 79, 167, 184-185, 224; and the Isthmian Canal negotiations, 24, 31; and the 1902-3 Anglo-Venezuela Dispute, 37, 41-42, 46, 48-49, 51, 54-55, 57-58, 62-63; establishes Committee of Imperial Defence, 84; and attitude to tariff reform, 86; and the Alaska Boundary dispute, 99, 108, 114, 118, 122; and the Anglo-French negotiations of 1904, 145, 189; on Indian defence, 165; and the international struggle for power in China, 167, 170; attitude towards the 1902 Anglo-Japanese Agreement, 172-173; on the threat of a Russo-Japanese war, 179-184, 187-188; remains firm on British diplomatic neutrality during the Russo-

Japanese War, 192, 220; and the Dogger Bank incident, 193; sends Spring Rice to Washington, 195-196; renewal of the Anglo-Japanese Agreement, 197, 214-215; and Anglo-American diplomacy to end the Russo-Japanese war, 198-200, 206, 212, 218; leaves office, 221
Bax-Ironside, Sir Outram, 68-74
Benkendorff, Count, 176, 189-190, 193
Beresford, Lord Charles, 37, 59
Bernstorff, Count, 56
Bertie, Sir Francis, 61, 171-172, 178, 197, 203, 206, 215
Blaine, James G., 133, 135
Bond, Sir Robert, 85, 133, 226; and American-Newfoundland reciprocity, 134-137, 139-143, 146-149; and Newfoundland fisheries issues, 135, 138; and Anglo-French negotiations on the Newfoundland Treaty Shore, 145
Borden, Sir Frederick, 81, 89, 92
Bowen, Herbert, 47, 53-54, 57-58, 66-68, 71
Bowles, Gibson, 184
Broderick, St John, 14, 84, 89, 178
Bryce, James, 11, 149
Bulwer, Sir Henry, 21

Cabrera, Manuel E., 43-44
Cambon, Paul, 135, 138, 145
Campbell-Bannerman, Sir Henry, 59-60, 76, 105, 173, 197, 221